portraits

THE FRENCH LIST

portraits

(Situations IV)

JEAN-PAUL SARTRE

TRANSLATED BY CHRIS TURNER

LONDON NEW YORK CALCUTTA

Seagull Books 2009

© Editions GALLIMARD, Paris, 1964

English translation © Chris Turner 2009

First published in English by Seagull Books, 2009

ISBN-13   978 1 9064 9 717 0

British Library Cataloguing-in-Publication Data
A catalogue record for this book is available
from the British Library

Typeset by Seagull Books, Calcutta, India
Printed and bound in Great Britain by
the MPG Books Group, Bodmin and King's Lynn

contents

PART ONE

portrait of a man unknown

One of the oddest features of our literary age is the appearance here and there of enduring, totally negative works that might be termed anti-novels. I shall place the works of Nabokov in this category, together with those of Waugh and, in a sense, Gide's *Counter-feiters.*[1] These are not essays attacking the novel genre, such as *Puissances du roman* by Caillois,[2] which I would compare, with all due allowances, to Rousseau's *Lettre sur les spectacles.*[3] Anti-novels retain the appearance and outlines of the novel; they are works of the imagination that present us with fictional characters and tell us their story. But they do so only the better to deceive: the aim is to use the novel to contest the novel; to destroy it before our eyes as it is apparently being constructed; to write the novel of a novel that does not become one, that cannot become one; to create a fiction that is to the great compositions of Dostoyevsky and Meredith what Miró's canvas, *The Murder of Painting* [*El asesinato de la pintura*], is to the pictures of Rembrandt and Rubens. These strange works, which are difficult to classify, do not attest to the weakness of the novel genre, but merely indicate that we are living through a period of reflection and that the novel is currently reflecting on itself. Nathalie Sarraute's is a novel of this kind: it is an anti-novel that reads like a detective story. It is, indeed, a parody of the 'quest novel' and she has introduced into it a kind of impassioned amateur detective who is fascinated by a quite ordinary couple, an ageing father and a daughter no longer very young; he spies on them, tails them and sometimes remotely divines their thoughts by a kind of mental transference, but without ever knowing very clearly what he is after nor who they are. And indeed he will find nothing, or *almost* nothing. He will abandon his investigation as a result of a metamorphosis: as though Agatha Christie's detective, on the point of unmasking the villain, suddenly turned criminal.

It is the bad faith of the novelist—that *necessary* bad faith—that horrifies Nathalie Sarraute. Is he 'with' his characters, 'behind' them or outside? And when he is behind them, does he not try to convince us that he remains inside or outside? Through the fiction of this soul-detective, who hits up against the 'outside', against the shells of these 'enormous dung-beetles' and dimly senses the 'inside' without ever touching it, Nathalie Sarraute seeks to preserve her good faith as a storyteller. She does not want to come at her characters from either the inside or the outside, because we are—for ourselves and for others—wholly outside and inside at one and the same time. The outside is a neutral ground; it is this *inside* of ourselves that we want to be for others and that others encourage us to be for ourselves. This is the realm of the *commonplace*. And this fine word has several meanings: it refers, doubtless, to the most hackneyed of thoughts, but these thoughts have become the meeting-place of the community. Everyone finds himself in them and finds the others too. The commonplace is everyone's and it belongs to me; it belongs in me to everyone and it is the presence of everyone in me. It is, in its essence, *generality*; to appropriate it requires an act: an act by which I strip away my particularity in order to adhere to the general, to become generality. Not in any sense *similar* to everyone, but, to be precise, the *incarnation* of everyone. By this eminently social adherence, I identify myself with *all* others in the indistinctness of the universal.

Nathalie Sarraute seems to distinguish three concentric spheres of generality: the sphere of character, the sphere of the moral commonplace and the sphere of art, which precisely includes the novel. If I act the kindly rough diamond, like the old father in *Portrait of a Man Unknown*,[4] I confine myself to the first sphere. If, when a father refuses to give his daughter money, I declare: 'How sad to see that. And to think she's all he has in the world . . . Ah, he can't take it with him now, can he?' I project myself into the second. If I describe a young woman as a Tanagra, a landscape as a Corot or a family story as being like a Balzac novel, then I move into the third. The others, who have easy access to these domains, approve and understand right away; by reflecting my attitude, judgement or comparison, they impart a sacred character to it. This is reassuring for others and reassuring for myself, since I have taken refuge in this neutral, common zone that is neither entirely objective—since I am there by decree—nor entirely subjective—because everyone can reach me and be at home there—but may be termed both the subjectivity of the objective and the objectivity of the subjective. As I claim to be nothing other than this, and protest that I have no hidden dimensions, I am permitted, at this level, to chatter away, to be stirred or even indignant, to show 'a character', even to be 'an eccentric'—in other words, to assemble commonplaces in an unprecedented way: there is even such a thing as the 'common paradox'. All in all, I am free to be subjective within the limits of objectivity. And the more subjective I am within these narrow bounds, the more I will be thanked for it, since I shall show thereby that the subjective is nothing and one should not be afraid of it.

In her first work, *Tropisms*, Nathalie Sarraute showed us how women spend their lives *communing* in the commonplace:

> They talked: 'They have awful scenes about nothing at all. I must say that he's the one I feel sorry for in it all. How much? Oh, at least two million. And if only what she inherited from her Aunt Josephine . . . No . . . How could it? He won't marry her. What he needs is a good housewife . . . Housewife . . . Housewife . . .' They had always heard it said, they knew it: the sentiments, love, life, these were their domain. It belonged to them.[5]

This is Heidegger's 'chatter', the realm of his impersonal *das Man* (the 'they') and, in a word, of inauthenticity. And many authors have no doubt brushed against or scraped along the wall of inauthenticity, but I know none who have deliberately made it the subject of a book: the fact is that inauthenticity is not novelistic. Novelists strive, rather, to persuade us that the world is made up of irreplaceable individuals, all of them exquisite, even the wicked ones, all of them passionate and individual. Nathalie Sarraute shows us the wall of the inauthentic; she shows it to us everywhere. And what is there behind this wall? Well, there is precisely *nothing*. Or almost nothing. Vague efforts to evade something one divines in the shadows. *Authenticity*, a real relationship with others, with oneself, with death, is everywhere suggested, but remains invisible. We sense it because we flee it. If, as the author invites us, we take a glance inside people, we glimpse a teeming sprawl of spineless evasions of authenticity. There is the escape into objects that peacefully reflect permanence and the universal, the escape into daily occupations, the escape into pettiness. I know of few more impressive pages than those that show us 'the old man' only just managing to escape the panic fear of death by charging, barefooted in his nightshirt, into the kitchen to check whether his daughter is stealing soap from him. Nathalie Sarraute has a protoplasmic view of our inner world: roll away the stone of the commonplace and you find flows of liquid, trickles of slobber, mucus, and hesitant, amoeboid movements. She has an incomparably rich vocabulary for suggesting the slow centrifugal reptations of these viscous, living elixirs. '[L]ike some sort of sticky slaver,

their thought filtered in to him, lined him internally.'
And here we have the pure girl-woman: 'sitting silent
in the lamplight, looking like some frail, gentle under-
seas plant, entirely lined with mobile suckers . . .'[6] The
fact is that these stumbling, shameful evasions that
dare not speak their name are also relations with others. Thus, hallowed conversation, that ritual exchange
of commonplaces, conceals a 'half-voiced conversation' in which the suckers brush up against each other,
lick and suck each other. There is, first, a sense of *unease*: if I suspect that you *are not* quite simply, quite
plainly the commonplace you *utter*, then all my formless monsters are roused and I am afraid:

> She was sitting crouched on a corner of the
> chair, squirming, her neck outstretched, her
> eyes bulging: 'Yes, yes, yes, yes,' she said, and
> she confirmed each part of the sentence
> with a jerk of her head. She was frightening,
> mild and flat, quite smooth, and only her
> eyes were bulging. There was something dis-
> tressing, disquieting about her and her mild-
> ness was threatening.
>
> He felt that she should be set straight,
> soothed, at any cost, but that only someone

endowed with superhuman strength would be able to do it . . . He was afraid, he was on the verge of panic, he must not waste a second trying to reason it out, to think. And, as usual, as soon as he saw her, he assumed the role that, through compulsion, through threats, it seemed to him she forced him to assume. He started to talk, to talk without stopping, about just anybody, just anything, tossing from side to side (like a snake at the sound of music? like birds in the presence of a boa? he no longer knew). He must hurry, hurry, without stopping, without a minute to lose, hurry, hurry while there's still time, to restrain her, to placate her.[7]

Nathalie Sarraute's books are full of these terrors: people are talking, something is about to explode, is about to illuminate suddenly the murky depths of a soul, and everyone will feel the shifting mire of his own. And then, no: the threat averted, the danger avoided, it is back to trading commonplaces again. Yet, at times these break down and a horrible, protoplasmic nudity appears:

11

It seemed to them that their outlines were breaking up, stretching in every direction, their carapaces and armours seemed to be cracking on every side, they were naked, without protection, they were slipping, clasped to each other, they were going down as into the bottom of a well . . . down where they were going now, things seemed to wobble and sway as in an undersea landscape, at once distinct and unreal, like objects in a nightmare, or else they became swollen, took on strange proportions . . . a great flabby mass was weighing on her, crushing her . . . she tried clumsily to disengage herself a bit, she heard her own voice, a funny, too neutral-sounding voice.[8]

In fact, nothing happens: nothing ever happens. With one accord, the interlocutors draw a veil of generality over this transient moment of weakness. So we should not look to Nathalie Sarraute's book for what she is not trying to give us; for her, a human being isn't a character or, primarily, a history or even a skein of habits, but the ceaseless, flabby toing-and-froing between the particular and the general. Sometimes the shell is empty; a 'Monsieur Dumontet' comes in suddenly; having artfully sloughed off all particulars, he is merely a charming, lively assemblage of generalities. Everyone then breathes easily and recovers hope: it was possible, after all! It is, after all, still possible. A deathly calm accompanies him into the room.

These few remarks are meant merely to guide the reader through this excellent, difficult book; they are not intended as an exhaustive treatment of its content. The best thing about Nathalie Sarraute is her stumbling, groping style, so honest and full of misgivings; it comes at its object with pious precautions, sidesteps it suddenly out of a kind of modesty or timidity at the complexity of things and, in the end, presents us suddenly with the drooling monster, but almost without having touched it, doing so merely by the magic of an image. Is this psychology? Perhaps Nathalie Sarraute, a great admirer of Dostoyevsky, wants to persuade us that it is. For my part, I believe that, by allowing us to sense an elusive authenticity, by showing this incessant toing-and-froing from the particular to the general, by tenaciously depicting the reassuring, desolate world of the inauthentic, she has developed a technique that enables her to attain, beyond psychology, human reality in its very *existence*.

Preface to Nathalie Sarraute, *Portrait d'un Inconnu* (Paris: Gallimard, 1957).

the artist and his conscience

You have asked me, my dear Leibowitz, to append a few words to your book. The fact is that I happened to write some time ago on the subject of literary commitment and, by linking our names together, you wish to indicate that artists and writers stand shoulder to shoulder in their common concerns in any one period. If friendship had not been sufficient, the concern to show this solidarity would have made up my mind for me. But now I have to put pen to paper, I confess I feel very awkward.

I have no particular competence in music and I don't want to invite ridicule by repeating badly and in inappropriate terms what you have put so well in the appropriate language. Nor would I foolishly presume to introduce you to readers who already know you extremely well and who follow you passionately in your threefold career as composer, conductor and music critic. It would be a pleasure to say how good I think your book is—it is so simple and clear, it taught me so much, it clears up the most confused and intricate problems, teaching us to take a new perspective on them—but what purpose would that serve? The reader doesn't need me for that: to appreciate its virtues, he simply has to open the book. In the end, the best I can do is to assume we are chatting, as we have done so often, and unburden myself of the concerns and questions your work raised for me. You have convinced me, yet I feel uneasy and have misgivings. I must tell you about them. In so doing, I am, of course, a layman questioning an initiate, a pupil talking over the lesson with the teacher. But, after all, many of your readers are lay people and I imagine my feelings reflect theirs. All in all, this preface has no other aim than to ask you, in their name and mine, to write a new book, or just an article, in which you would remove our last remaining doubts.

The queasy condition of the Communist boa, incapable either of keeping down or coughing up the enormous Picasso, gives me no cause for amusement. In the Communist Party's indigestion, I discern the symptoms of an infection that extends to the whole of our age.

When the privileged classes are happily ensconced in their principles, when they have good consciences, when the oppressed, duly convinced that they are inferior creatures, pride themselves on their servile condition, the artist is at ease. Since the Renaissance, the musician has, you say, constantly addressed himself to an audience of specialists. Yet what was this audience but the ruling aristocracy, which, not content with exerting military, judicial, political and administrative power over the whole land, at some point also appointed itself the arbiter of taste? Since this divine-right elite decided what was or was not human, the cantor or *Kapellmeister* could direct their symphonies or cantatas to the whole of humanity. Art could call itself humanistic because society remained inhuman.

Is it the same today? This is the question which torments me and which, in turn, I put to you. For the ruling classes of our Western societies can no longer dream of claiming that they are, themselves, the measure of humanity. The oppressed classes are conscious of their strength; they possess their own rites, techniques and ideology. Of the proletariat Rosenberg says, admirably:

> On the one hand, the present social order is permanently threatened by the extraordinary potential power of the workers; on the other, the fact that this power is in the hands of an anonymous category, a historical 'zero', gives all modern mythmakers the temptation to treat the working class as the raw material for new collectivities, through which society can be subjugated. Cannot this history-less proletariat be so easily converted into *anything*, as into itself? Holding in suspense the drama between revolution by the working class on its own account and revolution as an instrument for others, the pathos of the proletariat dominates modern history.[9]

Now music, to speak only of this one art, has indeed undergone a metamorphosis. The art of music took its laws and limits from what it believed to be its essence; you have shown brilliantly how, at the end of a rigorous and yet free development, music wrested itself from alienation and set about creating its essence for itself by freely providing its own laws. Could it not, then, for its humble part, influence the course of history by helping to present the working classes with the image of a 'total man' who, having wrested himself from alienation and from the myth of human 'nature', forges in daily battle his essence and the values by which he judges himself?

When it recognizes *a priori* limitations, music, in spite of itself, reinforces alienation, celebrates *the given* and, while manifesting freedom in its own way, indicates that that freedom is bounded by nature. It is not uncommon for the 'mythmakers' to employ music to mystify audiences by communicating a sacred emotion to them, as is the case, for example, with military bands or choirs. But if I understand you aright, should we not see in the more recent forms of this art something like the presentation of the raw power of creation? And I believe I grasp here what sets you against those Communist musicians who signed the *Prague Manifesto*: they would like the artist to subject himself to an object-society and to sing the praises of the Soviet world as Haydn sang the praises of the divine Creation.[10] They call on him to copy what *is*, to imitate without transcending and to offer his audience the example of submission to an established order; if music defined itself as a permanent revolution, would it not risk, for its part, awakening in its listeners the desire to transport that revolution into other fields? You, by contrast, wish to show man that he is not pre-fabricated, that he never will be, and that he always and everywhere retains the freedom to act and to *make himself*, above and beyond any kind of 'prefabrication'.

But here's what troubles me: haven't you established that an inner dialectic took music from monody to polyphony and from the simplest polyphonic forms to the most complex? This means that it can go forward, but not back: it would be as naïve to wish to return it to its earlier forms as to wish to reduce our industrial societies to pastoral simplicity. This is all well and good, but, as a result, music's increasing complexity reserves it—as you recognize yourself—for a handful of specialists who are necessarily recruited from within the privileged class. Schönberg is further removed from the workers than Mozart was, in his day, from the peasants. You will tell me that most bourgeois have no understanding of music, and that would be true. But it is also true that those who can appreciate it belong to the bourgeoisie, enjoy the advantages of bourgeois culture and are generally members of the professions. I know that its *amateurs* are not rich; they are to be found mainly among the middle classes; it is rare for a big industrialist to be a music-lover. However, that does happen, whereas I don't remember seeing a worker at your concerts.

It is certain, then, that modern music breaks with established patterns, spurns convention and marks out its own path. But to whom does it speak of liberation, freedom, will and the creation of man by man? To a stale, genteel audience, whose ears are clotted with an idealist aesthetic. It says, 'permanent revolution' and the bourgeoisie hears 'Evolution and Progress'. And even if some among the young intellectuals understand it, won't their present impotence lead them to see this liberation as a fine myth but not as *their* reality?

Let us be clear about this: it is the fault neither of the artist nor the art. Art has not changed *from within*: its movement, negativity and creative force remain what they always were. Today, as yesterday, what Malraux wrote remains true: 'All creation is, initially, the struggle of a potential form against an imitated one.'[11] And it has to be that way. But in the heavens above our modern societies, the appearance of those enormous planets, the masses, overturns everything, transforms artistic activity from a distance, without even touching it, strips it of its meaning and undermines the artist's good conscience: simply because the masses are *also* struggling for man, but blindly, because they run the constant risk of going astray, of forgetting what they are, of allowing themselves to be seduced by the voice of a mythmaker, and because the artist does not have the language that would enable them to hear him. It is indeed of *their* freedom that he speaks—for there is only one freedom—but he speaks of it in a foreign language.

The disarray in which the cultural policy of the USSR finds itself would be sufficient to prove that what is involved here is a historical contradiction essential to our age, not some bourgeois outrage due to the subjectivism of artists. Of course, if one takes the view that the USSR is the Devil, one may suppose that its leaders take an evil delight in carrying out purges that bewilder artists and exhaust them. And if one thinks that God is Soviet, there is no difficulty either: God acts justly and that is all there is to it. But if we dare for a moment to argue the new, paradoxical thesis that the Soviet leaders are human beings—human beings in a difficult, virtually untenable position, who are trying to do what seems right to them, who are often overtaken by events and who are sometimes carried further than they would like; in short, human beings like us—then everything changes, and we may suppose that they take no pleasure in making these sudden changes of tack that are in danger of throwing the whole machine out of kilter. In destroying classes, the Russian Revolution proposed to destroy elites, that is to say, those exquisite, parasitic organs one finds in all societies of oppression—organs that

produce values and works like papal bulls. Wherever
an elite functions—the aristocracy of the aristocracy
limning out for aristocrats the figure of the total
man—then, instead of enriching the oppressed, the
new values and the works of art increase their im-
poverishment in absolute terms: for the majority of
human beings, the products of the elite are rejections,
absences and limits. The taste of our 'art-lovers' necessarily defines the bad taste or tastelessness of the
working classes, and, when a work is fêted by refined
minds, there is in the world one more 'treasure' that
the workers will not possess, one more thing of
beauty they can neither appreciate nor understand.
Values can be a positive determination for each only
if they are the common product of all. A new acquisition on the part of society, be it a new industrial
technique or a new form of expression, being made
by everyone, must, for each person, be an enrichment
of the world and a path opening up—in short, it must
represent that society's innermost potential. Instead
of the total man of the aristocracy defining himself
by the totality of the opportunities he denies to everyone, as the person who knows what others do not,

who appreciates what they cannot appreciate, who does what they do not do—in short, as the most irreplaceable of human beings—the total man of the socialist societies would be defined at birth by the totality of opportunities that all offer to each and at his death by the new opportunities—however small they may be—that he has offered to all. In this way, *all* are the path of each to himself and each is the path of all to all.

But at the same time as it sought to bring a socialist aesthetic into being, the needs of administration, industrialization and war prompted the USSR to implement first a policy of training *cadres*: it needed engineers, functionaries and military leaders. Hence the danger that this *de facto* elite, whose culture, occupations and standard of living were in marked contrast to those of the masses, would in turn produce values and myths; the danger that 'art-lovers' would arise within it who would create a *special* demand for artists. The Chinese text that you quote, revised by Jean Paulhan, sums up quite appositely the threat that hovers over a society under construction: if horse-lovers are enough to bring fine steeds into being, then an elite that formed itself into a specialist audience would be enough to bring into being an art for the elite. There is a danger that a new segregation may occur: a culture of cadres will be born, with its accompaniment of abstract values and esoteric works, whereas the mass of the workers will fall back into a new barbarism that can be gauged precisely by their failure to understand the products aimed at that new elite. This, I believe, is one of the explanations for those infamous purges that revolt us: as the cadres strengthen their position, as the bureaucracy is in danger of transforming itself if not into a class then at least into an oppressive elite, a tendency towards aestheticism develops in the artist. And, while drawing on support from this elite, the leaders have to strive to maintain, at least ideally, the principle of a community producing its values as a whole. They are most surely forced into contradictory projects, since they are conducting a general policy of producing cadres and a mass-based cultural policy: with one hand they are creating an elite, while with the other they are attempting to wrest its ideology from it, though this is constantly re-emerging and always will. But, conversely, there is indeed confusion among the opponents of the USSR when they criticize its leaders for simultaneously creating both an oppressor class and yet wishing to smash class aesthetics. What is true is that the Soviet leaders and the artists of the bourgeois societies are faced with the same impasse: music has developed according to its own dialectic; it has become an art based on a complex technique; it is a regrettable fact, but *a fact nonetheless*, that it needs a specialized audience. In short, modern music requires an elite and the working masses require music. How is this conflict to be resolved? By 'giving form to the deep popular sensibility'? But *what* form? Vincent d'Indy made serious music 'on a French mountain air'. Do we believe the mountain-dwellers would have recognized their song? And then the popular sensibility creates its own forms. Folk songs, jazz, African chants have no need of being reworked by professional artists. On the contrary, the application of a complex technique to the spontaneous products of that sensibility would necessarily distort them. This is the tragedy of the Haitian artists who cannot manage to connect their formal culture to the folk subjects they

27

would like to treat. The *Prague Manifesto* says, more or less, that we have to lower the level of music while at the same time raising the cultural level of the masses. Either this means nothing or it is an admission that art and its public can unite only in absolute mediocrity. You are right to point out that the conflict between art and society is eternal because it relates to the essence of each. But, in our day, it has assumed a new, more acute form: art is a permanent revolution and, for forty years, the fundamental situation of our societies has been revolutionary. Now, social revolution demands an aesthetic conservatism, whereas the aesthetic revolution, in spite of the artist himself, demands a social conservatism. Picasso, a sincere Communist condemned by the Soviet leaders, and purveyor of works of art to rich American art-lovers, is the living image of this contradiction. As for Fougeron, his paintings have stopped pleasing the elite but never stirred up any interest among the proletariat.

Moreover, the contradiction becomes deeper and sharper when we come to the sources of musical inspiration. It is a question, says the *Prague Manifesto*, of expressing 'the sentiments and the lofty progressive ideas of the popular masses'. I can agree on the sentiments, but how on earth are 'the lofty progressive ideas' to be turned into music? For music is, in the end, a *non-signifying* art. Unrigorous minds have happily spoken of a 'musical language'. But we know very well that the 'musical phrase' does not refer to any object: it is itself an object. How could this dumb thing evoke man's destiny for him? The *Prague Manifesto* offers a solution of entertaining naivety: 'the musical forms that enable us to achieve these goals' will be cultivated: 'in particular, vocal music, opera, oratorio, cantatas and choral works, etc.' Why, of course: these hybrid works have the gift of the gab; they are musical chatterers. There could be no better way to say that music is to be merely a pretext, a means of enhancing the glory of the word. It is words that will hymn Stalin, the Five Year Plan and the electrification of the Soviet Union. With other words, the same music might celebrate Pétain, Churchill, Truman or the Tennessee Valley Authority. Change the lyrics and a hymn to the Russian dead of Stalingrad will become a funeral oration for the Germans who fell before that same city.

What can sounds provide? A great blast of sonorous heroism; it is the word that will bring specificity. There could be musical commitment [*engagement*] only if the work were such that it were susceptible to only one verbal commentary; in short, the sound structure would have to *repel* some words and *attract* others. Is this possible? In some privileged cases, perhaps: and you yourself quote *A Survivor from Warsaw*.[12] And yet Schönberg has not been able to avoid recourse to words. How, without the words, would we recognize in this 'gallop of wild horses' the counting of the dead? We would hear a gallop. The poetic comparison is not in the music, but in the relation of the music to the words. But, you will say, here at least the words are part of the work; they are of themselves a musical element. That is so, but must we give up the sonata, the quartet, the symphony? Must we devote ourselves to 'operas, oratorios and cantatas', as the *Prague Manifesto* urges? I know you do not think so. And I agree with you when you write that, 'the subject chosen remains a *neutral* element, something like a raw material that will have to be subjected to a purely artistic treatment. It is only in the last analysis that the

quality of this treatment will prove or disprove that
. . . extra-artistic concerns and emotions belong to the
purely artistic project.'

Only, in that case, I can no longer very clearly see
where musical commitment lies. I fear it may have fled
the work to take refuge in the artist's conduct, in his
attitude to art. The life of the musician may be exemplary—his voluntary poverty, his rejection of easy
success, his constant dissatisfaction and the permanent revolution he pursues against others and himself—but I fear the austere morality of his person may
remain a commentary external to his work. The musical work is not *by itself* negativity, rejection of traditions and liberatory movement; it is the positive
consequence of this rejection and negativity. As a
sound object, it no more reveals the doubts, crises of
despair or final decision of the composer than the inventor's patent reveals the torments and worries of
the inventor. It does not show us the dissolution of
the old rules: it shows us *other rules*, which are the
positive laws of its development. Now, the artist must
not be the commentary on his work for the public: if
the music is committed music, then it is in the sound

object as it presents itself immediately to the ear, without reference to the artist or to earlier traditions, that the commitment, in its intuitive reality, will be found.

Is this possible? It seems we run up here, in another form, against the dilemma we encountered initially: by enlisting music, a non-signifying art, to express pre-established significations, one alienates it; but by rejecting the significations into what you call 'the extra-artistic', doesn't musical liberation run the risk of leading to abstraction and presenting the composer as an example of that formal, purely negative freedom Hegel calls Terror? Servitude or Terror: it is possible that our age offers no other alternative to the artist.[13] If I have to choose, I confess that I prefer Terror: not for itself but because, in these lean years, it maintains the properly aesthetic demands of art and enables it to await more propitious times without suffering too much damage.

But I must confess that, before I read your book, I was less pessimistic. I present here my very naïve sense as a relatively uncultured listener: when someone performed a musical composition in front of me, I found no signification of any kind in the succession of sounds, and it was of no matter to me whatever whether Beethoven had composed one of his funeral marches 'for the death of a hero' or whether, at the end of his first Ballade, Chopin had wanted to suggest the satanic laughter of Wallenrod; on the other hand, it did seem to me that that succession had a *meaning*, and it is that meaning I liked. I have, in fact, always distinguished meaning from signification. It seems to me that an object signifies when one aims, through it, at another object. In this case, the mind does not attend to the sign itself, but passes beyond it to the thing signified; it frequently happens, even, that this thing remains present to us when we have long forgotten the words that made us conceive it. Meaning, on the other hand, is not distinct from the thing itself, and the more we attend to the thing it inhabits, the more manifest it is. I shall say that an object has a *meaning* when it is the incarnation of a reality that transcends it but which one cannot grasp outside of it and which its infinite nature makes impossible to express adequately by any system of signs; it is always a totality that is involved: the totality of a person, of a milieu, of an age or of the human condition. Of the *Mona*

Lisa's smile I shall say that it does not 'mean' *to say* anything, but that it has a meaning: through it is realized
the strange mixture of mysticism and naturalism, of
self-evidence and mystery that characterizes the Renaissance. And I need only look at it to distinguish it
from that other, equally mysterious, but more troubling, stiffer, ironic, naïve and sacred smile that floats
vaguely on the lips of the Etruscan Apollo or the
'hideous', secular, rationalistic, witty smile shown in
Houdon's *Voltaire*. Of course, Voltaire's smile had a
significance; it appeared on particular occasions and *intended to say*, 'I'm not fooled' or, 'Listen to this fanatic!'
But, at the same time, it is Voltaire himself, Voltaire as
ineffable totality: of Voltaire you can speak *ad infinitum*; his existential reality cannot be encompassed in
words. But as soon as he smiles, there you *have* the
whole of him, effortlessly. Now, it seemed to me that
music was a pretty, dumb creature with deeply meaningful eyes. When I hear a Brandenburg Concerto, I
never *think* of the eighteenth century, of the austerity
of Leipzig, the Puritan ponderousness of the German princes, of that moment in the history of the
mind when reason, in full possession of its tech-

niques, remained nonetheless subordinate to faith and when the logic of the concept transformed itself into a logic of judgement. And yet it is all there, given in the sounds, in the same way as the Renaissance smiles on the lips of *La Gioconda*. And I have always thought that the 'average' listener who, like me, has no particular precise knowledge about the history of musical composition, could immediately date a work by Scarlatti, Schumann or Ravel—even if he might get the composer's name wrong—on account of that silent presence in any sound-object of the entire age and its *Weltanschauung*. Is it not conceivable that commitment in music resides at this level? I know what you are going to say to me: if the artist has painted himself wholly in his work—and his century with him—then he did so involuntarily: his only concern was to make music. And it is audiences today who, a hundred years later, discern intentions that are in the object without having been put there: the listener of the last century perceived only the melody; he saw absolute and *natural* rules in what we retrospectively regard as postulates that reflect the age. This is true: but can we not conceive today of a more self-aware artist who, by thinking about his art, might attempt to embody his human condition in it? I merely ask the question; it is you who are qualified to answer it. But, I confess that if, with you, I condemn the absurd *Prague Manifesto*, I cannot help being disturbed by certain passages in the famous speech by Zhdanov that inspired the whole cultural policy of the USSR.[14] You know as well as I do that the Communists are guilty because they are wrong in their way of being right, and they make us guilty because they are right in their way of being wrong. The *Prague Manifesto* is the extreme, stupid consequence of an entirely defensible theory of art and one that does not necessarily entail aesthetic authoritarianism. We must, said Zhdanov, 'know life, so as to be able to depict it truthfully in works of art, not . . . depict it in a dead, scholastic way, not simply as "objective reality", but . . . depict reality in its revolutionary development.' What did he mean other than that reality is never inert?—it is always changing and those who appreciate it or depict it are themselves changing. The deep unity of all these unavoidable changes is the future meaning of the whole system. So, the artist must smash those habits that have already crys-

tallized and that make us see *in the present* those institutions and customs that are *already outdated*. To provide a truthful image of our age, he must view it from
the heights of the future it is fashioning for itself,
since it is tomorrow that decides the truth of today. In
a sense, this conception connects with your own: have
you not shown that the committed artist is 'ahead of'
his time and that he is watching the present traditions
of his art with future eyes? There is, most certainly, an
allusion in your writing, as in Zhdanov's, to negativity
and 'overcoming', but he does not confine himself to
the moment of negation. For him, the work's value
derives from a positive content: it is a lump of the future that has fallen into the present; it is some years
ahead of the judgement we shall pass on ourselves; it
opens up our future possibilities; at one and the same
time, it follows, accompanies and precedes the dialectical progression of history.

I have always thought there was nothing sillier than
those theories that attempt to determine the mental
level of a person or a social group. There are no *levels*:
for a child to be 'his age' is to be simultaneously above
that age and below it. It is the same with our intellec-

tual and sensory habits. Matisse has written, 'Our senses have a developmental age that derives not from the immediate ambience, but from a moment of civilization.'[15] This is right. And, conversely, they transcend that moment and obscurely perceive a host of objects that we shall see tomorrow; they discern another world in this one. But this is not the product of some prophetic gift: it is the contradictions and conflicts of the age that over-excite the senses to the point of giving them a kind of double vision. It is true, then, that a work of art is both an individual production and a social fact. What we rediscover in *The Well-tempered Clavier*[16] is not just the religious, monarchical order: to those prelates and barons, victims and beneficiaries of oppressive traditions, Bach offered the image of a freedom which, while appearing to contain itself within traditional frames, passed beyond tradition in the direction of new creations. He countered the closed tradition of the little despotic courts with an open tradition; he taught how to find originality by consenting to a discipline—in a word, how to live: he showed the play of moral liberty within religious and monarchical absolutism, he depicted the proud dignity of the subject who obeys his king, of the believer who prays to his God. While being fully in his age, all of whose prejudices he accepts and reflects, he is at the same time outside it and judges it wordlessly in terms of the still implicit rules of a pietistic moralism that will give rise, half a century later, to the ethics of Kant. And the infinite variations he executes, the postulates he forces himself to respect, bring his successors to the brink of changing the postulates themselves. Admittedly, his life was an example of conformism and I do not suppose he ever aired any very revolutionary views. But is his art not simultaneously the magnification of obedience and the transcendence of that obedience, which he *judges*, in the very moment that he seeks to *show* it to us, from the standpoint of an individualist rationalism as yet unborn? Later, with no loss of his aristocratic audience, the artist gains another one: through his thinking on the recipes of his art and the continual adjustments he makes to received custom, he reflects to the bourgeoisie, ahead of time, the calm, non-revolutionary progression it wishes to accomplish. Your conception of musical commitment, my dear Leibowitz, seems to me to suit that happy age: the match between the aesthetic demands on the artist and the political demands on his listeners is so perfect that a single critical analysis serves to demonstrate the wicked futility of internal customs barriers, tolls and feudal rights, and the futility of the prescriptions that traditionally govern the length of the musical theme, the number of its repetitions and the way it is developed. And that critique respects the foundations of both society and art: the tonal aesthetic remains the natural law of all music, property the natural law of all community. I have, naturally, no intention of explaining tonal music in terms of the regime of property ownership: I merely point out that there are, in every age, deep correspondences between the objects on which, in all fields, negativity exerts itself, and between the limits that negativity runs up against, at the same time, in all directions. 'There is a human nature, do not tamper with it!' Such is the shared signification of social and artistic prohibitions in the late eighteenth century.

Oratorical, pathos-laden and, at times, long-winded, Beethoven's art offers us, with a little delay, the musical image of the revolutionary Assemblies; it is Barnave, it is Mirabeau and, at times, alas, it is Lally-Tollendal. And I am not thinking of the *significations* he sometimes liked to give to his works, but of their *meaning*, which ultimately expressed his way of throwing himself into an eloquent, chaotic world. But, in the end, this torrential rhetoric and these floods of tears seem held in abeyance in a freedom of almost deathly calm. He did not overturn the rules of his art; he did not transgress its limits and yet one might say that he was beyond the triumphs of the Revolution, beyond even its failure. If so many people have chosen to seek consolation in music, it is, it seems to me, because it speaks to them of their troubles in the voice they will use to speak of them themselves once they have found consolation, and because it makes them see those troubles from the viewpoint of the day after tomorrow.

Is it impossible, then, today, for an artist, without any *literary* intention and any concern for *signifying*, to throw himself into our world with enough passion, to love it and hate it with such force, to live its contradictions with such sincerity, to plan to change it with such perseverance that that world—with its savage violence, barbarism, refined technologies, slaves, tyrants, deadly menaces and our fearful, imposing freedom—will transform itself, through him, into music? And if the musician has shared the fury and hopes of the oppressed, is it impossible for so much hope and rage to carry him beyond himself, so that he hymns this world today with a voice of tomorrow? And if this were the case, could we still speak of 'extra-aesthetic' preoccupations? Of 'neutral' subjects? Of signification? Could we distinguish the subject matter from its treatment?

It is to you that I put these questions, my dear Leibowitz, to you, not to Zhdanov. I know *his* reply, for, just when I thought he was showing me the way, I realized he was going astray. Hardly had he mentioned overcoming objective reality when he added, 'In addition to this, the truthfulness and historical concreteness of the artistic portrayal should be combined with the ideological remoulding and education of the toiling people in the spirit of socialism.' I had thought he was inviting the artist to live the problems of the age *in their totality* and to do so intensely and freely, so that the work would reflect them to us in its own way. But I see it is merely a question of ordering didactic works from functionaries—works they will execute as directed by the Party.

Since, instead of being allowed to find it, the artist has his conception of the future imposed upon him, it matters little that, where politics is concerned, this future remains to be made; for the musician, it is made already. The entire system sinks into the past. Soviet artists, to borrow an expression they are fond of themselves, are *backward-looking*; they hymn the future of the USSR the way our Romantics hymned the past of the monarchy. Under the Restoration, it was a question of counterbalancing the immense glory of our revolutionaries with an equal glory they claimed to find in the early days of the *Ancien Régime*. Today, the golden age has been shifted; it has been projected into the future. But this roving golden age remains, nonetheless, what it was: a reactionary myth.

Reaction or terror? Art free but abstract, art concrete but encumbered? A mass audience that is uneducated, a specialist listenership, but a bourgeois one? It is for you, my dear Leibowitz, for you, who live out, in full awareness of what you do and without mediation or compromise, the contradiction of freedom and commitment, to tell us whether this conflict is eternal or just a moment in history and, if the latter is the case, whether the artist has in him today the means to resolve it or whether we have to wait for a profound change of social life and human relations to bring a solution.

Preface to René Leibowitz, *L'Artiste et sa conscience* (Paris: Éditions de l'Arche, 1950).

of rats and men

They rectified his squint with glasses, his lisp with a metal loop, his stammer with mechanical exercises, and he spoke perfectly, but in a voice so fast and low that his mother was forever complaining, 'What are you saying? Talk louder! What are you mumbling about now?' and they nicknamed him 'Mumbler' . . .[17]

You are about to hear this muted, steady, courteous voice, and from this moment on you will be able to distinguish it from all others. To whom does it belong? To no one. It is as though language had begun speaking all by itself. There is an occasional mention of the word 'I' and we think we catch a glimpse of the Speaker of this Speech, the subject choosing the terms. This is a pure mirage; the subject of the verb is itself merely an abstract word; the sentence has gone along its familiar path and has taken a personal slant out of sheer convenience. In fact, *someone is here*: 'a thin fellow with hollow cheeks and eyes, a sloping forehead and chin, a long tortoise's neck arched forward from a slightly stooping back: he moves like a bird with miserly gestures, as if trying to contain his being within himself.' But he says nothing. He is an 'object'. Every proposition rearranges him, designates him. Were it not for this mute creature, his voice would be quite deserted; he lives in it, extends his verbal body through the words; the voice informs us that *he* is anxious, that *he* has completed a philosophical work and that *he* is preparing to take it to a certain Morel's.

You will ask what concern of ours this anonymous whispering can be. We want books that are properly put together, with real authors: in the case of literature, as in that of a trapeze act, our sole pleasure lies in being able to appreciate the artist's work;

we attach no more importance to the *frissons* that run through abandoned language than to the wind shaking the reeds. If this is your view, then put down this book. On its last page, indeed, a certain Gorz, emerging from the depths, asserts his retrospective rights over the language that has engendered him. 'I didn't want to make a work of art,' he says. You will readily believe him. Almost as soon as you heard this abandoned voice, you discerned in it both the uncertain flabbiness of natural things and some sort of arid, unselfconscious questing always on the verge of getting bogged down in words. Now, art is a calm image of movement; when you begin reading a novel or even a confession, everything has long since been settled; 'before' and 'after' are merely conventional markers; the birth and death of love exist simultaneously, each extending into the other in the eternal indistinctness of the moment. To read is to carry out a time transfusion: it is our lives that lend life to the hero; his ignorance of the future and of the perils besetting him is, in reality, our ignorance; it is out of our patience as readers that he manufactures a parasitic span of time for himself, the thread of which we break off and pick up again as the fancy takes us. As for style, that great flourish of the vainglorious, it is death. Its illusory speed carries us back to the author's past. And the author may groan all he likes, he may torture himself before our very eyes, but he feels nothing, he is simply telling his story. By the time he picks up his pen, matters have long since been settled: his friend has betrayed him, his mistress has left him and he has taken the decision to hate them or to hate the human race. He is writing to convey his hatred: style is a hammer that crushes our resistance, a sword to cut our reasoning to shreds. Everything about it is ellipsis, syncope, flea-jumps and false connivance; rhetoric becomes terror; rage and insolence, calculated humiliation and pride control the 'attack' and the crafting of the sentences. The great writer, that mad-man, hurls himself upon language, subdues it, enslaves it, mistreats it, *for want of a better way*; alone in his study, he is an autocrat. If he streaks a bolt of lightning across his pages that will dazzle twenty generations, it is because he, through this verbal *diktat*, is after the symbol of the respectability and the humble powers that his contemporaries stubbornly refuse to grant him. It is the vengeance of a dead man, for scorn killed him long ago. Behind these lightning strokes lies a dead child who prefers himself to anything else: the child Racine, the child Pascal, the child Saint-Simon— these are our classics. We like to stroll among the tombs of literature, that peaceful cemetery, deciphering the epitaphs and resuscitating eternal meanings momentarily. It is reassuring that such phrases *did* once live: their meaning is fixed forever; they will not take advantage of the brief survival we deign to lend them to move off unexpectedly and drag us towards some unknown future. As for the novelists who are not yet so fortunate as to be in their coffins, they play dead. They will go and find words in their stock ponds, kill them, gut and season them and serve them up to us grilled, *meunière* or *au bleu*.

The Traitor can be regarded as both less and more than a literary undertaking. This Gorz is not dead; he even has the impertinence, at the beginning of his book, not to be born yet. So there is no rhetoric. Who would there be to persuade us? And of what? Nor is there any question of siphoning off our time to sustain a fictional hero or of guiding our dreams with words. There is only this voice: a voice that searches, but does not know what it is searching for; that wants, but does not know what it wants; that speaks in the void, in the dark—perhaps to give a meaning *through words* to the words it has just let slip, or perhaps to conceal its fear.

It is afraid: of that we can be in no doubt. It said, '*He* is afraid, *he* is anxious, because *he* has finished his book.' It aspired to impassiveness, but it was merely a soundscape in which various objective meanings gathered. It enumerated the passions of a hollow-eyed, thin chap, but it did not feel them. We are not fooled: confined initially in this alien body, in *the individual being spoken about*, the passions have spread beyond their envelope; we can no longer pin them down. The whole voice is permeated with anxiety; anxiety accounts for the inert urgency of this mumbling. These groping, scrupulous, modest words are fevered ones: it is the voice of Care that we hear. This time we have understood: the individual *being talked about* is the one *who is speaking*; but the two do not succeed in becoming one. There is at least one man on earth who eats, drinks, works, sleeps—in short, someone who seems just like us, but who is condemned by some obscure, evil spell to remain *another* in his own eyes.

Has his inner life been pounded and ground down to the point where only a swarm of words is left in a decomposed body? Or is his—intact—consciousness so deeply buried that it views him from afar as something alien and does not recognize him? No one knows yet, since this fissured creature is no one. There is the dummy with hollow eyes, this pure object that does not know itself; there is this little tumult of words that unravels in the empty darkness and does not hear itself. Who, in fact, is this voice speaking to? To us? Certainly not. To address human beings, you have first of all to be fully a human being. It is not concerned with being listened to: it is the fissure itself gaping ever wider as it strives to close; it is a dropped stitch in language that has begun to unravel. Without reference points and prompted by a nameless anxiety, the words perform their labour: if they strive determinedly to designate this carcase of a man, it is because they are obscurely trying to lay hold of it, to dissolve it into them. The voice was born of a danger: one must either lose oneself or win the right to speak in the first person.

That is why this soliloquy is so disconcerting: we stumble upon it unawares. You will smile at my naivety. You will say, 'After all, Gorz *did publish* his book.' Yes, *when there was* a Gorz to make the decision; but he has added nothing and taken nothing away from this beginning, which seemed to be going nowhere and was intended for no one. Whenever I chattered too much as a child, I remember being told, 'Be quiet, you babbling stream.' And there'll be a babbling stream flowing through you, made up of these long caterpillar-crawling sentences, interrupted by asides, swelled by the addition of further retrospective considerations, abbreviated by erasures for reasons of scruple or regret and suddenly upended by leaps into the past. Where is Order? Where is Ceremony? Where is mere politeness? Vainly would you try to cling on to the earlier declarations: they are constantly being transformed by the ones that follow: on page 80 you learn that what you read on page 30 is not what *one* really thought—*one* merely supposed one did. And on page 150 you learn *one* did not even believe it, and on page 170 that *one* hadn't in fact written it but that *one* wrote a certain sentence imagining *one* was writing another; and on page 200 you learn that the imagined and written meanings are strictly interchangeable and are, in fact, both wrong. But you should not assume we are witnessing a confession that is initially mendacious and gradually discovers its own sincerity. There is neither confessor nor confessional—nor even anything to confess. When the voice struck up—I know this and can attest to it—it had nothing to say and its truth did not exist. It uttered words at random, since a beginning had to be made: these words are transparent, they refer only to themselves. And do not try to find some ruse of exposition in this artless stammering: no undertaking could be more sincere or less artificial. It begins in anguish, in penury, *here* before your very eyes and with these very words; it wanders off and we wander off with it; *it is true* that it loses itself and will re-find itself; *it is true* that it breaks free from itself and grows richer.

Being used to the exercises of the mind, we believe, from the very first words, that we grasp the movement of this thought, the intention governing the construction of a paragraph: these rapid anticipations, these implicit conjectures, these expectations are what ordinarily enable us to understand the way of the world and men's actions. So we leapfrog the developments that are to come and settle ourselves comfortably at the finishing line, waiting for this language to unfold itself. But in the present instance this is no way at all to proceed. We had discovered an intention and we were not wrong to do so. But that intention changed along the way: there was no one there to maintain it; 'the Master is in the Styx' or, rather, 'in Limbo'; there are these snippets of sonorous inanity which change as they find body, each of which, by its mere presence, modifies all the others. Leaning against the last milepost, we see the verbal flow moving towards us, then suddenly it gathers, contracts and slides off down another slope, leaving us in the lurch. The indefinite recurrence of such disappointments will cause us at first to see a prattling disorder in what will later seem to be an order in the making.

For it *is* an order, this slow, unpredictable wandering: it is a truth in the process of becoming, organizing itself in minute detail; it is a whole human existence passing from the abstract to the concrete, from poverty to riches, from the universal to the individual, from anonymous objectivity to subjectivity. There are excuses for our astonishment: books are dead bodies and yet here is one which, hardly have we picked it up, becomes a living creature. We have, of course, had to open it, turn the pages and revive the signs; but the mere movement of reading will give rise to an unforeseeable event, with neither its moments nor its end given in advance; you imagine you are lending it your own time, and it is the book that imposes its time on you; you will discover the laws of this venturesome discourse only as it generates them, but you will know at the same time that they will not stop changing and that the whole system will transform those laws even as it dances to their tune.

This flinty, muffled—breaking—voice will live on in your ears: its slowness is a genuine speed, since it is guiding us towards a *real future*, the *only* one that is not a masquerade of memories; towards a place no one knows, which does not exist, and yet *will be*. It strips down its 'appearances': neither lukewarm, nor flabby, nor fluid, it discloses to us the inflexible order of *enrichment*. Each sentence gathers all the preceding ones into it; each is the living milieu in which all the others breathe, endure and change. Or there is, rather, only one sentence, moving over all kinds of terrain, nourished by all soils, ever thicker, rounder and denser, which will swell until it bursts, until it becomes a human being. At every moment, it runs a *real* risk: it may be that it explodes, that it comes to a woeful halt and collapses back on itself, a great inert ball, frozen in the desert of the present. We feel this risk within ourselves; we read anxiously. The book seems, of course, to have been completed; after this page there are others. But what does that prove? Everything may peter out into nothing or, worse still, get hopelessly bogged down. What reassures us, however, is that, beyond the hesitations of life and language, we glimpse a sharp, ice-cold, arid passion, a steel wire stretched between the lacerations of the past and the uncertainty of the future. An inhuman, blind passion—a questing malaise, a manic silence at the heart of language—drives a hole in the reader's time and pulls this whole cavalcade of words along behind it; we shall trust it.

Since the work of art shouts to the four winds the name of the artist, that great dead man who determined it all, *The Traitor* is not a work of art. It is an event, a sudden precipitation, a disorder of words

ordering themselves. You hold in your hands this surprising object—*a work* in the process of creating *its*
author. Of that author we know nothing, save this one
negative feature: he will not be—cannot be—that sacred monster called the Writer. If, at the end of his
struggle, he finds himself, it will be as everyman, as a
man like the rest, for the voice is in search of a man,
not a monster. Do not, then, expect that *gesture* that is
style; everything here is in action. But if, in our great
authors, you enjoy a certain savour for words, a particular cast of phrasing, a depiction of feelings and
thought, then read *The Traitor.* You will, at first, lose
everything, but all will be restored to you. Its abandonment, its passionate questing, its breaking—all
these things lend an inimitable tone to this voice. In
this subjectless writing, the radical impossibility of
style ultimately becomes a transcendence of all known
styles, or, if you prefer, the style of death gives way to
a style of life.[18]

Some will not like what Gorz has done. We like
those who like us: if you want to be read, you have to
give yourself, to nip the words surreptitiously so as to
send a tremor through them, contrive a husky-voiced
affection: but *he,* the object, the third person, the

third-rater, how could he like us? How could the voice like us? We are dealing with a man split in two, who is trying to reconcile the parts of himself with each other: it's an occupation that leaves no time for leisure; the whoring is for tomorrow, if that's possible. To which you will doubtless reply that you haven't much time yourself and soldering problems don't interest you. But what do you know?

I sometimes read science-fiction stories. And I always enjoy them: they give a precise indication of just how frightened we are of ourselves. One story in particular captivated me—about a human landing on Venus. The colonizers-to-be have barely stepped out of their rocket when they set about joyously hunting the natives, their future colonial subjects, though these do not initially show themselves. You can imagine the pride of the King of Nature, his exhilaration at his triumph and his new freedom. But everything quickly collapses in the face of an unbearable realization: the conquerors are behind bars and every move they make is anticipated. The paths they take are ones preordained for them. The Venusians, watching unseen over the glass cage, are subjecting these higher mammals to intelligence tests. This, it seems to me, is our shared condition, except that we are our own Venusians and our own guinea-pigs. Open *The Traitor*: you are would-be colonizers; you look on, with a shake of your head, at a strange animal—perhaps a native—running around in a great panic on the surface of Venus. But I dare say it wouldn't be two minutes before you see that the native is a rat and that that rat is none other than yourself. The book was a trap and we have fallen into it; at present, we are hightailing it through the corridors of an oversized maze under the gaze of the experimenters—that is to say, under *our own* gaze. The experiment is under way: the question at issue is whether there is in this falsified world a single act of which we can say, '*I* did that.' Can we *recognize* our undertakings? Is their nature not *changed* by being brought to fruition? Is it not *others* who pursue them in our stead, others dearer to us than ourselves, who are nourished by our blood? Scarcely has this stranger in my heart of hearts decided my behaviour for me than I hear the shouts of the crowd within: a great ferment seizes hold of all these people I do not know; they condemn my initiative and protest that I must take sole responsibility for it. 'I am another,' says the voice of the Traitor. I find it extremely restrained; in its place, I would say that I am *others* and would speak of myself in the third-person plural. Each of my acts, registering itself in the passivity of being, forms itself into a whirligig whose imperious inertia defines me as *its man*, or, in other words, *its slave*—the other that I have to be to give it its initial impulsion and keep on renewing it *ad infinitum*. My most casual acts, my most sincere commitments, produce only inanimate patterns; I have to slip into these merry-go-rounds and move around inside them, like a showground horse, to make them turn. *He*, the author writing this preface, is an Other at this very moment, an Other I do not like. I enjoyed the book and I agreed to preface it, because one always has to pay to have the right to like what one does. But as soon as I took up my pen, an invisible little carrousel was set in motion just above the paper: it was the foreword as literary genre that calls for the attentions of the specialist, a fine old fellow, all passion spent, a member of the Académie française. Was I *not* a member of the Académie? No matter: *he* would become one for the nonce. How could one dare to present another person's book, unless one were at death's door? *He* got inside the character; he turned himself into the great diaphanous-and-admiring elder; *he* wrote all of the foregoing with a long, pale hand manipulating my stubby little one. He sinks his tentacles into me, he sucks up my words and ideas to extract from them his somewhat dated blessings. If I try to wrest myself from his grasp and write naturally, it is worse: I no longer have any naturalness—*he* sifts it and transforms it into *bonhomie*. He will continue to hold the pen until the end of this exercise and then vanish. But, whatever I may undertake subsequently, be it pamphlet, lampoon or autobiography, other Vampires await me, future intermediaries between my consciousness and the written page.

At least I can hope the intruder will go away. But sometimes he stays; sometimes I fall victim to his long-term installation—even collude in it. One day, *Mirandola* found himself compelled to publish, under the pseudonym *Jouvence*, one of those angry, healthy books that exhort their reader to show courage and which, for that reason, is called 'courageous'. The work met with some success. Reading between the lines, sad, weary men saw an austere, sacred figure who restored their hope. In short, Mirandola's book, as it cooled, created Jouvence, its real author. Jouvence is recognized today as a general influence for good, his virtues are taught in our primary schools; he is seen as a national treasure and often represents France abroad. He lives off Mirandola and, through him, Mirandola has died. The other day, at some first night or other, there was only a measly little foldaway seat reserved for the two of them. Now, Mirandola is modest by nature—almost shy. Yet he took the offence to heart and, shaking with rage, made a scene. 'Personally, I wouldn't have said anything,' he explained as he was leaving, 'but I *couldn't* let them do *that* to Jouvence.'

What wrong had he done? What wrong have you done? After all, we don't wish these undesirable guests upon ourselves: it is the Others who force them on us. The others or the instruments of the Others, those stiff fingers constantly pointing at us: it is his leather bag and the patient that make a hare-brained, fat man into the *Doctor*, that angelic dictator, that enlightened despot, who seeks to do us good despite ourselves and after whose orders, admonishments and adorable severity we hanker.

We sometimes feel the urge to muzzle the Vampires and show ourselves as we are: no one is listening; it is *They* who are expected. In response to this disappointment, or to the general indifference, we say wryly to ourselves, 'Well, if that's what everyone wants,' and then we release the monsters. It always ends badly. In the early days after the war, I met a foreign painter. He had come over from London and we were chatting in a cafe. He was another Traitor—at least, he thought he was. He liked himself so little that people detested him: it was his name they liked. I found him very charming. Weak and authoritarian, distrustful and naïve, madly proud and filled with shame, wicked and affectionate, fascinated by his fame and inconvenienced by it, he was still quite astounded to have a considerable body of work behind him which, nonetheless, he scorned. This Don Quixote could not gain his own esteem unless, on another terrain, he won a battle that he knew he would never even manage to engage. Everything ended, in fact, two years later in gales of laughter. Unstable, unhappy and romantic, he was dependent on the hour, on the light, on a note of music, on women and, above all, on men—all men. *All working together*, we could have saved him; lacking that unanimity, he wavered between haughtiness and a defenceless kindness: sometimes, to forget that old, poorly-medicated venereal disease, his Treason, he allowed himself to be swallowed whole by the prestigious being he represented for other people; on those occasions, all that remained of him was a gleaming insect. At other times, fear, affection and good faith changed him into himself, into an unexceptional man who painted. That day, sitting at another table, was a little old man who could not take his eyes off him. I knew him to be one of the painter's compatriots, also an *émigré*, but one who had not enjoyed the same good fortune. In the end, no longer able to restrain himself, the old man rose, came over and introduced himself to my companion, who, with his guard down, innocently returned his smile. The fame and the genius were together extinguished; there were just two exiles there, acknowledging, but not knowing, each other, neither of them happy, talking as friends.

It was the more unfortunate of the two who re-lit the halo around his interlocutor's head: there had been a misunderstanding; it hadn't been the man he had been addressing but the Painter. We must not ask too much of artists: summoned up by too manifest a respect, by some servile inflections, the Great Man appeared. He was sheer perfection: understanding, modest, so simple in his genius that he put his companion to flight: the latter hurriedly picked up the papers lying on the table and left the cafe with a rancorous, disappointed air, not understanding that he had engineered his own downfall. We remained alone and, after an embarrassed silence, the great personage murmured these words which I shall never forget: 'Another failure!' This meant, 'He had told himself he would forget his name, his fame and his voluminous presence, that *he* would simply be an exile with another companion in exile.' But since he was expected to play the Incomparable Artist, *he* resigned himself and lent his body and voice to that Other who is not even his own, *personal* parasite but one that simultaneously sucks the blood of a good thousand people from Peking to Moscow and from Paris to Valparaiso. And he heard that Other speaking in his own mouth with the terrible sweetness that meant: 'But no, it's nothing, I'm nothing, I'm no better than you, it's just that lady luck has smiled on me.' And he realized he had once again missed the *opportunity*; it might recur each day at any moment, and every day, on each occasion, he would miss it.

The test is not over—we have not finished trotting round the maze, the voice has not finished speaking. The investigation does not concern these tourists, these travellers who inhabit us by the month or by the day. We shall not be asked to account for the furnished rooms, the mirror-lined salons we let out to our passing clientele. Everyone will be released after the customary identity-checks except for one mysterious guest who claims to be the jailer but who is, in reality, merely our oldest tenant. This is the character the voice insists on calling 'He'. And listen to that voice—already it is no longer quite the same. In the beginning, it confined itself to commenting on the occupant's actions; then it revealed that that particular character was under observation; it described the tests he had been subjected to and published the results. Stronger now, tenacious, at times even violent, it is an *interrogating* voice: the Venusians have turned into cops and the rats into suspects. Naturally, we are told at first that we are merely *witnesses* in a police enquiry. No one seems concerned with us. It's a certain Gorz who's in the hot seat. His name has just been mentioned. There's no let-up to his questioning; they try to break his alibis, to force him to contradict himself. What was he doing in Vienna on a particular day in winter 1936? And before that, as a small child? And afterwards, at the time of the *Anschluss*? He acknowledges he went about with young Nazis; that he admired them. Why? He claims he subsequently broke with them. Is that really true? Did he do so of his own accord? Can he say, 'I *broke* with them'? Wasn't he forced into it by circumstances? By his *objective nature*? And where does that nature come from? From whom? From what? Silent and embarrassed, we watch the questioning and do our best to feel indiscreet. What good fortune if we could say, '*I* wasn't in Vienna in Chancellor Dollfuss' day; that business has nothing to do with me.' But no: we are stuck and we know it. At the point when we demonstrate to the officers that our presence in the torture chamber can be explained as a simple misunderstanding, we have long since begun to confess. Torturers and victims—as ever it is we, the cops, who 'put' the traitor 'to the question'. But as soon as he starts to talk, as soon as he denounces his first 'inhabitant'—that misshapen dwarf who may, we think, have died, or who may in fact be hiding (and it may be his puckish face that has just pressed itself against the window and is making rude gestures at us)—we suddenly remember the little cripple that has lived inside us for so long and try to reconstruct the suspicious circumstances of his disappearance. In 1920, I existed and *he* still existed: *who, then*, had so cruelly mutilated him? I remember I didn't like him much. Then I stopped seeing him; there was a murder, I think. But which of us killed the other? The voice is still speaking: it has found words for the fissure running through us; the first guilty parties left their fingerprints on a knife and it will not be long before we identify them.

It seems, in fact, that there are still savages on Earth who are so stupid as to see their newborn children as reincarnated ancestors. The weapons and necklaces of the dead are waved over the infant's head; if, in response, he moves, a great shout goes up: great uncle is reborn! The old man will suckle, will soil the straw beneath him and they will call him by his name. The survivors from his generation will take pleasure in seeing their comrade of the hunt and the battlefield waving his little legs about and exercising his lungs. As soon as he can speak, they will inculcate memories of the dead man into him. Strict training will restore his previous character; he will be reminded that *he* was angry, cruel or big-hearted and will remain convinced of it, despite experience suggesting otherwise. What barbarity: they take a living child and sew him up in a dead man's skin; he will stifle in this senile childhood, where he has no other occupation than the exact reproduction of avuncular gestures, no other hope than to poison future childhoods after his death. After this, should we be surprised that he speaks of himself with the greatest of precaution, under his breath and often in the third person? This sad character is fully aware that he is his own great-uncle.

These backward aborigines are to be found in Fiji, Tahiti and New Guinea, in Vienna, Paris and

Rome—indeed, wherever there are human beings. They are called parents. Long before we were born, even before they conceived us, our families defined our personas. They applied the word 'he' to us years before we could say 'I'. We existed first *as absolute objects*. Through our families, society assigned us a situation, a being, a set of rules; social struggles and the contradictions of history determine in advance the character and destiny of the coming generations.

Algeria, 1935: the parents are exploited, oppressed and reduced to poverty in the name of a racism that refuses them the status of human being; Arabic is taught as a dead language; French schools are so few in number that the great majority of Algerians are illiterate. Rejected by France, without rights, culture or past, they find succour only in religion, in the negative pride of a nascent nationalism. Are their sons, the *fellagha* of 1957, not *made in advance*? And who made them but the colonialists? Who, from Bugeaud's[19] time onwards, prescribed this destiny of anger, despair and blood for them? Who built these infernal machines that must one day explode and blow up colonialism? The roles are there—everywhere—

just waiting for the human beings to fill them: for the one, the role of Jew, for another, the part of landowner. But these functions are still too abstract: within the family, they are particularized. We have all been forced to reincarnate *at least one* dead person, generally a child that has fallen victim to its nearest and dearest, killed at a young age, his desolate ghost outliving himself in adult form: our own father or mother, those living dead. Barely is he out of the womb and every child is mistaken *for someone else*; he is pulled and pushed around to force him into his persona, like those children the *Comprachicos* jammed into porcelain vases to prevent them from growing. At least, you will say, *they* were not their molesters' sons: sometimes they were bought, often they were stolen. That was doubtless the case: but who is not, more or less, a stolen child? Stolen from the world, stolen from his fellow man, stolen from himself? The custom has perpetuated itself: out of stolen children, child thieves are made.

All this we knew: we had always known it; a lone voice kept telling us it was so, but we preferred to say nothing. It spoke in the desert—in *our* desert: *he* did this or that in our stead and we were *his* straw men.

Out of cowardice or connivance, we said, 'I did it.'
And everyone pretended to believe us, on the understanding that we would return the favour. In this way,
for millennia, humanity, ashamed of giving in to fear
and blackmail, has hidden from itself the revolving
racket that has lived off its back. Fortunately, someone has just spilled the beans: a traitor, a man like one
of those American dockers who, from disgust at their
own cowardice, inform on the gang exploiting them
and are found, shortly afterwards, in the Hudson,
washed up on the tide. A traitor: a fissured character
like all of us, but one who could no longer bear the
duplicity. He has broken the silence and refused to
underwrite the acts of the intruder assuming his identity—refused to say 'I'. This has immediately left the
Others naked—the *zar*s, the *loa*s, the black angels, the
sons of Cain, all our parasites. Naked but not dead: we
are torn between scandal and terror; at any minute,
we expect the Union to strike back and bump off the
'stoolpigeon'. We have, in fact, gained no victory: we
have merely found the cracks in ourselves once more,
rediscovered our occupying forces. But we have lost
our illusions: we thought that the little gnawing noise

came in through our ears. But no: it was born in our hearts. This time we recognize the universal murmuring of slavish minds, the Human Voice—and we are not about to forget it.

This does not, of course, prevent the Traitor from belonging to a very peculiar species: he has his own way of being just anyone. Neither the Foolish Scholars nor the Preening Heroes have chosen to take up residence inside him. If he speaks of himself in the third person, he does so not from excess but from lack: he would regard the measured acts performed in his name as *his own* if only he could find the motives for them. He has carried out a hundred searches, but never with any result. The conclusion has to be that he cares about nothing. *He* travels without wishing to travel; *he* meets people; *he* visits their homes; *he* has them round without enjoying their company; at other times *he* goes to ground, *he* shuts himself away without any wish to be alone. Is he merely sated? He cannot be: to turn one's back on the good things of life, one must first have cared for them. And, above all, let us not criticize him for his 'seen-it-all-before' attitude. For he doesn't give the impression of having been or seen anything. He hasn't left the spot: that is his real misfortune. And why not? Because he hadn't enough desire. His heart shows no trace of that haughty dissatisfaction that has served three generations of French writers as an alibi. The Infinite, the eternal Elsewhere, the Dream—he doesn't, thank God, give a damn for these things. I know people who feel entitled to scorn the world because they compare it with some perfect prototype. But the Traitor scorns nothing and no one. So are we talking of the 'empty suitcase' Drieu la Rochelle[20] spoke of? No: the suitcase trick was fine for the inter-war years: you opened it, you asked the onlookers to see for themselves that there was nothing inside but pyjamas and a toothbrush. We know today that it had a false bottom, that it was used for trafficking arms and drugs: the gilded youth craftily hid in it everything that could serve the destruction of the human race and hasten the coming of the Inhuman. But the Traitor will have nothing to do with blowing up the world: the Inhuman is already *his lot* because he doesn't share the same ends as other human beings. In a word, I class him among the Indifferent. This is a group of recent origin, its representatives are no older than thirty and no one knows yet what will become of them. But we must say right away that we shall fail to understand them if we insist on ascribing to them an aristocratic nonchalance. What sets them apart is their bustling zeal. Gorz holds down a job, cultivates his body and mind; he has taken a wife. If you met him at the Palais de Justice or the Stock Exchange, carrying his smart briefcase, you would take him for a man of your own kind. He is punctual, even finicky, in his work, and no one is more affable. He shows just a hint of reserve in his daily dealings, which his colleagues smilingly explain away as shyness; but if you ask him a favour, he will drop everything and run—race—to perform it. The most superficial people will regard him as insignificant: he does not, in fact, speak much; *he is like everyone*; this self-effacement and this perfectly imitated similarity to others will ensure his popularity. But when we examine him closer, the impostor is unmasked by his zealousness. Most people, sharing a conviction that they are human beings (one that has been handed down, since Adam, from father to son), treat their human nature rather negligently; they have such an ancient, uncontested entitlement to it that they calmly follow their personal inclinations with a certainty that they can take a pee if they want to or kill quite humanely. But the Indifferent individual knows no inclinations; whether he is having a drink or fighting, he has to make his mind up to do so; he drinks without thirst, takes revenge without anger for an affront he has not felt—*in order to do as the others do*. His first impulse is to have no impulse: this is what has to be ceaselessly hidden and denied. Terrified of falling to the level of the angels or of tamed animals, this curious product of our societies strives to imitate the Adamites in every respect. In so doing, he loses himself. In an excellent little book in which he told the story of his war, Paulhan called himself an 'assiduous warrior'.[21] The Indifferent one becomes suspect for the simple reason that he is an 'assiduous' human being.

Too assiduous to be honest: if he wants to be taken for my fellow man that is because he *is not*. So, might we say the human community contains fake human beings who are indistinguishable from the real ones? How, in that case, can we know whether the real ones exist? Who will check their *bona fides*? I've heard it said that man is the future of man and, on other occasions, that man is his past: I've never heard it said that man is man's present. We are all fakes. For the second time, the Traitor has let the cat out of the bag: by the passion he puts into *making himself* human, he reminds us that our species does not exist.

The author of this book is, as one might suspect, a rat. And, moreover, a rat possessed. By another rat? By the Rat-in-itself? No, this Other, of which a lone voice speaks to us constantly, this pure object, this receding perspective, this absence—is Man, our tyrant. We are unmasked as rats that are prey to Man. The insane undertaking of the Indifferent one becomes immediately apparent: it is our undertaking. We are all running after a ghost in the corridors of an experimental maze and Gorz is in the lead. If he catches and eats this parasite he has long been feeding with his anxieties and weariness, if he absorbs it into his own substance, our species is possible. Somewhere, between the angels and the rats, it is being born; we *shall* get out of the maze.

Once again, the aim of the book has changed. It is not a question of knowing life now, but of changing it. We are not yet the ones being addressed, but, like it or not, it is we who are being asked the fundamental question: by what activity can an 'accidental individual'[22] achieve, within himself and for everyone, human personhood? As I have already pointed out, this work has been organized like a machine with 'feedback': the present is constantly transforming the past from whence it came. In the first pages of the book, it seemed the voice was taking up words at random, just anywhere, to escape anxiety and so that there should at least be *something* behind it—anything but silence. And it was true: *at that moment* it was true. But the question of the human being was posed and, with it, a new light is cast over the beginning of the undertaking; a change takes place: *before the voice*, Gorz already existed, he was already pained by his indifference and combated it with the means at his disposal. Suddenly, he changes tactics and reverses his relation to himself. That break represents in itself an absolute event; but we would be wrong to see it as an inner adventure whose chief merit would be to have given rise to the book: it is, in fact, *in* the book that the adventure takes place; it is through it and by it that it develops and becomes conscious of itself. *The Traitor* does not claim to *tell us* the story of a convert; it *is* the conversion itself.

Gorz is thirty-two. For thirty-two years, whatever he did, it immediately seemed to him he could have done the opposite and the outcome would have been the same—that is to say, worthless or, worse, meaningless. For thirty-two years his existence has escaped him; he has no other evidence of it than an insurmountable boredom: I am bored, therefore I exist. But he has deliberated on the matter; he has searched and he believes he has found the response. He said to himself,

> Since I'm from nowhere, no group, no project, since I'm the exile from all groups and all projects, there is only the following alternative: to be on the fringes of society and history, the supernumerary of the human race, reduced to *ennui*, to the acute awareness of the contingency of everything around me; or to raise myself, in my mind, to the absolute—in other words, to ground everything philosophically as a moment of the spiritual adventure and, having done this, having started out from this speculative interest, to regain a taste for the concrete; . . . I can connect with . . . the real only by starting out from the Idea.

In other words, because he is made in such a way that he doesn't feel he has any particular desires, he will turn his indifference to advantage: for want of being able to be—or wanting to be (nothing is decided yet)—*a certain* Gorz, he will make himself Universal Man. He will determine his behaviour by concepts and will obey this rule: act always in such a way that the circumstances and the moment serve as a pretext for your acts, in order to bring about, both within and outside you, the generality of the human species. It was for this reason that he undertook to write a work of philosophy at the age of twenty: when you are im-munized from birth against the violence of fear, con-cupiscence or anger, you must either do nothing or ground everything in reason—even the act of opening an umbrella if it is raining.

Everything is explained now and no one will be surprised any longer at his betrayal: he is one of those fellows who have their heads full of words, who analyse everything, who always want to know the whys and the wherefores—a critical, destructive mind. In a word, a filthy intellectual. The point cannot be denied; that is even why I like him: I am one too. A literary paper asked the prince of counterfeiting what he hated the most. He had no hesitation: 'Intellectuals'. I am amiably disposed towards this counterfeiter: he is a true poet and a good man. But I do wonder what got into him that day. Everyone knows his hunted airs, his monologues on destiny, on time, on life, these congestions of words in his throat, purple patches from a perpetual, imploring anthology; his fascinating hands that are words too, their palms turning outward to plead for forgiveness; his thinking, vexed and tired, that presses on regardless, jumping nimbly from one idea to another, not noticing it is merely spinning round inside its cage; these stunning improvisations whose groundlines are to be found in the previous day's writings, which, as they fade, allow us to glimpse the incurable sadness of a frozen stare. This is a man who seeks out a tribunal merely to corrupt it: meeting you, he appoints you judge and jury, spares you no detail of his conduct and will not let you leave until you have acquitted him. But do not be deceived: he knows everything. The sentence he is trying to avoid is the one he knows he passed on himself at the beginning of the century. He knows he is doing hard labour for it and has been for fifty years, for he has condemned himself to plead into old age the cause his adolescence judged lost. What would you call this Devil's Advocate but an *intellectual*?

Of course, I know others who like to set the great silences of the earth, or of the peasants, against such chatter. But if you open them up—what a din! Their heads are buzzing with the words to describe other people's silences. Gorz is the first, I think, to have formulated the problem concretely; and I am grateful to him for it. It matters little that one speaks about language or silence, about the confused intuitions of the poet or clear ideas: what counts is that these speakers are compelled to speak. To defend the dark corners of the heart, the counterfeit man put forward more arguments than Kant to establish the claims of Reason. He was forced to: speeches, concepts, reasoning— these are our lot. Why? Because intelligence is neither a gift nor a defect: it is a drama or, if you prefer, a provisional solution that turns, most often, into a life sentence. Someone once told our traitor, 'You stink of intelligence the way some people stink from their armpits.' And it's true: intelligence stinks. But no more than stupidity: there are odours to suit every taste. Stupidity smells like a wild animal, intelligence like a human being. The fact is that some riven, exiled, condemned individuals attempt to overcome their conflicted natures and loneliness by pursuing the insane image of unanimity. It is this that is reflected in their eyes, shyly offered in their smiles. Unanimity over everything and nothing: the appeal is there, permanently etched on their faces; whatever they say, their voices call for universal agreement. But human beings, laden as they are with particularities, densely packed interests and passions, loathe the idea that someone wants to dissolve their differences and hatreds in the purely formal harmony of assent.

And then, intelligence is meticulous. It wants to start everything over again from the beginning, even the things everyone can do: it takes walking and breathing apart and puts them together again; it learns how to wash, how a nose is blown—all from first principles. It is intelligence that makes intellectuals seem like severely disabled people undergoing rehabilitation. But we have to show some understanding here: each of them is reinventing intelligence to compensate for the enormous clearance sale of all their drives and doggedness. They need it to replace the signals that weren't etched into their flesh, the habits that weren't bestowed on them, the paths that weren't cleared for them—in short, they need it *in order to live*. I remember seeing a puppy after its cerebellum had been partially removed: it could move around the room and seldom bumped into the furniture, but it had become reflective: the animal established its itinerary carefully and thought long and hard before evading an obstacle; it took it a lot of time and thought to accomplish the movements it previously made quite unconsciously. In the language of the day, they said its cortex had taken over the functions of the lower centres: it was, in short, an intellectual dog. I don't know whether it was very useful or very harmful to its fellows but we can quite well imagine that it had lost what another exile, Genet, so aptly termed 'sweet native confusion'; in a word, it had either to die or reinvent the dog. And we de-brained rats are so constituted that we have to either die or reinvent man. We are, as it happens, perfectly well aware that man will constitute himself without us, through labour and struggle, that our models become outdated overnight, and that nothing will remain of them in the finished product, not even a knuckle-bone. On the other hand, that making would be done blindly—by cobbling things together and patching them up—if we de-cerebrated individuals were not there constantly repeating that we must work from principles, that it isn't a question of making-do and mending but hewing and building; that our species will, in a word, be either the concrete universal or nothing at all.

Gorz's intelligence strikes you at the very first glance: it is one of the nimblest, acutest intelligences I know; he must have had great need of this instrument to have honed it to this point. Yet, when he sets about writing his philosophical treatise, he does not avoid contradiction, as is the case with intellectuals. He wants to act as a function of the human condition alone. Yet, as soon as acts are accomplished, they are buried in the particular: what remains is the fortuitous realization of one possibility out of a thousand. But why, precisely, just *this one*? The worst of it is that it compromises him: he cannot even breathe without adding a new touch to the model-less portrait that is none other than his own self-portrait. He would have to become all possible Gorzes at once for these empty equivalences to cancel each other out, to be *only man* by becoming *the whole of man*. But no, 'We are born several and we die one only,' says Paul Valéry's Socrates.[23] Gorz cannot prevent himself from living, or from shrinking with use: his universal intelligence outstrips his personal adventure and looks on with distaste as the physiognomy emerges of that Gorz who will be '*one only*'. It rejects it; it does not even want to recognize it; it would joyfully have accepted him being just anyone. Yet he is not even that: a succession of accidents has lent him a definite individuality that is distinguished by little trifles from the others.

We—that is to say, we intellectuals—are all familiar with this distracted, cloying anxiety. We thought ourselves universal because we toyed with concepts and then, suddenly, we see our shadows at our feet; we are *here*, we are doing *this* and not something else. Once in Brooklyn, I got myself into a terrible spin. It was my own fault: I was walking. You don't walk in the USA. I was crossing roads, walking past buildings, looking at the passers-by. And, from one street to another, the buildings, roads and passers-by were all identical—at least, they seemed to be. I turned right and left, retraced my steps and pressed forward, but each time I found the same brick houses, the same white steps in front of the same doors, the same children playing the same games. At first, I enjoyed this; I had discovered the city of absolute equivalences. Universal and commonplace, I had no more reason to walk on *this* sidewalk than on *the same one* a hundred blocks away. The wave of stone, a thousand times recommenced, carried me onward, made me share in its inert renewal. What gradually wearied me was this constant advancing *to get nowhere*; I speeded up until I was almost running and yet I remained on the same spot. Suddenly, I was aware of a massive rejection: all these mass-produced blocks, all these sections of street, running along side by side, resembled each other further in being equally empty of me—except, that is, for one, which was in no way different from the others, and in which I had no more reason to be than in the neighbouring segments; and which, for un-known reasons—or for no reason at all—tolerated my presence. Suddenly, my movements, my life and even my weight seemed illegitimate: I wasn't a real person since I had no particular reason to be at this point of the forty-second parallel than any other. And yet I was a singular, irreducible individual, since my latitude and longitude defined me precisely. Neither everyone, nor someone, nor entirely some*thing*: a spatial determination, a guilty, contagious dream haunting the overheated asphalt in places, a lack of being, a flaw. A stubborn body in motion, my presence in the mechanical universe of repetition became a sheer accident, as mindless as my birth. Ubiquity would have saved me; I had to be legion, to stride along a hundred thousand sidewalks at once: that alone would have enabled me to be any old stroller in any old street in Brooklyn. Being unable either to leave myself behind or multiply, I hurled myself into the subway. I came back to Manhattan and, in my hotel, rediscovered my ordinary reasons for being—in no way compelling, but human.

There is no subway for the young Gorz, and no hotel or reason for being. Even in his room, he is outside; hence, he is illegitimate everywhere. And mystified to his bones: he believes he can escape his

insignificant persona by parading the disgust it inspires in him; but it is, first and foremost, that disgust
that lends him his singularity; the particularity of intellectuals is nothing other than their futile desire for
universality.

But he has just finished his philosophical treatise.
He steps back to look at it and the entire mystification disappears; universal thinking has narrowed and
condensed; it has assumed a particular countenance:
it looks like him. He is at the origin of a supernumer-
ary object, this bunch of typewritten sheets, and, in
the process, he has imprisoned himself in it. For a
long time, the others have claimed to see the whole
of him in his commonest gestures—his way of eating,
of sitting, of opening a telegram. 'Oh, that really is
you; that's you all over; I really see you in that; what
you're doing there, that's pure Gorz.' God knows, it irritated him. But what has he just done, if not make a
large-scale gesture of this kind that has now closed
around him? The others will be only too happy. They
will lean over the transparent walls of his prison and
recognize him: 'that way of writing, old pal, that way of
correcting yourself, of feeling your way into the

subject, putting your toe in the water before you jump in, that is you, that really is you, it's you to a T; and these ideas, old chap, my dear old chap, that really is Gorz, it's pure Gorz and no mistake!' A devil in a bottle. He really has just one single approach to opening a tin can, other people's thoughts or an umbrella; a single approach to entering the mind of a seventeenth-century philosopher or the flat of a fellow student or a young woman. He re-examines the sentences in his book one by one: gestures, gestures, gestures! Gorz is there, before his very eyes, stretching out his long neck, pinching his thin lips: the Gorz that eternity will make of him.[24] All in all, he has tried to live and he has failed. He knows now that he was forced to fail and, moreover, that he was secretly resolved to do so.

At this precise moment, the Voice struck up. A little, barely intelligible murmur, born of anxiety and recrimination, ruminating on this surprising, yet foreseen defeat. The Voice acknowledges a simple fact: it's him, it definitely is him, it's his spitting image. This is enough to change everything: it was the others who claimed to know this parasite that was growing fat on his acts; the universal gaze of the Indifferent passed through him like light through a windowpane. He is suddenly there, opaque and unwieldy: 'Admit it! You've seen him, you've spoken to him, we know. Your line of defence won't convince anyone; we know when and where you met. The game's up.' The voice begins to confess: 'Yes, all right. I know him better than anyone. I've always known him. I'll tell you what I know about him.'

Wasn't I right a moment ago when I said one should speak of oneself in the plural? There are two people living off this poor unfortunate: there is Universal Man, that elusive, well-armed tyrant, and then there is the other one, the one left over. *One* makes oneself *a certain Gorz* by trying just to be Man; and, to be absolutely truthful about it, one tries to become *the whole of Man* because one refuses to be a certain Gorz. Yet who is refusing to be Gorz but Gorz himself? This refusal explains and defines him. If one *could accept* being—or, in other words, accept having been—the long-necked miser who wants to preserve his futile universality; if one spoke of him constantly; if one enumerated all his particular obstinacies; if, instead of passing through him, the intellectual gaze *saw into his soul,* wouldn't this 'eccentric' disappear, along with the stubborn negation that was the source of his eccentricity? It would not, admittedly, be future Man that came to take his place, but another individual whose basic obstinacies would merely risk being more positive. What would be gained? Is the game worth the candle? It is, in fact, too late to count the profits and losses: the voice is speaking, the undertaking has begun. The Traitor has chosen his own particularity as his goal.

It is not a question of knowing that particularity, nor entirely of changing it, but, *first and foremost,* of changing oneself by the will to know it. The Indifferent one does not have the foolish plan of depicting himself: he wants to modify the fundamental relationship that binds him to Gorz. When he turns towards the child, the adolescent that he was, when he interrogates his persona, his investigation is, in itself, an action: he suddenly halts his headlong flight, he forces himself to view himself without disgust; he brings his taste for totalizations to bear upon himself and, for want of being the whole of mankind, aspires first to become for himself *the whole of Gorz.*

This is not so simple: having neglected himself for so long, being in the midst of himself is like being a Robinson Crusoe on a desert island. How can he find the lost paths?—everything is covered in vines and briars. One can still latch on to memories, but what is a memory? What is the truth of this inert little picture? And what importance does it have? Is it the past exploding in the present like a bomb? Is it the present dressing itself up as the past? Or both? These two questions must have replies: *who* is this Gorz that I am? Who has made me in such a way that I both am Gorz and so fiercely refuse to be? But how are we to decide? Where are the tools for such a decision? Of course, there is no shortage of answers: there are tried and tested methods that offer themselves in haste and even perform little test demonstrations to show their efficacy: 'Your class,' says the one,

> is completely decadent. Without principles or hope, it expends all its energies just keeping itself in being and no longer has the heart or, if you prefer, the naivety, to undertake anything new: your indifference is an expression of its anxious uncertainty. Existence

seems purposeless to you because bourgeois life no longer has any meaning. Don't look anywhere else for the origins of your philosophical malaise: the bourgeoisie no longer even has confidence in its ancient idealism, it attempts to hide it beneath old glad rags. But you have held these worn-out fabrics in your hand and seen how threadbare they are; you are still disgusted with them, though you aren't able either to be content with these outworn notions or to find a new form of thinking.

He listens, he agrees, but he is not entirely convinced. He has no difficulty conceding that he is a young bourgeois. Without needs, entirely abstract, 'a pure consumer of water, air, bread and the labour of others, reduced to an acute awareness of the contingency of all that surrounds him.' But he knows lots of other bourgeois of his age who are not like him. Admittedly, he could, without abandoning the method, recover the historical and social circumstances that may explain his peculiarities: he informs us himself that he is Austrian, half-Jewish, that he had to leave Austria at the time of the *Anschluss* and that he lived for some years in Switzerland. He is persuaded that these factors have some influence on his current attitude. But *what sort of influence*? And how is it exerted? And, at a more general level, is there anything more surprising or obscure than the action of people, events or objects on the development of a human being? All around him, everyone is in agreement: we are conditioned. He cannot find anyone to doubt the existence of this conditioning or to question its nature; these are things that are handed down from father to son; the arguments begin when they try to classify the various conditions and determine their importance. But all these people are inheritors: these presuppositions, these allegedly obvious facts are part of a very ancient heritage that each generation hands on to the next and that no one has ever catalogued exhaustively. The Indifferent one, by contrast, has inherited none of their convictions: the Exile from all groups must also be an exile from all ideologies. When he comes to consider both that he is 'the son of a Jew' and that he has an 'acute awareness of the contingency of everything', he wonders at the isolation, opacity and lofty irreducibility of these two facts that are so different: looking at them naïvely, you would say they were two miniature cities surrounded by ramparts and ditches; each is painted on an old canvas confined within a frame, both are hanging from the picture rail: between them *there is no visible path* because they do not exist in the same world. He is not, however, unaware that people come and go in their own little personal museum, that they move from a Circumcision to a Flagellation without even looking for the artists' names and say, '*This* is the cause of *That*, I am the unfortunate product of my race, of my father's Judaism, of the anti-Semitism of my schoolmates,' as though the true connection between these mysterious images of himself were quite simply the wall on which the paintings that enclose them are hung. But when he thinks of the peaceful self-assurance of these heirs, he falls into the profoundest bewilderment.

It is at this point that the other method offers itself, that strange dogmatism based on an absolute scepticism: does he remember his earliest years, the estrangement from the Jew she had married that his mother felt—and managed to inspire in him—the unbearable tension within the family group, the severe training he was made to undergo as soon as he could speak? Let him ask then whether he was not the victim of an abusive, castrating mother and whether he shouldn't date from that obscure time, from that distractedly experienced oppression, the appearance of the 'complexes' that cut him off from the world today. Isn't 'he', ultimately, the honorary Aryan, the persona an insulted wife wants to impose on her son because she reproaches a certain Israelite constantly with having been the only husband she could find? The docility of a moulded child might be said to survive in the adult in the form of apathy.

To which he replies that his upbringing did, in fact, leave him with complexes: his mother tried to turn him into the Other that he in part became; in his earliest years he suffered, as he does now, from a worried, zealous indifference. But he cannot manage to understand how these famous 'complexes' persist: he was apathetic at eight, and he is apathetic today. *Is it the same apathy*? Has it been preserved by an inert perseverance of being? But he will not believe so easily in human passivity: all his experience rejects this ever so convenient idea and the metaphysics that underpins it. Will he, rather, admit that he has nurtured and coddled his complexes; that he indulges them, fattens them up; that the adolescent and the adult have, by a kind of ongoing creation, taken over, re-emphasized and enriched the first characteristics of the child? In that case, he might be said to bear the responsibility for everything: it would be he, on a daily basis, who would be making himself indifferent.

He cannot reach a conclusion so quickly: none of these interpretations is entirely satisfactory, none is entirely clear in his eyes. A betrayer once again, like Hans Christian Andersen's child who sees that the emperor has no clothes, he draws up the inventory of our philosophical heritage, finds the coffers empty and ingenuously says so. Why, indeed, would he have himself interrogated by other people's methods, why would he give himself up to the psychiatric or Marxist police? It is, in fact, down to him to call these investigative procedures into question in the question he asks about himself. This Oedipus directs his investigation on to his own past and the validity of his memories, on to the rights of experience and the limits of reason—in a word, on to the legitimacy of the prophetic gifts claimed by our Tiresiases. But he turns his back on the universal: as regards method, he invents one by reflecting on his own case and the proof of that method will lie in its success. To bring himself to light as a particular totality, he has to confine himself within the experience of his particularity; he has to invent himself by inventing his own questioning and the means to respond to it. The Traitor wipes the slate clean and starts himself over again: this is what he gives us today: the opportunity to read a *radical* book.

For a long time we have listened to 'His Master's Voice'. Now it is Gorz speaking: the end of the monologue returns to its beginning, enwraps it and absorbs it. The meaning of the work appears now in full daylight. It was at first a question asked, in the shadows, by *no one*: on what conditions will the man known as Gorz be able to say 'I'? But immediately afterwards, an as-yet-indistinct being emerges from the darkness: it is not just a question of determining these conditions; the book becomes Gorz's living effort to fulfil them. *He* knows now that *he* will have done nothing if he does not wring the neck of the Vampires that wash him, clothe him and fatten him

up, in order to grow fat on him: the first act that will
be born on its own from my hands, that will depend
on itself alone and on the obstacles to be surmounted,
that will fold back on itself to lay hold of itself and
control itself—it is this act that will say my first 'I';
this imperceptible sliding of an action against itself
will be me. And what is preventing him from acting?
He knows this too: it is the over-hasty desire to be
prematurely universal. He repeatedly tells himself now
that his future action will necessarily make use of *his*
eyes, *his* mouth, *his* arms, that it will have the look of
his face about it. And, above all, that he will be more
strictly defined each day by the ephemeral agitation
that his action conveys to the surrounding objects.
Looked at from the outside, this is all a man is: an anxiety working over material within the limits of a
strictly defined area. Old individual projects impose
their individuality on a new project that goes back
over all the others and individualizes them the more.
I am this constant toing-and-froing. If he acts, he will
be *himself*; but, if he is to act, he has first to *accept* himself. What is preventing him from doing so? What underlies his futile desire for universality? He discovers

a heap of rubbish piled up in his heart: his childhood. He sets about breaking it down, but his efforts are not sufficient. He can no longer conceal from himself that he is perpetually reinventing his bastardy, the burden of his old miseries and infirmities. Because he cannot be everything, it is he *today* who pitches himself into a haughty passivity, to let everyone understand that he is externally determined and does not consent to this. It is he who annihilates himself of his own free will or, at least, who absents himself, leaving it to the habits that others have ingrained in him to keep him walking upright, performing the natural, social functions of his body. It is he who, in all freedom, has decided, like Saint John of the Cross, but without mysticism, that he will never do anything, so as freely to 'be nothing at all'. Is he, then, free? Of course he is: he has never doubted it. They have fabricated him, marked him and poured him into the plaster mould— *and* he is free? Yes: unfree or free will are one and the same thing where he is concerned. How can this be? He will try to say why, to explain why to *himself*, but his aim remains a practical one. The issue for him is to find the dialectical movement that is able to totalize the changing relations between past, present and future, between objective and subjective, between being and existence, between the apparatuses and freedom, so as to be able both to assert himself and to dissolve himself endlessly to the point where at last a genuine impulse is generated in his heart that is harrowing, that comes out through his hands and finds completion outside him in that holocaust of objects we call an *act*.

This is his task and he has just understood it. He puts down what he has understood on paper and, at that very moment, he notices that his innermost desire leaves his heart through his hands; that he is *already* embarked on an undertaking, that the words of today, yesterday and last month gather together and form themselves to reflect his new face to himself; that he is currently unmaking himself by words, in order one day to be able to make himself by acts; that this destruction is creating him, that it is determining him irreversibly; that it is transforming him gradually into that incomparable being of one sort or another that we each are for ourselves during the sleep of our Vampires; that he has at last 'taken the plunge', 'got himself involved' and condemned himself, whatever he may do, to have no other springboard again but himself. This is the moment: *hic Rhodus, hic salta*. His undertaking now takes on a different coloration; it takes on the thousand inner recesses of consciousness, the thousand circuits of reflection; it rubs against itself, feels itself, sees itself: the undertaking was the Voice. The Voice recognizes itself: in it, action discovers itself and says 'I'. *I* am creating this book, *I* am searching for myself, *I* am writing. Somewhere, a hollow-eyed chap sighs, intimidated: 'How pompous it is to talk in the first person!' And then he dissolves and Gorz appears: I am Gorz, *it was my voice* that was speaking, I write, I exist, I suffer myself and make myself—I have won the first round.

Is it worth shouting 'victory'? Who is Gorz, after all? A 'man of no social importance', a failed aspirant to universality who has left behind abstract speculation to become fascinated, instead, with his insignificant person. What has been gained by this? Where is the progress? I do not imagine that Gorz will reply to this question, but we can answer it for him. For we have followed this fantastical Cuvier[25] step by step as he found a bone, reassembled the whole animal from that minute vestigial element and ended up noticing that the reconstructed beast was actually himself. The method was valid for him alone—this he has said and re-said a hundred times; he was able to test it out only on his own case. But we have followed him; we have understood the meaning of his acts at the same time as he did. We have watched his experiments and seen the muscles being reborn around the knucklebone; we have seen the organism being gradually reconstructed and seen the author and the book being produced by each other. Now, what we understand belongs to us; the Gorz approach is ours; when he attempts to interpret his life by the Marxist dialectic and by psychoanalysis, without every *entirely* managing to do so, his failure is our concern; we shall know how to attempt the experiment and we know the outcome in advance. And when he asks his own object—namely, himself—to devise his method for him, we immediately grasp the significance of this peculiar endeavour: for we are his fellows inasmuch as each of us is, like him, a unique anybody. What then is this object that turns itself into a subject under the appellation 'method'? Is it Gorz, or you and I? You are not 'Indifferent ones'; you will have other questions to ask yourselves about yourselves. In inventing *himself*, Gorz has not absolved you of the duty of inventing *yourselves*. But he has proved to you that totalizing invention was possible and necessary. Closing the book, every reader is consigned back to their own brush land, to the poisonous trees that people their own jungle. It is for them to cut their own ways through, to clear a path, to chase off the Vampires, to break out of the old iron stays, the old, worn-out actions to which resignation, fear and self-doubt have confined them. Can we be said to have rediscovered the universal by concentrating on the particular? No, that would be too much to hope for. We are no longer entirely animals, though we are not quite human beings. We have not yet turned to our advantage that appalling catastrophe that has befallen certain representatives of the animal kingdom: namely, thought. In short, we shall remain, for a long time yet, stricken mammals. This is the age of fury, fetishes and sudden terrors; universality is merely a dream of death amid separation and fear. But our world has been changing in the last few decades; reciprocity is being discovered even in the depths of hatred; even those who like to exaggerate their differences are clearly trying to conceal a basic identity from themselves. This agitation that is so novel, this modest, but strenuous attempt to communicate across the incommunicable is not the insipid—and always rather foolish—desire for an inert and already achieved universality. It is what I would call, rather, the movement of universalization. Nothing is possible yet; no agreement is in sight between the laboratory animals. We are separated by our universals, which afford constant opportunities for individual massacres. But if one of us turns away, anxiety-ridden, from the Idea and rejects abstract thinking; if one of us re-examines his singularity *in order to overcome it*; if one of us tries to recognize his loneliness in order to escape it, somehow to build bridges—in a strange, trial-and-error language similar to the one the aphasic reinvents—between the islets of our archipelagos; if one of us replaces our intransigent loves—that are really masked hatreds—with firm preferences; if one of us searches in the always singular, time-specific circumstances to unite with others, of whom he barely approves and who disapprove of him, to make the realm of Injustice a little less unjust, he will force the others to reinvent this same assiduous effort, to unite by recognizing their diversity. This is what Gorz has attempted: this traitor has smashed the tablets of the Universal, but he has done so to recover the movement of life, that slow universalization that is achieved by the affirmation and transcendence of the particular. The immediate consequence is that, at the very moment when he can at last say, *I* am doing this, *I* am responsible for it, he realizes that he is addressing *us*. For there are only two ways of speaking about oneself today: the third-person singular and the first-person plural. You have to be able to say 'we' if you are to be able to say 'I': this much is beyond dispute. But the converse is also true: if some tyranny, in order first to establish the 'we', deprived individuals of subjective thought, then the whole of inwardness would disappear at a stroke and, with it, relationships of mutuality: *they* would have won a definitive victory and we would never stop trotting round the experimental maze, crazed rodents in the grip of Vampires.

Gorz's book concerns us all. If at first he stammers and doesn't know where he's going, if he is perpetually transforming himself and if we feel his icy fever in our hands, if he contaminates us without seeing us and if, last of all, he addresses himself directly and intimately to every reader, this is because he is altogether shot through with the movement that drives us today, the movement of our age. Radical and modest, vague and rigorous, commonplace and inimitable, this is the first book *from after the defeat*. The Vampires created a memorable mayhem; they crushed hope. We have to get our breath back, play dead for a while and then raise ourselves, leave the killing fields and begin everything again; we have to invent new hope, to try to live. The great massacres of the century have made a corpse out of Gorz: he has revived by writing an Invitation to Life.

Foreword to André Gorz, *Le Traître*
(Paris: Edition de Seuil, 1958).

Notes

1 André Gide, *Les faux-monnayeurs* (1925); first published in *Nouvelle Revue Française*; *The Counterfeiters* (Dorothy Bussy trans.) (New York: Alfred A. Knopf, 1927). [Trans.]

2 Robert Caillois, *Puissances du roman* (Marseille: Sagittaire, 1942). [Trans.]

3 Jean-Jacques Rousseau, *Lettre à M. d'Alembert sur les Spectacles* (1758)—a refutation of d'Alembert's article 'Genève' in Denis Diderot and Jean le Rond d'Alembert (eds), *Encyclopédie ou Dictionnaire raisonné des sciences, des arts et des métiers* (Paris: 1751–77, 32 vols), VOL. 7 (1757), p. 578. [Trans.]

4 Nathalie Sarraute, *Portrait d'un inconnu* (Paris: Robert Marin, 1948; first edition); *Portrait of a Man Unknown* (Maria Jolas trans.) (New York: Braziller, 1958). [Trans.]

5 Nathalie Sarraute, *Tropismes* (first edition: Paris: Denoël, 1939); *Tropisms* (Maria Jolas trans.) (London: John Calder, 1963). [Trans.]

6 Sarraute, *Portrait of a Man Unknown*, p. 30. [Trans.]

7 Ibid.

8 Ibid. p. 57.

9 See Harold Rosenberg, 'Le Prolétariat comme héros et comme rôle', *Les Temps modernes*, 56 (June 1950): 2151.

10 On 20–29 May 1948, the Second International Congress of Composers was held in Prague. The conclusions of the congress, where it had been argued that contemporary Western music was in a state of crisis, were formulated in one of the official Congress documents, entitled the Proclamation (*Provolani*) but also known as the *Prague Manifesto*. [Trans.]

11 André Malraux, *The Voices of Silence. Man and His Art* (Princeton: Princeton University Press, 1978).

12 *A Survivor from Warsaw, Op. 46 (Ein Überlebender aus Warschau*) is a work for narrator, men's chorus, and orchestra written by the Austrian composer Arnold Schönberg in 1947. The initial inspiration was a suggestion from the Russian émigrée dancer Corinne Chochem for a work to pay tribute to the Jewish victims of the German Third Reich. [Trans.]

13 Let me make clear that the artist, in my view, differs from the writer [*littérateur*] in that he cultivates non-signifying arts. I have shown elsewhere that the problems of literature are very different.

14 Speech of 17 August 1934 to the First Soviet Writers' Congress. [Published as 'Soviet Literature—The Richest in Ideas, The Most Advanced Literature', in H. G. Scott (ed. and trans.), *Problems of Soviet Literature: Reports and Speeches at the First Soviet Writers' Congress* (Westport, Connecticut: Hyperion Press, Inc.,

1935), pp. 15–24. Also available at: www.marxists. org/subject/art/lit_crit/sovietwritercongress/ zdhanov.htm—Trans.]

15 Henri Matisse, 'Statements to Tériade: On the Purity of Means' [1936], in Jack D. Flam (ed.), *Matisse on Art* (California: University of California Press, 1995), p. 123 (translation modified). [Trans.]

16 *The Well-tempered Clavier (Das Wohltemperirte Clavier)* is a collection of solo keyboard music composed by Johann Sebastian Bach. He first gave the title to a book of preludes and fugues in all 24 major and minor keys, dated 1722, composed 'for the profit and use of musical youth desirous of learning, and especially for the pastime of those already skilled in this study'. He later compiled a second book of the same kind, dated 1742, but titled 'Twenty-four Preludes and Fugues'. The two works are now usually considered to comprise *The Well-tempered Clavier* and are referred to respectively as Books I and II. [Trans.]

17 Andre Gorz, *The Traitor* (Richard Howard trans.) (London: Verso, 1989) (translation modified). [All subsequent quotations are from this edition—Trans.]

18 I do not claim to establish Gorz's superiority, but his originality. Along with everyone else, I love death as much as life, for both are part of our fate.

19 Thomas Robert Bugeaud (1784–1849): appointed Governor-General of Algeria in 1840. [Trans.]

20 Pierre Drieu la Rochelle (1893–1945): prominent French fascist novelist and essayist; wrote *La Valise vide* (The Empty Suitcase) in 1921. [Trans.]

21 Jean Paulhan, *Le guerrier appliqué* (Paris: Sansot, 1917).

22 The expression is Marx's in German Ideology. [*Die Deutsche Ideologie*, 1845–46; first published in 1932—Trans.]

23 Paul Valéry, *Eupalinos* (Paris: Gallimard, 1944), p. 71. Valéry's Socrates actually makes this assertion in the singular: 'I told you that I was born *several* and I died *one.*'

24 Sartre alludes here to the first line of Stéphane Mallarmé's 'Le tombeau d'Edgar Poe' ['The Tomb of Edgar Poe', in Sara Sigourney Rice (ed.), *Edgar Allan Poe: A Memorial Volume* (Baltimore: Turnbull Brothers, 1877)—Trans.]

25 Baron Georges Cuvier (1769–1832): perhaps the foremost comparative anatomist of his day. [Trans.]

PART TWO

gide alive

We thought him sacred and embalmed: he dies and we discover how alive he still was; the unease and resentment that show through beneath the funerary wreaths so grudgingly woven for him demonstrate he still had the power to offend and will have for some time. He managed to unite right-thinking people of both Right and Left against him and you have only to imagine the joy of a few august old fogies as they exclaim, 'Thank you, Lord! So he really was in the wrong, since I'm the one who's still alive,' or to read, in *L'Humanité*, 'It is a corpse that has just died,' to see what an enormous influence this man of eighty, who had virtually given up writing, still had on the literature of our day.

There is a geography of thought. Just as a Frenchman, wherever he goes, cannot take a step on foreign soil without *also* moving closer to, or further from, France, so any step in our thinking *also* took us closer to Gide or further from him. His clarity, lucidity, rationalism and rejection of pathos gave others licence to venture into murkier, more uncertain, areas of thinking: one knew that, at the same time, a brilliant intelligence was upholding the rights of analysis, of purity and of a certain tradition. Had one foundered on one's voyage of discovery, one would not have dragged the mind down into the wreckage. The whole of French thought over the last thirty years, whether it liked it or not, and whatever its other points of reference—Marx, Hegel or Kierkegaard—had to define itself *also* in relation to Gide.

For my own part, the mental restrictions, the hypocrisy and, all in all, the contemptible foulness of the obituaries penned for him have annoyed me too much to contemplate setting down here what separated us from him. It is better to recall the inestimable gifts he bestowed on us.

I have learned from the pen of fellow journalists—who never struck me much by their boldness—that he 'lived dangerously beneath three layers of flannel'. What idiotic scoffing! These timorous creatures have invented a curious defence against the daring of others: they deign to acknowledge it only if it shows itself in all fields simultaneously. It seems Gide would have been forgiven for the risks he took with his thinking and reputation if he had also taken risks with his life and if, somewhat oddly, he had braved pneumonia. These people affect not to know that there are *different kinds* of courage and that they vary between people. Yes, Gide was cautious, he weighed his words, hesitated before signing anything, and, if he was interested in a movement of ideas or opinion, he saw to it that he gave it only conditional backing, remaining on the fringes, always ready to withdraw. But the same man dared to publish the profession of faith that is *Corydon*, the indictment that is *Travels in the Congo*,[1] and he had the courage to stand by the USSR when it was dangerous to do so and the greater courage publicly to reverse his opinion when he formed the view, rightly or wrongly, that he had been mistaken. It is perhaps this mix of wariness and audacity that makes him exemplary: generosity is a virtue only in those who know the price of things and, similarly, nothing is more moving than considered temerity. Written by an irresponsible person, *Corydon* would have been a mere moral scandal. But if its author is this wily, pernickety 'Oriental' who weighs everything, the book becomes a manifesto, a *testimony*, the significance of which goes far beyond the outrage it inspires. This wary audacity should be a 'Rule for the Guidance of the Mind': withhold one's judgement until the matter is clear and then, when one is firm in one's convictions, accept that one pays the price down to the very last penny.

Courage and caution: this judiciously balanced mixture explains the inner tension of his work. Gide's art seeks to strike a compromise between risk and rule. In him are balanced the Protestant law and the non-conformity of the homosexual; the proud individualism of the *grand bourgeois* and the Puritanical preference for social constraint; a certain curtness of manner, a difficulty in communicating and a humanism of Christian origin; a lively sensuality and yet a view of that sensuality as innocent. Observance of the rule is united here with the quest for spontaneity. This balancing act underlies the inestimable service Gide rendered contemporary literature: he it was who lifted it out of the symbolist rut. The second symbolist generation had convinced themselves that the writer demeaned himself if he ventured beyond a very narrow range of subjects, all of them very elevated, but that he could, on these clearly defined subjects, express himself in any manner he wished. Gide freed us from this naïve focus on subject matter: he taught us, or re-taught us, that *anything* could be said—that was his audacity—but according to certain rules of literary elegance—that was his caution.

From this cautious audacity came his perpetual turnabouts, his oscillations from one extreme to the other, his passion for objectivity, for what one should even term his 'objectivism'—a highly bourgeois characteristic, I admit—that made him look for Reason and for the right even in his opponent's positions and saw him fascinated by the opinions of others. I do not claim at all that these attitudes, so characteristic of the man, could serve us well today, but they enabled him to make his life a strictly conducted experiment that we can assimilate without any preparation; in a word, he *lived* his ideas. And one in particular: the death of God. I do not imagine that a single believer today was led to Christianity by the arguments of St Bonaventure or St Anselm, but I don't believe either that a single non-believer was turned from the faith by the opposite arguments. The problem of God is a human problem that concerns the relationships of human beings among themselves; it is a total problem to which everyone brings a solution by their whole life, and the solution one brings reflects the attitude one has chosen towards other human beings and oneself. The most precious thing Gide offers us is his decision to live out to the end the agony and death of God. He could, like so many others, have taken a gamble on concepts, plumped for faith or atheism at the age of twenty and held to that throughout his life. Instead of so doing, he wanted to *test out* his relation to religion, and the living dialectic that led him to his ultimate atheism is a path others can follow in his footsteps but not one that can be fixed in concepts or notions.

His interminable discussions with the Catholics, his outpourings, shafts of irony, flirtations, sudden breaks, advances, spells of marking time, backslidings, the ambiguity of the word 'God' in his work, his refusal to abandon it even when he believed only in humanity—all this rigorous experimentation has, in fact, done more to enlighten us than a hundred demonstrations. He lived *for us* a life we have only to relive by reading him; he enables us to avoid the traps he fell into or to get out of them as he did; the opponents on whom he brought discredit, if only by publishing their correspondence with him, no longer have any attraction for us. All truth, says Hegel, *has become* truth. Too often we forget this; we see the point of arrival, not the journey; we take the idea as a finished product without realizing that it is nothing other than its slow maturation, than a succession of necessary errors correcting themselves, of partial views that complement and expand one another. Gide is an irreplaceable example because he chose, on the contrary, to *become his truth*. Had he opted for it abstractly at twenty, his atheism would have been false; but   conquered slowly, as the crowning glory of a half- century's quest, that atheism becomes his concrete truth and our own. Starting from this point, the men of today can become new truths.

Les Temps modernes, 65 (March 1951).

reply to albert camus[2]

My dear Camus,

Our friendship was not easy, but I shall miss it. If today you break it off, doubtless that means it would inevitably have ended some day. Many things brought us together, few separated us. But those few were still too many: friendship, too, tends to become totalitarian; there has to be agreement on everything or a quarrel, and those who don't belong to any party themselves behave like members of imaginary parties. I shall not carp at this: it is as it must be. But, for just this reason, I would have preferred our current disagreement to be over matters of substance and that there should not be a whiff of wounded vanity mingled with it. Who would have said, who would have believed that everything would end between us in an authors' quarrel in which you played Trissotin to my Vadius?[3] I did not want to reply to you. Who would I be convincing? Your enemies, certainly, and perhaps my friends? And you—who do you think you are convincing? Your friends and my enemies. To our common enemies, who are legion, we shall both give much cause for laughter. That much is certain.

Unfortunately, you attacked me so deliberately and in such an unpleasant tone that I cannot remain silent without losing face. I shall, therefore, reply: without anger but, for the first time since I've known you, without mincing my words. A mix of melancholy conceit and vulnerability on your part has always deterred people from telling you unvarnished truths. The result is that you have fallen prey to a gloomy immoderation that conceals your inner difficulties and which you refer to, I believe, as Mediterranean moderation. Sooner or later, someone would have told you this, so it might as well be me. But do not fear, I shall not attempt your portrait; I do not want to incur the criticism you gratuitously level at Jeanson: I shall speak of your letter and of it alone, with a few references to your works if necessary.

It amply suffices to show—if I must speak of you the way the anti-Communist speaks of the USSR; alas, the way *you* speak of it—that you have carried through your Thermidorian Reaction. Where is Meursault, Camus? Where is Sisyphus? Where today are those Trotskyites of the heart who preached permanent revolution? Murdered, no doubt, or in exile. A violent, ceremonious dictatorship has established itself within you, basing itself on a fleshless bureaucracy and claiming to enforce the moral law. You wrote that my collaborator 'would like us to rebel against everything except the Communist party and state', but I fear, in my turn, that you rebel more easily against the Communist state than against yourself. It seems that the concern in your letter is to place yourself, *as quickly as possible*, beyond debate. You tell us this in the very first lines: it is not your intention to discuss the criticisms made of you, nor to argue with your adversary as an equal. Your aim is to *teach*. With the praiseworthy, didactic concern to edify the readers of the *Temps modernes*, you take Jeanson's article, which you assume to be symptomatic of the evil gnawing away at our societies and make it the subject of a lecture on pathology. It is as though we were in Rembrandt's painting, with you as the doctor and Jeanson the corpse, and you were pointing out his wounds to the astonished public. For it is of no matter to you at all, is it, that the offending article discusses your book? Your book is not at issue; a God guarantees its value. It will merely serve as a touchstone for revealing the guilty man's bad faith. In doing us the honour of participating in this issue of *Les Temps modernes*, you bring a portable pedestal with you. Admittedly, you do change method part way through and abandon your professorial demonstration and your 'tense serenity' to launch a vehement attack on me. But you were careful to say you were not defending your cause: what would be the point? Only Jeanson's criticisms—so tendentious that they leave you unscathed—run the risk of infringing inviolable principles and offending venerable personalities. It is these persons and principles you are defending: 'It is not me . . . he has treated unfairly, but our reasons for living and struggling and the legitimate hope we have of overcoming our contradictions. In the event, silence was no longer an option.'

But tell me, Camus, by what mystery can your works not be discussed without removing humanity's reasons for living? By what miracle do the objections made against you turn all at once into sacrilege? When *Passage du Malin* received the reception it did, I don't remember François Mauriac writing to *Le Figaro* to say the critics had imperilled the Catholic faith.[4] The fact is that you have a mandate: you speak, you say, 'in the name of that poverty that produces thousands of advocates and never a single brother'. If this is the case, we have to throw in the towel: if it is true that poverty came to you and said, 'Go and speak in my name,' we cannot but be silent and listen to its voice. Only I admit I don't follow your thinking very clearly: you speak in its name, but are you its advocate, its brother or its brother advocate? And if you are a brother to the poor, how did you become one? Since it cannot be by ties of blood, it must be a matter of the heart. But no, this cannot be either, since you *are selective about* your poor—I don't think you are a brother to the unemployed Communist in Bologna or the wretched day-labourer struggling against Bao-Dai and the colonialists in Indochina. Did you become a brother to the poor by your condition? You may have been so once but you are no longer; you are middle-class, like Jeanson and me. Is it by devotion, then? But if that devotion is intermittent, how close we are here to the lady bountiful and her charity. And if, to dare to call oneself a brother to the wretched, one must devote every moment of one's life to them, then you are not their brother: whatever your concern, it is not your sole motive and you don't greatly resemble Saint Vincent de Paul or a 'little sister of the poor'. Their brother? No. You are an advocate who says, 'These are my brothers' because these are the words most likely to move the jury to tears. You'll appreciate that I've heard too many paternalistic speeches: permit me to distrust that kind of brotherliness. And poverty did not give you any message. I have not the slightest intention, I assure you, of denying you the right to speak of it. But if you do, let it be, like us, at your own risk, accepting in advance the possibility of disavowal.[5]

But what does all this matter to you? If we take the poor away from you, you will still have plenty of allies. The former Resistance fighters, for example. Jeanson, poor man, did not remotely intend to offend them. He merely wanted to say that French people of our kind were faced with a political choice in 1940 (for we were of the same kind then: the same educational background, principles and interests). He was not claiming that resistance would have been easy; and, though he had not yet had the benefit of your lessons, he was not unaware of torture, shootings and deportations, nor of the reprisals that followed resistance attacks and the excruciating dilemmas of conscience they posed for some. He had been told of these things, you may rest assured. But these difficulties emerged out of action itself; to know them, one had already to have committed oneself. If he remains convinced that the decision to resist was not difficult to *make*, he is in no doubt either that it took great physical and moral courage to *sustain* it. Yet, he suddenly saw you appealing to the Resistance and—I blush here on your behalf—invoking the dead. 'He does not necessarily understand that the Resistance . . . never seemed to me either a happy or an easy form of history, any more than it did to any of those who really suffered from it, who killed or died in it.'

No, he does not necessarily understand that: he wasn't in France at the time but in a Spanish concentration camp, a result of trying to join the *armée d'Afrique*. But let us put these badges of honour aside. If Jeanson had lost an arm in the camp in which he almost died, his article would be neither better nor worse than it is. *The Rebel*[6] would be neither better nor worse if you hadn't joined the Resistance or had been sent to a concentration camp.

But here is another protestor. Jeanson—rightly or wrongly, I shall not get involved—criticized you for a certain ineffectiveness of thought. Immediately summoned up, the old political activist comes on stage: he is the offended party. You, however, confine yourself to gesturing towards him and informing us that you are tired. Tired of receiving lessons in efficacity, admittedly, but, *above all*, tired of seeing them given to mature family men by young upstarts. To this, one might, of course, reply that Jeanson was not speaking about political activists, young or old, but that he ventured, as is his right, an appreciation of that henceforth *historical* reality termed revolutionary syndicalism—for one may judge a movement ineffective while at the same time admiring the courage, spirit of enterprise, self-denial, even efficiency, of those who took part in it. Above all, one might reply that he was speaking about *you* who are not a political activist.

What if I were to quote an old Communist activist to you, after making him rich in years and loading him down with the ills best calculated to evoke emotional effect? What if I brought him on stage and had him make the following comments:

> I'm tired of seeing bourgeois like you bent on destroying the Party that is my one hope when they are incapable of putting anything in its place. I don't say the Party is above criticism; I do say you have to earn the right to criticize it. I have no truck with your moderation, Mediterranean or otherwise, and even less with your Scandinavian republics. Our hopes are not yours. And you may perhaps be my brother—fraternity costs so little—but certainly not my comrade.

What emotion, eh? I've trumped your activist with an activist-and-a-half. And we would lean, you and I, on the struts that hold up the scenery, receiving the applause of the public, each overcome by a healthy tiredness. But you know very well I do not play that particular game: I have never spoken except in my own name. And then, if I were tired, it seems to me I would be rather ashamed to say so: there are so many people who are more tired. If we are tired, Camus, let's go and rest, since we have the means to. But let us not hope to shake the world by compelling it to take stock of our weariness.

What name am I to give to these manoeuvres? Intimidation? Blackmail? At the very least, their aim is to terrorize: the unfortunate critic, surrounded all of a sudden by this host of heroes and martyrs, ends up jumping to attention like a civilian lost among soldiers. But what a confidence trick! Are you really asking us to believe they have lined up behind you? Nonsense, it is you who have put yourself at their head. Have you changed, then, so much? You used to condemn the use of violence everywhere and now, in the name of morality, you subject us to virtuous violence; you used to be the first servant of your moralism and now you are making it serve you.

What is disconcerting in your letter is that it is too *'written'*. I have no quarrel with its ceremoniousness, which comes naturally to you, but I object to the ease with which you wield your indignation. I recognize that our age has its unpleasant aspects and that it must at times be a relief, for red-blooded natures, to bang on the table and shout. But I regret the fact that upon this disorder of the mind, for which there may well be excuses, you have based a rhetorical order. One is not as ready to show indulgence to controlled violence as to the involuntary kind. With what cunning you play the cool customer, so that your outbursts will astonish us the more; how artfully you let your anger show through, only to conceal it immediately beneath a smile that seeks to be falsely reassuring! Is it my fault if these techniques remind me of the law courts! Only the Public Prosecutor knows how to affect irritation at the opportune moment, to retain control of his anger even in the wildest outbursts and to switch, if need be, to a burst of 'hearts and flowers'. Wouldn't the Republic of the Well-Meaning have appointed you its Public Accuser?[7]

I am here pulled aside and advised not to accord too much importance to stylistic devices. I would willingly give in, only it is difficult in this letter to distinguish devices in general from bad devices. You call me

Mr Editor, when each of us knows we have been friends for ten years: this is, I agree, merely a device; you address yourself to me when your clear intention is to refute Jeanson: this is a bad device. Is it not your aim to transform your critic into an *object*, into a dead man? You speak *of him* as though of a soup-tureen or a mandolin; you never speak *to him*. This indicates that he has placed himself beyond the bounds of the human: by your good offices, the resistance fighters, the prisoners, the activists and the poor turn him to stone. At times you succeed in annihilating him altogether, calmly writing '*your* article', as though I were its author. This isn't the first time you have used this trick: Hervé attacked you in a Communist journal and someone mentioned his article in *L'Observateur*, describing it as 'noteworthy' but offering no further comment. You asked the editor of that periodical how he could justify the adjective employed by his colleague and explained at length why Hervé's article was anything but 'noteworthy'. In short, you responded to Hervé but without addressing yourself to him: does one speak to a Communist? But I ask you, Camus, *who* are you to assume such a lofty stance? And what gives you the right to affect a superiority over Jeanson that *no one* grants you? Your literary merits are not in question; it matters little that you are the better writer and he the better thinker, or the other way about: the superiority you accord yourself, which gives you the right not to treat Jeanson as a human being, must be a *racial* superiority. Has Jeanson, by his criticisms, perhaps indicated that he differs from you in the way ants differ from human beings? Is there, perhaps, a racism of moral beauty? You have a handsome spirit and his is ugly: communication is not possible between you. And it is here that the device becomes intolerable because, to justify your attitude, you have to discover some blackness in his soul. And to discover it, isn't the easiest method first to put it there? For, what is this about? Jeanson didn't like your book. He said so and you didn't like it: so far, then, nothing exceptional. You wrote to criticize his criticism: you cannot be blamed for this; Monsieur de Montherlant does it every day.[8] You could go much further. You could say he had not understood a word and that I was a blockhead. You could cast aspersions on the intelligence of the whole editorial board of *Les Temps modernes*: all's fair in love and war. But when you write, 'Your collaborator would like us to rebel against everything except the Communist party and state,' I confess I feel uneasy: I thought I was faced with a man of letters and I am, in fact, dealing with an investigating magistrate handling the case on the basis of tendentious police reports. And if only you would be happy just to call him a 'Communist mole', but you have to make him a liar and a traitor: 'The author *has pretended* to mistake what he has read . . . I found (in the article) neither generosity nor honesty, but the *futile desire to misrepresent* a position he could not express without putting himself in a situation where he would have to debate it properly.' You propose to reveal the (evidently hidden) 'intention' that leads him to 'practice omission and traduce the book's argument . . . to make you say the sky is black when you say it is blue, etc.', to avoid the real problems, to conceal from the whole of France the existence of Russian concentration camps which your book revealed. What intention? Well, let's take a look! The intention to show that any idea that is not Marxist is reactionary. And why, when all is said and done, does he do that? Here you are a little less clear-cut, but, if I understand you aright, this shameful Marxist is afraid of the light. He was attempting with his clumsy hands to stop up all the openings of your thought, to halt the blinding rays of the obvious. For, if he had understood you fully, he *could no longer* call himself a Marxist. The unfortunate man believed it permissible to be both Communist and bourgeois: he was hedging his bets. You show him that he must choose: join the Party or become bourgeois like you.[9] But that is precisely what he will not see. Here, then, are the findings of the investigation: criminal intent, deliberate misrepresentation of another's thought, bad faith, repeated lies. You can no doubt imagine the mixture of stupefaction and merriment with which those who know Jeanson and Jeanson's sincerity, uprightness, scruples and concern for the truth, will greet this charge-sheet.

But what will be most appreciated, I suspect, is the passage in your letter when you invite us to come clean: 'I would find it normal and almost courageous if, tackling this problem openly, you were to justify the existence of these camps. What is abnormal and betrays embarrassment is that you do not mention them at all.' Here we are at police headquarters, the cop is pacing up and down and his shoes are squeaking, as they do in the cinema: 'We know the whole story, I tell you. Saying nothing isn't helping your case. Come on, admit you were involved. You knew these camps, didn't you? Just say you did and it will all be over. The court will take a favourable view of your confession.' In heaven's name, Camus, how *serious* you are and, to employ one of your own words, how frivolous! And what if you were wrong? What if your book merely revealed your philosophical incompetence? What if it were put together from second-hand information, hastily cobbled together? What if it merely afforded the privileged a good conscience, as might be attested by the critic who wrote the other day, 'With Monsieur Camus, revolt is changing sides'? And what if your reasoning were not so very correct? If your ideas were vague and banal? And if Jeanson had quite simply been struck by the indigence of those ideas? If, far from obscuring your radiantly plain facts, he had been forced to light lanterns to make out the contours of weak, obscure, garbled ideas? I do not say that this is the case, but could you not conceive *for one moment* that it might be? Are you so afraid of contradiction? Must you discredit all those who look you in the face as soon as you can? Can you accept only bowed heads? Was it not possible for you to defend your argument and maintain its correctness, while understanding that the other man thought it was wrong? Why do you, who defend *risk* in history, refuse it in literature? Why do you have to be defended by a whole universe of inviolable values instead of fighting against us—or with us—without divine intervention? You once wrote: 'We are stifling among people who believe they are absolutely right, either in their political machines or their ideas.' And it was true. But I'm very much afraid you may have gone over to the side of the stiflers and are abandoning forever your old friends, the stifled.

What really is too much is that you resort to the practice we heard criticized quite recently during a public meeting in which you took part—a practice termed, I believe, *conflation*. In certain political trials, if there are several defendants, the judge combines the charges so as to be able to combine the sentences: of course, this happens only in totalitarian states. Yet this is the procedure you have chosen. From one end of your indictment to the other, you pretend to confuse me with Jeanson. And how do you do this? It is simple, though it needed some thinking out: by an artifice of language, you disorient the reader to the point where he no longer knows which of us you are talking about. Step one: I am the editor of the journal, so it's me you are addressing—an irreproachable procedure. Step two: you invite me to acknowledge I am responsible for the articles published in it—I agree that this is the case. Step three: it *therefore* follows that I approve of Jeanson's attitude and, moving on quickly, that his attitude is also mine. Once this is established, it matters little which of us held the pen—in any event, the article is mine. Skilful use of the personal pronoun will complete the conflation: '*Your* article . . . *You* should have . . . *You* were entitled . . . *You* were not entitled . . . As soon as *you* spoke . . .' Jeanson, you imply, was merely embroidering on a canvas prepared by me. There is a double advantage here: you present him as my scribe and henchman, and there you have your revenge. And, then, here am I, a criminal in my turn: I am the one insulting the activists, the Resistance fighters and the poor; I am the one who covers his ears when the Soviet camps are mentioned; I am the one seeking to hide your light under a bushel. One example will suffice to expose the method here: it will be clear that the 'offence', which loses all substance if ascribed to its true author, turns into a crime when the charge is levelled against the person who did not commit it.

When you write, 'No review of my book can leave aside the fact (of the Russian camps),' you are addressing Jeanson alone. It is the critic you are taking issue with for not speaking, *in his article*, about the concentration camps. Perhaps you are right. Perhaps Jeanson could reply that it is farcical to have the author decide what the critic is to say; moreover, you don't speak much of the camps in your book and it's not easy to see why you suddenly demand their being taken into consideration, unless some poorly primed informers have led you to believe you would thereby be embarrassing us. In any event, this is a legitimate debate that you and Jeanson could have. But when you then write, '*You* retain the relative right to ignore the fact of the camps in the USSR, so long as you do not tackle the questions raised by revolutionary ideology in general and by Marxism in particular, *you* lose it if you tackle those questions, and *you* tackle them *by speaking* about my book,' or alternatively: 'I would find it normal . . . if *you* justified the existence of the camps,' then it is *me* you are addressing. Well, let me reply that these interpellations are deceitful: for you take advantage of the undeniable fact that Jeanson—*as was his right*—did not, in reviewing your book, speak of the Soviet camps, so that you may insinuate that I, the editor of a journal that claims to be politically committed, have never tackled the question—something which, if it were the case, might be said to be a serious offence against honesty. Only it just so happens that it is untrue: a few days after Rousset's declarations, we devoted several articles to the camps, together with an editorial to which I fully subscribed.[10] And, if you compare the dates, you'll see that the issue was put together *before* Rousset's declarations. But that matters little: I merely wanted to show you that we raised the question of the camps and took a stand at the very moment when French public opinion was discovering them. We returned to the subject a few months later *in another editorial* and clarified our point of view in articles and notes. The existence of these camps may enrage and horrify us; it may be that we are obsessed with them, but why should it *embarrass us*? Have I ever backed away when it came to saying what I thought about the Communist attitude? And if I am a 'crypto-communist', a shameful fellow traveller, why do they hate me and not you? But let us not boast about the hatreds we inspire: I will tell you honestly that I deeply regret this hostility; sometimes I might even go so far as to envy the profound indifference they show towards you. But what can I do about it, except precisely no longer say what I believe to be true? What are you claiming then, when you write, 'You retain the relative right to ignore . . .' etc.? Either you are insinuating that Jeanson does not exist and is one of my pseudonyms, which is absurd, or you are claiming I've never said a word about the camps, which is slanderous. Yes, Camus, like you I find these camps unacceptable, but I also find unacceptable the use the 'so-called bourgeois press' makes of them each day. I do not say that the Madagascan takes precedence over the Turkoman; I say we must not use the sufferings inflicted on the Turkoman to justify those *we* inflict on the Madagascan.

I have seen anti-Communists delight in the existence of these jails, I have seen them use them to salve their consciences; and I did not have the impression they were helping the Turkomans, but, rather, exploiting their misery in the same way as the USSR exploited their labour. We might truly term this full employment for the Turkomans. But let's be serious, Camus: tell me, if you will, what sentiment Rousset's revelations could have stirred in an anti-Communist's heart. Despair? Affliction? Shame at being human? Nonsense. It's difficult for a Frenchman to put himself in the shoes of a Turkoman, to feel sympathy for that abstract being, the Turkoman, when seen from France. At best, I will concede that, among the best of Frenchmen, the memory of the German camps reawakened a kind of very spontaneous horror. And then, of course, fear too. But, don't you see, in the absence of any relationship with the Turkoman, what must provoke indignation, and perhaps despair, was the idea that a socialist government, supported by an army of functionaries, could have systematically reduced human beings to slavery? Now *that*, Camus, cannot affect the anti-Communist, who *already believed the USSR capable of anything*. The only sentiment this information provoked in him was—and it pains me to say this—*joy*. Joy because he had, at last, his *proof* and that now 'we should really see something'. The point now was to act not on the workers—the anti-Communist isn't so foolish—but on all the good people who remained 'on the Left'; they had to be intimidated, stricken with terror. If they opened their mouths to complain about some outrage, it was closed immediately with a 'What about the camps?' People were *commanded* to denounce the camps on pain of collusion with them. An excellent method, in which the unfortunates either offended the Communists or were made to collude in 'the greatest crime on earth'. It was around this time that I began to find these blackmailers despicable. For, in my view, the scandal of the camps puts us all on our mettle. You as much as me. And everyone else: the Iron Curtain is merely a mirror and the two halves of the world reflect each other. To every turn of the screw *here* there is a corresponding turn *over there*; we both turn the screw and feel its bite. A tougher line in the USA, which expresses itself in a renewed outbreak of witch-hunting,[11] causes a harder line on the part of the Russians, which will perhaps be expressed in increased arms production and a higher number of forced labourers. The opposite may, of course, be true too. Those who condemn today must know that our situation will force them tomorrow to do worse things than they have condemned; and when I see this joke scrawled on the walls of Paris—'Take your holidays in the USSR, land of liberty' over grey shadowy figures depicted behind bars, it isn't the Russians I find disgusting. Don't misunderstand me, Camus: I know you have on a hundred occasions denounced and fought Franco's tyranny or the colonial policy of our government with all the powers available to you; you have won the *relative* right to speak of the Soviet concentration camps. But I shall make two criticisms of your position: you were fully entitled to mention the camps in a serious work, the aim of which is to provide us with an explanation of our times; indeed, it was your *duty*; what seems unacceptable to me is that you use this today as a piece of clap-trap and that you, like the others, exploit the Turkoman and the Kurd the more surely to crush a critic who did not praise you.

And then I'm sorry you produce your sledge-hammer argument to justify a quietism that refuses to distinguish between the different masters. For, as you say yourself, it is the same thing to treat all masters as the same as to treat all slaves as the same. And if you do not make any distinction between slaves, you condemn yourself to have only a theoretical sympathy for them. Particularly as it often happens that the 'slave' is the ally of those you call the masters. This explains the embarrassment you get into over the war in Indochina. If we are to apply your principles, then the Vietnamese have been colonized and hence are slaves, but they are Communists and hence are tyrants. You criticize the European proletariat for not having publicly expressed disapproval of the Soviets, but you also criticize the governments of Europe because they are going to admit Spain into UNESCO; in this case I can see only one solution for you: the Galapagos Islands. It seems to me, by contrast, that the only way to help the slaves over there is to take the side of the slaves over here.

I was going to close on this, but, re-reading your letter, I get the impression that your indictment claims also to take in our ideas.[12] It would seem, in fact, that in employing the words 'unbridled freedom', you have our conception of human freedom in your sights. Should I insult you by believing these to be your words? No, you are incapable of such an error; you have no doubt picked up the words 'unbridled freedom' from the study by Troisfontaines.[13] Well, I shall at least share with Hegel the distinction of not having been read by you. But what a bad habit you have of not going back to sources! Yet *you know very well* that only the real forces of this world can be 'bridled' and that the physical action of an object is restrained by acting on one of the factors affecting it. But freedom is not a force: this is not my decision; it is part of its very definition. Freedom either exists or does not, but, if it does, it lies outside the sequence of cause and effect; it is of another order. Would you not laugh if we spoke of Epicurus' unrestrained *clinamen*? Since that philosopher, the conception of determinism and, as a consequence, of freedom has become a little more complicated, but the idea of a break, a disconnection or 'solution of continuity' remains. I hardly dare advise you to refer here to *Being and Nothingness*;[14] to read it would seem to you pointlessly arduous: you detest difficulties of thought and are quick to decree that there is nothing to understand, so as to avoid in advance the criticism that you have not understood. The fact remains that in that book I explained precisely the conditions for this break. And if you had spent a few minutes reflecting on someone else's ideas, you would have seen that freedom cannot be restrained or bridled: it has neither wheels nor legs, nor jaws between which to put a bridle, and, since it is determined by the undertaking in which it is involved, it finds its limits in the positive, but necessarily *finite,* character of that undertaking.

We are on a journey, we have to choose: the *project* brings its own enlightenment and gives the situation its meaning, but, by the same token, it is merely one particular way of transcending that situation—of understanding it. Our project is ourselves: in the light of it, our relation to the world becomes clearer; the goals and the tools appear that reflect back to us both the world's hostility and our own aim. Having said this, you are quite at liberty to term 'unbridled' the freedom that can alone ground *your own demands,*

149

Camus (for if human beings are not free, how can they 'demand to have a meaning'? Only, you don't like to think about that.). But there will be no more sense to this than if you spoke of oesophagus-less freedom or freedom without hydrochloric acid, and you merely have revealed that, like so many, you confuse politics and philosophy. Unbridled: of course. Without police or magistracy. If we grant the freedom to consume alcoholic drink without setting limits, what will become of the virtuous wife of the drunkard? But French Revolutionary thinking is clearer on this than yours: the limit of one right (i.e. of one freedom) is another right (i.e. another freedom) and not some 'human nature' or other; for nature, whether 'human' or not, can crush human beings but it cannot reduce them to the status of object; if man is an object, he is so for another man. And it is these two ideas—which are, I agree, difficult—that man is free and man is the being by which man becomes an object, that define our present status and enable us to understand *oppression*.

You had believed—on whose authority?—that I first ascribed a paradisiacal freedom to my fellow creatures so as subsequently to clap them in irons. I am so far from this conception that I see around me only freedoms *already enslaved*, attempting to wrest themselves from their *congenital* slavery. Our freedom today is merely *the free choice to struggle to become free*. And the paradoxical aspect of this formula encapsulates the paradox of our *historical* condition. It is not a question, as you see, of *caging* my contemporaries: they are already in the cage; it is a matter, rather, of uniting with them to break down the bars.

For we too, Camus, are committed, and if you really want to prevent a popular movement from degenerating into tyranny, don't begin by condemning it out of hand and threatening to withdraw into the desert, particularly as your deserts are only ever a less frequented part of our cage. To earn the right to influence human beings in struggle, you have first to take part in their fight; you have first to accept a lot of things if you want to try to change a small number. 'History' presents few more desperate situations than ours—this is what excuses the pompous prophecies. But when a man sees the present struggles merely as the imbecilic duel between two equally despicable monsters, I contend that that man has already left us:

he has gone off alone to his corner and is sulking; far from seeming to me loftily to judge and dominate an age on which he deliberately turns his back, I see him as entirely conditioned by it and clinging obstinately to the refusal inspired in him by a very historical *ressentiment*. You pity me for having a bad conscience and that is not the case, but, even if I were entirely poisoned by shame, I would feel less alienated and more open than you: for, to keep your conscience in good order you need to condemn; you need a guilty party: if not yourself, then the universe. You pronounce your verdicts and the world responds with not a word; but your condemnations cancel themselves out on contact with it and you have perpetually to begin again. If you stopped, you might see yourself; you have condemned yourself to condemn, Sisyphus.

For us you were—and can again be tomorrow— the admirable conjunction of a person, an action and a body of writings. That was in 1945: we discovered Camus, the Resistance fighter, as we had discovered Camus, the author of *The Outsider*.[15] And when we compared the editor of the underground *Combat* with that Meursault who carried honesty to the point of refusing to say that he loved either his mother or his mistress and whom our society condemned to death, when we knew, above all, that you had not stopped being either of these, the apparent contradiction increased our knowledge of ourselves and the world, and you were little short of exemplary. For you summed up the conflicts of the age in yourself and transcended them through your fiery determination to live them out. You were a *person*, the most complex and richest of persons: the latest and timeliest of the heirs of Chateaubriand and the resolute defender of a social cause. You had every good fortune and all the qualities, since you combined a sense of greatness with a passionate taste for beauty, a *joie de vivre* with an awareness of death. Even before the war, and against the bitter experience of what you call the *absurd*, you had chosen to defend yourself by scorn, but you were of the opinion that 'every negation contains a flowering of *yeses*' and you tried to find the consent that underlay every rejection, 'to hallow the accord between love and revolt'. In your view, man is only entirely himself when he is happy. And 'what is happiness but the simple accord between a being and the existence he leads.

And what more legitimate accord can bind man to life than the twofold consciousness of his desire to endure and his mortal destiny?' Happiness was neither entirely a state nor entirely an act, but that tension between the forces of death and the forces of life, between acceptance and refusal, by which man defines the *present*—that is to say, both the moment and eternity—and turns into himself. Thus, when you described one of those privileged moments that achieve a temporary accord between man and nature and which, from Rousseau to Breton, have provided our literature with one of its major themes, you were able to introduce into it an entirely new note of *morality*. To be happy is to do one's job as a human being; you showed us 'the duty of being happy'. And that duty merged with the affirmation that man is the only being in the world who has a meaning, 'because he is the only creature to demand that he should'. The experience of happiness, similar to Bataille's 'Torment',[16] but richer and more complex, made you stand up to an absent God as a reproach but also as a challenge: 'Man must affirm justice in order to combat eternal injustice, and create happiness to protest against the universe of misery.' The universe of misery is not *so-cial* or, at least, not primarily so: it is indifferent, empty Nature, in which man is alien and condemned to die; in a word, it is 'the eternal silence of the Divinity'. So your experience closely combined the ephemeral and the permanent. Aware of being perishable, you wanted to deal only with truths 'that must necessarily rot'. Your body was one of those. You rejected the fraudulence of the Soul and the Idea. But since, in your own words, injustice is *eternal*—that is to say, since the absence of God is a constant throughout the changing course of history—the immediate relation, begun ever anew, of the man who demands that he *have* a meaning (that is to say, demands to be given one) to this God who eternally remains silent, is itself transcendent with respect to history. The tension by which man realizes himself—which is, at the same time, intuitive enjoyment of being—is, therefore, a veritable conversion that wrests him from daily 'agitation' and 'historicity' and reconciles him at last with his condition. We can go no further; no progress can have its place in this instantaneous tragedy. As an Absurdist *avant la lettre*, Mallarmé wrote: '(The drama) is resolved immediately in the time it takes to show the defeat that occurs with lightning speed' and he seems to me to have provided in advance the key to your theatrical works when he writes: 'The Hero *releases*—the (maternal) hymn that creates him and is restored in the Theatre which this was—from the Mystery in which that hymn was shrouded.'[17] In short, you remain within our great classical tradition which, since Descartes and with the exception of Pascal, is entirely hostile to history. But you, at last, achieved the synthesis between aesthetic pleasure, desire, happiness and heroism, between satisfied contemplation and duty, between Gidean plenitude and Baudelairean dissatisfaction. You topped off Ménalque's immoralism[18] with an austere moralism; the content was not changed.

> There is only one love in this world. Embracing a woman's body also means holding in your arms this strange joy which descends from sky to sea. In a moment, when I throw myself down among the wormwood plants to bring their scent into my body, I shall know, whatever prejudice may say, that I am fulfilling a truth which is that of the sun and which will also be that of my death.[19]

But since this truth belongs to everyone, since its extreme singularity is precisely what makes it universal, since you were breaking open the shell of the pure present in which Nathanael[20] seeks God and opening it to the 'profundity of the world', that is to say, to death, then at the end of this sombre, solitary pleasure, you rediscovered the universality of an ethics and human solidarity. Nathanael is no longer alone; he is 'conscious and proud of sharing' this love of life, stronger than death, 'with a whole race'. It all ends badly, of course: the world swallows up the irreconciled libertine. And you liked to cite this passage from *Obermann*: 'Let us go down resisting, and if nothingness is to be our fate, let it not be a just one.'[21]

You do not deny it then. You did not reject history because you have suffered from it and discovered its face to be horrendous. You rejected it before you had any experience of it, because our culture rejects it and because you located human values in man's struggle 'against heaven'. You chose and created yourself as you are by meditating on the misfortunes and anxieties that fell to you personally, and the solution you found for them is a bitter wisdom that strives to deny time.

However, with the coming of war you devoted yourself unreservedly to the Resistance; you fought an austere fight that offered no fame or elevation; the dangers incurred hardly brought one any glory: worse, one ran the risk of being demeaned and debased. That effort, always painful and often solitary, *necessarily* presented itself as a *duty*. And your first contact with history assumed for you the aspect of *sacrifice*. You wrote as much, in fact, and you have said that you were fighting 'for that nuance that separates sacrifice from mysticism.' Don't misunderstand me: if I say 'your first contact with history', it is not to imply that I had another and that it was better. Around that time, we intellectuals had only that contact; and if I refer to it as *yours*, it is because you experienced it more deeply and totally than many of us, myself included. The fact remains that the circumstances of this battle entrenched you in the belief that one must sometimes pay one's tribute to history to have the right, later on, to return to the real duties. You accused the Germans of tearing you away from your battle with heaven to force you to take part in the temporal combats of men: 'For so many years you have tried to *bring me into*

history.' And, further on, you write: 'You did the necessary, *we entered history*; and for five years, it was no
longer possible to enjoy birdsong.'[22] The history in
question was the war; for you that was *other people's
madness*. It does not create, it destroys: it prevents the
grass from growing, the birds from singing and
human beings from making love. It so happened, in
fact, that external circumstances seemed to confirm
your point of view: *in peacetime* you were fighting a
timeless battle against the injustice of our destiny and
the Nazis had, in your view, sided with that injustice.
In collusion with the blind forces of the universe, they
were trying to destroy humanity. You fought, as you
put it, 'to save the *idea* of mankind'.[23] In short, it was
not your intention to 'make history', as Marx says, but
to prevent it from being made. Proof lies in the fact
that, after the war, you merely had in mind a return
of the *status quo ante*: 'Our condition [continued to be]
desperate.' The meaning of the Allied victory seemed
to you to be 'the acquisition of two or three nuances
that will perhaps have no other use than to help some
of us to die better'.

After serving your five years with history, you thought you (and the whole of humanity with you) could return to the despair in which man must find his happiness, and go back to 'proving that we did not deserve so much injustice' (in whose eyes?) by resuming the desperate battle human beings wage 'against their repellent destinies'. How we loved you in those days. We too were neophytes of history and endured it with repugnance, not understanding that the war of 1940 was merely one mode of historicity—neither more nor less so than the years preceding it. When we thought of you, we thought of Malraux's phrase, 'May victory go to those who made war without liking it,' and we felt a little sorry for ourselves as we repeated it; at that time we were under threat, like you and in you, without our realizing it.

It often happens that cultures produce their richest works when they are about to disappear, and those works are the fruits of the lethal marriage of the old values and the new ones that seem to render them fertile but actually kill them off. In the synthesis you were attempting, the happiness and the yea-saying came from our old humanism, but the revolt and the de-

spair were intruders. They came from outside, from
an outside where persons unknown looked on at our
spiritual festivities with hatred in their eyes. You had
borrowed that gaze from them to turn it on our cultural heritage; it was their simple, stark existence that
threw our tranquil pleasures into question; of course, the
defiance of destiny, the revolt against absurdity all
came from you or passed through you: but, thirty or
forty years earlier, you would have been made to drop
these ill-bred ways and would have joined the ranks
of the aesthetes or the Church. Your Revolt assumed
the importance it did only because it was prompted
in you by this obscure crowd: you barely had time to
deflect it against the heavens, where it vanished. And
the moral demands you brought to light were simply
the idealization of very real demands welling up
around you that you had seized on. The equilibrium
you achieved between these things could happen only
once, for a single moment, in a single person: you had
had the good fortune that the common struggle
against the Germans symbolized for you, and for us,
the unity of all human beings against inhuman fate.
By choosing injustice, the German had, of his own

volition, ranged himself among the blind forces of Nature and you were able, in *The Plague*,[24] to have his part played by microbes without anyone realizing the mystification. In short, you were, for a few years, the symbol and evidence of solidarity between the classes. This is also what the Resistance seemed to be and it is what you demonstrated in your earliest works: 'Men rediscover their solidarity in order to enter the struggle against their repellent destinies.'

In this way, a combination of circumstances, one of those rare concordances that, for a time, turn a life into the image of a truth, enabled you to conceal from yourself that man's struggle against Nature is both the cause and effect of another struggle, just as old and even more ruthless: the struggle of man against man. You were rebelling against death but, in the belts of iron that ring our cities, other people were rebelling against the social conditions that increase the mortality rate. When a child died, you condemned the absurdity of the world and that deaf, blind God you had created so as to be able to spit in His face. But the child's father, if he were a labourer or unemployed, condemned human beings: he knew very well that the absurdity of our condition isn't the same in Passy as it is in Boulogne-Billancourt.[25] And, in the end, the microbes were almost hidden from him by human beings: in the poor districts, the child mortality rate is twice what it is in the wealthy suburbs and, since a different distribution of income could save them,[26] half of the deaths, among the poor, seem like executions, with the microbe merely playing the hangman's final role.

You wanted to achieve—within yourself, through yourself—happiness for everyone by way of a *moral* tension. The sombre masses we were beginning to discover called on us to give up our happiness so that they could become a little less unhappy. Suddenly, the Germans no longer mattered. It was almost as though they had never mattered. We had thought there had been only one way of resisting; we discovered that there were two ways of *seeing* the Resistance. And while you still personified the immediate past for us and were perhaps even the coming man of the near future, for ten million French people who did not recognize their only too real anger in your ideal rebellion, you had already become one of the privileged. The death, life, earth, rebellion and God you spoke of, the 'yes' and the 'no' and the

'love' were, they told you, mere aristocratic amuse-
ments. To others, they seemed like something out of a
circus. You had written: 'Only one thing is more tragic
than suffering and that is the life of a happy man.' And:
'a certain continuity in despair can give birth to joy.'
And: 'I was not sure that this splendour of the world
was not [the justification] of all men who know that an
extreme point of poverty always connects us back to
the luxury and riches of the world.'[27] And admittedly,
being like you, one of the privileged, I understood what
you meant and I believe you have paid your dues to be
able to say it. I imagine you have been closer to a certain kind of death and deprivation than many people,
and I think you must have known genuine poverty, if
not destitution. Coming from your pen, these lines *do
not have* the meaning they would in a book by Messrs.
Mauriac or Montherlant. Moreover, when you wrote
them, they seemed natural. But the key thing today is
that *they no longer do*: we know that it takes, if not wealth,
then at least culture, the inestimable and unjust riches
of culture, to find luxury in the depths of deprivation. One feels that the circumstances of your life—
even the most painful of them—have chosen you to
attest that personal salvation was accessible to all; and

the predominant thought in everyone's heart, a menacing, hate-filled thought, is that this is possible only for
a few. A hate-filled thought, but what can we do about
that? Hatred gnaws away at everything. Even in you,
who tried not even to hate the Germans, there is a hatred of God that shows through in your books, and it
has been said that you are even more of an 'anti-theist'
than an atheist. The whole value that oppressed persons may still have in their own eyes, they put into the
hatred they bear to other human beings. And their
friendship for their comrades also involves the hatred
they bear for their enemies; neither your books nor
your example can do anything for them; you teach an
art of living, a 'science of life', you teach us to rediscover our bodies, but their bodies when they get them
back in the evening—after having them stolen from
them all day—are merely great wretched things that
encumber and humiliate them. These men are *made* by
other men; their number one enemy is man, and, if
the strange nature they find in the factory and the
building site still speaks to them of man, this is because it is men who have transformed these places
into prisons for them.

What options remained open to you? To modify yourself in part, so as to retain some of your old loyalties, while satisfying the demands of these oppressed masses. You would perhaps have done this, had not their representatives insulted you, as is their wont. You stopped dead the slide that was taking place within you and insisted, with renewed defiance, on demonstrating to everyone the union of men in the face of death and the solidarity between classes, when the classes had already resumed their struggles before your very eyes. Thus, what for a time had been an *exemplary reality* became the utterly empty affirmation of an *ideal*—all the more so as this false solidarity had changed into struggle even in your own heart. You found history to be in the wrong and, rather than interpret its course, you preferred to see it as just one more absurdity. Basically, you resumed your initial attitude. You borrowed some sort of idea of the 'divinization of man' from Malraux, Carrouges and twenty other writers and, condemning the human race, you took your stand alongside it, but outside its ranks, like the last of the Mohicans.

Your personality, real and vital so long as it was fed by events, is becoming a mirage. In 1944 it was the future; in 1952 it is the past. And what seems to you the most repellent injustice is that all this is happening to you from outside and without your having changed. It seems to you that the world offers the same riches as it did in the past and that it is human beings who no longer wish to see them. Well, try holding out your hand and you will see if it doesn't all vanish: even Nature has changed its meaning because the relationship of human beings to that Nature has changed. The memories and the language you are left with are increasingly abstract; you are only half living among us and you are tempted to leave us altogether to withdraw into some solitude where you can rediscover the drama that was supposed to be that of mankind and is no longer even your own—in other words, into a society that has remained at a lower level of technical civilization. What is happening to you is, in a sense, quite unjust. But, in another, it is pure justice: you had to change if you wanted to remain yourself and you were afraid of changing. If you find me cruel, have no fear: I shall speak of myself shortly, and in this same tone. There is no point trying to hit back at me; but, trust me, I shall see to it that I pay for all this. For you are absolutely unbearable, but you are, nonetheless, by force of circumstance, my neighbour.

Though engaged, like you, in history, I do not see it as you do. No doubt it has this absurd, fearful countenance for those who view it from Hades: this is because they no longer have anything in common with the human beings who are making it. And if it were a history of ants or bees, I am sure we would see it as a silly, macabre succession of crime, mockery and murder. But if we were ants, perhaps we would take a different view. Until I re-read your *Letters to a German Friend*, I did not understand your dilemma—'Either history has a meaning or it does not,' etc.—but it all became clear to me when I found there this remark which you address to the Nazi soldier, 'For years you have been trying to get me to enter history.' 'Good Lord,' I said to myself, 'since he believes he stands *outside* history, no wonder he lays down his conditions before coming *inside*.' Like a girl testing the water with her toe and asking, 'Is it warm?', you regard history warily. You stick in a finger, then very quickly pull it out again, asking, 'Has it a meaning?' You didn't hesitate in 1941, but then you were being asked to make a sacrifice. It was quite simply a question of preventing the Hitlerian madness from smashing a world where solitary elation was still possible for some, and you were willing to pay the price for your future moments of elation.

Things are different today. It is no longer a question of *defending the status quo* but of changing it. This is something you will agree to only with the firmest of guarantees. And if I thought, as you do, that history is a pool full of mud and blood, I would do as you do, I imagine, and look twice before diving in. But let us suppose that I am already in it; let us suppose that, from my point of view, your very aloofness is proof of your historicity. Suppose you receive the answer Marx would give you: 'History does nothing . . . It is men, real living men who do everything; history is merely the activity of human beings pursuing their own ends.' If this is true, the person who believes he is moving away from history will cease to share his contemporaries' ends and will be sensible only of the absurdity of human restlessness. But if he rails against that restlessness, he will, against his will, re-enter the historical cycle, for he will involuntarily provide the side that is on the ideological defensive (that is to say, the one whose culture is dying) with arguments for discouraging the other. The person who, by contrast, subscribes to the aims of concrete human beings will be forced to choose his friends because, in a society torn apart by civil war, one can neither accept nor reject everyone's aims at the same time. But, as soon as he chooses, everything acquires a meaning: he knows why the enemies resist and why he fights. For only in historical action is the understanding of history vouchsafed. 'Does history have a meaning?' you ask. 'Does it have a purpose?' In my view, it is the question that is meaningless. For history, considered apart from those who make it, is merely an abstract, static concept, and we can neither say that it has a purpose nor that it does not. And the problem is not one of *knowing* its purpose but of *giving* it one.

Moreover, no one acts *solely* with an eye to history. Human beings are, in fact, engaged in short-term projects, lit by distant hopes. And there is nothing absurd about these projects: on the one hand, we have Tunisians rising up against the colonial power, on the other, miners striking for better conditions or on grounds of solidarity. Whether there are values transcendent to history is not the question: we shall merely note that *if there are* such values, they manifest themselves through human actions that are, by definition, historical. And this contradiction is essential to human beings: they become historical through pursuing the eternal, and discover universal values in the concrete action they take to achieve a particular outcome.

If you say this world is unjust, you have lost the game: you are already outside, comparing a justiceless world to a contentless Justice. But you will discover justice in every effort you make to order your undertaking, to divide tasks between your comrades, to submit yourself to discipline or to apply it. And Marx never said history would have an end: how could he have? You might as well say that men would one day have no objectives. He merely spoke of an end to prehistory or, in other words, of an objective that would be achieved within history itself and then left behind, as all objectives are. It is not a matter of establishing whether history has a meaning and whether we deign to participate in it, but, given that we are in it up to our necks, of trying to give it what seems to us the best meaning, by not refusing our participation, no matter how small, in any of the concrete actions that require it.

Terror is an abstract violence. You became terroristic and violent when history—which you rejected—rejected you in turn: this is because you were merely, then, the abstraction of a rebel. Your distrust of human beings led you to presume that any accused person was, *first and foremost*, a guilty one: hence your police methods with Jeanson. Your morality turned first into moralism; today it is merely literature; tomorrow it will perhaps be immorality. What will become of us I do not know: perhaps we shall end up on the same side, perhaps not. The times are hard and confused. In any event, it has been good to be able to tell you what I have been thinking. The review is open to you if you want to reply, but I shall make no further reply to you. I have said what you were for me and what you are at present. But, whatever you may do or say in return, I refuse to fight with you. I hope our silence will lead to this polemic being forgotten.

Les Temps modernes, 82 (August 1952).

albert camus

Six months ago, even yesterday, we were wondering, '*What is he going to do?*' Riven by contradictions we must respect, he had, for the time being, chosen silence. But he was one of those rare men you can happily wait for because they choose slowly and stand by their decisions. One day, he would speak. We would not even have dared to conjecture what he would say. But we thought that he changed with the world, as each of us does: that sufficed for his presence to remain a living one.

We had quarrelled, he and I. A quarrel is nothing—even if you were never to see each other again: it is just another way of living *together*, without losing sight of each other in the narrow, little world allotted to us. This didn't prevent me from thinking of him, from sensing his gaze on the page of the book or the newspaper he was reading and asking myself, 'What's he saying about it, what's he saying about it *right now*?'

His silence which, depending on events and my mood, I thought at times too cautious and, at others, painful, was a quality of each day, like the heat or the light, but a *human* quality. One lived with or against his thought, as revealed to us in his books—*The Fall*,[28] in particular, perhaps the finest and least understood—but always through it. It was a singular adventure of our culture, a movement whose phases and final term one tried to divine.

In this century, and running counter to history, he was the current heir to that long line of moralists whose works perhaps constitute what is most original in French literature. His stubborn humanism, narrow and pure, austere and sensual, fought an uncertain battle against the massive, misshapen events of our times. But, conversely, through the unyielding nature of his refusals, in the heart of our age, against the Machiavellians and the golden calf of realism, he re-asserted the existence of morality.

He *was*, one might almost say, that unshakeable affirmation. If one read or thought, then one ran up against the human values he held in his tightly clenched fist: he called the political act into question. You had either to bypass him or fight him: he was, in a word, indispensable to that tension that constitutes the life of the mind. His very silence in recent years had a positive aspect: this Cartesian of the Absurd refused to leave the sure ground of morality and tread the uncertain paths of *practice*. We sensed this, and we sensed also the conflicts on which he remained silent: for morality, taken on its own, both demands revolt and condemns it.

We were waiting, we had to wait, we had to know; whatever he might have done or decided subsequently, Camus would never have ceased to be one of the chief forces in our cultural field or to represent, in his way, the history of France and of this century. But we would have known, perhaps, and understood his itinerary. He had done everything—produced an entire body of work—and, as ever, everything still remained

to be done. He said as much: 'My work lies before me.'
It is finished. The particular scandal of this death is
the way that the inhuman has overridden the order of
men.

The human order is still merely a disorder: it is
unjust and precarious; people are killed in it, they die
of starvation. But at least it is founded, maintained
and combated by human beings. In that order, Camus
should have lived: this man on the march called us
into question; he was himself a question in search of
an answer; he was living *in the middle of a long life*. For
us, for him, for those who enforce order and those
who reject it, it was important that he end his silence,
that he decide, that he conclude. Others die old; others, under constant stay of execution, may die at any
minute without the meaning of their lives—or *of
life*—being changed. But for us, uncertain and disori-
ented as we are, *we needed* our best men to get to the
end of the tunnel. Seldom have the characteristics of
a work and the conditions of the historic moment so
clearly demanded that a writer live.

I call the accident that killed Camus a scandal because it showed up, at the heart of the human world,

the absurdity of our profoundest exigencies. Camus, suddenly struck down at twenty by a disease that turned his life upside down,[29] discovered the Absurd, that imbecilic negation of mankind. He came to terms with it, he *thought through* his unbearable condition and came through it. And yet we would think that his early works alone tell the truth of his life, since this restored invalid has now been snuffed out by an unforeseeable death from out of the blue. The absurd would be that question no one asks him any more, that he no longer asks anyone, this silence that is no longer even a silence, that is absolutely *nothing* any more.

I do not believe this. As soon as it shows itself, the inhuman becomes part of the human. Every arrested life—even that of such a young man—is *both* a gramophone record being smashed to smithereens and a complete life. For all those who loved him, there is an unbearable absurdity in this death. But we shall have to learn to see this mutilated *oeuvre* as a total one. To the very extent that Camus' humanism contains a *human* attitude to the death that was suddenly to overtake him, insofar as his proud search for happiness implied and called for the *inhuman* need to die, we shall

recognize in this work, and in the life that is inseparable from it, the pure, victorious attempt of a man to
reclaim every moment of his existence from his future
death.

France-Observateur, 505 (7 January 1960).

paul nizan

I

Feeling bored one day, Paul Valéry went over to the window and, gazing into the transparency of a pane, asked, 'How to hide a man?' Gide was present. Disconcerted by this studied laconicism, he said nothing. Yet there was no lack of possible answers: any method would do, from poverty and hunger to formal dinners, from the county jail to the Académie française. But these two excessively renowned bourgeois had high opinions of themselves. Each day they buffed up their twin souls in public and believed they were revealing themselves in their naked truth. When they died, long afterwards, the one morose, the other contented—

179

both in ignorance—they had not even listened to the young voice crying out for all of us, their grand-nephews: 'Where has man hidden himself? We are stifling; we are mutilated from childhood: there are only monsters!'

The man denouncing our actual situation in these terms more than suffered in his own skin: while alive, there was not an hour that he did not run the risk of ruin. Dead, he faced an even greater danger: to make him pay for his clear-sightedness, a conspiracy of cripples tried to erase him from memory.

He had been in the Party for twelve years when, in September 1939, he announced he was leaving. This was the unpardonable crime, this sin of despair that the God of the Christians punishes with damnation. The Communists do not believe in hell: they believe in oblivion. It was decided that Comrade Nizan would be consigned to oblivion. One of many exploding bullets had hit him in the back of the neck, but that liquidation satisfied no one: it was not enough that he had ceased to live; he had to have never existed. They persuaded the witnesses to his life that they had not really known him: he was a traitor, a

Judas; he worked secretly for the Ministry of the Interior and receipts had been found there bearing his signature. One comrade volunteered an exegesis of the works he had left behind, discovering in them an obsession with treason. 'How can an author who puts informers in his novels know about their ways,' asked this philosopher, 'unless he were an informer himself?' A profound argument, one must admit, but a dangerous one. The exegete has, in fact, himself become a traitor and has just been expelled; should we criticize him now for having projected his own obsessions on to his victim? At any rate, the trick worked: the suspect books disappeared; the publishers were intimidated and left them rotting in cellars, as were the readers, who no longer dared ask for them. This grain of silence would germinate. Within ten years it would produce the most radical negation: the dead man would exit from history, his name would crumble into dust, his very birth would be excised from our shared past.

The odds were with them initially: a grave-robbery at night in a poorly guarded cemetery was no great task. If they lost the first phase of the battle, it was because they were too contemptuous of us. Blinded by mourning and glory, the Party intellectuals saw themselves as a chivalric order. They referred to each other as 'the permanent heroes of the age' and it was around this time, I think, that one of my former students informed me, with sweet irony, 'We Communist intellectuals suffer, do you see, from a superiority complex!' In a word, subhumans unaware of their subhumanity. Hence their arrogance carried them so far as to try out their slanders on Nizan's best friends: to test them, as it were. The encounter proved decisive: challenged publicly to produce their evidence, they scattered in disarray, blaming us for never trusting them and for really not being very nice.

The second round in this battle spelled defeat for us: to confound them was a small matter; we needed to convince, to push home our advantage, to cut off our enemies' retreat. Our victory frightened us: at bottom we quite liked these unjust soldiers of Justice. Someone said, 'Don't push it, they'll end up getting annoyed.' We heard no more of the story, but it did the rounds of the Communist Party by word of mouth and new recruits in Bergerac and Mazamet

learned in dispassionate but absolutely certain terms
of the ancient crimes of an unknown by the name of
Nizan.

When I think of it, our negligence seems suspect;
at a pinch, I will admit we had honestly assumed that
his innocence as a man had been re-established. But
his works? Was it acceptable for us to do nothing to
rescue them from oblivion? It was their aim to be dis-
agreeable: that is their greatest strength; and I am certain at present that we found them so. I recall, indeed,
that we had acquired beautiful, new souls, so beautiful that I still blush to think of it. Not wanting to
waste anything, the Nation decided to entrust to us
those empty, insatiable pools in which it had no interest: pools of buried pain, the unsatisfied demands
of the deceased—in short, all that is beyond recov-
ery. These martyrs' merits were ascribed now to us;
alive, we received posthumous decoration. We were,
all in all, honorary dead men: a whispering campaign
dubbed us Righteous; smiling, frivolous and funereal,
we took this noble vacuity for plenitude and concealed
our unparalleled promotion beneath the simplicity of
our manners. Alongside whisky, Virtue was our chief

diversion. We were everyone's friends! The enemy had invented classes in order to ruin us: in defeat, he took them with him. Workers, bourgeois and peasants all communed in the sacred love of the Fatherland. In the authorized circles, we thought we knew that self-sacrifice was rewarded in cash, that crime did not pay, that the worst does not necessarily happen and that moral advance brings technical progress. We proved by our very existence and self-conceit that the bad are always punished and the good always rewarded. Wreathed in glory and pacified, the Left had just entered upon the inexorable death throes that were to see it perish thirteen years later to the strains of military bands. Idiots that we were, we thought it was in fine fettle. Soldiers and politicians came home from Britain and Algeria; they crushed the Resistance before our eyes and spirited away the Revolution and we wrote in the newspapers and our books that everything was in fine order: our souls had absorbed the exquisite essence of these annihilated movements into themselves.

Nizan was a killjoy. His was a call to arms and hatred. Class against class. With a patient, mortal enemy, no quarter can be given: it is kill or be killed, there is no middle way. And no time for sleep. All his life, with his graceful insolence and his eyes lowered to his fingernails, he had repeated, 'Don't believe in Father Christmas.' But he was dead. The war had just ended. In every French hearth, shoes and boots were laid out and Father Christmas was filling them with tins of American food. I am sure that those who thumbed through *Aden, Arabie* or *Antoine Bloyé*[30] at that time quickly broke off reading with lordly pity: 'pre-war literature, simplistic and decidedly passé'. What need had we of a Cassandra? Had he lived, we thought he would have shared in our new subtlety or, in other words, our compromises. What had preserved his violent purity? A stray bullet, no more and no less. That was nothing to boast about. This wicked corpse was gently chuckling to himself: in his books he had written that, past the age of forty, a French bourgeois is merely a carcase. And then he disappeared. At thirty-five. At present we, his classmates and comrades, bloated with that flatulence we call our souls, are running about the town with garlands for both Right and Left. And we are forty. Protecting innocence is our job; we are the just and we dispensed Justice. But we

left *Aden, Arabie* in the hands of the Communists because we loathed all those who disputed our merits.

This attitude is an offence in French law: refusal
to come to the assistance of a person in danger. If we
had not morally liquidated this former colleague, it
was because we did not have the means to do so. The
rehabilitation was a farce. 'Talk, talk, that's all you can
do.'[31] We talked: our beautiful souls spelled death for
others; our virtue reflected our total impotence. It
was, in fact, the job of the young to resurrect Nizan
the writer. But the young people of the day—today
quadragenarian carcasses—gave no thought to that.
Having just escaped an epidemic, what did the en-
demic disease of bourgeois death matter to them?
Nizan asked them to look into themselves at a point
when they believed they could at last look outwards.
Of course they would die. 'Socrates is mortal.'
'Madame is dying, Madame is dead': they had been
given some famous passages to learn at school: *Le Lac*,
a sermon by Bossuet.[32] But there is a time for everything, and this was the time for living because for five
years they had thought they were going to die. As adolescents they had been stunned by defeat: they had

been heartbroken at no longer being able to respect anyone—either their fathers or the 'best army in the world' that had run away without fighting. The biggest-hearted had given themselves to the Party, which had repaid them royally: with a family, a monastic rule, tranquil chauvinism and respectability. In the aftermath of war, those young people went wild with pride and humility: they found pleasure in a sudden passion for obedience. I have said they were contemptuous of us all—by way of compensation. They twisted the arm of tomorrow to make it yield a radiant socialist future; one can imagine how the brassy song of these birds drowned out the thin, chill voice of Nizan, the short-lived voice of death and eternity. Other adolescents found their relaxation in cellars: they danced, made love, went to each other's houses and threw their parents' furniture out of the windows in great, revolving potlatch ceremonies: in a word, they did all a young man can do. Some of them even read. In despair, of course. All of them were in despair: it was the fashion. And despairing of everything, except of course of the vigorous pleasure of despairing. Except of life. After five years, their futures were thawing: they had plans, the guileless hope of renewing literature through despair, of knowing the weariness of great global journeys, of the unbearable tedium of earning money or seducing women or, quite simply, of becoming a despairing pharmacist or dentist and remaining one for a long time, a very long time, without any other care than those of the human condition in its generality. How joyful they were! Nizan had nothing to say to them: he spoke little of the human condition and much of social matters and our alienations; he knew terror and anger better than he did the *douceurs* of despair; in the young bourgeois of his acquaintance he hated the reflection of himself, and, whether they were despairing or not, he despaired of them. His books were kept for the lean years, and rightly so.

Then, at length, came Marshall: the cold war hit this generation of dancers and vassals like a blow to the heart. We old-timers took a bit of a battering, as did our virtues. 'Crime pays. Crime is rewarded.' With the return of these fine maxims, our beautiful souls perished in a dreadful stench. And good riddance to them. But our juniors paid for everyone. The nightclubbers became dumbfounded, old young men. Some are going grey, some balding, others have a paunch. Their relaxed attitude has frozen into inertia. They do what has to be done, and do it simply; they earn their corn, own a Peugeot 403 and a country cottage, have a wife and children. These young men were getting ready for life, they were 'starting out': their train came to a stop somewhere in the countryside. They will go nowhere now and do nothing. Sometimes a confused memory comes back to them from the glorious turbulent years; when this happens, they ask themselves, 'What did we want?' and cannot remember. They are well-adapted, yet suffer from a chronic maladaptation that will kill them: they are tramps without poverty; they are well-fed, but they perform no service. I can see them at twenty—so lively, so joyous, so eager to relieve the old guard. I look at them today, their eyes ravaged by the cancer of astonishment, and I think to myself that they did not deserve this fate. As for the faithful vassals: some have not renewed their vows of fealty, others have fallen to a lower rank of vassalage. They are all wretched. The first group buzz around at ground level, never able to land: dismayed mosquitoes who have lost everything, including weight. The second group, sacrificing their organs of locomotion, have taken root in the sand: the slightest breath of wind can whip up these plants into a swarm. Nomadic or sedentary, they are united in stupor: where did their lives go? Nizan has an answer. For the desperate and for the vassals. Only I doubt whether they are willing or able to read it: for that lost, mystified generation, this vigorous dead writer tolls the knell.

But they have twenty-year-old sons, our grandsons, who register their defeats and ours. Until recently, the prodigal sons told their fathers where to get off, packed up and joined the Left. The rebel, following the classical pattern, became an activist. But what if the fathers are on the Left? What is to be done? A young man came to see me: he loved his parents, but, he said severely, 'They're reactionaries.' I have aged and words have aged with me: in my head, they are as old as I am. I mistook him. I thought I was dealing with the scion of a prosperous family that was rather sanctimonious, with free-market beliefs perhaps, voting for Pinay.[33] He put me right: 'My father's

been a Communist since the Congress of Tours.' Another, the son of a socialist, condemned both the
SFIO[34] and the CP: 'The one lot are traitors, the others are in a rut.' And what if the fathers were conser-
vatives? What if they supported Bidault?[35] Do we
believe this great upturned, worm-ridden cadaver, the
Left, can attract the young? It is a stinking, decaying
carcase; the power of the military, and dictatorship
and fascism are being—or will be—born from its rotting corpse; it takes a strong stomach not to turn away
from it. We, the grandfathers, were made by the Left;
we lived by it; in it and by it we shall die. But we no
longer have anything to say to the young: fifty years of
living in this backward province that France has become is degrading. We have shouted, protested, signed
and signed again. Depending on our habits of thought,
we have declared, 'It is not acceptable . . .' or 'The proletariat won't stand for . . .'. And yet, in the end, here we
are; we have accepted everything. How to convey our
wisdom and the fine fruits of our experience to these
young unknowns? From abdication to abdication we
have learned only one thing: our total powerlessness.
Now, I admit that this is the beginning of Reason, of

the struggle for life. But we have old bones, and, at an age when people are usually thinking about writing their wills, we are discovering that we have achieved nothing. Shall we tell them, 'Be Cubans, be Russians or Chinese, as you like, be Africans'? They will tell us it is rather too late to change their place of birth. In short, accountants or tearaways, technicians or teddy boys, they are battling alone and without hope against asphyxiation. And do not think those who choose job and family are showing resignation: they have turned their violence inwards and are destroying themselves. Reduced to impotence by their fathers, they cripple themselves out of spite. The others smash every- thing, hit anyone and everyone with everything and anything—a knife, a bicycle chain: to escape their malaise, they will send everything up in smoke. But nothing does go up in smoke and they end up at the police station, covered in blood. It was a great Sunday; next week they'll do better. Dishing out violence or taking it is all the same to them: there just has to be blood. In the daze that follows the brawls, only their bruises hurt; they have the funereal pleasure of empty minds.

Who will speak to these 'Angry Young Men'? Who can explain their violence? Nizan is their man. Year by year, his hibernation has made him younger. Not so long ago he was our contemporary; today he is theirs. When he lived we shared his anger, but, in the end, none of us performed 'the simplest Surrealist act' and now here we are, grown old. We have betrayed our youth so many times that mere decency demands we do not speak of it. Our old memories have lost their claws and their teeth. I must have been twenty once, but I'm fifty-five now and I would not dare write, 'I was twenty. I won't let anyone tell me it's the best time of life.' So much passion—and so lofty. Coming from my pen it would be demagogy. And then I would be lying: the unhappiness of the young is total, I know—I may perhaps have felt it once— but it is still human because it comes to them from human beings who are their fathers or their elders; ours comes from our arteries; we are strange objects half eaten away by Nature, by vegetation and covered with ants, we are like lukewarm drinks or the idiotic paintings that amused Rimbaud. Young and violent, the victim of a violent death, Nizan can step out of the ranks and speak to young people about youth: 'I won't let anyone . . .' They will recognize their own voices. To some he can say, 'Your modesty will be the death of you, dare to desire, be insatiable, let loose the terrible forces that are warring and whirling inside you, do not be ashamed to ask for the moon—we must have it.' To the others, 'Turn your rage on those who caused it, don't try to run away from your pain but seek out its causes and smash them.' He can say anything to them because he's a young monster, a fine young monster like them, who shares their terror of dying and their hatred of living in the world we have made for them. He was alone, became a Communist, ceased to be one and died alone near a window on a stairway. His life is explained by his intransigence: he became a revolutionary out of a sense of rebellion; when revolution was necessarily eclipsed by the war, he rediscovered his violent youth and ended as a rebel.

We both wanted to write. He finished his first book long before I penned a word of mine. At the point when *La Nausée*[36] appeared, if we had valued such solemn presentations, *he* would have prefaced *my* book. Death has reversed the roles. Death and systematic defamation. He will find readers without my assistance: I have said who his natural readership will be. But I thought this foreword was necessary for two reasons: to show everyone the cunningly abject nature of his detractors and to warn the young to lend his words their full weight. They were once young and hard, those words; it is we who have caused them to age. If I want to restore to them the brilliance they had before the war, I must recall the 'marvellous age' of our refusals and make it live again, with Nizan, the man who said 'no' to the very end. His death was the end of a world: after him, the Revolution became constructive and the Left came to define itself by assent—to the point where, one day in Autumn 1958, it expired, with a last, dying 'yes' on its lips.[37] Let us attempt to recover the days of hatred, of unquenched desire, of destruction, those days when André Breton, barely older than we were, spoke of wishing to see the Cossacks watering their horses in the fountains of the Place de la Concorde.

II

The error I want to avoid readers committing is one I made myself during his lifetime. Yet we were close— so close that we were sometimes mistaken for each other. In June 1939, Léon Brunschvicg[38] met the two of us at the publisher Gallimard's offices and congratulated me on having written *Les Chiens de garde*:[39] 'although,' as he told me without bitterness, 'you were rather hard on me.' I smiled at him in silence. Alongside, Nizan smiled too: the great idealist left without our having disabused him. This confusion had been going on for eighteen years; it had come to define us socially and, in the end, we accepted it. From 1920 to 1930, in particular, as schoolboys and then students, we were indistinguishable. Nevertheless, I did not see him as he was.

I could have drawn his portrait: medium height, dark hair. He squinted, as I did, but in the opposite direction, that is to say attractively. My divergent strabismus turned my face into an unploughed field; his was convergent, and lent him a mischievous faraway look, even when he was paying attention. He followed fashion closely, insolently. At seventeen, his trousers were so tight around the ankles that he had difficulty pulling them on. A little later they flared into bell-bottoms, to the point where they hid his shoes. Then, all of a sudden, they turned into plus fours, up around his knees and billowing out like skirts. He carried a rattan cane and wore a monocle, wing collars or little round ones. He exchanged his iron-rimmed spectacles for enormous tortoise-shell ones which, with a touch of the Anglo-Saxon snobbery that raged among the youth of the time, he called his 'goggles'.

I tried to emulate him, but my family mounted effective resistance, even going so far as to bribe the tailor. And then someone must have put a spell on me: when I wore them, fine clothes changed into rags and tatters. I resigned myself to gazing at Nizan in amazement and admiration. At the École normale, no one gave much thought to how they dressed, with the exception of a few provincials who proudly wore spats and sported silk handkerchiefs in their waistcoat pockets. However, I don't remember anyone disapproving of Nizan's outfits: we were proud to have a dandy among us.

Women liked him, but he kept them at arm's length. To one who came right up to our very room and offered herself to him, he replied, 'Madam, we would be defiling each other.' In fact, he liked only girls, and he chose the virgins and the fools among them, drawn by the dizzying secret of stupidity—our only true profundity—and by the glossy brilliance of a flesh with no memories. Indeed, during the only liaison I ever knew him to have, he was constantly tormented by the most needless jealousy: he could not bear the thought that his mistress had a past. I found his behaviour quite incomprehensible, and yet it was very clear. I stubbornly insisted on seeing it as a personality trait. I also saw his charming cynicism and his 'black humour' as personality traits, together with his quiet, implacable aggressiveness; he never raised the tone of his voice; I never saw him frown nor heard him strain his voice: he would bend back his fingers and, as I have said, fall to contemplating his nails, loosing his violent remarks with a sly, deceptive serenity.

Together we fell into every trap there is: at sixteen, he offered me the role of superman and I eagerly accepted. There would, he said, be the two of us. Since he was a Breton, he gave us Gaelic names. We covered all the blackboards with the strange words R'hâ and Bor'hou. He was R'hâ. One of our classmates wanted to share our new-found status. We devised ordeals to test him. He had, for example, to declare out loud that the French army and the flag could go to hell; these remarks were not so daring as we imagined: they were commonplace at the time and reflected the internationalism and anti-militarism of the old pre-war days. However, the aspirant declined the task and the two supermen remained alone, eventually forgetting their superhumanity.

We would spend hours, days, strolling around Paris: we discovered its flora, its fauna and its stones, and were moved to tears when the first electric signs appeared; we thought the world was new because we were new in the world. Paris was the bond between us; we loved each other through the crowds of this grey city, beneath its light spring skies. We walked and talked; we invented our own language, an intellectual slang of the kind all students make up.

One night, the supermen climbed the hill of Sacré-Coeur and turning, saw a disorderly collection of jewels spread out beneath their feet. Nizan stuck his cigarette into the left-hand corner of his mouth, which he twisted into a horrible grimace, and announced, 'Hey, hey, Rastignac.' I repeated, 'Hey, Hey!' as I was meant to, and we walked down again, satisfied at having so discreetly marked the extent of our literary knowledge and the measure of our ambition. No one has written about those walks or that Paris better than my friend. Re-read *La Conspiration*[40] and you will recapture the fresh, yet quaint charm of that world-capital, quite unaware as yet that it would later become a provincial backwater. The ambition, the sudden mood-swings, the gentle, livid rages—I took it all in my stride. That was the way Nizan was, calm and perfidious, charming. That was how I loved him.

He described himself in *Antoine Bloyé* as 'a taciturn adolescent, already plunged into the adventures of youth, deserting childhood with a kind of avid exhilaration'.[41] And that is how I saw him. I experienced his taciturnity to my own cost. In *hypokhâgne*,[42] we fell out for six months, which I found painful. At the École normale, where we roomed together, he went for days without speaking to me. In the second year, his mood grew even darker: he was going through a crisis and could see no way out. He disappeared, and was found three days later, drunk, with strangers. And when my fellow students asked me about his 'escapades', I could answer only that he was 'in a foul mood'. Yet he had told me of his fear of death, but, being mad enough to believe myself immortal, I criticized him for this and thought that he was wrong: death wasn't worth a thought. Nizan's horror of death was like his retrospective jealousy—eccentricities that a healthy morale should combat.

When he couldn't stand things any longer, he left: he became a tutor with an English family in Aden. This departure scandalized the rest of us, rooted in the École as we were, but, since Nizan intimidated us, we found a benign explanation: love of travel. When he came back the following year, he did so at night when no one was expecting him. I was alone in my room. I had been plunged into a state of pained indignation since the previous day by the loose morals of a young lady from the provinces. He entered without knocking. He was pale, a bit breathless and rather grim. He said, 'You don't look too cheerful.' 'Neither do you', I replied. Whereupon we went off to have a drink and set the world to rights, happy that the good feeling was restored between us.

But this was simply a misunderstanding: my anger was a mere soap bubble, his was real. He gagged on the horror of returning to his cage with his tail between his legs. He was looking for the sort of help no one could give him. His words of hate were pure gold, mine were false coin. He ran off the very next day. He lived with his fiancée, joined the Communist Party, married, had a daughter, nearly died of appendicitis; then, after passing the *agrégation*, taught philosophy at Bourg and stood for election to parliament. I saw him less. I was teaching at Le Havre and there was also the fact that he had a family. His wife had given him a second child—a son—but it was mostly the Party that came between us: I was a sympathizer, but not an initiate. I remained his friend from adolescence, a petty-bourgeois that he liked.

Why did I not understand him? There was no lack of signs: why would I not see them? It was out of jealousy, I think: I denied the feelings that I couldn't share. I sensed from the very first that he had incommunicable passions, a destiny that would separate us. I was afraid and I blinded myself to these things. At fifteen, this son of a pious woman had wanted to take holy orders: I found out only many years afterwards. But I can still remember my scandalized bewilderment when, walking round the schoolyard with me, he said, 'I had lunch with the pastor.' He saw my stupor and explained in a detached tone, 'I may convert to Protestantism.' 'You,' I said, indignantly, 'But you don't believe in God.' 'Well, no,' he replied, 'but I like their morality.'

Madame Nizan threatened to cut off his allowance and the plan was dropped, but the moment had been enough for me to glimpse, beyond this 'childish whim', the impatience of a sick man writhing around to escape his pain. I did not want him to have this inaccessible pain: we shared superficial melancholies and that was enough; otherwise, I tried to force my optimism on him. I kept telling him we were free: he did not reply, but his thin, sidelong smile was eloquent.

On other occasions, he proclaimed himself a materialist—we were barely seventeen—and I was the one smiling scornfully. Materialist, determinist: he felt the physical weight of his chains; I did not want to feel the weight of mine. I hated him engaging in politics because I felt no need to do so myself. He was a Communist, then a follower of Georges Valois,[43] then a Communist again. It was easy to mock him and I wasn't slow to do so; in fact, these enormous swings were evidence of his stubbornness: there was nothing more excusable than that he should hesitate between two extremes at the age of eighteen.

What did not vary was his extremism: whatever happened, the existing order had to be destroyed. For my part, I was quite happy at the existence of that order and the opportunity to hurl my bombs—my words—in its direction. This real need to unite with other men to move away the stones that were weighing them down seemed to me a mere dandy's extravagance: he was a Communist in the same way that he was a monocle-wearer, out of a trivial desire to shock.

He was unhappy at the École normale and I criticized him for it: we were going to write, we would write fine books that would justify our existences. Since I wasn't complaining, why was he? In the middle of the second year, he suddenly declared that literature bored him and he was going to be a cameraman; a friend gave him a few lessons. I was annoyed with him. In explaining to me that too much reading and writing had turned him against words and he now wanted to act on things and transform them into silence with his hands, he was, as I saw it, merely compounding his offence: this defector from the word could not condemn writing without passing sentence on me. It never occurred to me that Nizan was seeking, as we said at the time, his salvation, and these 'written cries' do not save.

He did not become a cameraman and I was delighted. But only briefly: his departure for Aden annoyed me. For him it was a matter of life and death, as I guessed. To reassure myself, I chose to see it as a further eccentricity. I had to admit to myself that I did not mean much to him, but, I ask myself today, whose fault was that? Where would you find a more stubborn refusal to understand and, hence, to help? When he came back from one of his binges, his panic-stricken flights, drunk and with death at his heels, I would welcome him tight-lipped without a word, with the dignity of an old wife who has resigned herself to such outrages, so long as it is understood that she is keeping score. It is true he was hardly encouraging. He would go and sit down at his table, gloomy, his hair tousled, his eyes bloodshot; if I happened to speak to him, he would give me a distant, hate-filled look. No matter, I still reproach myself for the fact that I had only these four words in my head: 'What an awkward so-and-so!' and that I never tried, even out of curiosity, to find an explanation for these escapades. His marriage I got all wrong. I was friendly with his wife, but bachelorhood was a moral principle with me, a rule of life. It could not, I assumed, be otherwise for Nizan. I decided he had married Rirette because that was the only way he could have her. In all honesty, I didn't realize that a young man in the grip of a dreadful family can break free only by starting one of his own. I was born to be a bachelor all my days. I did not understand that the single life weighed down the bachelor living at my side, that he detested casual affairs—because they have a taste of death about them—just as he detested travel, and that, when he said 'man is a sedentary animal' or 'give me my field

. . . my needs, my men,' he was simply demanding his share of happiness: a home, a wife and children.

When he published *Aden, Arabie*, I thought it a good book and I was delighted. But I saw it only as a lightweight pamphlet, a whirl of frivolous words. Many of his classmates made the same mistake: we were set in our thinking. For most of us, for me, the École normale was, from the very first day, the beginning of independence. Many can say, as I do, that they had four years of happiness there. But here was a wild man flying at our throats: 'The École normale . . . a ridiculous and more often odious thing, presided over by a patriotic, hypocritical, powerful little old man who respected the military.' In his eyes, we were 'adolescents worn out by years of lycée, corrupted by a classical education, and by bourgeois morality and cooking.'[44] We chose to laugh about it: 'He didn't moan about the place when he was here, did he? He seemed to have quite a good time with the worn-out adolescents.' And we would recall our harmless pranks, in which he had gladly taken part. Forgetting his escapades, his scorn, and the great breakdown that took him off to distant Arabia, we saw his passion merely as excessive rhetoric. Personally, I felt foolishly offended because he tarnished my memories. Since Nizan had shared my life at the École, he had to have been happy there, or else our friendship was dead even then. I preferred to rescue the past. I said to myself, 'It's all a bit over the top!' Today, I think our friendship was already dead, through no fault of our own, and that Nizan, consumed with loneliness, needed to be fighting among men rather than bandying words with an unfaithful and all-too-familiar reflection of himself. I was the one who maintained our friendship and embalmed it, by premeditated ignorance, by lying. In truth, our paths had always been moving apart. It has taken many years, and I have had to come at last to understand my own path through life, before being able to speak sure-footedly about his.

The more dismal life is, the more absurd is death. I do not claim that a man busy with his work and full of hope, cannot be struck, as if by lightning, by an awareness of death. I do say that a young man is afraid of death when he is unhappy with his fate. Before he is led by the hand to the seat that is kept for him, a student is the infinite, the undefined: he passes easily from one doctrine to another, detained by none of them; he finds all systems of thought equivalent. In fact, what we call 'classics' in school curricula is merely the teaching of the great errors of the past. Shaped by our republics in the image of Valéry's Monsieur Teste—that ideal citizen who never says or does anything but who knows what the score is all the same[45]—these young men will take twenty years to understand that ideas are stones, that there is an inflexible order to them and they have to be used for building. So long as worn-out old men, discreet to the point of transparency, carry bourgeois objectivity so far as to ask their students to adopt the standpoint of Nero, Loyola and Monsieur Thiers, each of these apprentices will take himself for pure Mind, that colourless, tasteless gas that at times expands to the galaxies and at others condenses into formulae. The young elite are everything and nothing: in other words, they are supported by the state and by their families; beneath this vaporous indistinctness their life burns away; suddenly pure Mind is brought up short against the stumbling block of Death. In vain does it try to encompass it in order to dissolve it: death cannot be thought. A body is struck down by an accident; a brute fact must put an end to the brilliant indeterminacy of ideas. This shocking realization awakens more than one terrified adolescent at night: against capital punishment and its incomprehensible particularity, universal Culture provides no defence. Later, when the individuality of his body is reflected in the individuality of the work he has undertaken, a young man will integrate his death into his life and view it as just one more risk among others—among all those that threaten his work and family. For those men who have the rare good fortune to be able to enjoy what they do, the final disaster, the less terrifying as one approaches it, is converted into the small change of everyday concerns.

I have described our common fate. That is nothing; but when the anxiety outlasts adolescence, when it becomes the profound secret of the adult and the mainspring of his decisions, the invalid knows his afflictions: his terror at the idea that he will soon be no more simply reflects his horror at still having to live. Death is the irremediable sentence; it condemns the wretched, for eternity, to have been only that: disgusting calamities. Nizan dreaded that fate: this monster crawled randomly among monsters; he feared one day he would burst and nothing would remain. He had known for a long time when he put these words into the mouth of one of his characters, that death was the definitive illumination of life: 'If I think about my death, it's for a good reason. It's because my life is hollow and death is all it deserves.' In the same book, Bloyé takes fright at 'the uniform countenance of his life . . . and [this fear] comes from a deeper region than the bleeding places in the body where the warnings of disease are formed.'[46]

What, when all is said and done, did he suffer from? Why did I sound ridiculous to him, more than to anyone else, when I talked about our freedom? If he believed, from the age of sixteen, in the inflexible chain of causes, it was because he felt constrained and manipulated: 'We have within us divisions, alienations, wars, debates . . .' 'Every man is split between the men he can be . . .'[47] Having been a solitary child, he was too conscious of his singularity to throw himself, as I did, into universal ideas: having been a slave, he came to philosophy to free himself, and Spinoza provided him with a model: in the first two types of knowledge, man remains a slave because he is incomplete; knowledge of the third type breaks down the partitions, the negative determinants: so far as the mode is concerned, it is one and the same thing to return to infinite substance or to achieve the affirmative totality of one's particular essence. Nizan wanted to beat down all walls: he would unify his life by proclaiming his desires and assuaging them.

The easiest desire to name comes from sex and its frustrated appetites: in a society that reserves its women for old men and the rich, this is the first source of unhappiness for a poor young man and a premonition of his future troubles. Nizan spoke bitterly of the old men who slept with our women and sought to castrate us. But, all in all, we were living in the age of the Great Desire: the Surrealists wanted to awaken that infinite concupiscence whose object is simply Everything. Nizan was looking for remedies and took what he could find; through their works he came to know Freud, who became part of his pantheon. As revised by Breton and by a young writer in peril, Freud looked like Spinoza: he tore away the veils and cobwebs, he imposed harmony on the enemies massacring each other in our tunnels, dissolved our raging monsters in light, and reduced us to the unity of powerful appetites. My friend tried him for a while, not without some felicity. Even in *Antoine Bloyé* we find traces of this influence. It gave us the following fine sentence, for example: 'As long as men are not entire and free, they will dream at night.' Antoine dreams: about the women he has not had and has not even dared to long for. On waking, he refuses to hear 'this voice of wisdom'. The fact is that 'the wakeful man and the sleeper seldom see eye to eye.'[48] Antoine is an old man, but here Nizan speaks from experience, I know; he used to dream, he dreamed until the day of his death: his wartime letters are filled with his dreams.

But it was only a working hypothesis, a temporary way of unifying himself. He adored the passing women in the street, those pale forms eclipsed by the light, by the smoke of Paris, those fleeting tokens of love; but he loved, above all, their being inaccessible to him: this well-behaved, literary young man intoxicated himself with privations; that is useful to a writer.

But let us not suppose that he found chastity difficult to bear: one or two affairs—short and painful—and, the rest of the time, nice young girls whom he touched lightly as they slipped by. He would have been only too happy to find in himself merely a conflict between the flesh and the law; he would have decided the matter by finding the law guilty: 'Morality is an arsehole,' he used to say at twenty. In fact, taboos are more insidious, and our very bodies collude with them. Morality never showed itself but, with all women other than virgins, his unease was accompanied by a strong sense of revulsion. Later, when he had his 'field' and his 'men', he praised the beauty of the *whole* female body to me with a shocked, but precise, sense of wonder. I had wondered what had kept him from such a general discovery at the time of his devastating affairs. Now I know: it was disgust, an infantile repugnance for bodies he regarded as stale from past caresses. As adolescents, when we looked at women, I wanted them all; he wanted only one, and one who would be his. He could not conceive that it was possible to love unless one loved from dawn till nighttime, or that there could be possession when you did not possess the woman and she did not possess you. He thought that man was a sedentary being and that casual affairs were like travel—abstractions. A thousand and three women are a thousand and three times the same, and he wanted one woman who would be a thousand and three times another; as a promise against death, he would love in her even the secret signs of fecundity.

In other words, the non-satisfaction of the senses was an effect, not a cause. Once married, it disappeared: the Great Desire fell back into line, became one need among others again, a need one satisfies poorly, too quickly or not at all. In fact, Nizan suffered from his present contradictions only because he deciphered them by the light of the future. If he formed the intention, one day, of killing himself, it was to put an immediate end to what he believed merely to be a recommencement. He was marked from childhood by Breton piety; too much or too little for his happiness; contradiction had settled beneath his roof. He was the child of old parents: the two adversaries had begotten him during a ceasefire; by the time he was born, they had resumed their quarrel. His father, first a manual worker, then an engineer on the railways, provided him with an example of adult, atheistic, technical thinking and, when he talked, betrayed a sorrowful loyalty to the class he had left behind. This mute conflict between a childish old *bourgeoise* and a renegade worker was something Nizan internalized from his earliest childhood; he made it the future foundation of his personality. However humble his position may be, the child of a charwoman has a part in the future of his family: his father makes plans. The Nizans had no future: the yardmaster was almost at the height of his career—what had he to look forward to? A promotion that was due to him, a few honours, retirement and death. Madame Nizan lived both in the crucial moment—when the onions have to be 'browned' or the juices 'sealed' in the chops—and in that fixed moment termed Eternity. The child was not far from his starting point and the family not far from its point of fall: carried along in this fall, he wanted to learn and build, whereas everything was visibly coming apart, even the marital quarrel. Externally, it had transformed itself into indifference; it existed nowhere, except within him. In

the silence, the child heard their dialogue: the ceremonious, futile babble of Faith was occasionally interrupted by a harsh voice, naming plants, stones and
tools. These two voices consumed each other. At first
the pious language seemed to be winning out: there
was talk of Charity, Paradise, of Divine Purpose, and
all this eschatology did battle with the precise activity
of the technicians. What was the point of building locomotives? There are no trains to heaven. The engineer would leave the house as soon as he could.
Between the ages of five and ten, his son would follow
him into the fields, take his hand and run along at his
side. At twenty-five, he had fond memories of those
men-only walks that were so obviously directed against
the wife, against his mother. I note, however, that he
gave his preference not to the Sciences but to the
weary urbanity of the Word. A worker becomes an engineer, feels the deficiencies in his education and his
son tries to get into the École Polytechnique; the pattern is a classic one. But Nizan showed a suspect repugnance for mathematics: he did Greek and Latin.
As the stepson of a Polytechnique graduate, I had the
same dislike, but for different reasons: we liked vague,

ritualistic words, myths. Yet his father took his revenge: under the influence of his positivism, my friend sought to wrest himself from the baubles of religion. I have mentioned the stages of this release: the mystical transport—the last gasp of Catholicism—that almost took him into holy orders, his flirtations with Calvin, and the metamorphosis of his pious Catharism into political Manichaeism, royalism, and, in the end, Marxism. For a long time the two of us continued to use a Christian vocabulary: though atheists, we had no doubt we had been brought into the world to find our salvation, and, with a little luck, the salvation of others. There was only one difference: I felt certain I was one of the elect, Nizan often wondered if he were not damned. From his mother and Catholicism he got his radical scorn for the things of this world, the fear of succumbing to worldly temptations, and the taste—which he never lost—for pursuing an absolute Purpose. He was persuaded that, hidden within him, beneath the tangle of daily concerns, was a beautiful totality, flawless and unsullied; he had to hoe and weed, to burn the brushwood, and the indivisible Eternity would manifest itself in all its purity. And so, at this period, he

regarded his father's job as manic, pointless agitation: the order of supreme purposes was being sacrificed to that of mere technical resources; man was being lost to the machine. He soon stopped believing in the white pills of life called souls, but he retained the obscure feeling that his father had lost his.

These ancient superstitions do not prevent you from living, *provided that you have the Faith*. But technology, ruled out of court, took its revenge by wringing the neck of religion. Nizan's dissatisfactions stayed with him, but they were rootless now and disconnected. Worldly activities are farcical, but, if nothing exists but the earth and the human animals scraping a living from it, then the children of men must take over and begin scraping: for there is no other occupation, short of doctoring the old Christian words. When Nizan offered me the strange prospect of becoming a superman, it was not so much pride that drove him as an obscure need to escape our condition. Alas, it was merely a matter of changing names. From that time on, until he left for Aden, he carried a constant millstone around his neck and kept on forging symbols of escape.

But one would understand nothing of Nizan's *angst* if one did not recall what I said earlier: he deciphered this arduous, disenchanted present, broken as it was only by brief periods of exhilaration, in the sinister light of a future that was nothing other than his father's past. 'I was afraid. My departure was a product of fear.' Fear of what? He says it right here in this book: 'mutilations . . . awaited us. After all, we knew how our parents lived.'[49] He expanded upon this sentence in a very fine, long novel, *Antoine Bloyé*, where he recounts the life and death of his father. As for Nizan, though he barely appears in the book, he continually speaks of himself: first, he is the witness to this process of decay; and second, Monsieur Nizan confided in no one—all the thoughts and feelings attributed to him are torn from the author's own person and projected into that old, disordered heart. This constant dual presence is a sign of what psychoanalysts term 'identification with the father'.

I have said that, in his early years, Nizan admired his father, that he envied that sterile but visible strength, those silences and those hands that had toiled. Monsieur Nizan used to talk about his former comrades: fascinated by these men who knew the truth about life and who seemed to love each other, the little boy saw his father as a worker and wanted to be like him in every way—he would have his father's earthly patience. It would take nothing less than the obscure inner density of things, of matter, to save the future monk from his mother, from Monsieur le Curé, and from his own idle chatter. 'Antoine,' he said admiringly, 'was a corporeal being. He did not have a mind so pure that it separated itself from the body that nourished it and for so many years had provided it with the admirable proof of existence.'[50]

But the admirable man stumbled; suddenly, the child saw him begin to come apart. Nizan had committed himself unreservedly to his father: 'I shall be like him.' He now had to watch the interminable decomposition of his own future: 'That will be me.' He saw matter come to grief; the maternal prattle triumphed—and with it the Spirit, that foam that remained after the shipwreck. What happened? Nizan tells the story in *Antoine Bloyé*: for reasons I do not understand—because, while staying quite close to the truth in his book, he undoubtedly changed the circumstances—the man who served as the model for Antoine sought, as early as forty years of age, to take stock of his life. Everything had begun with that false victory, a 'crossing of the line', at a time when the bourgeoisie was promising everyone a 'great future of equal opportunity,' a time when every working-man's son carried in his schoolbag . . . 'a blank certificate of membership of the middle classes.' Since the age of fifteen, his life had been like the express trains he would later drive, trains 'carried along by a force that was all certainty and breathlessness'. And then, in 1883, he graduated from the École des Arts et Métiers, eighteenth out of a class of seventy-seven. A little later, at twenty-seven, he married Anne Guyader, his yardmaster's daughter. From that point on, 'everything was settled, established. There was no going back.' He sensed this at the very moment the *curé* united them and then he forgot his worries: years passed, the couple went from town to town, constantly moving house without ever settling. Time wore on, and life remained provisional; yet every day was like all the others in its abstraction. Antoine dreamed, without too much conviction, that 'something would happen.' Nothing happened. He consoled himself: he would show what he was made of in the real battles. But while he waited for the great events, the little ones ate into him and imperceptibly wore him down. 'True courage consists in overcoming small enemies.' Yet he rose irresistibly. First, he experienced 'the most insidious peace', he heard the bourgeois siren song: he was able to derive from the false duties assigned to him—towards the Company, towards Society, *even* towards his former comrades—what might be called a vital minimum of good conscience. But 'the years piled up'; desires, hopes and memories of youth drove down 'into that shadowy realm of condemned thoughts into which human forces sink'. The Company devoured its employees: for fifteen years there was no man less self-aware than Antoine Bloyé: he was driven by, 'the demands, the ideas and the judgments of work'; he barely even scanned the newspapers: 'the events they speak of take place on another planet and are of no concern to him.' He passionately devoured 'descriptions of machines' in technical journals. He lived, or rather his body imitated the attitudes of life. But the mainsprings of his life, the motives for his action were not in him. In fact, 'complex powers prevent him from having his feet firmly set on the earth.' Changing just a few words, changing nothing, one could apply to him what Nizan writes about a rich Englishman in Aden: 'Each of us is divided among the men he might be, and Mr. C. has allowed to triumph within him that man for whom life consists of making the price of . . . Abyssinian leather go up or down . . . Fighting abstract entities such as firms, unions, merchants' guilds—are you going to call that action?'[51] Of course, Bloyé does not have so much power, but what of that? Isn't everything about his job abstract: the plans, the specifications, the paperwork—isn't it all *pre-ordained* somewhere else, a long way away, by other people? The man himself is merely a subsidiary of the company: this 'full employment' of himself leaves him both unoccupied and available. He sleeps little, works unstintingly, carries sacks and beams on his back, is always the last to leave his office, but, as Nizan says, 'all his work conceals his essential lack of an occupation.' I know. I spent ten years of my life under the thumb of a *polytechnicien*. He worked himself to death—or rather, somewhere, no doubt in Paris, his work had decided it would kill him.

He was the most trifling of men: on Sundays he would withdraw into himself, find a desert within and lose himself in it; he held on, though, saved by his somnolence or by rages of wounded vanity. When they retired him, it was, fortunately, during wartime: he read the newspapers, cut out articles and glued them into a notebook. At least he was straight about it: his flesh was abstract. For young Bloyé, however, the scandal lay in an unbearable contradiction: Antoine had a real body that was tough, capable and had once been eager; and that body imitated life: driven by distant abstractions, scuppering his rich passions, he transformed himself into a creature of the mind:

> Antoine was a man who had a profession and a temperament, that was all. That is all a man is, in the world in which Antoine Bloyé lived. There are nervous shopkeepers, full-blooded engineers, morose workers and irascible solicitors: people say these things and think they have worked on defining a man; they also say a black dog, a tabby cat. A doctor . . . had told him, 'You're the highly-strung, full-blooded type, you are.' There, that said everything. Everyone could handle

225

him like a coin of known value. He circu-
lated with the other coins.[52]

The boy worshipped his father: I do not know if
he would have noticed this inner wretchedness on his
own. Nizan's misfortune lay in the fact that his father
was better than the next man: after ignoring many
danger signs, Monsieur Nizan came—too late—to see
what he was and was horrified at his life; in other
words, he saw his death and hated it. For almost half
a century he had lied to himself, he had tried to persuade himself he could still 'become someone new,
someone different, who would be truly himself.' He
realized suddenly that it was impossible to change.
This impossibility was death in the midst of life: death
draws the line and tots up the score; but, for Nizan's
father, the line was already drawn, the score already
counted. This schematic, half-generalized creature
shared a bed with a woman who was no more a particular person than he was, but more a relay station for
the pious thoughts manufactured in Rome, and one
who had no doubt, like himself, repressed simple, vo-
racious needs. He proclaimed their double failure to his
frightened son. He would get up in the night:

He carried his clothes over his arm and dressed at the foot of the staircase . . . He would go out . . . 'I'm surplus to requirements,' he would tell himself, 'I'm not wanted, I'm useless, already I don't exist; if I threw myself into the water no one would notice, there would just be the announcement of my death. I'm a failure, I'm finished . . .' He would come back in . . . shivering; he would draw his hand over his face and feel how his beard had grown during the night. Near the house, his wife and son, awakened, would be looking for him, calling to him: he could hear their high-pitched cries from a way off, but did not reply; he left them to worry till the very last moment, as if to punish them. They were afraid he had killed himself . . . When he got near them, stifling his anger, he would say, 'Haven't I the right to do as I like?' and he would go back up to his room without any concern for them.[53]

These nocturnal escapades are no novelist's invention: Nizan talked to me about his father and I know all this is true. Meditating on death inclines you to suicide, out of a feverishness, an impatience. I ask

you to imagine the feelings of an adolescent whose
mother wakes him at night with the words, 'Your father isn't in his bedroom; this time I'm sure he's going
to kill himself.' Death enters him, hunkers down at
the crossroads of all his possible routes in life; it is
the end and the beginning: dead in advance, his father
wants to join the lists ahead of time—this is the
meaning and conclusion of a stolen life.

But this paternal life occupied Nizan like a foreign power; his father infected him with the death that
was to be his end. When this disenchanted old man—
the doctors called him 'neurasthenic'—fled the house
goaded by fear, his son feared two deaths in one: the
first, in its imminence, presaged the other and lent it
its aspect of horror. The father bayed at death[54] and
the child died of fright each night. In this return to
nothingness of a life that was nothing, the child believed he saw his destiny; 'everything was settled, established. There was no going back'. He would be this
superfluous young man, then this empty shell, then
nothing. He had identified with the strong maturity
of another man; and when that man displayed his
wounds, my friend was alienated from that mortal

wretchedness. The engineer's unseemly nocturnal wanderings increased when Nizan turned fourteen; now, between fifteen and sixteen, the adolescent took out an insurance policy on eternal life: in one last effort, he asked the Church to grant him immortality. Too late: when the faith is lost, disgust with one's times is not enough to restore it. He lived out his alienation: he believed himself to be another, interpreted every moment in the light of another existence. Everywhere he came upon the traps that had been laid for his father. Kindly and deceitful people got round him with flattery or by granting him false victories: academic honours, little gifts, invitations. The engineer's son would enter the teaching profession. And afterwards? Teachers, like railway yardmasters, move around a lot, pass hurriedly from town to town, take wives from the provincial lower middle class and align themselves, out of self-interest or weakness, with their masters. Are they less divided than the technicians? And which is better: building locomotives to serve a few overlords and the bourgeois state, or imparting a foretaste of death to children by teaching them dead languages, a loaded history and a mendacious morality?

Do academics show more indulgence 'for their great pain, for the adventures coiled in the crevices of their bodies'? All these petty-bourgeois are alike: they have an imbecilic dignity imposed on them, they unman themselves, they have no sense of the real purpose of their work and they wake up at fifty to watch themselves die.

From the age of sixteen, I thought we were united by the same desire to write; I was wrong. As a clumsy hunter, I was dazzled by words because I always missed them; the more precocious Nizan had a game-bag full of them. He found them everywhere—in dictionaries, in books, even at large on people's lips. I admired his vocabulary and the way he dropped into the conversation, with ease and at the first attempt, the terms he had just acquired—among others, 'bimetallism' and 'percolator'. But he was far from fully committed to literature: I was inside it; the discovery of an adjective delighted me. For his part, he wrote better and watched himself write, doing so with his father's cheerless eyes. The words died or turned into withered leaves: can you justify yourself with words? The smouldering fires of death made literature seem a mere party game, a variant on canasta. It is quite natural for a teacher to write; he is encouraged to do so. And the same traps will work with both the engineer and the writer: flattery and temptation. At forty, all these flunkeys are mere shells of themselves. Valéry was buried beneath honours; he met with princes, queens and powerful industrialists and dined at their tables. And he did so because he was working for them: the glorification of the word serves the interests of people in high places; you teach people to take the word for the thing, which is not so costly. Nizan understood this: he was afraid of wasting his life gathering together mere wisps of voices.

He set about *repeating* his father's dark follies: he recommended that man's nocturnal excursions and escapades. He would be walking in the street and suddenly 'he felt he was going to die (and) was suddenly a man apart from all the passers-by . . . It was a thing he knew in a single act of cognition, a thing of which he had a particular, perfect knowledge.'[55] It wasn't an idea, but 'an absolutely naked anxiety . . . far beyond all individual forms.' At such moments he believed he possessed a fundamental, material insight; he believed he understood the undivided unity of his body through the unity of its radical negation. But I don't think it was anything of the sort: we do not even have that, do not even have such unmediated communication with our nothingness. In reality, a shock had revived his old, learned pain-response: in him his father's life was draining away, the eye of *other death* reopened, tainting his modest pleasures: the street became a hell.

In those moments he loathed us: 'the friends he met, the women he glimpsed were life's accomplices, drawing drafts on time.' He would not even have dreamed of asking our help: we lacked awareness, we would not even have understood him: 'Which of these madmen loved him so shrewdly as to protect him from death?'[56] He fled our rapacious faces, our eager mouths, our greedy nostrils, our eyes ever set on the future. Gone missing. A three-day suicide, ending in a hangover. He was *reproducing* his father's night-time crises; these grew more acute and ended in drink—and yet more words: I think he exaggerated the tragic element, being unable to achieve the perfect, gloomy sincerity of the fifty-year-old. No matter: his anxiety did not lie; and if you want to know the deepest, most specific truth, I would say that it was *this* and this alone: the death throes of an old man gnawing at the life of a very young one. He had fire and passion about him, and then that implacable stare froze everything; to judge himself on a daily basis, Nizan had placed himself beyond the tomb. In fact, he was going round in circles: there was, of course, the rush to get to the end, and the panic fear that he would do so; there was the time that was wearing away, 'the years piling up', and those traps he just managed to avoid, that manhunt, the sense of which he didn't quite understand; but there was also, in spite of everything, his muscles, his blood: how could you stop a well-fed young bourgeois from trusting in the future? He did have times of sombre enthusiasm, but his own excitement frightened him, aroused mistrust: what if it were a trap, one of the lies you tell yourself to choke back your anxiety and pain? The only thing he liked in himself was his revolt: it proved he was still holding out, that he was not yet on the track that leads, irresistibly, to life's sidings. But when he thought about it, he was afraid that his resistance might weaken: they have thrown so many blankets on me that they've almost got me; they will

233

start again. What if I were to get used, little by little, to the condition they are preparing for me?

Around 1925–26, this was what he feared madly: habituation. 'So many ties to break, secret timidities to conquer, little battles to fight . . . One is afraid of being . . . unbearably singular, of no longer being just like anyone . . . false courage waits for great opportunities; true courage consists in defeating the little enemies each day.'[57] Would he manage to defeat these gnawing enemies? And in five or six years' time, would he still be capable of breaking all these ties, which daily increased in number? He was living in enemy country, surrounded by the familiar signs of universal alienation: 'Just try, while still in your arrondissements and sub-prefectures, to forget your civic and filial obligations.'[58] Everywhere there were invitations to slumber, to abandonment, to resignation: he had got to the point of cataloguing his abdications: 'the terrible old habits'. He was also afraid of that alibi so dear to the cultured: the empty noise in his head of torn and precious words. Meditation on death has, in fact, other consequences, more serious than these intermittent conversations: it disenchants. I was running after sparks that for him were merely ashes. He wrote, 'I tell you, all men are bored.' Now, the worst damage done by boredom, 'that continuous forewarning of death', is to generate a by-product for sensitive souls: the inner life. Nizan feared his very real loathings might end up by giving him an over-refined subjectivity, and he was afraid that he might lull his grievances to sleep with the purring of 'empty thoughts, and ideas that are not ideas at all'. These aborted offspring of our impotence deflect us from facing up to our wounds, our bleeding. But Nizan, with his eyes wide open, felt sleep rising in him.

So far as the sons of the bourgeoisie are concerned, I think this revolt can be termed exemplary, because it has neither hunger nor exploitation as its direct cause. Nizan sees all lives through the cold window-pane of death: in his eyes, they become balance-sheets; his fundamental alienation is the source of his insight: he can sniff out any kind of alienation. And how serious he is when he asks each of us, in the presence of our death, like a believer, 'What did you do with your youth?' What a deep, sincere desire to knit together the scattered strands in each of us, to contain our disorders in the synthetic unity of a form: 'Will man never be anything but a fragment of man—alienated, mutilated, a stranger to himself; how many parts of him left fallow . . . how many things aborted!'[59]

These cries of protest on the part of a 'sub-human' form the outline in negative of the man he wanted to be. He put his mystical flights to one side, his taste for adventure and his word-castles. The inaccessible image remains simple and familiar: man can be said to be a harmonious, free body. There is a bodily wisdom—constantly stifled, but constantly present since Adam; 'in the most obscure part of our being are hidden our most authentic needs.' It is not a question here of being madly in love or of undertakings that exceed our powers: man is sedentary; he loves the earth, because he can touch it; he enjoys producing his life. The Great Desire was just empty words: *desires* remain, modest but concrete, balancing each other out; Nizan felt an affection for Epicurus, on whom he later wrote very well:[60] *there* was a man who spoke to everyone, to prostitutes and to slaves, and he never lied to them.

We may be reminded here of Rousseau and not without reason: out of loyalty to his childhood, Nizan the town-dweller retained a kind of rustic naturalism. We may also wonder how this noble savage could have adapted to the needs of socialist production and interplanetary nomadism. It is true: we shall not recover our lost liberty unless we invent it; there can be no looking back, even to gauge the extent of our 'authentic' needs.

But let us leave Epicureanism and Rousseau to one side: to do otherwise would be to take fleeting hints to extremes. Nizan began with individualism, like all the petty-bourgeois of his day: he wanted to be *himself* and the entire world was separating him from himself; against the abstractions and symbolic entities they tried to slip into his heart, into his muscles, he defended his own, individual life. He never wasted effort describing the fullness of moments or passions: for him it did not exist. It is what is stolen from us. But he said that love was true and we were prevented from loving; that life could be true, that it could bring forth a true death, but that we were made to die even before we were born. In this upside-down world, where ultimate defeat is the truth of a life, he showed that we often have 'encounters with death' and each time confused signs awaken 'our most authentic needs'. A little girl is born to Antoine and Anne Bloyé; she is doomed and they know it; grief draws closer together these abstract characters, who have been living in solitude despite being crowded together. For only a short while, the singularity of an accident will never be able to save individuals.

From the age of fifteen, Nizan had understood the key things about himself: this had to do with the nature of his suffering. Some alienations are, in fact, the more formidable for the fact that they are covered up by an abstract sense of our freedom. But he never felt free: there had been *possession*; his father's 'bungling unhappiness' occupied him like a foreign power; it imposed itself upon him, destroying his pleasures and impulses, governing by *diktat*. And one could not even say this wretched fate had been produced by the ex-worker; it came from all quarters, from the whole of France, from Paris. Nizan had tried for a time—in the days of mysticism, of R'hâ and Bor'hou—to struggle alone, by way of words and moral uplift, against his revulsions and the discords within him. But to no avail: the fabric of our social being crushes us. Spinoza came to his aid: you have to act on the causes. But what if the causes are not in our hands? He deciphered his experience: 'What man can overcome his dividedness? He will not overcome it on his own for its causes are not within him.' This is the juncture at which to bid a scornful farewell to spiritual exercises: 'I was under the impression that human life disclosed itself through revelation: what mysticism!'[61] It is clearly the case that one has to fight and that one can do nothing on one's own. Since everything comes from elsewhere—even the innermost contradictions that have produced the most singular features of one's character—the battle will be waged elsewhere and everywhere. Others will fight for him *there*; *here*, Nizan will fight for others: for the moment, it is simply a question of seeing clearly, of recognizing one's brothers-in-darkness.

As early as his second year at the École normale, he had been drawn to the Communists: in short, his decision was made. But decisions are taken in the night and we battle for a long time against our own will, without recognizing what that will is. He had to knock on all the doors, to try everything, to test out solutions he had long since rejected. He wanted, I think, to experience the good things of this world before making his vow of poverty. He left in order to bury his bachelor life. And then the fear mounted and he had to break it off. Aden was his last temptation, his last attempt to find an individual way out. His last escapade too: Arabia attracted him in the same way as, on certain evenings, the Seine had attracted his father. Did he not later write of Antoine Bloyé that he 'would have liked to abandon this existence . . . to become someone new, someone foreign, who would really be himself'? He imagined himself '. . . lost, like a man who has left no address and who is doing things and breathing.' He had to get away from us and from himself.

We lost him, but he did not shake himself off. He was gnawed at now by a new abstraction: to run from one place to another, to chase after women was to hold on to nothing. Aden is a compressed version of Europe, heated to a white-hot temperature. Nizan one day did what his father—when still living—never dared: he took a car and set out on the road without a helmet at noon. They found him in a ditch, unconscious but unharmed. This suicide attempt swept away some old terrors. On coming round, he looked about him and saw 'the most naked state, the economic state'. The colonies lay bare a regime that is seen only through a mist in the home countries. He came back: he had understood the causes of our servitude; the terror within him became a force of aggression: it turned to hatred. He was no longer fighting insidious, anonymous infiltrations; he had seen exploitation and oppression in the raw and understood that his adversaries had names and faces: they were human beings. Unhappy, alienated human beings, no doubt, like his father and himself. But 'defending and preserving their unhappiness and its causes with cunning, violence, obstinacy and cleverness'. On the night of his return, when he came knocking at my door, he knew he had tried everything, that he was up against it, that all the exits were blind alleys except one: war. He came back to his enemies' heartland to fight: 'One must no longer be afraid to hate. One must no longer be ashamed to be a fanatic. I owe them some pain. They almost did for me.'[62]

It was over: he found his community and was received into it; it protected him from them. But, since I am presenting him here to the young readers of today, I must reply to the question they will unfailingly ask: did he at last find what he was looking for? What could the Party offer to this sensitive soul, wracked to the core of his being by the horror of death? We have to ask this conscientiously: I am telling the story of an exemplary existence, which is the absolute opposite of an edifying life. Nizan turned over a new leaf and yet the old man—the old, young man—remained. Between 1929 and 1939, I saw less of him, but I can give an impression of these meetings which, though shorter, are the more vivid for it. I am told people choose family ahead of politics today. Nizan had chosen both—together. Aeneas had tired of carrying gloomy old Anchises for so long: with a heave of his shoulders he dropped him flat on his back; he became a husband and father in great haste, in order to kill his own father. But fatherhood alone is an insufficient remedy for childhood. Far from it. The authority of the new head of the family condemns him to repeat the age-old childishnesses that Adam bequeathed to us through our parents. My friend knew the score: he wanted to strike a definitive blow against the father who, in the passage from father to son, is repeatedly murdered and repeatedly revived. To do so, he would become *a different person* and, through a public discipline, would take care to avoid family quirks. Let us see whether he succeeded.

The doctrine fully satisfied him. He detested reconciliation, and among conciliators he most detested Leibniz, their Grand Master. Forced by the syllabus to study the *Discourse on Metaphysics*, he took his revenge by making a talented drawing of Leibniz in full flight, wearing a Tyrolean hat, with the imprint of Spinoza's boot on his right buttock. From the *Ethics* to *Capital*, by contrast, the transition was easy. Marxism became second nature for Nizan, or, rather, became equivalent to Reason itself. His eyes were Marxist, and his ears too. And his head. He was at last able to explain to himself his incomprehensible wretchedness, the holes in his life, his anxiety: he saw the world and saw himself in it. But, above all, the doctrine—while lending legitimacy to his hatreds—reconciled in him the opposing voices of his parents. Technical rigour, scientific exactitude and the patience of reason—everything was preserved. But, at the same time, the pettiness of positivism was overcome and its absurd refusal to 'know through causes'; the sad world of means—and of means to means—was left to the engineers. For the troubled young man trying to save his soul, there were absolute goals on offer: playing midwife to history, making revolution, readying Man to come into his kingdom. There was no talk of salvation or personal immortality, but survival, in fame or anonymity, was granted as part of a shared undertaking that ended only when the human race came to an end. He put everything into Marxism: physics and metaphysics, the passion for action and for rehabilitating his actions, his cynicism and his eschatological dreams. Man was his future: but this was a time for cleaving things apart; others would have the job of stitching them back together; to him fell the pleasure of merrily smashing everything to pieces for the good of humanity.

Everything suddenly took on substance, even words: he had distrusted them because they served bad masters. Once he could turn them against the enemy, everything changed. He used their ambiguity to confound, their dubious charms to beguile. With the Party's guarantee, literature could even become idle chatter; the writer, like the ancient sage, would, if he wanted, turn a triple somersault. All the words belonged to man's enemies; the Revolution gave permission to steal them; that was all. But it was enough: Nizan had been pilfering for ten years and suddenly he came forth with the sum total of his thefts: his vocabulary. He understood his role as a Communist writer and understood that discrediting the enemies of man or discrediting their language were, for him, one and the same thing. It was 'no holds barred', the law of the jungle. The masters' Word is a lie: we shall take apart their sophisms and shall also invent sophisms against them; we shall lie to them. We shall even go so far as to clown around, so as to prove, as we speak, that the masters' speech is clownish.

These games have become suspect today: Eastern Europe is building; it has given our provinces a new respect for the 'trinkets of high-sounding inanity'.[63] I have said we were serious, caught between two kinds of false coin, one coming from the East, the other from the West. In 1930, there was only one sort and, with us in France, the Revolution was simply at the destructive stage: it was the intellectual's mission to spread confusion and muddle the threads of bourgeois ideology; marauding troops were setting fire to the brush and whole linguistic sectors were being reduced to ashes. Nizan seldom played the fool and had little time for sleight of hand. He lied, like everyone in that golden age, when he was quite certain he would not be believed: slander had just been born, a nimble, joyous thing verging on poetry. But he found these practices reassuring: we know that he wanted to write against death, and death beneath his pen had turned words into dead leaves; he had been afraid of being duped, afraid of wasting his life toying with trifles. Now he was being told he had not been wrong, that literature was a weapon in the hands of our masters, but he was being given a new mission: in a negative period, a book can be an act if the revolutionary writer applies himself to de-conditioning language. Everything was permitted—even to create a style for himself: for the wicked, this would be a gilding of a bitter pill; for the good, it would be a call to vigilance: when the sea sings, do not jump in. Nizan studied the negative form: his hatred produced pearls; he took the pearls and cast them before us, delighted that it fell to him to serve common ends by producing so personal a body of work. Without changing its immediate target, his battle against the particular dangers menacing a young bourgeois became a sacred charge: he spoke of impotent rage and hatred; he wrote of the Revolution.

The writer, then, was made by the Party. But the man? Had he at last found 'his field'? His fulfilment? Was he happy? I do not believe so. The same reasons deprive us of good fortune as make us forever incapable of enjoying it. And then, the doctrine was clear and chimed with his personal experience: his alienations, being linked to the present structures of society, would disappear when the bourgeois class disappeared. Now, he did not believe that he would see socialism in his lifetime nor, even if he saw it in the last days of his life, that such a metamorphosis of the world would leave time to transform the old habits of a dying man. Yet he had changed: his old bouts of desolation never returned; he was never again afraid he was wasting his life. He had an invigorating violence about him, and felt joy: he accepted in good heart being only the *negative man*, the writer of de-moralization and de-mystification.

Was there enough in this to satisfy the serious child he had continued to be? In a sense, yes. Before he joined the Party, he clung to his rejections. He clung to the idea that, since he could not achieve true being, he would be empty: he would derive his sole value from his dissatisfaction, from his frustrated desires. But, sensing a torpor coming over him, he was terrified of letting go and of one day subsiding into consent. As a Communist, he consolidated his resistances: up until then he had continually feared that dunce, the 'social man'. The Party socialized him without tears: his collective being was none other than his individual person; it was enough merely that his restless agitations were now *sanctioned*. He saw himself as a monstrous, misbegotten thing; he was heaved on to the stage, where he showed off his wounds, saying, 'See what the bourgeois have done to their own children.' Once he had turned his violence against himself: now he made it into bombs which he hurled at the palaces of industry. The buildings sustained no damage, but Nizan found deliverance. He presided over a sacred fury, but he no more felt it than a fine singer hears his own voice; this *mauvais sujet* turned himself into a terrible object.

It was not so easy to free himself from death, or rather from the shadow it cast over his life. But the adolescent ravaged by an alien anxiety acquired, as an adult, the right to die his own death. Marxism revealed his father's secret to him: Antoine Bloyé's loneliness was the product of betrayal. This worker-turned-bourgeois thought constantly of:

> the companions he had had in the yards of the Loire and among the watchmen at the goods depots, who were on the side of the hirelings, on the side of life without hope. He said . . . something he would strive to forget, which would disappear only to reappear at the time of his decline, on the eve of his own death: 'So I am a traitor.' And he was.[64]

He had crossed the line, betrayed his class and ended up as a simple molecule in the molecular world of the petty-bourgeois. On a hundred occasions, he felt his friendlessness—one day in particular, during a strike, seeing the demonstrators marching by:

These men of no importance bore far away from him the strength, friendship and hope from which he was excluded. That evening, Antoine felt he was a man of solitude. A man without communion. The truth of life lay with those who had not 'succeeded'. They are not alone, he thought. They know where they are going.[65]

This renegade had fallen apart; now he was whirling around in the bourgeois pulverulence. He knew alienation, the misfortune of the rich, as a result of having thrown in his lot with those who exploited the poor. This communion of 'the men of no importance' could have armed him against death. With those men, he would have known the fullness of misfortune and friendship. Without them, he remained unprotected: dead before his time, a single blow of the scythe had severed his human bonds and cut short his life.

Was Mr Nizan really this tearful deserter? I do not know. At any rate, his son saw him that way: Nizan discovered or thought he discovered the reason for the thousand tiny resistances he put up against his father: he loved the man in him, but loathed the betrayal. I beg those well-intentioned Marxists who have studied my friend's case, and have explained it by the obsession with betrayal, to re-read his writings with open eyes, if they can, and not reject the glaring truth. This son of a traitor does, admittedly, often speak of betrayal; in *Aden* he writes, 'I could have been a traitor, I might have suffocated.' And in *Les Chiens de garde*, he writes: 'If we betray the bourgeoisie for humanity, let us not be ashamed to admit that we are traitors.' A traitor to men, Antoine Bloyé; a traitor still, in *La Conspiration*, the sad Pluvinage, the son of a cop and a cop himself. And what does it mean, then, this word repeated so often? That Nizan was in the pay of Daladier? When they speak of others, the right-thinking characters of the French Left are shamefully hungry for scandal; I know of nothing dirtier or more puerile, except perhaps 'decent' women gossiping about a free woman. Nizan wanted to write, he wanted to live: what need had he of thirty pieces of silver from secret political funds? But as the son of a worker who had become a bourgeois, he wondered what he might become: bourgeois or worker? His chief concern was undoubtedly this civil war within him; as a traitor to the proletariat, Mr Nizan had made his son a betraying bourgeois; this bourgeois-despite-himself would cross the line in the opposite direction: but that is not so easy. When the Communist intellectuals want a bit of fun, they call themselves proletarians: 'We do manual work in our garrets.' Lacemakers, so to speak. Nizan, more clear-sighted and more demanding, saw them—saw himself, indeed—as petty-bourgeois who had chosen the cause of the people. That does not actually close the gap between a Marxist novelist and an unskilled worker: they can exchange smiles from either side of the intervening gulf, but if the author takes a single step, he falls in. All this is true when we are speaking about a bourgeois who is the son and grandson of a bourgeois: against the fact of birth, fine feelings are powerless. But Nizan? He was close to his new allies by ties of blood: he remembered his grandfather who 'remained on the side of the hirelings, on the side of life without hope'; he had grown up, like the sons of the railwaymen, in landscapes of iron and smoke; yet a diploma in the 'liberal arts' had been enough to make his a lonely childhood, to force an irreversible metamorphosis on the whole family. He never crossed the line again: he betrayed the bourgeoisie without rejoining the enemy army and had to remain something of a 'Pilgrim' with one foot on either side of the frontier; right to the end he was the friend—but he never managed to become the brother—of 'those who have not succeeded'. It was nobody's fault but those bourgeois who had taken his father into their class. This discreet absence, this emptiness always troubled him a little: he had heard the bourgeois siren song. Retaining his scruples, he remained anxious: for want of participating in the 'communion of hirelings, of those who live without hope,' he never saw himself as sufficiently protected from temptations, from death; he knew the comradeship of fellow militants without escaping his loneliness, which was the legacy of a betrayal.

His life would not be stolen from him; released now from an alien death, he contemplated his own: it would not be the death of a railway yardmaster. But this negative man, robbed of the humblest plenitude, knew he would ultimately suffer an irreparable defeat. With his passing, nothing might be said to have happened but the disappearance of a refusal. All in all, a highly Hegelian demise: it would be the negation of a negation. I doubt if Nizan drew the slightest consolation from this philosophical view. He made a long journey to the USSR. On his departure, he had told me of his hopes: over there perhaps, these men were immortal. The abolition of classes closed up all the divides. United by a long-term undertaking, the workers would change themselves by death into other workers, and those into others in their turn; the generations would succeed each other, always different and always the same.

He came back. His friendship for me did not entirely exclude the propagandist's zeal: he told me the reality had exceeded all his expectations. Except on one point: the Revolution freed men of the fear of living, but it did not remove the fear of dying. He had questioned the best among them: they had all replied that they thought about death and that their zeal for the shared task gave no protection from that obscure personal disaster. Disabused, Nizan forever renounced the old Spinozist dream: he would never know that affirmative plenitude of the finite mode which, at the same time, shatters its own limits and returns to infinite substance. In the midst of the collective commitment, he would retain the particularity of his disquiet. He tried not to think of himself any more, and he succeeded, concentrating only on objective necessities: yet he remained, as a result of this hollow, indissoluble nothingness—this bubble of emptiness within him—the most fragile and the most 'irreplaceable' of human beings. Individualized in spite of himself, a few scattered phrases show that he ended up choosing the most individual solution: 'It takes a great deal of strength and creation to escape nothingness . . . Antoine understood, at last, that he could only have been saved by creations he had produced, by exercising his power.'[66] Nizan was not an engineer. Nor a politician. He wrote; he could exercise power only through the practice of style. He put his trust in his books: he would live on through them. Into the heart of this disciplined existence, which grew more militant each day, death injected its cancer of anarchy. This lasted somehow for ten years. He devoted himself to his party, lived a dissatisfied life and wrote with passion. From Moscow there came a squall—the Trials—which shook, but did not uproot him. He held out. But to no avail: this was an unblinkered revolutionary. His virtue and his weakness were that he wanted everything *right now*, the way young people do. This man of negation did not know renunciation of assent. About the trials he remained silent and that was all there was to it.

I regarded him as the perfect Communist, which was convenient: in my eyes, he became the spokesman for the Political Bureau. I saw his moods, illusions, frivolities and passions as attitudes agreed by the Party leadership. In July 1939, where I met him by chance for the last time, he was cheerful: he was about to take a ferry to Corsica. I read in his eyes the cheeriness of the Party; he spoke about war, expressing the view that we were going to escape it. I immediately translated in my head: 'the Political Bureau is very optimistic, its spokesman declares that the negotiations with the USSR will bear fruit. By the Autumn,' he says, 'the Nazis will be on their knees.'

September taught me it was prudent to dissociate my friend's opinions from Stalin's decisions. I was surprised by this. And annoyed: though apolitical and reluctant to commit myself in any way, my heart was on the Left, as was everyone's. Nizan's rapid career had flattered me; it had given me some sort of revolutionary importance in my own eyes. Our friendship had been so precious and we were still so often confused for one another that it was I too who wrote the foreign politics leaders in *Ce Soir*—and I knew quite a bit about all that! Now, if Nizan knew nothing, what a come-down: we were back to being a pair of real clots. Sent back to the ranks. Unless he had deliberately deceived me. This conjecture amused me for a few days: what a fool I was to have believed him; but this way he retained his high-flying role, his perfect insight into what in those days we called 'the diplomatic chessboard'. Deep down, I preferred this solution.

A few days later in Alsace, I learned from the newspapers that the spokesman for the Political Bureau had just left the Party, making a great splash about the break. So I had been wrong about everything, from the very outset. I don't know why I wasn't completely stunned by this news: perhaps my frivolousness protected me; and then, at this same time, I discovered the monumental error of a whole generation—our generation—which had actually been sleepwalking. Through a fierce period of preparation for war, when we thought we were strolling on the calm lawns of Peace, we were actually being impelled towards massacres. At Brumath I experienced our immense anonymous awakening; I lost my distinctiveness once and for all and was drawn in.[67]

Today I recall this learning experience without displeasure and I tell myself that at the same time, Nizan was engaged in *unlearning*. How he must have suffered! It is not easy to leave a party: there is its law, which you have to wrench from yourself if you are to break it, its people, whose beloved, familiar faces will become filthy enemy 'mugs', that sombre crowd continuing on its stubborn march which you will watch disappear into the distance. My friend became an interpreter: he found himself alone in the north of France among British soldiers: alone among the British, as he had been at the worst time of his life in Arabia, fleeing beneath the sting of the gadfly, separated from everyone and saying 'no'.

He gave political explanations, of course. His former friends accused him of moralism; he criticized them for not being Machiavellian. He approved, he said, of the lofty cynicism of the Soviet leaders: all means were permitted when it came to saving the socialist fatherland. But the French Communists had neither imitated this cavalier attitude, nor understood that they had to distance themselves in appearance from the USSR; they were going to lose their influence for failing to put on a timely act of indignation.

He was not the only one to give these reasons—how frivolous they seem today! In fact, this recourse to Machiavelli was merely a riposte to his critics: Nizan was attempting to prove his realism; he was a tactician condemning a tactic: nothing more—and, above all, he didn't want anyone to think that he was resigning for emotional reasons or because his nerves were shot! His letters prove, on the other hand, that he was distraught with anger. We know the circumstances and documents better today, we understand the reasons driving Russian policy: I tend to think his decision was a headstrong one and that he should not have broken with his friends, with his real life. Had he lived, I believe the Resistance would have brought him back into the fold, like so many others. But that is none of my business: I want to show that he was cut to the quick, wounded to the heart, that his unexpected turnabout revealed his nakedness to him again, sent him back to his desert, to himself.

He was writing for *Ce Soir* at the time; he had been put in charge of foreign affairs, where a single theme prevailed—union with the USSR against Germany. He had argued this so many times that he had become convinced of it. When Molotov and Ribbentrop were putting the last touches to their pact, Nizan, in his harshest tones, was demanding a Franco-Soviet *rapprochement* with menaces. In the summer of 1939, he saw some of the leaders in Corsica: they talked with him in a friendly way, congratulated him on his articles and, when he had gone to bed, held long secret meetings. Did they know what was in store for us? There is some chance they did not: the September revelation struck a holidaying Party like a thunderbolt. In Paris we saw journalists assuming the most serious responsibilities blindly and with a sense of dismay. At any rate, Nizan never doubted for a moment that he had been lied to. It pained him, not in his vanity, nor even in his pride, but in his humility. He had never crossed the class boundary—he knew; suspect in his own eyes, he saw the silence of his party bosses as a sign of the people's distrust. Ten years of obedience had not allayed it: they would never forgive this dubious ally for his father's betrayal.

That father had worked for others, for gentlemen who robbed him of his strength and life; against this, Nizan had become a Communist. Now he learned that he was being used as a tool, with the real objectives hidden from him; he learned that lies had been put into his mouth and he had repeated them in good faith: from him too, unseen, remote individuals had stolen his strength, his life. He had put all his obstinacy into rejecting the gentle, corrosive words of the bourgeoisie and, all of a sudden, in the Party of the revolution, he was back with what he feared most: alienation from language. Communist words, so simple, virtually raw—what were they? Leaking gas. He had written that his father '[had performed] solitary acts that had been imposed on him by an external, inhuman power, . . . acts that had not been part of an authentic human existence, that had produced nothing enduring. They were merely recorded in bundles of dusty files . . .'[68] At present, his actions as a militant

261

came back to him and they were virtually identical to those of the bourgeois engineer: 'nothing enduring'; articles scattered in dusty newspapers, hollow phrases imposed by an external power, the alienation of a man to the necessities of international politics, a frivolous life emptied of its substance, 'the vain image of that headless human being walking in the ashes of time, with hurried tread, directionless and disorientated'.[69]

He came back to his eternal concern: he became politically active to save his life and the Party stole his life from him; he was fighting death and death was coming to him from the Party itself. He was, I think, wrong: it was the Earth that gave birth to the slaughter and it broke out in all parts at once. But I am relating what he felt: Hitler had a free hand now, he was going to hurl himself against us; Nizan, dumbfounded, imagined that our army of workers and peasants would be exterminated with the consent of the USSR. To his wife he spoke of another fear: he would return too late and exhausted from an interminable war; he would survive only to ruminate on his regrets and his rancour, haunted by the false coin of memory. Against these rediscovered threats, only revolt remained—the old desperate, anarchic revolt. Since human beings were betrayed on all sides, he would preserve the little bit of humanity that remained by saying 'no' to everything.

I know the angry soldier of 1940, with his prejudices, principles, experience and intellectual resources was not much like the young adventurer who set out for Aden. He wanted to be rational, to see things clearly, weigh everything up and maintain his links with 'those who have not succeeded in life'. The bourgeoisie awaited him, affable and corrupting: they had to be thwarted. Having been betrayed, as he saw it, by the Party, he felt anew a pressing duty not to betray in his turn; he persisted in calling himself a Communist. He pondered patiently how he was to correct the deviations without falling into idealism? He kept notebooks and logs; he wrote a great deal. But did he really believe he could redirect the inflexible thrust of these millions of human beings on his own? A lone Communist is lost. The truth of his last months was hatred. He had written that he wanted 'to fight real men'. At that juncture, he had in mind the bourgeois, but the bourgeois has no face: the person you think you detest slips away, leaving behind Standard Oil or the Stock Exchange. Right up to his death, Nizan harboured particularized grudges: out of cowardice, such and such a friend hadn't supported him; another had encouraged him to break with the Party, then condemned him for it. His anger was fuelled by some undying memories; in his mind's eye he saw eyes, mouths, smiles, skin tones, a harsh or sanctimonious look and he hated these all-too-human faces. If ever he had an experience of fullness, it was in these violent moments when, selecting these hunting trophies, his rage turned to delight. When he was totally alone, 'directionless and disorientated', and reduced to the inflexibility of his refusals, death came and claimed him. *His* death, stupid and savage, in keeping with his constant fears and forebodings.

An English soldier took the trouble to bury his private notebooks and his last novel, *La Soirée à Somosierra*, which was almost finished. The earth devoured this testament: when his wife, following precise instructions, tried to recover his papers in 1945—the last lines he had written about the Party, the war or himself—there was nothing left of them. Around this

time, the slander against him began to be taken seriously: the dead man was found guilty of high treason.
What a funny old life: a life alienated, then robbed,
then hidden, and saved even in death because it said
'no'. Exemplary too, because it was a scandal, like all
the lives that have been lived, like all the lives that are
manufactured today for young people; but a conscious
scandal and one that publicly declared itself such.

Here is his first book. We thought he had been
obliterated; he is reviving today because a new audience demands it. I hope we shall soon have restored
to us his two masterpieces: *Antoine Bloyé*, the finest,
most lyrical of funeral orations, and *The Conspiracy*.
But it is no bad thing to begin with this raw revolt: at
the origin of everything, there is refusal. So now, let
the older generation withdraw and let this adolescent
speak to his brothers: 'I was twenty. I won't let anyone
tell me it's the best time of life.'

March 1960. Foreword to Paul Nizan, *Aden, Arabie*
(Paris: Éditions François Maspéro, 1960).

merleau-ponty

How many friends I have lost who are still alive. It was nobody's fault: sometimes it was them, sometimes me. Events made us and brought us together; they also separated us. And Merleau-Ponty, I know, said just this when he happened to think of the people who had been part of his life and left it. Yet he never lost me, and he has had to die for me to lose him. We were equals, friends, but we were not alike; we had understood this immediately and our differences amused us at first. And then, around 1950, the barometer plummeted: a stiff breeze blew through Europe and the world; the swell it whipped up knocked us against each other, then a moment later tossed us to opposite poles. Though so often strained, the ties between us were never severed: if you ask me why, I must say we had a lot of luck and, sometimes, a degree of merit. We each tried to remain true to ourselves and loyal to the other, and we more or less succeeded. Merleau is still too alive for it to be possible to paint his portrait; it will be easier to achieve a likeness—perhaps unconsciously—if I tell the story of that quarrel that never took place: our friendship.

At the École normale, we knew each other without being part of the same set. He lived outside the college and I was a boarder: each of these two groups regarded themselves as an elite and the others as mere footsloggers. Then came military service: I was a private, he became a second lieutenant: two different orders again.[70] We fell out of touch with each other. He had a chair at Beauvais, I think; I taught at Le Havre. Yet, without knowing it, we were preparing to meet: each of us was trying to understand the world as best he could with the resources at hand. And we had the same resources—which were then called Husserl and Heidegger—because we were part of the same world.

One day in 1947 Merleau told me he had never got over a peerless childhood: it was a time of the cosiest happiness, and only age drove him out of it. Being from adolescence a Pascalian, even before reading Pascal, he experienced his singular selfhood as the singularity of an adventure: a person is something that happens and fades, though not without tracing out the lines of a future ever new and ever renewed. What was his life but a lost paradise? An amazing piece of undeserved good luck—a free gift—turned, after the Fall, into adversity; it depopulated the world and disenchanted it in advance. The story is an extraordinary one and yet it is common: our capacity for happiness depends on a particular balance between what our childhood has granted and denied us. If we are entirely deprived or entirely satisfied, we are doomed. The lots that fall to us are infinite in number: it was his lot to have won in life too early. Yet he had to live: it remained for him to make himself, until the end, as events had made him. As they had made him and different: seeking the golden age. His archaic simplicity, crafting from that golden age his myths and what he has since termed his 'style of life', set up preferences

—both for traditions, which recall the ceremonies of childhood, and for the 'spontaneity' that evokes its superintended freedom—discovered the meaning of what is happening from what *has happened* and, lastly, turned inventory and acknowledged fact into prophecy. This is what he felt as a young man, without being able to express it yet; these are the byways by which he came to philosophy. He felt a sense of wonderment and that is all there is to it: everything is played out in advance and yet you carry on; why? Why lead a life discredited by absences? And what is it to live?

Our masters, serious and ineffectual, knew nothing of history: they took the view that such questions should not be asked, that they were badly framed or—as a stock response of the time had it—that 'the answers were in the questions'. To think is to measure, said one of them, who did neither. And all of them argued that man and nature can be treated in terms of universal concepts. This was precisely what Merleau-Ponty couldn't accept: tormented by the archaic secrets of his pre-history, he felt irritation at these well-meaning souls who saw themselves as bees and whose philosophy soared above the earth, forgetting that we are bogged down in it from birth. They pride themselves, he was later to say, on looking the world in the face: are they not aware that it envelops and produces us? The most penetrating mind bears the mark of this and one cannot form a single thought that is not deeply conditioned, from the outset, by that Being about which it claims to speak. Since we are each of us ambiguous histories—good and bad fortune, reason and unreason—the origin of which never lies in knowing but in events, it isn't even imaginable that we could express our lives, these unravelling stitches, in terms of knowledge. And what can be the value of human thinking about human beings, since the human being himself is both making the judgement and vouching for it? This was how Merleau 'ruminated on his life'. But the comparison with Kierkegaard is not apposite here: it is too early for that. The Dane was thoroughly averse to Hegelian knowledge; he invented opacities for himself out of a horror of transparency: if the light passed through him, Søren would be done for. With Merleau-Ponty, it was precisely the opposite: he wanted to understand, to understand *himself*; it wasn't his fault if he discovered in practice that universalist idealism was incompatible with what he would call his 'primordial historicity'. He never claimed to grant unreason precedence over rationalism: he merely wanted to bring history into play against the immobilism of the Kantian subject. It was, as Rouletabille said, coming at reason from the right end and nothing more.[71] In short, he was looking for his 'point of anchorage'. We can see what he lacked for beginning at the beginning: 'intentionality', 'situation' and twenty other tools that were to be had in Germany. Around this time I, for quite other reasons, had need of the same instruments. I came to phenomenology through Levinas and went off to Berlin where I stayed for almost a year. When I came back, we were both, without realizing it, at the same point; until September 1939, we went on with our reading and research; at the same pace, but separately.

Philosophy, as is well-known, has no direct efficacy: it took the war to bring us together. In 1941, groups of intellectuals formed all over France, aspiring to resist the victorious enemy. I belonged to one of them, 'Socialism and Liberty'. Merleau joined us.

Our meeting again was no chance matter: being each of us a product of the Republican petty-bourgeoisie, our tastes, tradition and professional consciousness prompted us to defend the freedom of the writer. It was through this freedom that we discovered all the others. Apart from this, we were innocents. Born in enthusiasm, our little unit caught a fever and died a year later, for want of knowing what to do. The other groups in the occupied zone met the same fate, doubtless for the same reason: by 1942, none was left. A little later, Gaullism and the Front National swept up these early resistance fighters. As for the two of us, despite our failure, 'Socialism and Liberty' had brought us together. The times helped us too: there was an unforgettable openness of heart between Frenchmen, which was the reverse side of hatred. By way of this national friendship, which liked everything about everybody from the outset so long as they hated the Nazis, we recognized each other; the essential words were spoken: phenomenology, existence; we discovered our real concerns. Being too individualistic to pool our research, we developed a reciprocity, while remaining separate. Left to ourselves, each of us would have persuaded himself too easily that he had understood the phenomenological idea; together, we embodied its ambiguousness for each other: this was because each of us regarded the alien—and sometimes hostile—labours the other was engaged in as an unexpected deviation from his own work. Husserl became at once the distance between us and the foundation of our friendship. On that terrain, we were, as Merleau, writing about language, has rightly put it: 'differences without terms or, rather, terms engendered by the differences which appear among them.'[72] He retained a nuanced recollection of our talks. Ultimately, he merely wanted to deepen his own understanding and discussions distracted him. And then I made too many concessions to him, and too hastily: he criticized me for this later, in the dark times, and for having exposed *our* viewpoint to third parties without taking account of *his* reservations; he told me he attributed this to pride, to some kind of contempt for others. Nothing can be more unjust: I have always taken the view, and take the view now, that Truth is one and indivisible; on the points of detail it seemed to me then that I had to abandon my views if I had not been able to convince my interlocutor to abandon his or hers. Merleau-Ponty, by contrast, found security in the multiplicity of perspectives: he saw in it the facets of Being. As for remaining silent about his reservations, if I did so it was in good faith. Or almost: does one ever know? My fault was, rather, to drop the decimals so as to achieve unanimity more quickly. In any event, he was not too displeased with me, as he retained the thoroughly amicable idea that I was a reconciler. I do not know if he derived any benefit from these discussions: sometimes I doubt it. But I cannot forget what I owe to them: a thinking that had been aired. In my opinion, this was the purest moment of our friendship.

Yet he did not tell me everything. We no longer spoke about politics except to comment on the news on the BBC. I had lapsed into a distaste for politics which I did not overcome until I was able to join up with a well-established organization. Merleau, formerly more reserved about our joint venture, was slower to forget it: it offered him in miniature the image of an event: it transported the human being back to what he was—to the accident that he was and continued to be, the accident he produced. What had they been through, what had they wanted and, in the end, what had they done, those teachers (including ourselves), students and engineers, suddenly thrown together and just as suddenly separated by a whirlwind?

Merleau-Ponty was, at the time, enquiring into perception; it was, he thought, one of the beginnings of the beginning: this ambiguous testing-out yields up our body by way of the world and the world by way of our body; it is the pivot and the *point of anchorage*. But the world is also history; perhaps we are historical first. In the margins of the book he was slowly writing, he reflected on what, ten years later, seemed to him the fundamental anchoring point. *Phenomenology of Perception*[73] bears the marks of these ambiguous meditations, but I was not able to recognize them; it took him ten years to get to what he had been seeking since adolescence, this *being-event* of human beings, which we may also term existence. Should I say that phenomenology remained a 'static' in his thesis and that he was going to transform it gradually into a 'dynamic' by a deepening, of which *Humanism and Terror*[74] represented the first stage? This would not be wrong; exaggerated, no doubt, but clear. Let us say that this magnification at least enables us to glimpse the movement of his thought: gently, cautiously, inflexibly, it turned round on itself to reach back, through itself, to the original. In these years preceding the Liberation he had not got far: he knew already, however, that History cannot, any more than Nature, be looked straight in the face. The fact is that it envelops us. How? How did it envelop us, the totality of future time and time past? How were we to discover the others in ourselves as our deep truth? How were we to perceive ourselves in them as the rule of their truth? The question already arises at the level of perceptual spontaneity and 'intersubjectivity'; it becomes more concrete and urgent when we resituate the historical agent within the universal flow. Our labours and travails, our tools, government, customs and traditions—how were persons to be 'inserted' into this? Conversely, how could they be extracted from a web they were constantly spinning and that was, in its turn, constantly producing them?

Merleau had expected to make a peacetime living; a war had made him into a warrior and he, for his part, had made war. What if this strange whirligig marked the scope and limits of historical action? He had to look closely into this. As investigator, witness, defendant and judge, he went back and, in the light of our defeat and of the future German defeat—of which, after Stalingrad we felt assured—examined the false war he had fought, the false peace he had thought he was living through, and himself, as ever, at the pivot of these things, the biter bit, the mystifier mystified, both victim and accomplice, despite a good faith that was not in doubt and yet had, nonetheless, to be questioned.[75] All this went on in silence: he had no need of a partner to cast this new light on the singularity of his times, on his own singularity. But we have the evidence that he was constantly reflecting on his times; as early as 1945 he wrote: 'When all is said and done, we have learned history and it is our contention that we must not forget it.'[76]

This was a courtesy 'we': it would take me a good few years yet to learn what he knew. Having known deep satisfaction from birth, then frustration, he was destined, by his experience, to discover the force of circumstance, the inhuman powers that steal our acts and thoughts from us. As a man invested with a role and yet encircled, a man predestined but free, his original intuition disposed him to understand *the event*, that adventure that comes out of everywhere and nowhere, with no consistency or signification until it has filled us with its hazardous shades, until it has forced us to grant its iron necessity freely and in spite of ourselves. And then he suffered from his relations with others: everything had been too good too quickly; the Nature that at first enveloped him was the Mother Goddess, his mother, whose eyes bestowed upon him what he saw; she was the *alter ego*; by her and in her he lived that 'intersubjectivity of immanence' he has often described and which causes us to discover our 'spontaneity' through another. With childhood dead, love remained, just as strong, but disconsolate. Being sure that he could never recover the lost intimacy, he didn't know what to ask of his friends: everything and nothing; at times too much, at others not enough. He moved quickly from demands to lack of interest, not without suffering from these failures which confirmed his exile. Misunderstandings, estrangements, separations with wrong on both sides: private life had already taught him that our acts register themselves in our little world in a manner different from what we had wished, making us other than we were by retrospectively lending us intentions we did not have but will have had from now on. After 1939 he saw these errors of reckoning, these unnecessary expenses that must be accepted because one has failed to foresee them, as the very characteristics of historical action. In 1945 he wrote, 'We have been led to accept and regard as our own not only our intentions, the meanings our acts have for us, but also the consequences of those acts externally, the meaning they assume in a certain historical context.'[77] He saw 'his shadow cast on history as on a wall, that form which his actions assumed for the outside world, that objective Spirit that was himself.'[78] Merleau felt sufficiently engaged to have constantly a sense of restoring the world to the world, sufficiently free to objectivize himself in history by that restitution. He was happy to compare himself to a wave: one crest among others, with the whole of a head sea holding in a hem of foam. As a mix of strange chance occurrences and generalities, historical man appears when his act, performed and planned remotely, to the point of the most alien objectivity, introduces the beginnings of reason into the original irrationality. To his adversaries, Merleau replied, in all certainty, that his feeling for existence did not set him in opposition to Marxism and, in actual fact, the well-known saying, 'Men make history, but not in circumstances of their own choosing' could pass, in his eyes, for a Marxist version of his own thinking.

The Communist intellectuals made no mistake on this point. As soon as the lull of 1945 was over, they attacked me: my political thinking was confused, my ideas could do harm. Merleau, by contrast, seemed close to them. A flirtation began: Merleau-Ponty often saw Courtade, Hervé and Desanti;[79] his traditionalism found solace in their company: after all, the Communist Party is a tradition. He preferred its rites, its thought baked and hardened by twenty-five years of history, to the speculations of those who belonged to no party.

He was not, however, a Marxist: he did not reject the Marxist idea, but he rejected Marxism as dogma. He did not accept that historical materialism was the sole light of history, nor that that light emanates from an eternal source which stands, in principle, outside the vicissitudes of historical events. He criticized this objectivistic intellectualism, like classical rationalism, for looking the world in the face and forgetting that in fact it enwraps us. He would have accepted the doctrine if he could have seen it merely as a net cast upon the sea, unfurled and refurled by the swell, its truth dependent, precisely, on its perpetual participation in the sea's endless commotion. He could see it as a system of reference, but, on condition that, in referring to it, we change it; he could see it as an explanation, on condition that it change shape as it explain. Should we speak of 'Marxist relativism'? Yes and no. Whatever the doctrine, he mistrusted it, fearing he might find it to be a construction of that philosophy that 'soars above the earth'. A relativism, then, but a precautionary relativism; he believed in just the one absolute: our point of anchorage, life. What, then, ultimately was his criticism of the Marxist theory of history? Crucially this and nothing else: it allowed no room for contingency:

> Every historical undertaking has something
> of an adventure about it, being never guar-

anteed by any *absolutely* rational structure of things. It always involves a utilization of chance, one has always to be crafty with things (and with people) since one has to extract from them an order that was not given with them. The possibility of an enormous compromise remains, of a corruption of history in which the class struggle, which is powerful enough to destroy, would not be powerful enough to build, and in which the broad outlines of history as mapped out in the *Communist Manifesto* would fade away.[80]

The contingency of each and all, the contingency of the human adventure; within this, the contingency of the Marxist adventure—we come back here to Merleau-Ponty's fundamental experience. He had first reflected on the singularity of his life, then, moving on to contemplate his historical existence, he had discovered they were both cut from the same cloth.

With these reservations, he accepted historical materialism as a grid, as a regulative idea or, if one prefers, as a heuristic schema:

There have been enough writers in the last fifteen years who have falsely gone beyond

Marxism for us to take care to distinguish ourselves from them. To go beyond a doctrine, you have first to have come up to its level and you have to explain what it explains better than it does itself. If we raise some questions with regard to Marxism, this is not to prefer a conservative philosophy of history that would be even more abstract.

In short, he was a Marxist for want of anything better.

Let us be clear about this: Marxism is basically a practice that has its origins in class struggle. Deny that struggle and nothing remains. In 1945—and so long as the Communist Party shared power with the bourgeois parties—that struggle was not clearly decipherable. The Party's young intellectuals believed in it devoutly. They were not wrong; I say they *believed* in it because they could not *see* it behind the deceptive mask of national unity. Merleau-Ponty often irritated them because he only half believed in it. He had reflected on the consequences of victory: no more allies, two giants face to face. These latter, concerned to avoid friction, had recast the globe at Yalta: I'll have the sunset lands, you have the sunrise; for peace they had little concern; it was beyond doubt that there would be a Third World War; each of the two, anxious to win it as soon as possible, came to an arrangement with the other, to postpone it until such time as they had acquired the better positions. The balance of forces remained, however, temporarily in favour of the West: hence, in that moment of history, revolution became impossible in Europe; neither Churchill, Roosevelt, nor in the end Stalin, would have tolerated it. We know what happened to the Greek resistance and how it was liquidated. Everything is clear today: the whole earth became united in a single history; there ensued this contradiction, indecipherable at the time, that the class struggle transformed itself in places into conflicts between nations—hence into deferred wars. Today the Third World shows us the truth of this; in 1945, we could neither understand the change that had taken place nor accept it. In short, we were blind; Merleau-Ponty, who had one good eye, came to conclusions that were astonishing because they seemed inevitable: if the revolution can be halted from outside by the concern to preserve the international balance, if external forces can nip it in the bud, if the workers must look not to themselves but to a planetary conflict for their emancipation, then the revolutionary class has gone on leave. The bourgeoisie continued to exist, surrounded by the immense mass of workers it exploited and atomized. But the proletariat, that invincible force that passed sentence on capitalism and whose mission was to overturn it, was out to lunch. It was quite possible that it would return; perhaps tomorrow, perhaps in half a century; it may, also, never return. Merleau-Ponty registered this absence, deplored it as seemed fitting and proposed that we organize immediately just in case it should continue. He went so far as to outline a programme in a text which I quote from memory, though I'm certain I do so quite accurately: 'In the meantime, let us undertake to do nothing that might prevent the rebirth of the proletariat; better, we should do all we can to help it to reconstitute itself; in short, we should follow Communist Party policy.' I can, at any rate, vouch for these last words, as I was so struck by them: born out of the class struggle, the Communist Party developed its policy as a function of that struggle; in the capitalist countries, it would not survive the disappearance of the proletariat. Now, Merleau-Ponty no longer believed in civil war, contesting by that very token the legitimacy of Communist organization: the paradox is that he proposed, at the same moment, that we should align ourselves with the Party.

There was another paradox. Go and find a bishop and, just as an experiment, tell him: 'God is dead, I doubt he'll revive but, in the meantime, I'm with you.' You will be thanked for your kind offer, but it will not be possible to accept it. Now, Merleau's Communist friends had taken the opposite stance: they said some harsh things to him in polite terms, but they didn't reject him. Thinking about it, this is no surprise. The Party had come out on top from the Resistance: it was less strict about the choice of its fellow travellers. But, above all, its intellectuals were uneasy about their lives: being radical by their position, they would have liked the proletariat to set about gaining new ground, to resume its forward march; the bourgeoisie, terrorized by the publicity given to its betrayals, would have put up no opposition. Instead of this, action was postponed. They said, 'Let's seize power' and the reply came back: the British and Americans would land within the hour. A new contradiction appeared within the movement for political advance since, to save peace and the socialist countries, a revolution demanded from the inside by the masses could be countermanded from the outside. These young people who had come to the Party through the Resistance, did not lose their trust in it; but there were doubts and frictions. After all, France was a bourgeois democracy; what was the Communist Party doing in the tripartite government? Was it not a hostage to capital? They faithfully transmitted the slogans that troubled them: 'you have to know how to end a strike' and 'the reconstruction of the country is the revolutionary objective'. But they couldn't stop Merleau's conclusions worrying them a little. At the edges. After all, he approved of the Party's reformist policy, that policy of which they themselves, out of sheer obedience, were the agents. Could they blame him for repeating out loud what they sometimes said under their breath: where is the proletariat? In actual fact, it was there. But bridled and muzzled. And by whom? They became irritated a little more each day by Merleau-Ponty, that Cassandra; Merleau-Ponty became irritated with them—each as wrongly as the other.

Merleau misunderstood the rootedness of his friends. He returned to the question fifteen years later, in the preface to *Signs*. There, by contrast, he stresses the status of the party activist who is embedded and entrusted with a mission and who must, nonetheless, contribute by his allegiances and actions to making the party that makes him. It is an ambiguous expression of regret, which leads him, above all, to justify resignations from the Party: it is all very well to have fun judging a policy calmly and serenely from the outside. When those who produce that policy on a day-to-day basis, if only through their acquiescence, discover its meaning, and when they see their shadows cast on the wall, they have no alternative but to break with it. But the argument can be turned around and I believe he knew it: for all these young people of 1945, floundering about between their sincerely held beliefs and their sworn allegiance, by way of actions they assumed daily and whose meaning they saw change in their hands, on more than one occasion the thinker 'soaring' above the fray was Merleau-Ponty.

His friends were mistaken about him in their turn: they did not know the path he had followed. From some conversations we had later, I was left with the feeling that he had been closer to Marxism before 1939 than he ever was afterwards. What distanced him from it? I imagine it was the trials; the fact that he spoke about them at such length in *Humanism and Terror* shows that he continued to be very affected by them. After that, the Nazi-Soviet Pact made little impression on him: he amused himself by writing rather 'Machiavellian' letters to 'apportion roles'. Friends and the writings of Rosa Luxemburg had converted him to the idea of that 'spontaneity of the masses' that saw the general movement as being closely related to its particular form; when he saw Reason of State gleaming out from behind it, he turned away.

He had been a Christian at twenty but ceased to be so because, as he said, 'You believe you believe, but you don't believe.' More exactly, he wanted Catholicism to reintegrate him into the unity of immanence and that was precisely what it couldn't do: Christians love each other in God. I shall not say that he went straight from there to socialism: that would be too schematic. But there came a time when he encountered Marxism and asked what it had to offer: he concluded that it offered the future unity of a classless society and, in the meantime, a warm friendship in struggle. After 1936, there can be no doubt: it was the Party that troubled him. One of his most constant characteristics was to seek the lost immanence everywhere, to be thrown back by that immanence itself towards some transcendent entity and thereupon to take his leave. Yet he did not remain at this level of the original contradiction: between 1950 and 1960, he gradually conceived a new connection between being and inter-subjectivity; but in 1945, though he dreamed perhaps of going beyond it, he had found no way to do so.

In short, he had been through a great deal when, despite the feelings of revulsion he had at times experienced, he proposed his severe, disillusioned, *attentiste* Marxism. And it was true that he had 'learned history' without having any taste for it, from his vocation and out of obstinacy. It was true, too, that he was never again to forget it. This is something his Communist friends did not see at the time, tending, as they did, more towards unconditional commitments than precise, limited agreements. For his part, being concerned only with deepening his relation to history, he would have offered no purchase for their criticisms, I imagine, and would have remained stubbornly silent, if we had not, by chance, founded *Les Temps modernes*. He now possessed the instrument of expression and was virtually compelled to express the detail of his thinking.

We had dreamed of having the review since 1943. If the Truth is indivisible, I thought, then we must, as Gide said of God, seek it 'only everywhere'. Every social product, every attitude—the most private and the most public—are allusive embodiments of it. An anecdote reflects a whole age as effectively as a political Constitution. We would be seekers after meaning; we would speak the truth about the world and our lives. Merleau thought me over-optimistic: was I sure there was meaning everywhere? To which I might have replied that the meaning of non-meaning exists and it was up to us to find it. And I know what he would have replied in turn: cast as much light on barbarism as you will, you will not dispel its obscurity.

The discussion never took place: I was more dog-matic, he was more nuanced, but that is a matter of temperament or, as they say, of character. We had a single desire: to get out of the tunnel, to see things clearly. He wrote: 'Our only recourse lies in a reading of the present that is as complete and faithful as pos-sible; a reading that does not prejudge its meaning and even recognizes its chaos and non-meaning where they are to be found, but is not averse to discerning a direction and an idea in that present, where they exist.'[81]

This was our programme. Today, after Merleau's death, it is still the programme of the review. We would have to say that the real difference was our in-equality. After he had learned history, I was no longer his equal. I was still stuck in the questioning of facts while he was already attempting to make events speak.

Facts *repeat* themselves. They are, of course, al-ways new—but what of it? The annual play by the boulevard playwright is new. He had to come up with the idea and then he thought about it and worked on it; every speech was a stroke of inspiration, and the actors in their turn had to 'get inside' the piece. For days they said 'I don't feel the part' and then, suddenly, 'I feel it.' And in the end, on the day of the dress rehearsal, the unexpected happens: the play became what it was—namely, just the same as all the others. Facts confirm and begin anew: they reveal customs, old contradictions and sometimes, more deeply, structures. The same adultery has been committed for fifty years, every evening, before the same bourgeois audience in the heart of Paris. By looking only for permanencies of this kind, I was hoping unconsciously that we would become the ethnographers of French society.

Merleau-Ponty didn't hate these permanencies. Indeed, he loved the child-like return of seasons and ceremonies. But for this very reason, pining hopelessly for his childhood, he knew it would not return. It would be something too wonderful if, in the world of adults, the adult could be visited by the grace of his earliest years: life would be too perfect. Merleau, the exile, had *felt* at an early stage what I could only *know*: you cannot go back; you cannot take a second turn; by its irreversibility, the sweet contingency of birth transforms itself into a destiny. I was not unaware that you descend life's course and never reverse its direction; but, duped by the bourgeois myth of progress, I cherished for a long time the illusion that I was a little better each day. Progress: the accumulation of capital and virtue; you keep everything. In short, I was approaching excellence; it was the masking of death, which today stands naked. He was moving away from it: being born to die, nothing could restore the immortality of his earliest years; this was his original experience of *the event*.

In the middle of the last century, he would have lived time backwards, though in vain, as Baudelaire did after the *'fêlure'*: the golden age is past; there is room now only for decline. It is to Merleau's credit that he avoided this reactionary myth: let there be as much decline as you will, but it is our decline, we cannot suffer it without creating it or, in other words, without producing man and his works through that decline. The event swoops on us like a thief and throws us into a ditch or hoists us up on to a wall; dazed, we see nothing. Yet hardly has it scarpered away than we find ourselves so deeply changed that we no longer even understand how we could love, live and act before. Who in 1945 would have remembered the 1930s? They were preparing quietly for retirement; the Occupation had killed them off; only bones remained. Some still dreamed of a return to pre-war days. Merleau knew it would not happen and it was criminal and futile to wish for it: when he wondered in 1945 whether the human adventure would sink into barbarism or rescue itself through socialism, he was putting the question to universal history as though it were his own life: time lost? time regained? Divergence, deviation, drift—these words from his pen, a hundred times rewritten, attest to the fact that we gain nothing without a loss, that the future, even the nearest, most docile future, betrays our hopes and calculations. But most of the time it betrays them by bringing them to fruition: our past acts come back to us, from the depths of future time, unrecognizable, but nonetheless our own; one either had to despair or find in those acts the changing reason for change and, not being able to restore the old facts, at least establish them in the heart of the event that repudiates them. We would try to govern the strange slippage we call history from within, by seeking, in the movement that carries us along, the implicit objectives of human beings, so as to propose those objectives to these human beings explicitly. This meant questioning the event in its unpredictability—without pre-judging any-thing—to find a logic of temporality in it. One might be tempted to call that logic 'dialectical' if Merleau had not already objected to that term and had not, ten years later, more or less repudiated it.[82]

All in all, the pre-war period denied time: when a cyclone had blown down our walls, we searched for the survivors among the rubble and told them, 'It's nothing.' The most extraordinary thing is, they be-lieved us. Merleau-Ponty 'learned history' quicker than we did because he took a full and painful pleasure in passing time. This is what made him our political commentator, without his even having wished to be and without anyone even noticing.

Les Temps modernes had at that point an editorial board that was anything but homogeneous: Jean Paul-han, Raymond Aron and Albert Ollivier were all friends of ours, of course. But, though no one knew this, least of all ourselves,[83] we did not share any of their ideas. In fact, our inert coexistence had been, not so long before, a lively comradeship: some had just come from London, others from underground. But the Resistance fragmented: everyone returned to their natural home, some to *Le Figaro*, others to the RPF, yet others to the *Nouvelle Nouvelle Revue Française*. The Communists themselves, having participated in the first issue in the person of Jean Kanapa, took their leave. This was a heavy blow for those of us who remained: we lacked experience. Merleau saved the review by agreeing to take charge of it: he was editor-in-chief and political editor. This happened naturally. He didn't offer me his services and I didn't take the liberty of 'selecting' him: we both realized, after a certain time, that he was filling these two posts and that he couldn't leave them without the review going under. We discussed only one matter: since the editorial board had disappeared from the cover, I suggested printing Merleau's name there alongside my own: we would have been the two 'directors'. He turned me down flat. I put the same offer to him a hundred times in the ensuing years, always on the simple grounds that it would have been a truer reflection of the actual position. A hundred times, relaxed and smiling, he turned me down again, citing circumstantial reasons, but never the same ones. Since his reasons changed constantly, but his position did not, I concluded that he was concealing his true motives from me. I confronted him with this and he rejected the idea, though with no great vigour: he was not trying to deceive me, but merely wanted to put a stop to the discussion. And then, whatever the subject, he never liked the debate to get to the crux of the matter. On this point, he won: I know no more of his reasons today than I did in 1945. Was it modesty? I doubt it: this wasn't about sharing honours but responsibilities. On the other hand, I have been told, 'At the time you were better known: he was too proud to accept the fruits of that fame.' It is true that I was better known and it was nothing to boast of: it was the time of the *rats de cave*,[84] of existential suicides; the respectable newspapers heaped dirt on me and so did the gutter press: I had fame, but it was born of misconceptions. But those who read *Samedi Soir*'s interesting account of a virgin whom I apparently lured to my room to show her a camembert did not read *Les Temps modernes* and were not even aware of its existence. On the other hand, the real readers of the review knew both of us equally; they had read our essays and preferred the one or the other of us, or felt no great preference but no animosity either. Merleau knew this as well as I did: we had received letters and shown them to each other. All in all, his audience and mine—the audience of *Les Temps modernes*—were the same people. And the best people one could wish for, not shooting the pianist, and judging him on his work and not concerning themselves with other matters. From my dubious reputation Merleau could neither suffer nor profit. Was he perhaps afraid of being compromised? Nothing was less like him: he proved this in the review itself, publishing articles that provoked scandal and signing them with his own name. So, what can we say? Why did he stubbornly persist in signing editorials with the letters T. M., when, though I accepted them unreservedly, he had conceived and written every word? All the writings to which he didn't own up were randomly attributed to me: there was some logic to this, since I claimed to be in sole charge. And last year, leafing through some foreign bibliographies, I discovered that I was the author of his article on the Soviet camps—the very one he recognized and legitimized in his last book.[85] Why had he not signed it in 1950, given that he was later to republish it? Why did he republish it ten years later, when he hadn't wanted to sign it? Why create all these 'bastards' for the review when it was wholly within his power to 'regularize' their status? This is the question; I cannot claim to have an answer. Yet one had to get on with life; I contented myself with the most convenient explanation: he valued his independence and would have felt as a burden any bond but the tacit understanding, renewed with each issue, that committed no one and that either of us could break at a moment's notice. This is a possible explanation, and yet I think today that he mistrusted me: he knew my incompetence, and he feared my zeal; if I should begin talking politics, then where would we be? I have no evidence of this distrust except for the following. In 1947, I published 'What is Literature?' in the review. He read the first proofs and thought he had found in them a sentence which, as was the fashion at the time, equated fascism with 'Stalinism' beneath the common appellation of 'totalitarian regimes'. I was in Italy and he wrote to me immediately; I received the letter in Naples and I remember my stupefaction. It said, more or less: 'If you really apply the same yardsticks to communism and Nazism, then I beg you to accept my resignation.' Fortunately, as I was able to prove to him, it was simply a typographical error. We left matters there. But when I reflect on it, it reveals the extent of his distrust: first, the text, at the proof stage, was incomprehensible and clearly mangled; second, as Merleau knew, I had never indulged in that kind of silliness; last, his resignation was offered rather too eagerly. All in all, it is very clear that he was expecting the worst. But what strikes me most is that his fear was that I would defect to the *Right*. Why? Did he see me as temperamentally right-wing? Or was he simply afraid that the hyena with the fountain pen, frozen out by the jackals, would seek admission to the Pen Club? In any event, he was taking precautions against possible blunders on my part: if one should prove inexcusable, he could be away within twenty-four hours. This emergency exit was still in place five years later when a political disagreement drove us apart: yet Merleau did not use it; so long as he could hope that our contradictions would be overcome, he remained. His letter of 1947 proves he would have left the review there and then if I had let it fall into a Rightist rut. When I moved to the Left, he accepted being compromised: he believed he could already see the ditch and that we would imminently be pitched into it, yet he remained at my side, determined to jump only as a last resort. For a long time I thought he was wrong not to have joined me in the stocks: public collaboration would have forced us, I told myself, to make concessions on both sides; we would have been tactful with each other to save the collegiate editorship. Yet for some time now I have tended to believe he was right: in 1952, our differences could neither be masked nor overcome. They arose not out of our temperaments but from the situation: since the name of Merleau wasn't mentioned, we were able to delay matters a little longer. The secret nature of the bond between us, which had been conceived to make withdrawal easy for him, enabled us to stay together till the last moment. The separation was a quiet one, we had no need to proclaim it or, in other words, to turn it into a publicized quarrel. This is perhaps what saved our friendship.

In our closest circles, all these precautions afforded him the reputation of an *éminence grise*. This was quite wrong, particularly as he was nobody's adviser: master of his sphere, as I was of mine, his role—like mine—was to make decisions and write.

He was, however, extremely keen that I should read his articles, both those which he signed T. M., which spoke in the name of the review, and the others bearing his own name, which committed only himself. Let me be clear here: this attitude *seems like* that of an employee, a functionary having his actions 'covered' by the competent authority. It was, in fact, quite the opposite: Merleau was entirely his own boss. He knew his way around the ambiguous world of politics better than I did and I knew that. It would be an understatement to say I trusted him: it seemed to me that, when I read him, he revealed my own thinking to me. But our gentlemen's agreement demanded that he consult me: writing anonymously, he did not want me to be saddled with his writings. He was as tactful as possible about it: I was still a stammerer in this new language he already spoke and he was not unaware of this. Reluctant either to coerce or inveigle me, he brought me his manuscripts without comment. In the early days, he had to make a lot of effort to be read: the political labyrinth confused me, I approved everything in advance and in haste, and then ran off. He'd find out my hiding place and track me down to it. I'd find him suddenly standing there, smiling and holding out his manuscript: 'I agree,' I'd stammer. 'That's good,' he'd reply, not moving, 'But all the same,' he'd add patiently, indicating with his left hand the sheets of paper in his right, 'you should read these.'

I read and learned, and in the end I was passionate about my reading. He was my guide; it was *Humanism and Terror* that caused me to take the plunge. That little book, so densely written, showed me the method and the object: it gave me the nudge I needed to wrest me from my immobilism. As is well-known, it provoked scandal everywhere. Communists who see no harm in it today loathed it at the time. But, particularly to our Right, it raised a fine hullabaloo. One sentence in particular, which equated opponents with traitors and traitors with opponents, triggered the reaction. In Merleau's mind, this sentence applied to those anxious, threatened societies that huddle together around a revolution. But attempts were made to present it as a sectarian condemnation of any opposition to Stalin. In just a few days, Merleau became the bloodthirsty revolutionary. When Simone de Beauvoir visited them in New York, the editors of the *Partisan Review* made no effort to conceal their disgust: we were being manipulated; it was the hand of Moscow that held the pen of our *père Joseph*.[86] What idiots! One evening, at Boris Vian's, Camus took Merleau to task, accusing him of justifying the Moscow trials. It was painful: I can still see them, Camus outraged, Merleau-Ponty courteous and firm, a little pale, the one permitting himself, the other forbidding himself, the splendours of violence. Suddenly Camus turned away and left. I ran after him, accompanied by Jacques Bost, and caught up with him in the empty street. I tried as best I could to explain Merleau's thinking, which Merleau himself had not deigned to do. The only result was that we parted on bad terms; it took more than six months and a chance meeting to bring us together again. This is not a pleasant memory for me: what a stupid idea to try to play the peacemaker! I was, admittedly, to the right of Merleau and to the left of Camus; what black humour can have prompted me to play go-between to two friends who were both not long afterwards to criticize my friendship for the Communists, and who are both dead, unreconciled?

In fact, with this little sentence which caused such a violent reaction, but which everyone accepts today as a basic truth with a universal validity beyond the limits set for it by its author, Merleau had done nothing but apply to other circumstances what the war had taught him: we shall not be assessed on our intentions alone. As much as, and more than, the intended effects of our acts, the basis on which we are judged will be the unintended consequences that we have divined and exploited, and for which, in any event, we have assumed responsibility. 'The man of action,' he wrote later, quoting Hegel, 'has the certainty that, through his action, necessity will become contingency and contingency necessity.' In so doing, he was asking the true philosophical question of history: what is a detour and what does it mean to veer off course? We started out in rough weather and a headwind, we battled on stoically and have grown old in hard times;

this, here, is what we have achieved. What remains of the old goals? What has disappeared? A new society has been born along the way, shaped by the undertaking and deflected by its deflection. What can it accept? And what must it reject or risk doing itself a serious mischief? And, whatever the heritage, who can say whether we have travelled the shortest path or whether we must attribute the meanderings to everyone's failings?

Through this rough justice of injustice, in which the bad are saved by their works and men of good faith condemned to hell for acts committed with a pure heart, I finally discovered the reality of the event. In a word, it was Merleau who converted me: at heart I was an anarchist laggard, I saw a chasm between the vague fantasies of collectivities and the precise ethics of my private life. He set me straight: he taught me that this ambiguous undertaking that is both rational and mad, ever unpredictable and always foreseen, attaining its objectives when it forgets them, missing them when it tries to remain loyal to them, destroying itself in the false purity of failure and dissipating itself in victory, abandoning its prime mover on the way or denouncing him when he no longer believes himself responsible for it, was something I found everywhere, both in the most intimate recesses of my life and in the broad daylight of history, and that there is only one undertaking and it is the same for everyone—the event that makes us by becoming action, the action that unmakes us by becoming, through us, event— and, since Hegel and Marx, it bears the name *praxis*. In a word, he revealed to me that I made history in the same way as Monsieur Jourdain made prose. The course of events broke down the last ramparts of my individualism and swept away my private life, and I discovered myself in just those very places where I began to slip beyond my own grasp. I came to know myself: and I was more obscure, in the full light of day, than I believed myself to be, and two billion times richer. The time had come: our age demanded a dissertation on French politics from all men of letters. I prepared myself for that ordeal; Merleau instructed me without teaching, by his experience, by the consequences of his writings. If philosophy is to be, as he said, an 'educative spontaneity', I may say he was for me the philosopher of his politics. As for his politics, it is my claim we could have had no other and that it was appropriate. If one is to last, one must begin well: the beginning came from him and it was excellent. Proof of this is that our readers have taken all the subsequent twists and turns with us; it will soon be seventeen years since we published the first issue of *Les Temps modernes*; we have regularly gained subscribers and at the very most a few dozen have left us.

It was possible in 1945 to choose between two positions. Two and no more. The first and best was to address ourselves to the Marxists, to them alone and to denounce the way the Revolution had been nipped in the bud, condemn the murder of the Resistance and bemoan the fragmentation of the Left. A number of periodicals adopted this line courageously and disappeared, unheeded; it was the happy time when people had ears so as not to hear and eyes so as not to see. Far from believing that these failures condemned the attempts, I take the view that we could have imitated them without going under: the strength and weakness of these publications was that they confined themselves to the political sphere; ours published novels, literary essays, reportage and non-fiction material:

these kept it afloat. However, in order to denounce the betrayal of the Revolution, one had first to be revolutionary: Merleau was not, and I was not yet. We didn't even have the right to declare ourselves Marxist, despite our sympathies for Marx. Now, Revolution is not a vague sentiment: it is a daily practice illuminated by a theory. And, though it is not enough to have read Marx to be a revolutionary, you connect with him sooner or later when you campaign for revolution. The conclusion is clear: only men shaped by that discipline could criticize the Left effectively; at the time, then, they had to belong, in one way or another, to Trotskyist circles; but, without it being at all their fault, that affinity disqualified them: within that mystified Left that dreamt of unity, they were regarded as 'splitters'. Merleau-Ponty saw the threats clearly too; he noted that the working class' forward march was halted and he knew the reasons for it. But if he had shown the workers gagged, chained, mystified and defrauded of their victory, this petty-bourgeois intellectual—even if he had wept hot tears for them, even if he had made his readers weep them—would have been laying the demagogy on thick. When, on the other hand, he concluded that the proletariat had gone on holiday, he was being sincere and true to himself, and I was being true to myself when I backed his conclusions. Revolutionaries, us? Come off it! At the time, Revolution seemed the most likeable of myths, a Kantian idea, so to speak; I repeated the *word* with respect, but I knew nothing of the *thing*. We were moderate intellectuals whom the Resistance had pulled to the Left; but not enough; and then again, the Resistance was dead; left to ourselves, what could we be but reformists?

There remained the other attitude. We had no choice to make; it forced itself upon us. As products of the middle classes, we attempted to form a link between the intellectual petty-bourgeoisie and the Communist intellectuals. That bourgeoisie had engendered us; its culture and values were our heritage; but the Occupation and Marxism had taught us that neither the culture nor the values were to be taken for granted. We called on our friends in the Communist Party to supply us with the requisite tools to wrest humanism from the bourgeoisie. And we asked all our friends on the Left to do the work with us. Merleau wrote: 'We were not wrong in 1939 to want freedom, truth, happiness, and openness between human beings, and we are not renouncing humanism. [But] the war . . . taught us that these values remain nominal . . . without an economic and political infrastructure to bring them into existence.'[87] I can see that this position, which might be termed eclectic, was not viable in the long term, but I can also see that the French and international situations made it the only one possible. Why would we have taken things to extremes? We had, admittedly, forgotten the class struggle but we were not alone in that. Events had chosen us to bear witness to what the petty-bourgeois intelligentsia wanted in 1945, at the moment when the Communists had lost both the means and the intent to overthrow the regime. Paradoxically, that intelligentsia, as it seems to me, wanted the Communist Party to make reformist concessions and the French proletariat to regain its revolutionary aggression. The paradox is merely an apparent one: this chauvinistic class, exasperated by five years of occupation, was afraid of the USSR, but would have come to an accommodation with a 'home-grown' revolution. There are, however, degrees in being and thought: whatever the appeal of this revolutionary, chauvinistic reformism, Merleau did not care for being the herald of a proletariat in French colours. For his part, he had undertaken—as did others in other countries at around this same time—an enormous labour of confrontation: he threw our abstract concepts out to the Marxists, and their Marxism changed, as they assimilated those concepts, into what we know it to be today.

Today, the task is easier: this is because the Marxists—Communists or otherwise—have taken it up themselves. In 1948, it was very thorny, particularly as the Communist party intellectuals felt no compunction about telling these two suspect, empty-handed bourgeois, who had volunteered themselves as fellow travellers, where to get off. We had to defend Marxist ideology without concealing our reservations and hesitations; to travel with men to whom we expressed our goodwill and who, in return, called us *intellectuels-flics*; to make our ripostes without being insulting or breaking off relations; to criticize, moderately but freely, these hypersensitive souls who could not tolerate any reservations; to assert, despite our solitude, that we were marching at their side, alongside the working class—the bourgeois fell about laughing when they read us—and yet allow ourselves, when necessary, to run ahead of the Communist Party, as we did at the beginning of the war in Indochina; to struggle for peace and détente in our little magazine, as though we were running a mass-market daily; to deny ourselves any righteous passions, particularly self-importance and anger; to speak in the wilderness as though we were addressing the assembled nation and yet not lose sight of our extreme smallness; to remember at every moment that you don't need success to persevere but that the point of persevering is to achieve success. Despite the jibes and the cheap shots, Merleau-Ponty did the work decently, tastefully and unflinchingly: it was his job. He cannot claim to have uncovered the reality of the second half of the 1940s (who can?), but he took advantage of illusory French unity to stay as close as possible to the Communists, to begin necessary—and yet impossible—negotiations with them, and to lay the foundations, beyond Marx, of what he sometimes called 'a Left-wing thought.' In a sense, he failed: left-wing thought is Marxism, no more and no less. But history salvages everything except death: if Marxism is becoming *the whole of left-wing thought* today, we owe this, in the first place, to the efforts of a handful of people of whom he was one; the petty-bourgeoisie, as I have said, were veering to the Left; efforts to stop their slide came from all directions, but it came to a halt on some advanced positions: to the shared desire for democratic union and reforms Merleau gave the most radical expression.

Two years of calm and then the outbreak of the cold war. Behind Marshall's homilies, Merleau was immediately able to see, and denounce, the generosity of an ogre. It was the time when groups were forming. The Communist Party hardened its line, our right fled off towards the centre; at the same point, we were beginning to hear the sound of the RPF rousing its support. The bourgeoisie raised its head again, dubbed itself 'the third force' and developed the policy of the *cordon sanitaire*. We were being pressed to take sides and Merleau refused. He had at times to cling tightly to the tiller: the Prague Coup, revolving strikes, the end of the tripartite government, the

Gaullist landslide at the municipal elections. He had written, 'The class struggle is masked'; it unmasked itself. We persisted stubbornly with our offers of mediation, which no one took seriously, all the more confident that we were, in our two persons, achieving the unity of the Left because it had at the time no other representative. The RDR[88] was born, a mediating neutralism between the blocs, between the advanced fraction of the reformist petty-bourgeoisie and the revolutionary workers. I was asked to join and, allowing myself to be persuaded it shared our objectives, I accepted. Merleau, receiving requests from elsewhere, joined nevertheless so as not to disown me. It did not take me long to see I had been wrong. To live in the closest proximity to the Communist Party, to have it accept certain criticisms, we had, first, to be politically ineffectual and they had to sense that we were effectual in other ways. Merleau-Ponty was just that, standing alone with neither supporters or champions, his thought, ever new and ever recommenced, relying entirely on its own merits. By contrast, the Rassemblement, small as it was and small as it consented to be, put its faith in force of numbers. As a result, despite its immediate desire to suspend hostilities, it immediately triggered them: where would it recruit its revolutionary supporters from, if not from Communist or related circles? The Party, up in arms, treated it from the first as an enemy, to the astonishment of the Rassemblement's members. It was the ambiguity of this situation that gave rise to our internal divisions: some, in disgust, allowed themselves to drift to the Right—in general, these were the 'organizers'. The others—the majority—sought to remain unshakeable and to align themselves with the social action of the PCF.[89] This latter group, which included us, criticized the others for abandoning the initial programme: 'Where's your neutralism?' we asked and they immediately retorted, 'Where's yours?'

Did Merleau discover our mistake before I did? Did he learn that political thinking cannot easily be embodied unless it is pushed to its own logical extreme and taken up somewhere by those who have need of it? Was it not rather that, in 1948 as in 1941, he couldn't help feeling a little scorn for groups that were too young, that had no roots and traditions? The fact is that he never came to the Steering Committee, even though he was a founder member: this, at least, is what I've been told as I did not often go either. He may justifiably have feared that we were distorting his project and that *Les Temps modernes* might come to be seen as the monthly organ of the RDR: he said nothing of this to me, either because he shared my incautiousness or because he did not want to reproach me with it, counting on events to remove the scales from my eyes. In short, he carried on editing the review as usual and let me carry on battling, alone and intermittently, under the banner of neutrality. In the spring of 1949, however, we were agreed that the RDR was not viable. The Mouvement de la Paix, led at the time by Yves Farge, was to hold a congress in Paris.[90] As soon as we became aware of this, the suggestion came up within the Rassemblement that we should invite a number of American personalities and, a few days after the congress, devote some 'Study Days' to peace. Clearly, we could count on the right-wing press to spread the news; in short, these pacifist 'days' were merely a political machination, backed, if not indeed inspired, by the Americans. Having been invited a little too insistently by the US Embassy to take part, a worried Richard Wright came to see me: where were we heading? Merleau joined us: we decided that the three of us would not appear at these events and we wrote a letter in all our names to explain why we were staying away; the war between the two peaces was waged without us; at the *Vél d'Hiver*, an American was to be heard vaunting the merits of the atom bomb but we were not present. The activists were outraged; in June 1949, they went to the leadership to tell them what they thought of them and I took their side. We killed off the RDR and I left for Mexico, disappointed but at peace with myself. Merleau had not appeared at the congress but there could be no doubting his opinion: I realized I needed this unpleasant experience to appropriate his thought in its entirety. In fact, the so reasonable unreason of politics had been within an inch of tipping us into an anti-Communism which we execrated and to which we would, nonetheless, have had to sign up.

I saw him again in autumn: I told him I had understood his position. There would be no more active politics: the review and the review alone. I put some plans to him: why not devote an issue to the USSR?

We were, it seemed, in entire agreement on this: we were becoming interchangeable. I was, then, all the more astonished that so little came of my proposals. It would have been all right if he had shown me they were absurd: but he simply let them drop, silently and glumly. The fact was that we were getting wind of the Soviet camps. Documents were sent to us at the same time as Rousset received them, but from another source. Merleau's editorial appeared in the January 1950 issue; it was to be republished in *Signs*; this time I went so far as to ask him to show it to me even before he had offered. I attended closely to every word and approved the whole piece, not least the author's consistency with his previous positions. He laid out the facts and ended the first paragraph in the following terms:

> If there are ten million concentration camp inmates—while at the other end of the Soviet hierarchy salaries and standard of living are fifteen to twenty times higher than those of free workers—then quantity changes into quality. The whole system swerves and changes meaning; and in spite of nationalization of the means of production, and even though private exploitation of man by

man and unemployment are impossible in the USSR, we wonder what reasons we still have to speak of socialism in relation to it.[91]

How could the Soviet workers tolerate this disgraceful return of slavery on their soil? It was, he answered, because it had come about gradually 'without deliberate intention, from crisis to crisis and expedient to expedient'.[92] Soviet citizens know the [Corrective Labour] Code, they know there are camps: what they are not perhaps aware of is the extent of the repression; if they discover it, it will be too late: they have become habituated to it in small doses.

> A good number of young Soviet heroes . . . [and] many civil servants who were favourably endowed . . . who never knew discussion and the critical spirit in the sense of 1917, continue to think the prisoners are hotheads, asocial persons, men of bad will . . . And communists throughout the world expect that, by a sort of magical emanation, so many canals, factories and riches shall one day produce whole men, even if in order to produce them it is necessary to reduce ten million Russians to slavery.[93]

The existence of the camps, he said, made it possible to gauge how deluded the Communists were today. But he immediately added:

> It is . . . this illusion which forbids confusing communism and fascism. If our Communists accept the camps and oppression, it is because they expect the classless society to emerge from them . . . No Nazi was ever burdened with ideas such as the recognition of man by man, internationalism, classless society. It is true that these ideas find only an unfaithful bearer in today's communism . . . The fact remains that they are still part of it.[94]

He added even more explicitly:

> We have . . . the same values as a Communist . . . We may think he compromises them by embodying them in today's communism. The fact remains that they are ours, and that on the contrary we have nothing in common with a good number of communism's adversaries . . . [T]he USSR is on the whole situated . . . on the side of those who are struggling against the forms of exploitation

known to us . . . [W]e do not draw the conclusion that indulgence must be shown towards communism, but one can in no case
make a pact with its adversaries. The only
sound criticism is thus the one which bears
on exploitation and oppression, inside and
outside the USSR.[95]

Nothing could be clearer: whatever its crimes, the
USSR had this formidable advantage over the bourgeois democracies: the revolutionary aim. An Englishman said of the camps, 'They are their colonies.'
To which Merleau replies, 'Our colonies are, then, *mu-
tatis mutandis*, our labour camps.' But those camps have
no other aim than to enrich the privileged classes; the
Russians' camps are perhaps even more criminal since
they betray the revolution; the fact remains that they
were built in the belief of serving it. It may be that
Marxism has been bastardized, that domestic difficulties and external pressure have distorted the regime,
warped its institutions and deflected socialism from
its course: still Russia cannot be compared with other
nations; it is permissible to judge it only if one accepts
its project and in the name of that project.

In short, five years after his first article, in a moment of extreme seriousness, he was going back to the principles of his politics: alongside the Party, cheek by jowl with it, never inside it. We oriented ourselves by the Party alone and outside opposition was our only attitude to it. To attack the USSR alone was to absolve the West. This uncompromising position echoes Trotskyist thinking: if the USSR is attacked, said Trotsky, we have to defend the foundations of socialism. As for the Stalinist bureaucracy, it is not for capitalism to deal with that; the Russian proletariat will see to it.

But Merleau's voice grew sombre: he spoke coldly and even his anger lacked passion and was virtually lifeless. It was as though he were feeling the first symptoms of that weariness of soul that is our general malaise. Look again at the 1945 articles and compare them and you will be able to gauge his disappointments, the attrition of his hopes. In 1945, he wrote, 'We pursue the policy of the Communist Party with no illusions.' In 1950: 'we have the same values as a communist.' And, as if the better to demonstrate the weakness of this purely moral bond:

324

'A Communist, it will be said, has no values . . . He has values *in spite of himself*.'[96] To be in agreement with the Communists was to attribute our maxims to them while knowing they rejected them; as for a political understanding, there was no longer the slightest prospect of it. In 1945, Merleau forbade himself any thought or action that could possibly hinder the re-birth of the proletariat. In 1950, he simply refused to attack oppression in Russia alone: it should either be denounced everywhere or nowhere. The fact was that the USSR of 1945 seemed 'ambiguous' to him. There were 'both signs of progress and symptoms of re-gression'.[97] It was a nation emerging from a terrible ordeal and hope was permissible. In 1950, after the revelation of the concentration-camp system: '[W]e wonder what reasons we still have to speak of social-ism in relation to it.'[98] One single concession: the USSR was, all in all, on the right side of the fence, with the forces fighting exploitation. No more than that: the revolutionary objective of 'produc[ing] whole men' was reduced in the 1950 context to being merely an illusion of the Communist parties. We might say that Merleau was, around this time, at the parting of the ways, but he was still reluctant to choose. Was he going to continue favouring the USSR in order to remain true to himself and the disadvantaged classes? Was he going to lose interest in this society based on concentration camps? If it were proved that it was made of the same clay, why would one expect any more from it than from the predatory powers? One last scruple held him back: 'The decadence of Russian communism does not make the class struggle a myth . . . or Marxist criticism in general null and void.'[99]

Were we so sure we could reject the Stalinist regime without condemning Marxism? I received an indignant letter from Bloch-Michel. In substance, he wrote: 'How is it that you cannot understand that the Soviet economy needs a servile labour force and that each year it systematically recruits millions of underfed, overexploited workers?' If he were right, Marx had pitched us from one barbarism into another. I showed the letter to Merleau who was not convinced by it. We thought there was a legitimate passion in it, reasons of the heart but no actual Reason. No matter: perhaps if it had been better thought-out, backed by proven facts and by argument, who knows whether it would not have won us round? The difficulties of industrialization in a period of socialist accumulation, encirclement, the resistance of the peasantry, the need to secure food supplies, demographic problems, distrust, terror and police dictatorship—this whole set of facts and consequences were quite enough to overwhelm us. But what would we have said or done if it had been demonstrated that the concentrationary regime were required by the infrastructure? We would have needed to have a better knowledge of the USSR and its production regime: I went there some years later and was delivered from these fears at the point when the camps were being opened. During the winter of 1950, we were still grimly uncertain: the Communists' strong point was that we couldn't worry about them without worrying about ourselves; however inadmissible their politics might be, we could not distance ourselves from them—at least in our old capitalist countries—without resolving on some sort of betrayal. To ask, 'How far can they go?' was the same as asking, 'How far can I follow them?' There is a morality of politics—a difficult subject that has never been clearly examined—and when politics has to betray its morality, choosing morality means betraying politics. Just try to sort all that out—especially when politics has set the coming of humanity's rule as its objective. At the point when Europe was discovering the Soviet camps, Merleau was at last catching the class struggle without its mask; strikes and repression, the massacres in Madagascar, the war in Vietnam, McCarthyism and the Red Scare in America, the Nazi revival and the Church in power everywhere, mealy mouthed, protecting renascent fascism beneath its cloak: how could we not smell the stench of the decaying carcase of bourgeois rule? And how could we publicly condemn slavery in Eastern Europe without abandoning the exploited here at home to their exploiters? But could we agree to work with the Party if it meant putting France in chains and covering it with barbed wire? What were we to do? To kick out unheedingly to Right and Left at two giants who would not even register our blows? This was the least bad solution: Merleau suggested it, for want of anything better. I could see no other way, though I was worried: we had not moved an inch, but our 'yes' had

simply changed to a 'no'. In 1945, we said, 'Gentlemen, we are everyone's friends and, first and foremost, friends of our dear Communist Party.' Five
years later, we were saying, 'We are everyone's enemies
and the Party's only privilege is that it is still entitled
to the full measure of our severity.' Without even talking about it, we both sensed that this 'soaring' objectivity would not take us far. When everyone was being
forced to choose, we had not chosen; and we had perhaps been right. At present, our universal peevishness
could perhaps put off the choice for a few months
more. But we knew that, had we been editors of a
daily or a weekly, we should long ago have had to take
the plunge or go to the wall. The relatively small-
circulation character of the review gave us some
respite, but our—initially political—position was in
danger of turning gradually into moralism. We never
descended to the level of the 'beautiful soul', but fine
sentiments flourished in our vicinity while manuscripts became scarcer: we were losing momentum,
people no longer wanted to write for us.

In China, they showed me the statues of two traitors in a ditch; people have been spitting on them for

a thousand years and they are all shiny, eroded by human saliva. We were not yet shiny, Merleau and I, but the process of erosion had begun. We were not being forgiven for rejecting Manichaeism. On the Right, butchers' boys had been recruited to insult us: they were given *carte blanche*; they showed their behinds to the critics and the critics doffed their hats to them, proclaiming them the 'new generation'. Ultimately, all the fairies had watched over their cradles but one, the 'talent fairy', and they disappeared for lack of it: they needed just a hint of it, no more, but it had been denied them at birth. They would be starving to death today if the Algerian War were not feeding them: crime pays. They made a lot of noise, but did little harm. On the other flank, things were more serious: our friends in the Communist Party had not come to terms with the article on the camps. We had left ourselves open to attack and we really got it from them. It didn't bother me. I was called a rat, a hyena, a viper and a polecat, but I liked this bestiary; it took me out of myself. Merleau was more upset by it: he still remembered the comradely relations of 1945. There were two phases: at first, he was insulted in the morning in the public prints, then late in the evening his Communist friends made their highly secretive excuses. This went on until a day came when, in order to simplify matters, these same friends combined the two jobs, writing the articles at dawn and apologizing for them at dusk. Merleau suffered less from being insulted by intimates than from no longer being able to respect them. I would say today that they were possessed by a literally insane violence that was the product of a war of attrition being fought elsewhere, the effects of which were felt in our provincial backwater: they were trying to see themselves as other than they were and couldn't quite manage it. Merleau saw their faults, I think, and not their problem, this provincialism. This is understandable, since he knew them in everyday life. In short, he moved away from them because they wanted him to: the Communist Party had tolerated these fringes of critical sympathy on its periphery, but it had not liked them. From 1949 onwards, it decided to eliminate them: the friends outside the Party were requested to shut their mouths. If any of them publicly expressed reservations, they sickened him until he turned into an enemy. In this way the

Party proved to its activists—and each activist thought he proved to himself—that free examination of the dogma was the beginning of betrayal. It was *themselves* that Merleau's friends loathed in him. How much anguish there was in all this and how it all came out after the seismic shock of the Twentieth Congress! Merleau knew the score: the Communists' bad tempers did not reduce him to anti-Communism. He took the blows but gave none back: his attitude was simply to do right and let others say what they wanted. In short, he carried on with the project. No matter: they denied him oxygen; they exiled him once again into the thin atmosphere of solitary life.

The Communist Party, born of a historical upheaval, a party that had its traditions and its constraints, had appeared to him in the past, even from afar, as offering a possible community: now he lost it. He had many friends who were not Communists, of course, and who remained true to him: but what did he find in them or for them, but the affectionate indifference of the pre-war period? They met together around a table and ate together, so as to pretend for a moment they had a common task: but these very varied human beings, still shattered by history's intrusion into their private lives, shared nothing but a scotch or a leg of lamb. This amounted, of course, to recognizing that something had died: he realized at last that the Resistance had crumbled; but these perceptions have no deep truth to them unless we feel them to be our own death gaining ground on us. I saw Merleau often in the winter and spring; he showed little sign of nerves, but was extremely sensitive: without entirely understanding him, I felt he was dying a little. Five years later, he would write: 'The writer well knows that there is no possible comparison between the rumination on his life and the clearer, more precise things it may have produced (in his work).' This is true: everyone ruminates; one broods on the insults one has suffered, the disgust one has felt, the accusations, recriminations and pleadings—and then one tries to piece together fragmented experiences that have neither rhyme nor reason to them. Like each of us, Merleau knew those wearisome repetitions from which a sudden enlightenment sometimes springs. That year, there was neither light nor a bolt from the blue. He tried to take the measure of things, to put himself back at that crossroads where his own story intersected with the history of France and the world, where the course of his thinking emerged from the course of events: this is what he had tried to do, and succeeded in doing, as I have said, between 1939 and 1945. But in 1950 it was both too late and too early. 'I'd like to write a novel about myself,' he told me one day. 'Why not an autobiography?' I asked. 'There are too many questions without answers. In a novel I could give them imaginary solutions.' We must not let this recourse to the imagination mislead us: I would remind the reader of the role phenomenology allots to it in the complex movement that ends in the intuiting of an essence. And yet, even so, his life defied explanation; in meditating upon it, patches of shade emerged, breaks in continuity. Didn't the fact that he had pitched himself, against his will, into this open conflict with his former friends mean that he had made a mistake at the outset? Or was he not bound to take upon himself—at the risk of becoming torn by it—the shifts and turns of an immense movement that had produced him, the mainsprings of which lay beyond his control. Or, alternatively—as he had suggested in 1945 as a mere conjecture—had we not fallen, for a period at least, into non-meaning? Perhaps there was nothing left for us to do but *endure* by holding on to a few rare values? He kept his post at *Les Temps modernes* and chose not to change any of his activities. But 'ruminating on his life', taking him back towards his origins, slowly took him away from day-to-day politics. This was his good fortune; when people leave the marginal zone of the Communist Party, they have to go somewhere: they usually walk for a time and end up on the Right; Merleau never committed this betrayal: rejected, he took refuge in the depths of his inner life.

Summer came. The Koreans began fighting each other. We were separated when the news reached us: each of us commented off our own bat, as we saw fit. We met up at Saint-Raphaël, in August, for a day: too late. We were happy to see each other's gestures again, hear each other's voices, to meet up again with all those familiar oddities for which friends the world over love their friends. There was only one flaw: our ideas, already formed, were incommunicable. From morning to night we talked only of the war, first sitting still by the water, then over dinner, then on the terrace of a cafe surrounded by scantily clad holidaymakers. We debated as we walked and then again at the station as I waited for my train. But to no avail; we were deaf to each other. I spoke more than he did, I fear, and not without vehemence. He replied gently and curtly: the sinuous thinness and child-like mischievousness of his smile made me hope he was still hesitating. But no: he never trumpeted his decisions; I had to accept he had made up his mind. He repeated gently, 'All that remains is for us to keep silent.'

'Who is us?' I said, pretending not to understand.

'Well, we at *Les Temps modernes*.

'You want us to shut up shop?'

'No, but I want us to say no more about politics.'

'Why?'

'They're fighting.'

'Yes, they are, in Korea.'

'Tomorrow they'll be fighting everywhere.'

'But even if they were fighting here, why would we keep quiet?'

'Because . . . It's brute force that will decide. Why speak, since brute force has no ears?'

I got on the train. Leaning out of the window, I waved, as one does, and I saw he was waving back, but I sat dumbfounded till I reached my destination.

I charged him, very unjustly, with wanting to gag criticism at the point when the guns were beginning to rumble. This was far from his mind; he had merely come up against an overwhelming fact: the USSR, he thought, had attempted to compensate for its inferiority in weaponry by acquiring a strategic position. The first thing this meant was that Stalin thought war inevitable: it was no longer a question of averting war, but of winning it. But war had only to appear inescapable to one of the blocs for it to become so. It would have been all right if the capitalist world had attacked first: the world would have been blown up, but humanity's venture would have retained a meaning, even when shattered. Something would be dead, but it would at least have made an effort to be born. But since the preventive aggression was coming from the socialist countries, history would merely have been the winding-sheet of our species. The game was up. For

Merleau-Ponty, as for many others, 1950 was the crucial year: he thought he saw the Stalinist doctrine without its mask and he judged it to be a Bonapartism.
Either the USSR was not the homeland of socialism—
in which case, socialism existed nowhere and was, no
doubt, unviable—or else socialism was indeed this—
this abominable monster, this police state, this predatory power. In short, Bloch-Michel had been unable
to convince Merleau that socialist society rested on
serfdom; but Merleau convinced himself that it had
engendered—whether by chance, necessity or both together—an imperialism. This did not, of course, mean
that he had opted for the other monster, capitalist imperialism. 'But what can you say?' he said. 'They are as
bad as each other.' This was the great change: he had
no desire to rail against the Soviet Union—'Why
should I? People are exploited, massacred and plun-
dered the world over. Let's not take it all out on the
one party.' It merely lost all privilege in his eyes; it was
a predatory power like all the others. He believed at
this point that the internal workings of history had
perverted its course once and for all; it would carry on
in a state of paralysis, deflected by its own *dejecta*, till it

finally came to grief. All meaningful discourse could only, therefore, be lies: all that remained was to withhold one's complicity, to remain silent. He had wanted at first to retain what he felt to be valid in the two systems; he wanted to make a gift to the better one of what the other had achieved. In his disappointment, he had subsequently resolved to denounce exploitation wherever it occurred. After further disappointment, he calmly decided not to denounce anything anywhere ever again, till such point as a bomb, from either East or West, put an end to our brief histories. Being first affirmative, then negative, then silent, he had not shifted an inch. This moderation would be difficult to understand, however, if one did not see it as the calm exterior of a man committing suicide: I have already said that his worst acts of violence were depth charges that harmed only himself. Even in the most wildly raging anger, some hope remains: in this calm, funereal refusal, there was none.

I didn't think these things through as he did; that is what preserved me from melancholy. Merleau made light of the Koreans, but I could see nothing else. He moved too quickly to global strategy and I was mesmerized by the blood: the fault, as I saw it, was with the horse traders at Yalta who had cut the country in two. We were both wrong, out of ignorance, but not without some excuse: where at the time would we have acquired our knowledge? Who would have revealed to us that a military canker was gnawing at the USA and that civilians, in Truman's day, already had their backs to the wall? How in August 1950 would we have guessed MacArthur's plan and his intention to take advantage of a conflict to give China back to the Chinese lobby? Did we know of Syngman Rhee, the feudal prince of a state reduced to poverty, and of the designs of the agricultural South on northern industry? The Communist press barely spoke of any of this: they knew little more about it than we did and merely denounced the crime of the imperialist forces, i.e. the Americans, without taking the analysis any further. And, then, they compromised their credibility with a preliminary lie: the only fact that had been established was that the northern troops had been the first to cross the 38th Parallel; now, the Communist press stubbornly maintained the opposite. We know the truth today, which is that the US army, in league with Seoul's feudal overlords, drew the Communists into a trap: there were frontier incidents daily and they took advantage of them; the South made such obvious troop movements that the North, deceived, committed the enormous error of striking first to forestall an attack that was never intended. It is a failing of mass parties that they think they can connect with popular thinking—the only deep, true thought—by offering it truths adjusted to its taste. I no longer have any doubt, for example, that in this wretched business the warmongers were the feudal South and the US imperialists. But I have no doubt either that the North attacked first. The Communist Party's task was not easy: when it acknowledged the facts, if only to bring out their meaning, its enemies everywhere presented it as 'confessing' to them. If it denied the facts, its friends discovered the lie and backed away. It chose to deny them in order to remain on the offensive. But it was less than a year ago that we had discovered the existence of the Soviet camps: we were still distrustful and ready to believe the worst. In reality, the USSR deplored this conflict, which might drag it into a war that it could not easily win: yet it had to support the

North Koreans for fear of losing its influence in Asia. By contrast, the young China entered the fray, knowing itself to be the object of American designs, but everything required it to do so: revolutionary fraternity, its permanent interests and its international policy. We, however, had not enough information in the summer of 1950 to see who was playing which role. Merleau believed in Stalin's guilt because he had to believe in it. I didn't believe in anything; I was floundering about, uncertain. This was my good fortune; I didn't have the same temptation to believe that the lights were going out or that it was the year 1000 and the curtain was going up on the Apocalypse: I viewed this blaze from afar and could make out nothing distinct.

In Paris, I met up again with Merleau. Colder and darker. Some of our friends, his wife told me, were devoutly hoping I would blow my brains out the day the Cossacks crossed our borders. Naturally, they were calling for Merleau's brains too. Suicide did not tempt me and I laughed; Merleau-Ponty observed me and did not. Thoughts of war and exile came to his mind. Lightly, with that puckish air I always saw him adopt

when things might be turning serious: he would, he
said, be a lift attendant in New York. An embarrassing joke: this was another version of suicide. If war
broke out, it would not be enough just to stop writing,
you would have to refuse to teach. Imprisoned in a lift
cage, he would simply push buttons and mortify himself with silence. Such seriousness is not common and
may surprise the reader. Yet he had it, we had it, and
I do still. On one point we were in agreement with
the good people who wanted our skins: in politics, you
have to pay. We were not men of action, but wrong
ideas are crimes at par with wrong acts. How did he
judge himself? He did not say, but he seemed worried
and worrying: 'If ever,' I said to myself, 'he passes
judgement on himself, his concealed rage will push
him immediately to the point of carrying it out.' I
often wondered later how his cold anger against the
USSR could have turned into a surliness directed
against himself. If we had fallen into barbarism, then
we could not say a word or even keep silent without
behaving as barbarians: why did he blame himself for
sincere, carefully thought-out articles? The world's absurdity had simply stolen his thoughts; there was

nothing more to it. He answered this point in *Signs* with an explanation of Nizan that also covers his own case:

> One can understand, then, the objections Sartre makes today to the Nizan of 1939 and why they are without weight against him. Nizan, he says, was angry. But is that anger a matter of mood? It is a mode of understanding which is not too inappropriate when fundamental meaning-structures are at stake. For anyone who has become a Communist and has acted within the party day after day, things said and done have a weight because he has said and done them too. In order to take the change in line of 1939 as he should, Nizan would have had to have been a puppet. He would have to have been broken . . . I recall having written from Lorraine, in October, 1939, some prophetic letters which divided the roles between us and the USSR in a Machiavellian fashion. But I had not spent years preaching the Soviet alliance. Like Sartre, I had no party: a good position for severely doing justice to the toughest of parties.[100]

Merleau-Ponty was never, by any stretch of the imagination, a Communist; he was not even tempted to be. There was no question of him 'acting within the Party', but he lived its daily life through friends he had chosen. He did not blame himself for things said and done, but for the comments he had penned about them, for his decision never to offer a critique before having attempted to understand and to justify. He had been right, however, and one knows something only if one gives of oneself. But the consequence was that he suffered for having given of himself for nothing. He had said, 'Historical man has only one way of suffering barbarism, and that is to make it.' He was the victim of those he had defended so patiently because he had made himself their accomplice. In a word, he abandoned politics the moment he felt he had lost his way in it. With dignity, but guiltily: he had dared to live; now, he walled himself up. He was of course to change his mind about all this later and come to other conclusions; but that was in 1955: this sorrow weighed on his heart for five years.

There was no shortage of people to explain his turnabout in class terms: he was, they said, a liberal petty-bourgeois; he went as far as he could and then stopped. How simple that is! And those who say this are petty-bourgeois raised as liberals who, nonetheless, opted for the Manichaeism he rejected. It was, in fact, history's fault that the thread was broken: she wears out the men she uses and rides them to death like horses. She chooses actors, transforms them to their very core by the role she forces on them, then, at the slightest change, dismisses them and takes on entirely new ones, whom she throws untutored into the scrimmage. Merleau began work in the milieu that had been produced by the Resistance: with the Resistance's passing, he believed the unity it had produced lived on to a degree in some sort of future humanism which the classes, by their very struggle, could construct together. He 'followed the Communist Party line', yet refused to condemn the cultural heritage of the bourgeoisie out of hand. Thanks to this effort to hold on to both ends of the chain, the circulation of ideas in France was never entirely halted: as everywhere, there was a loathing for intelligence, but until 1958 we never knew any intellectual McCarthyism. Moreover, the official thinkers of the Communist

Party condemned his ideas, yet the best of them always knew those ideas had to be taken up and that it behoved Marxist anthropology to assimilate them. But for Merleau, is it conceivable that Tran Duc Tao would have written his thesis and attempted to annex Husserl to Marx?

In many archaic religions, there are sacred personages who perform the function of *binders*: everything has to be linked and attached through them. Politically, Merleau played such a role. He had come to politics in a time of union and refused to break up that union; his role was to bind. I believe the ambiguity of his heuristic Marxism—he said that it could not be sufficient, but also that we had nothing else—created a favourable climate for encounters and discussions that will continue. In this way, he made the history of this post-war period, as much as an intellectual can. Conversely, while being made by him, history also made him. Refusing to set his seal on breaches between people, hanging on with each hand to continents that were drifting apart, he returned in the end, without illusions, to his old idea of catholicity: on either side of the barricade there are only human beings; hence human inventiveness is being born everywhere: it is to be judged not on its origins, but on its content. It is enough that the 'binder' strain every sinew to keep the two terms of the contradiction together, that he hold back the explosion for as long as he is able: creative works, the product of chance and reason, will attest that the reign of the human is possible. I cannot decide whether this idea was behind its time or ahead of it in October 1950. One single thing is sure: it was not timely. The globe was cracking apart. There wasn't a single thought that didn't express some prejudice and aim to function as a weapon, not a single bond that didn't form without others breaking; to serve one's friends, everyone had to spill the blood of enemies. Let us be clear here: others, besides the 'binder', condemned Manichaeism and violence. But they did so precisely because they were Manichaean and violent: in a word, to serve the bourgeoisie. Merleau-Ponty was the only one who did not celebrate the triumph of discord, the only one not to tolerate—in the name of our 'catholic' vocation—love everywhere becoming the obverse of hatred. History had given him to us; well before his death, it took him away.

At *Les Temps modernes*, we had put politics on the back burner. It must be admitted that our readers did not notice this straight away: we were, at times, so far behind that we came round to talking about things when everyone had forgotten them. However, in the long run, people grew angry: being uncertain, they called for enlightenment and it was our bounden duty either to provide them with it or to confess that we were as lost as they were. We received irritated letters; the critics weighed in too; in an old issue of *L'Observateur* I recently found a 'Review of reviews' which took us sternly to task. We were each aware of these criticisms, sometimes learning of them from each other, but we never discussed them: that would have meant reopening the debate. It rather got on my nerves: did Merleau realize he was *imposing* his silence upon us? But then I would talk myself round: the review belonged to him, he had defined its political orientation and I had followed him; if our silence were the ultimate consequence of this, I had to go on following him. His smiling sullenness was harder to bear: he seemed to be reproaching us for having accompanied him into this hell-on-earth, and sometimes for having dragged him into it. The truth is that he could sense our discord growing and it pained him.

We emerged from this impasse without having made any decisions, without speaking. Dzelepy and Stone sent us good, well-informed articles which showed up the war, as it was happening, in a new light. I found that these articles confirmed my opinions. As for Merleau, they didn't contradict his own: we didn't go back over the origins of the conflict. However, he didn't like the articles much, but he was too honest to reject them: I didn't dare insist that we take them. I can't claim that we published them: they published themselves and we found them in the review. Others followed, finding the way to the printers by themselves. This was the beginning of a surprising transformation: having lost its political director, *Les Temps modernes* stubbornly went on obeying him, despite his change of heart. That is to say, it took a radical turn of its own volition. We had longstanding collaborators, most of whom did not meet us often: they changed position to remain as close as they could to the Communist Party, believing they were following us in this, when in fact they were dragging us along with them.

Young people came in to the review on the basis of the reputation Merleau had made for it: it was, they thought, the only publication which, in this age of iron, retained both its preferences and its clear-sightedness. None of these newcomers was a Communist, yet none wanted to veer from the Party line. In this way they put *Les Temps modernes* back, in other—more brutal—circumstances, in the position Merleau had given it in 1945. But this meant overturning everything: to keep our distance from the Communists, it was necessary in 1951 to break with all the rest of what still called itself the Left. Merleau remained silent: more exactly, he gagged himself with a hint of sadism. He forced himself, out of professionalism and the demands of friendship, to let through this stream of tendentious articles, which addressed themselves to our readership over his head and which, in a roundabout way—by way of anything, even a film criticism—gave vent to a confused, muddled, impersonal opinion that was no longer his without yet being entirely mine. In this way we both discovered that, over these six years, the review had acquired a kind of independence and that it directed us as much as we directed it. In a word, during the interregnum years 1950–52, a skipperless vessel itself recruited officers who kept it afloat. In those days, when Merleau looked at this little sardine rushing along in the wake of a whale, if he still told himself 'That is the fruit of my labours! . . .' then he must have swallowed many draughts of gall. He had fixed himself fast to the review, to which he had given life and which he kept alive day after day. I think he suddenly found himself in the position of a father who, having only yesterday treated his son as a child, suddenly finds himself face to face with a mulish, almost hostile adolescent, who has 'got into bad company'. Sometimes I tell myself that our common mistake was to remain silent *even then*, when we were still uncertain and uncommitted . . . But no, the die was cast.

The world developed a war psychosis and I developed a bad conscience. All over the West, people wondered in nonchalant tones but wild-eyed, what the Russians would do with Europe when they had occupied the whole of it. 'For they certainly will,' said the drawing-room generals. The same people spoke smugly of the Breton redoubt, that bridgehead the Americans would maintain in Finistère to facilitate future landings. Fine: if there was fighting on our soil, no problem: none of us would be spared. But other oracles thought the USA would look to other continents for the real battlefields and would abandon us, out of convenience, to the USSR. What would we do in that case? One answer was given by some young middle-class maidens: in a girls' grammar school in Paris, an entire class vowed to resort to collective suicide. The black heroism of these poor children said a great deal about the fright their parents felt. I heard some very dear friends, former Resistance fighters, coldly declare that they would take to the hills. 'This time,' I said, 'there's a danger you'll be shooting at Frenchmen.' I saw from their eyes that that would not trouble them, or rather that they had stubbornly arrived, out of hysteria, at this unreal decision. Others chose realism: they would take a plane to the New World. I was, in those years, a little less mad: for no other reason, perhaps, than a lack of imagination, I didn't believe in the Apocalypse. Yet my mood grew sombre; in the Metro a man shouted out, 'I'll be glad when the Russians get here!' I looked at him: his life-story was etched on his face; in his place, I would perhaps have said the same. I asked myself, 'What if, nonetheless, this war did take place?' People kept telling me, 'You'd have to leave. If you stay, then either you'll broadcast on Soviet radio or you'll go to a camp and we won't hear from you again.' These predictions didn't frighten me much, because I didn't believe in an invasion. Yet they made an impact on me: they were, in my eyes, mind games which, pushing things to extremes, revealed to everyone the need to choose and the consequences of their choices. Staying, they told me, meant collaboration or death. And leaving? To live in Buenos Aires with the wealthy of France, while abandoning my poor compatriots to their fate, would also be a way of collaborating: with the enemy class. But it was your class, you will say. Yet what does that mean? Is that any proof it is not still the enemy of humanity? If there must be betrayal, as Nizan said in *The Watchdogs*, let it be the smallest number doing it for the good of the largest. These gloomy fantasies made me feel really up against it. Everyone had chosen; in my turn, I tried for a moment to linger in neutralism: several of us supported Rivet's candidacy;[101] but the Communist Party had diverted away the potential supporters to his right: he suffered a crushing defeat.

Some Communists came to see me about the Henri Martin affair.[102] They were trying to bring together intellectuals of every stamp, from the well-regarded to the smarmy and the wanton, to bring the matter before the public. As soon as I'd taken a look at the business, it seemed so stupid that I joined in unreservedly with the protestors. We decided to write a book about the affair and I left for Italy; it was spring. From the Italian newspapers I learned of Duclos' arrest, the theft of his notebooks and the carrier pigeons farce.[103] These sordid childish tricks turned my stomach: fouler things were done, but none that was so revealing. My last ties were broken, my view transformed: an anti-Communist is a cur; this is my firm opinion and I shall not change it. People will think me very naïve and, indeed, I had seen many other things of this kind that had not stirred me. But after ten years of ruminations, I had reached breaking point; only the merest trifle was needed. In the language of the Church, this was a conversion. Merleau too had been converted, in 1950. We were both conditioned, but in opposite ways. Our disgusts, slowly accumulated, caused us in an instant to discover, in the one case, the horror of Stalinism, in the other, the horror of his own class. On the basis of the principles it had inculcated in me, on the basis of its humanism and its 'humanities', on the basis of liberty, equality and fraternity, I swore a hatred of the bourgeoisie that will end only when I do. When I hastily returned to Paris, I had to write or suffocate. I wrote, day and night, the first part of 'The Communists and Peace'.[104]

Merleau could not be suspected of any indulgence for the police methods of a dying regime: he seemed surprised by my eagerness, but he strongly encouraged me to publish this essay, which was supposed to be merely article-length. When he read it, he needed only a glance: 'The USSR wants peace,' I said, 'it needs it, the only threat of war comes from the West.' I said not a word about the Korean War, but, despite that precaution, it seemed I had premeditatedly taken a systematically opposite line to our political director, that I had contradicted his views point by point. I had in fact written at breakneck speed, with rage in my heart, joyously and tactlessly. When the best prepared conversions explode, one finds the joy of the storm: all around is blackest night, except where the lightning is striking. Not for a moment did I think to spare his feelings. For his part, he chose rather to be amused by my hotheadedness and was not angry. A while later, however, he pointed out that some of our readers were not with me on this: of course they shared my opinion on the way our government had acted, but in their view I was being too soft on the Communists. 'What do you tell them?' I asked. It so happened that printed below this first study were the words: 'To be continued.' 'I tell them,' he said, 'Next instalment in the next issue.' Around 1948, the non-Communist Left had, in fact, drawn up an essay plan that acquired classic status: 1. Thesis: rehearsal of the vileness of the government and its crimes against the working classes; the Communist Party was pronounced right; 2. Antithesis: the unworthiness of the Political Bureau was highlighted, together with the mistakes it had made; 3. Conclusion: both were as bad as each other and a middle course was pointed out, with unfailing mention here of the

Scandinavian countries. As Merleau saw it, I had developed only the thesis; he was still hoping—though without too many illusions—that the antithesis would follow.

It did not. Nor was the continuation printed in the next issue. I was, in reality, out of breath. And I realized I knew nothing. Just railing against a Prefect of Police doesn't bring insight into one's times. I had read everything, but everything had to be read again. I had only one guiding thread, but it was enough: the inexhaustible, difficult experience of the class struggle. I did the re-reading. I had some intellectual muscle and I set about using it, not without tiring myself. I met Farge. I joined the Peace Movement. I went to Vienna. One day I took my second article to the printers, though it was, in fact, merely an outline. I had entirely set aside the 'Third Force'-style essay plan: far from attacking the Communists, I declared myself a fellow traveller. At the end, once again, I wrote, 'To be continued', but there could no longer be any doubt. Merleau didn't see the article until the second proofs. Adding to my guilt, I didn't show them to him myself: he read them at the point when we had to make up the issue. Why hadn't I shown him my manuscript when he always showed me his without fail? Had I decided, once and for all, to take myself seriously? I don't believe so. And I don't believe either that I wanted to escape his admonishments or objections. I would blame, rather, that heedlessness of rage that aims straight for the goal and brooks no precautions. I believed; I knew; I had cast off my illusions: as a result, I would not climb down over anything. In our virtually private publication, you had to shout to be heard: I would shout; I would place myself alongside the Communists and would proclaim this to all and sundry. I shall not give the objective reasons for my attitude: they are of no importance here; I shall simply say that they alone counted, that I regarded them as urgent, and that I still do. As for the emotional reasons, I can see two: I was propelled along by the new team; they wanted us to take the leap; I could count on their approval. And then I now see that I bore a bit of a grudge against Merleau for having imposed his silence on me in 1950. The review had been drifting for two years and I couldn't bear it. Let each one judge: I have no excuse, I don't want any. What may be of interest in this adventure—which we both found painful—is that it shows in what ways discord may arise in the heart of the most loyal friendship and the closest agreement. New circumstances and an outdated institution—there were no other reasons for our conflict. The institution was our silent contract. Valid when Merleau spoke and I said nothing, this agreement had never clearly defined our respective domains. Each of us, without speaking of it even to himself, had appropriated the review. There was on the one hand, as in *The Caucasian Chalk Circle*, an official, nominal paternity, mine—and in everything connected with politics it was only that[105]—and, on the other, an adoptive paternity, five years of jealous care. Everything came to a head suddenly and exasperatedly. We realized that each of us, by his silences as much as by his words, was compromising the other. We needed to have only one set of ideas; and this was the case so long as I did not think for myself. But once there were two heads under the same hat, how were we to choose the right one? Looking at the matter from outside, it will seem that events themselves decided: this is true, but it is rather a facile explanation. It is true, in general, that empires crumble and parties collapse when they are not swimming with the tide of history. Even so, we must admit that this idea, which is perhaps the most difficult of all, is handled incautiously by most writers. But how can we use what may be applied— though not without care—to the great social forces, to explain, the growth, life and death of micro-organisms like *Les Temps modernes*? The overall movement was not without its small-scale catastrophes. And, then, however it might be, we had to live the venture ourselves, to accept the sentence passed on us, to carry it out and, as he said later, institute it. With wrong on each side and, in each of us a futile goodwill.

Merleau could have broken things off; he could have provoked a quarrel or written something against me. He abstained, eloquently, from all these things. For a time we remained this strange couple: two friends who still liked each other, each of whom was stubbornly opposed to the other and who had between them only one voice. I admire his moderation all the more for the fact that there were, at the time, several loudly trumpeted defections from the review: one of our longest-standing collaborators left us in a great hurry for the *Nouvelle Nouvelle Revue Française*, where he began by rounding on the 'Hitlero-Stalinists' and by speaking in glowing terms of Lucien Rebatet.[106] I wonder what there is left of him now: perhaps a rather too self-conscious smattering of *ennui*, somewhere in the provinces, and nothing more.

The years that followed brought several entertaining crack-ups of the same kind. To fill these gaps and drum up articles, I assembled our collaborators at my flat every other Sunday. Merleau-Ponty attended assiduously, being always the last to arrive and the first to leave, conversing in hushed tones with anyone and everyone on all subjects except *Les Temps modernes*. Yet he had allies in the camp: Claude Lefort, who disapproved of my position, Lefèvre-Pontalis,[107] who wasn't interested in politics, Colette Audry, who feared my excesses, and Erval.[108] It would not have been hard for Merleau to assume the leadership of a strong opposition: he refused to do so on principle—a review isn't a parliamentary assembly—and from friendship. He forbade himself to influence the group, while noting, without liking the fact, that the group was influencing me. The majority was, as it happened, lining up before his eyes behind the critical fellow-traveller position he had just abandoned; given the virulence of anti-Communism, the majority was even contemplating toning down the critical aspect and stressing the 'fellow-travelling'. Above all, I think Merleau found these meetings laughable and their product worthless. In the long run they became so and his silence had its part in bringing this about. But what would he have said? I never failed to ask his opinions; he never ventured them. It was as though he was letting me know it was no good asking me about details when I hadn't deigned to consulted him on the main issue. He probably took the view that I was salving my conscience cheaply and didn't want to help me in that. In fact, my conscience was clear and I felt Merleau was wrong to refuse to participate. This grievance will seem misplaced; when all is said and done, I was asking him to work on a venture he had openly disavowed. I recognize this: but, after all, he remained one of our number and then, from time to time, he couldn't stop himself taking some initiative—usually a felicitous one. Though he had abandoned his role of political director after 1950, he still remained editor. In these ambiguous situations, which one maintains in being to avoid a break, everything both parties do turns bad.

But there were more serious reasons for our mis-understanding and they were of a different order. I saw myself as remaining faithful to his thinking of 1945, while he was abandoning it. He saw himself as remaining faithful to himself and felt that I was be-traying him. I claimed that I was carrying on his work and he accused me of wrecking it. This conflict came not from either of us but from the world. And we were both right. His political thinking came out of the Resistance; in other words, it emerged from the united Left. Within that unity, it could slide towards the most extreme radicalism, but he needed this triple-entente environment: the Communist Party guaranteed the practical efficacy of common action; the allied parties assured him that that action would retain its human-ism and certain traditional values, while lending them real content. When, around 1950, everything broke apart, he saw only wreckage; in his eyes, it was my folly to cling to one bit of flotsam, expecting that the pieces of wreckage would rebuild the lost vessel on their own. For my part, I made my decision when the Left was smashed to pieces; my opinion was that it had to be reconstituted, though not at the top, but from the bottom up. We had, of course, no contact with the masses and hence no power. But our task remained clear: in the face of the unholy alliance between the bourgeoisie and the socialist leaders, there was no other course than to snuggle up to the Party and call on the others to join us. We had to attack the bourgeoisie unrelentingly, expose its policies and defuse its feeble arguments. We would not, of course, recoil from criticizing the Communist Party and the USSR. But we recognized that changing them was out of the question—an impossible task. We wanted to foreshadow future agreements for our readers by setting before them this tiny example of an accord with the Communists that had in no way detracted from our freedom of judgement. I was able, in this way, honestly to take the view that I was espousing Merleau-Ponty's attitude.

In fact, the contradiction was not in *us*, but, from 1945 onwards, in our position. To be for the whole was to refuse to choose between its parts. The privilege Merleau accorded the Communists wasn't a choice in their favour: merely a preferential regime.

When the moment to choose came, he remained faithful to himself and scuppered his own efforts, so as not to survive the shipwrecked unity. I, however, as a newcomer, chose the Party precisely in the name of unity: that unity could not be rebuilt, I thought, unless it were done around the Party. In this way, at a few years' remove, the same idea of union had led the one of us to reject a choice it had forced upon the other. Structures and events together determined everything; France is so constituted that the Party will not take power there on its own: we have therefore to think, first, in terms of alliances. Merleau could still see the tripartite government as a legacy of the Popular Front. But in 1952, without the demographic structure of the country having changed, I could no longer see the Third Force—a mere mask for the Right—as coterminous with the unity of the masses. Yet, power could not be taken from the Right without gathering together all the forces of the Left: the Popular Front remained the necessary means to triumph at the point when the cold war rendered it impossible. While waiting for an alliance to come about that seemed only a distant possibility, we had to maintain that possibility day after day by forming local alliances with the Party. Not choosing on the one hand, choosing on the other—but for the five years' difference, the two attitudes were pursuing the same objective. Two attitudes? There was, rather, just the one, which set us against each other as adversaries, by compelling each of us to stress one of its two contradictory components. In order to remain true to what he wouldn't accept, Merleau forgot his desire for union. And, to give future unity its chance, I forgot my universalism and chose to begin by increasing the disunion. These words will seem abstract; in fact we had to live through these historical determinations: that is to say, we put our whole life into them, our passions, our skins. I mocked his 'spontaneity': in 1945, union seemed to be achieved, he could just let himself be carried along. He mocked my naivety and voluntarism; in 1952, there was no union any longer; was wishing for it in the abstract enough to bring it about? The truth is that we each found the job to suit our talents: Merleau when it was time for subtleties, myself when the time of the hired killers had arrived.

Lefort and I had some lively discussions and I suggested that he criticize me in the review itself. He accepted and submitted a rather nasty article. I got angry and wrote a reply in the same tone. As a friend to both of us, Merleau found himself, against his wishes, with a new task: he had to play the role of mediator. Lefort had had the courtesy to submit his article to Merleau and I did the same with mine. My article exasperated him: with his customary sweetness, he informed me that he would leave once and for all if I didn't remove a certain paragraph, which was, as it seems to me, needlessly violent. I seem to remember that Lefort made some sacrifices too. All the same, our two texts had a spiteful tone to them. Merleau was fond of both of us and felt every one of the blows we dealt each other. Without being entirely in agreement with Lefort, he felt closer to him than to me: this freed his tongue. And mine. We launched into a long and futile argument that cascaded from one subject to another, one conversation to another. Is there such a thing as the spontaneity of the masses? Can groups derive their cohesion from themselves? Ambiguous questions which sent us off at times to politics, to the role of the Communist Party, to Rosa Luxemburg and Lenin, and at times to sociology, to existence itself or, in other words, to philosophy, to our 'styles of life', to our 'anchorage-points', to ourselves. With every word we bounced from a consideration of world affairs to the development of our own moods and back again. Beneath our intellectual divergences of 1941, which we had accepted so serenely when we were just arguing over Husserl, we discovered to our stupefaction, conflicts that had their source in our childhoods—and even in the elementary rhythms of our organisms. We went on to uncover the surreptitious presence in one of us of a slyness, a smugness and a mania for activism, that covered over his disorientation and, in the other, retractile sentiments and a determined quietism. Naturally, nothing in this was entirely true or entirely false: our ideas became confused because we were putting the same ardour into convincing, understanding and accusing each other. This passionate dialogue, carried on at a halfway point between good and bad faith, began in my office, continued in Saint-Tropez and was recommenced in Paris at the Café Procope and later at my flat. I travelled. He wrote me a very long letter. I replied, on a day when it was 40 degrees in the shade, which didn't improve matters. What were we hoping for? Ultimately, for nothing. We were doing our 'break-up work' in the sense in which Freud has so well demonstrated that mourning is 'work'. I believe this sullen two-handed rumination, this endless repetition that led us nowhere, was going to end in gradually exhausting our patience, in breaking the bonds between us one by one by little angry bursts, in casting shadows on the transparent nature of our friendship to the point of making us strangers to each other. If this undertaking had reached its end, we would have quarrelled. Fortunately, an incident intervened that interrupted it.

A Marxist I had bumped into by chance offered to write for us on 'the contradictions of capitalism'. This was, he said, a familiar subject, but little understood, and he would shed new light on it. He was not a member of the Party but a party unto himself and one of the most rigid; he had such a sense that he was doing me a favour that he talked me round. I forewarned Merleau, who knew the man but said nothing. I had to be out of Paris and the article was submitted in my absence. It was worthless. As editor-in-chief, Merleau-Ponty could not be persuaded to allow it to appear without adding an introductory paragraph, which was, all in all, an apology to our readers. He took the opportunity to criticize the author in two lines for not having even mentioned the contradictions of socialism: this would be for another day, no doubt? On my return, he told me nothing of all this; one of our collaborators put me in the picture and I got myself a set of proofs and read the article beneath its introductory paragraph. The less defensible the article seemed to me, the more irritated I was by that paragraph. Having put the issue 'to bed', as they say, Merleau was in his turn away from the office and I wasn't able to get hold of him. Alone and in a state of merry rage, I took out the introductory paragraph and the article appeared without it. You can guess the rest. A few days later, Merleau received the final proofs of the review, noticed his text had been cut and took it extremely badly. He grabbed the telephone and informed me of his resignation—for good this time. We spoke for more than two hours. Sitting in an armchair by the window, a very gloomy Jean Cau heard half the conversation and thought he was witnessing the last moments of the magazine.[109] We accused each other of abusing our power; I offered him an immediate meeting and tried in every way possible to make him reverse his decision: he was immovable. I didn't see him again for a few months; he didn't come to *Les Temps modernes* and never had anything else to do with it.

If I have told this idiotic story, I have done so, first and foremost, for its pointlessness. When I think back to it, I feel both that it was heartbreaking and that it 'had to end like that'. Like that: badly, stupidly, inevitably. The stage was set, the end decided in advance. As in *Commedia dell'Arte*, it only remained for us to improvise the break-up; we handled it badly, but, for good or ill, we acted out the scene and moved on to the next ones. I don't know which of us was the more guilty and it's not a question that excites me much: in fact, the ultimate guilt was a preordained part of our two roles; we had established, long before, that we would part with wrong on both sides and on some puerile pretext. Since we could no longer continue to work together, we had to part or have the review disappear.

Without *Les Temps modernes*, the events of 1950 would have had little impact on our friendship: we would have discussed politics more often or taken more care not to speak of it. Ordinarily politics affects people obliquely and they are unaware of anything except a muffled tremor or an indecipherable anxiety. Unless, that is, it seizes them by the throat and knocks them flying: even in that case, they will not realize what has happened to them. But chance has only to put the tiniest means of influencing or expressing the movement of history into their hands and the forces that shape our lives are immediately laid bare and show us the shadow we cast on the dazzling wall of objectivity. The review was nothing: it was just a sign of the times like a hundred others. But no matter: it belonged to history and through it the two of us experienced our standing as historical objects. It was our objectivization; through it the course of events provided us with our charter and our twofold role: we were at first more united than we would have been without it, then more divided. This is only natural: once caught in the mechanism, we are completely dragged into it; the little freedom that remains to us lies entirely in the moment when we decide whether to get involved or not. To put it succinctly, beginnings are our affair; thereafter we have to will our destinies.

The beginning was not a bad one. It was so for a single reason that is still a mystery to me: against the desire of all our collaborators, and against my desire, Merleau had claimed the weakest position from day one. The position of doing everything and not being named, of refusing to have a status to defend him against my moods or attacks: it was as though he had wanted to derive his power only from a living agreement, as though his fragility would be his most effective weapon, as though his moral authority would alone have to underwrite his functions. He had no sort of protection: for that reason, he was not bound by anything or anyone. He was present among us and as much in charge as I was. And he could be light and free as air. If he had agreed to his name going on the cover, he would have had to fight me and perhaps even overthrow me: but he had envisaged this possibility from the first day and declined on principle a battle that would have needlessly demeaned us both. When the fateful day came, a telephone call sufficed. He had made his decision, he informed me of it and disappeared. Yet there were sacrifices: for him, for me and for *Les Temps modernes*. We were all victims of this cleansing murder: Merleau cut off a part of himself, leaving me to grapple with fearful allies who, he thought, would grind me down or reject me as they had rejected him; he abandoned *his* review to my incompetence. This aggressive expiation must have absorbed the greater part of his resentment: in any event it allowed us to interrupt our break-up 'work' and rescue our friendship.

To begin with, he avoided me. Did he think the sight of me would revive his grievances? Perhaps. It seems to me, however, that he wanted to keep open the prospect of some kind of shared future. I would meet him at times; we stopped a moment to talk together; when we were about to part, I would suggest we meet up again the next day or the next week. He replied politely and firmly, 'I'll call you,' but he did not. Yet, another 'work' had begun: the stilling of grievances and a *rapprochement*. This was halted by grief: in 1953 Merleau lost his mother.

She meant as much to him as his own life; more exactly, she *was* his life. He owed his infant happiness to the attentions she had lavished on him; she was the clear-sighted witness of his childhood: thanks to that, when exile came, she remained its guardian. Without her, the past would have been swallowed by the sands; through her, it was preserved, out of reach but intensely felt; until the time came to mourn his mother, Merleau-Ponty experienced that golden age as a paradise that retreated a little more each day and as the fleshly, daily presence of the woman who had bestowed it on him. All the connivances of mother and son carried them back to ancient memories; thus, as long as she lived, Merleau's banishment retained a degree of sweetness and could be reduced at times to the bare difference that separates two inseparable lives. As long as there were two of them reconstructing and, at times, reviving the long prehistory of his actions, his passions and his tastes, he still had hope of regaining that immediate concord with everything that is the good fortune of children who have been loved. But when his mother died, the wind slammed all the doors shut and he knew they would never open again. Memories *à deux* are rites: the survivor is left only with dried leaves, with words. Meeting Simone de Beauvoir a little after this, Merleau-Ponty told her, quite casually

and with that sad cheerfulness with which he masked
his sincere remarks, 'I am more than half dead.' Dead
to his childhood—for the second time. He had
dreamed of achieving salvation: in his youth through
the Christian community, as an adult through his political companionships. Twice disappointed, he suddenly discovered the reason for these defeats: to 'save'
oneself on all levels, 'in all orders', would be to recom-
mence one's earliest years. We repeat ourselves endlessly, but we never begin again. Seeing his childhood
go under, he understood himself: he had never wished
for anything but to return to it and that impossible
desire was his particular vocation, his destiny. What
was left of it? Nothing. He had already been silent for
some time: silence not being enough any longer, he
turned into a recluse, leaving his office only to go to
the Collège de France. I did not see him again until
1956 and his best friends now saw him less.

I have, however, to indicate what was happening
in him during the three years that separated us. But, as
I have forewarned my readers, my object is merely to
recount the adventure of a friendship. I am, for this
reason, interested in the history of his ideas rather

than in the ideas themselves, which others will be able to describe in detail, and better than I would. It is the man I want to restore, not as he was for himself but as he lived in my life, as I experienced him in his. I do not know how truthful I shall be. I shall seem questionable and it will seem I am depicting myself negatively by the way I paint him: this I admit. I am, at any rate, sincere: I am describing what I took to be the case.

Pain is emptiness: others might have remained simulacra of hermits, hollow men. But, at the same time as it cut him off from us, his pain led Merleau back to his initial meditation, to the good fortune that had made him so unfortunate. I am struck by the unity of Merleau's life. Since the pre-war years, this young Oedipus who had revisited his origins had wished to understand the rational unreason that produced him. Just as he was getting close to it and writing the *Phenomenology of Perception*, history jumped at our throats. He wrestled with it without interrupting his quest. Let us call this the first period of his thinking. The second began in the last years of the Occupation and continued until 1950. His thesis completed, he seemed to

abandon that investigation and turn to the questioning of history and the politics of our time. But his
concern had changed only in appearance: everything
connects up, since history is a form of envelopment
and we are 'anchored' in it, since we have to situate
ourselves historically not in an *a priori* fashion, by
some 'soaring' thought, but through the concrete experience of the movement that carries us along: if we
read him closely, Merleau's commentaries on politics
are merely a political experience becoming, by itself
and in all senses of the term, a *subject* of meditation;
if writings are acts, let us say that he acts in order to
appropriate his action and to find himself, at a deep
level, in that action. From the general perspective of
history, Merleau is an intellectual from the middle
classes, radicalized by the Resistance and blown off
course by the fragmentation of the Left.[110] Seen for
himself, his was a life that turned round on itself to
grasp the emergence of the human in its singularity.
Cruel as it was, it is clear that his disappointment of
1950 was to be of use to him: it removed him from
our sad arenas, but, in so doing, it offered him an
arena that was neither quite the same nor entirely

different—that enigma that is the self. Not that he sought, like Stendhal, to understand the individual that he was but, rather, in the manner of Montaigne, he wanted to comprehend the person, that matchless mix of the particular and the universal. Yet that was not enough: there remained knots to untie; he was tackling these when the death of his mother supervened and cut through them. It is admirable that, in his sadness, he made this ill-fortune his own, elevating it to the status of strictest necessity. Though it had been foreshadowed for some years, the third period of his meditation began in 1953.

In the beginning, it was both a renewed investigation and a wake. Thrown back on himself for a third time by death, he tried to use it to cast light on his birth. To the newborn, this visible-seer who appears in the world of vision, something must *happen*: something, anything, even if it is only dying. This initial tension between appearance and disappearance he terms 'primordial historicity': it is in and through this that everything occurs; it hurls us, from the very first moment, into an inflexible irreversibility. To survive birth, if only for a moment, is an adventure; and it is an adventure also not to survive it: one cannot escape this unreason he terms our contingency. It is not enough to say that we are born to die: we are born to death.

But at the same time, being alive, he prevented his mother from disappearing entirely. He no longer believed in an afterlife; if, however, in his last years, he happened to reject being numbered among the atheists, this was not out of consideration for his one-time burst of Christianity, but to leave a chance for the dead. Yet this precaution was not enough: in reviving a dead woman through the worship of her, what was he doing? Was he reviving her in fantasy or *instituting* her?

Life and death; existence and being: to carry out his two-pronged investigation, he tried to pitch his tent at this crossroads. In a sense, none of the ideas he advanced in his thesis changed; in another, nothing was recognizable any longer: he plunged into the dark night of non-knowledge, in search of what he now called the 'fundamental'. In *Signs*, for example, we read: 'What interests the philosopher in anthropology is just that it takes man as he is, in his actual situation

of life and understanding. The philosopher it interests is not the one who wants to explain or construct
the world, but the one who seeks to deepen our in-
sertion in being.'[111]

At the level of presence and absence, the philosopher appears, blind and all-seeing: though *knowledge*
claims to explain or construct, he does not even want
to *know*. He lives in this mix of oxygen and thin gases
called the True, but he doesn't deign to itemize the
truths—not even to distribute them to our schools or
textbooks. He does nothing but deepen himself: he
allows himself to slide, while still alive, without interrupting his undertakings, into the sole, derisory abyss
accessible to him; to seek within himself the door that
opens on to the night of what is not yet self. This is
to define philosophy as a meditation in the Cartesian
sense of the word—that is to say, as an indefinitely
sustained tension between existence and Being. This
slim, ambiguous dividing line is the origin: to think,
one must *be*; the tiniest thought exceeds being, instituting it for others; this happens in a trice: it is birth,
absurd and definitive, that indestructible *e*vent that
changes into *ad*vent and defines the singularity of a

life by its calling to death: it is the work [*oeuvre*], opaque and wild, retaining being in its folds; it is the undertaking, an unreason that will endure in the community as its future *raison d'être*; it is, above all, language, this 'fundamental', for the Word is merely the Being cast into the heart of man to extenuate itself in a *meaning*; in short, it is man, emerging at a stroke, moving beyond his presence to Being and towards his presence to others, moving beyond his past and towards his future, moving beyond everything and himself towards the sign: for this reason, Merleau tended, towards the end of his life, to grant ever greater scope to the unconscious. He doubtless agreed with Lacan's formula, 'The unconscious is structured like a language.' But, as a philosopher, he had placed himself at the opposite pole to psychoanalysis: the unconscious fascinated him both as a fettered speech and as the hinge of Being and existence.

One day, Merleau-Ponty took against dialectics and abused it. Not that he didn't accept the division on which it is based; he explains in *Signs* that the positive always has its negative and vice versa; they will, as a consequence, pass eternally one into the other.

These things go round, so to speak, and the philosopher will go round with them. It is for him to follow the circuits of his object scrupulously and in a spirit of discovery; he must spiral down into the darkness. Merleau-Ponty acquired the habit of pursuing every 'No' until he saw it turn into a 'Yes' and every 'Yes' until it changed into a 'No'. He became so proficient, in his latter years, at this game of 'hide the slipper' that he positively made a method of it. I shall term this inversion. He jumped from one standpoint to another, denied and affirmed, changed more into less and less into more: all things are contraries and all are also true. I shall give just one example of this: 'At least as much as he explains adult behaviour by a fate inherited from childhood, Freud shows a *premature* adult life in childhood, and . . . for example, a first choice of his relationships of generosity or avarice to others.'[112] *At least as much*: in his writings contradictory truths never fight against each other; there is no risk of shackling the movement, of causing a break-up. And are they indeed, strictly speaking, contradictory? If this were even admitted, it would have to be acknowledged that contradiction, weakened by this giratory impulse, loses its role as 'engine of history' and represents in his eyes the sign of paradox, the living mark of fundamental ambiguity. In short, Merleau is quite happy with thesis and antithesis; it is the synthesis he rejects: he reproaches it with turning the dialectic into a construction set. By contrast, his revolving structures leave no room for a conclusion; each in its way illustrates the merry-go-round of Being and existence. As children of clay, we should reduce ourselves to imprints on the earth if we did not begin by denying it. Let us invert, then: we, whose most immediate existence is the negation of what is, what do we do from our first moment to our last but announce Being, institute it, restore it by and for others, in the milieu of inter-subjectivity? Institute it, announce it—all well and good. As for seeing it face to face, that we must not expect: we know only its signs. Thus the philosopher will never stop running round in circles, nor will the roundabout stop turning:

> This being—which is glimpsed through time's stirrings and always intended by our . . . perception and our carnal being, but to which there can be no question of our being

transported because to abolish its distance would be to take away its consistency of being—this being 'of distances', as Heidegger will put it, which is always offered to our transcendence, is the dialectical idea of being as defined in the *Parmenides*—beyond the empirical multiplicity of existent things and as a matter of principle intended through them, because separated from them, it would be only lightning flash or darkness.[113]

Merleau still has his flirtatious moments: he still speaks in this text of dialectics. Yet it isn't to Hegel he refers but to Parmenides and Plato. The appropriate method with meditation is to draw an outer line around one's subject and revisit the same places time and again. What is it, then, that meditation can make out? An absence? A presence? Both? Refracted by a prism, the outer being scatters, becomes multiple and inaccessible; but, as part of the same movement, it is also internalized, becomes the inner being—entirely and constantly present, yet not losing its intangibility. And, naturally, the opposite is also true: the inner being within us, our innermost recess, fiercely guarded and grave, constantly manifests its oneness with Nature, that indefinite deployment of outer being. Thus, circling and meditating, Merleau remains faithful to his spontaneous thinking, a slow rumination shot through with bolts of lightning: it is this which he sets up discreetly as a method, in the form of a decapitated dialectic.

In the end, it was this descent into Hell that enabled him to find the profoundest merry-go-round of all. It was a discovery of the heart, as is proved by its striking, sombre density. I shall tell how he informed me of it almost two years ago: the man paints himself, subtle and laconic as he was, in these remarks, tackling problems head on when he seems merely to be brushing at them from the side. I asked him if he was working. He hesitated: 'I'm perhaps going to write on Nature.' To whet my appetite, he added: 'I read a sentence in Whitehead that made an impression on me: "Nature is in tatters".' As the reader will already have guessed, not another word was added. I left him without having understood: at that time I was studying 'dialectical materialism' and for me the word 'Nature' evoked the full extent of our physical and chemical knowledge. Another misunderstanding: I had forgotten that Nature for him was the tangible world, that 'decidedly universal' world in which we encounter things and animals, our own bodies and others. I did not understand him until his last article, 'Eye and Mind', was published.[114] That long essay was, I imagine, supposed to form part of the book he was writing: at any rate, he constantly refers and alludes there to an idea that was going to be expressed, but remains unformulated.

More hostile than ever to intellectualism, Merleau enquires into painters and their manual, untutored thinking: he tries to grasp the meaning of painting from the works themselves. On this occasion, Nature reveals its 'threads and tatters' to him. How, he says more or less, does that mountain in the distance announce itself to us? By discontinuous and, at times, intermittent signals, sparse, insubstantial phantasms, shimmerings, shadowplay; this dusty thing strikes us by its sheeer insubstantiality. But our eye is, precisely a 'computer of Being';[115] these airy signs will settle into the heaviest of terrestrial masses. The gaze no longer contents itself with 'glimps[ing] . . . being . . . through time's stirrings': it would seem now that its mission is to form its—ever-absent—unity out of multiplicity. 'And so that unity does not exist?' we shall ask. It does and it does not, just like the defunct coat whose presence haunts the threads and tatters like Mallarmé's rose that is 'absent from all bouquets'. Being *is* through us, who *are* through it. All this, of course, requires the Other; this is how Merleau understands Husserl's 'difficult' assertion that 'transcendental consciousness is intersubjectivity.' No one, he thinks, can see, unless he is at the same time visible: how would we grasp what *is* if we *were not*? We are not speaking here of a mere '*noesis*', producing its noematic correlative through appearances. Once again, in order to think, one must first *be*. The thing, constituted by each of us out of all things—always a unity, but an indefinitely chamfered unity—consigns each of us, through the others, to our ontological status. We are the sea; as soon as it emerges each piece of driftwood is as uncountable as the waves, through them and like them absolute. The painter is the privileged artisan, the best witness of this mediated reciprocity. 'The body is caught in the fabric of the world, but the world is made of the stuff of my body.' A new spiralling, but deeper than the others since it relates to the 'labyrinth of embodiment'. Through my flesh, Nature is made flesh; but, conversely, if painting is possible, then the lineaments of being that the painter perceives in the thing and fixes on the canvas must designate, in the very depths of himself, the 'flexions' of his being. 'Only on condition of being self-figuring does the painting relate . . . to anything whatever among empirical things; it is a spectacle of things only by being the spectacle of nothing . . . showing how things make themselves things and the world a world.' It is just this that gives 'the painter's occupation an urgency that exceeds all others'. By representing outer being, he presents others with inner being, *his* flesh, their flesh. But 'present' is too weak a word here: culture, says Merleau, is a 'coming-into-being'. So the artist has this sacred function of instituting being amid men; this means going beyond the 'layers of raw being of which the activist is unaware' towards that eminent being that is *meaning*. The artist has this function, but each of us has it also. 'Expression,' he says, 'is the *fundamental* quality of the body.' And what is there to express except Being: we do not make a single movement without restoring being, instituting it and rendering it present. Primordial historicity, our being born unto death, is the surging from the deep through which the event becomes man and, by naming things, recites his being. This is also the history of groups in its most radical aspect: 'What but history are we to call this [milieu] in which a form burdened with contingency suddenly opens up a cycle of futurity and commands it with the authority of that which is established?'

These are, in their beginnings, his last thoughts: of his last philosophy, 'burdened with contingency', gnawing patiently at chance and interrupted by that chance, I have said that I saw it begin with a discovery of the heart. Against mourning and absence, it was he in his turn who was discovering himself: he was the true 'computer of Being'. He had a handful of memories and relics left, but our gaze reveals the being of the mountain with fewer resources than that: from the tatters of memory, the heart will wrest the being of the dead; out of the *e*vent that killed them it will make their *ad*vent; it is not simply a question of restoring their eternity to the lost smile and the words:

to live will be to deepen them, to transform them into themselves a little more each day, by our words and our smiles, without end. There is a progress of the dead and it is our history. In this way, Merleau made himself his mother's guardian, as she had been the guardian of his childhood; born through her unto death, he wanted death to be a rebirth for her. For this reason, he found more real powers in absence than in presence. 'Eye and Mind' contains a curious quotation: Marivaux, reflecting in *Marianne* on the strength and dignity of the passions, praises men who take their own lives rather than deny their being.[116] What Merleau liked about these few lines is that they uncovered an indestructible slab of stone beneath the transparency of the shallow stream that is life. But let us not be tempted to think he is returning here to Cartesian substance: hardly has he closed the quotation marks and taken up his pen on his own account than the slab shatters into discontinuous flickerings, becomes that ragged being that it is our lot to be, which is perhaps merely a disordered imperative, and which a suicide will sometimes put back together better than a living victory. By a movement of the same kind, since this is our rule, we shall institute the being of the dead in the human community by our own being, and our being by that of the dead.

How far did he go, then, in these dark years that changed him into himself? At times, reading him, one would say that Being invents man in order to be *manifested* by him. Did it not happen from time to time that Merleau, inverting the terms and standing things on their head, thought he glimpsed in us, 'ungraspable in immanence', some sort of transcendent mandate? In one of his articles, he congratulates a mystic on having written that God is below us. He adds, more or less, 'Why not?' He dreams of an Almighty who would need human beings, who would be in question in everyone's heart and would remain the total Being, the one that intersubjectivity is re-instituting infinitely, the only one we would push to the limit of its being and which would share with all of us the insecurity of the human adventure. This is clearly just a metaphorical indication. But the fact that he chose it cannot be seen as insignificant. It has everything in it: both stroke of inspiration and risk; if *L'Être*[117] is below us, a gigantic ragged pauper, it will take only an imperceptible change for it to become *our task*. God, the task of man? Merleau never wrote that, and he forbade himself to think it: there is nothing to say that he did not sometimes dream of it, but his researches were too rigorous for him to put forward anything he had not established. He worked unhurriedly; he was waiting.

It has been claimed that he had moved closer to Heidegger. There is little doubt of this, but we must be clear what we mean. So long as his childhood was safeguarded for him, Merleau had no need to radicalize his quest. With his mother dead, and his childhood swept away with her, absence and presence, Being and Non-Being flowed into each other. Merleau, through phenomenology and without ever leaving it, wanted to connect with the imperatives of ontology; that which is no longer, is not yet, never will be: it was for man to give Being to beings. These tasks emerged out of his life, out of his mourning; he found in them the opportunity to re-read Heidegger, to understand him better, but not to give in to his influence: their paths crossed and that was all. Being is the sole concern of the German philosopher; despite what is at times a shared vocabulary, man remains the main concern of

Merleau. When the former speaks of 'openness to being', I smell alienation. Admittedly, we should not deny that the latter has sometimes penned some troubling words. These, for example: 'The irrelative henceforth is not nature in itself or the system of the apprehensions of the absolute consciousness, nor indeed is it man, but that "teleology" that must be written and thought between quotation marks—the framework and articulation of the being that is accomplished through man.' The quotation marks don't make any difference. All the same, it was said only in passing. It is regrettable that a man can write today that the absolute is not man; but what he denies to the human realm, he does not grant to any other. His 'irrelative' is, in fact, a relation of reciprocity that is closed upon itself: man is designated by his basic calling, which is to institute Being, but Being is similarly designated by its destiny, which is to accomplish itself through man. I have told how, twice at least—in the Christian community and in the fraternity of political combat—Merleau had sought to envelop himself in immanence and had run up against the transcendent. While more than ever avoiding recourse to the Hegelian synthesis, his last thinking attempts to resolve the contradiction he experienced in his life: the transcendent will be poured into immanence; it will be dissolved in it, while being protected, by its very intangibility, from annihilation; it is now merely absence and supplication, merely infinite weakness dragging its omnipotence along. Is this not, in a sense, the fundamental contradiction of all humanism? And can dialectical materialism—in the name of which many will want to criticize this meditation—do without an ontology? Looking closer, indeed, and if we set aside the absurd theory of reflection, would we not find in it, discreetly announced, the idea of a layer of raw being producing and underpinning action and thought?

No, the man who a few months before his death wrote, 'When the lightning flash that is man blazes out, everything is given in that very instant,' never ceased to be a humanist. And then what? To accomplish Being is indeed to consecrate it: but that means to humanize it. Merleau does not claim that we should lose ourselves so that Being may be but, quite the contrary, that we shall institute Being by the very act that causes us to be born to the human [*naître à l'humain*].

More Pascalian than ever, he reminds us once again: Man is absolutely distinct from the animal species, but precisely in the respect that he has no original equipment and is the place of contingency, which sometimes takes the form of a kind of miracle . . . and sometimes the form of an unintentional adversity.[118]

This is sufficient to say that man is never either the animal of a species or the object of a universal concept but, from the moment he emerges, the splendour of an event. But he draws the same lesson from the humanist Montaigne: Montaigne 'rejects in advance the explanations of man a physics or metaphysics can give us, because it is still man who "proves" philosophies and sciences, and because they are explained by him rather than he by them . . .'[119] Man will never think man: he *makes* him at every moment. Is not this the true humanism: man will never be a total object of knowledge; he is the subject of history.

In the last works of the sombre philosopher, it is not difficult to find a certain optimism: nothing comes to anything, but nothing is lost. An endeavour is born, institutes *its* man at a stroke—the whole of the man in a lightning flash—and perishes with him or survives him extravagantly to end, in any event, in disaster; yet, at the very moment of calamity, it opens a door to the future. Spartacus struggling and dying is the whole of man: who can say better than this? A word is the whole of language gathered into a few sounds; a picture is the whole of painting. 'In this sense,' he says, 'there both is progress and there is not.' History is constantly establishing itself in our pre-   historic milieu; with each lightning flash, the whole is illuminated, instituted, frays at the edges and, deathless, disappears. Apelles of Cos, Rembrandt and Klee each in their turn *presented Being to the gaze* in a particular civilization and with the means available to them. And long before the first of them was born, the whole of painting was already made manifest in the caves of Lascaux.

Precisely because he is constantly summing himself up in this ever-recommenced lightning-flash, there will be a future for man. Contingency of Good, contingency of Evil: Merleau no longer either favoured or condemned anyone. Adversity had brought us within an inch of barbarism; miracles, always and everywhere possible, would bring us out of it. Since, 'spontaneously, every gesture of our body and language, every act of political life . . . takes others into consideration and surpasses itself, in its singularity, in the direction of the universal,' then even though it is in no sense necessary or promised, and even though we call on it not so much to improve us in our being as to clean up the detritus of our lives, a *relative* progress has to be the most probable conjecture: 'Experience will, very probably, end up eliminating the false solutions.' It is in this hope, I believe, that he agreed to write a number of political commentaries for *L'Express*. The Soviet and Western blocs were two growth economies, two industrial societies, each riven by contradictions. Above and beyond the different regimes, he would have liked to have identified common demands at the infrastructural level or lines of convergence at least: it was a way of remaining faithful to his own thinking. Once again, the point was to reject the Manichaean option. There had been unity; after the loss of that minor paradise, he had wanted to denounce exploitation everywhere, then he had walled himself up in silence: he came back out to seek after reasons for hope everywhere. Without any illusions—

'*la virtù*' and nothing more. We are twisted creatures: the ties binding us to others are distorted; there is no regime that could, in itself, rectify that distortion, but perhaps the men who will come after us—all men together—will have the strength and the patience to undertake this task.

The course of our thinking separated us a little more each day. His mourning and voluntary reclusiveness made a *rapprochement* more difficult. In 1955, we almost lost each other completely, by abstraction. He wrote a book on the Dialectic in which he attacked me fiercely.[120] Simone de Beauvoir replied no less fiercely in *Les Temps modernes*: it was the first and last time we argued in print. By publishing our differences, it seemed we would inevitably render them irremediable. Quite the contrary: at the point when friendship seemed dead, it began to blossom again imperceptibly. We had no doubt been too careful to avoid violence: it needed a little to eliminate the last remaining grievances and for him to get everything off his chest once and for all. In short, the quarrel was short-lived and we met up again not long afterwards.

It was in Venice in the early months of 1956, where the European Society of Culture had organized discussions between East and West European writers. I was there. As I sat down, I noticed that the seat alongside mine was empty. I leaned over and saw Merleau-Ponty's name on the card: we had been put together because they thought it would be to our liking. The discussion began, but I was only half listening; I was waiting for Merleau—not without trepidation. He came. Late as usual. Someone was speaking. He slipped behind me on tiptoe and touched me lightly on the shoulder; when I turned round, he smiled. The conversations went on for several days: we were not entirely in agreement, except that we both became irritated listening to an over-eloquent Italian and an excessively naïve Englishman who had been deputed to scuttle the project. But among so many people of such diversity, some older than us, others younger, we felt united by a self-same culture and experience, meaningful only to us. We spent several evenings together, a little uneasily and never alone. It was all right. Our friends who were present protected us from ourselves, from the temptation of prematurely re-establishing our intimacy. As a consequence, we merely talked to one another. Though neither of us had any illusions about the significance of the Venice discussions, we both wanted them to take place again the next year—he because he was a 'binder', I to 'privilege' the Left: when it came to drafting the final communiqué, we found ourselves of the same mind. It was nothing, and yet it was proof that a shared task could bring us together.

We met again—in Paris, in Rome and again in Paris. Alone: this was the second stage. The unease was still there, but was tending to disappear; another feeling emerged, one of tender affection: such disconsolate, mildly funereal affection brings together exhausted friends, to whom strife has left nothing in common but their quarrel and whose quarrel has one day ended for want of anything to argue over. That thing had been the review: it had united, then separated us; it no longer even separated us. Our cautiousness in our relations with each other had almost led us to fall out: aware of this now, we were careful never to spare each other's feelings. But too late. Whatever we did, each of us now failed to engage the other. When we explained our positions, it seemed to me rather as though we were exchanging news of our respective families—auntie Mary is having an operation, nephew Charles has got his 'A levels'—and we were sitting side by side on a bench with blankets over our knees, tracing out signs in the dust with the ends of our walking sticks. What was missing? Neither affection, nor esteem, but a shared undertaking. Our past activity had been buried without it having being able to separate us, but it took its revenge by making 'retired' old friends of us.

We had to wait for the third stage without forcing things. I waited, certain that our friendship would be recovered. We were united in condemning the war in Algeria unreservedly; he had sent his *légion d'honneur* back to the Guy Mollet government and we were both opposed to the fledgling dictatorship that was Gaullism. We were not perhaps agreed on how to fight it, but that would come: when Fascism is on the rise, it reunites lost friends. I saw him in the March of that same year. I was giving a lecture at the École normale and he came along. I was touched by this. For years it had been I who was always angling for meetings, proposing rendezvous. For the first time, he spontaneously went out of his way. Not to hear me rehearse ideas that he knew by heart, but to see me. At the end of the lecture, we met up together with Hyppolite and Canguilhem. For me, it was a happy moment. Later, however, I learned that he had apparently felt a persistence of the unease between us. This was not remotely the case, but unfortunately I had the flu and was rather groggy. When we parted, he had uttered no word of his disappointment but for a moment I sensed a stiffening. I took no notice of it: 'Everything is as it was,' I told myself, 'it will all begin again.' A few days later, I learned of his death and our friendship ended on this last misunderstanding. Had he lived, it would have been dissipated as soon as I returned. Perhaps. With his death, we shall remain for each other what we always were: unknowns.

Without a doubt, Merleau's readers can know him; he has 'made an appointment with them in his work'; every time I become his reader, I shall know him and know myself better. A hundred and fifty pages of his future book have been saved from the wreckage[121] and then there is 'Eye and Mind', which says everything, provided one knows how to decipher it: we shall, all of us together, 'institute' this thinking we find in tatters; it will be one of the prisms of our 'intersubjectivity'. At a moment when Mr Papon, the Prefect of Police, sums up the general view when he states that nothing surprises him any longer, Merleau provides the antidote by being surprised by everything. He is a child scandalized by our footling grownup certainties, a child who asks the scandalous questions the adults never answer: why do we live? Why do we die? Nothing seems natural to him— either the fact that there is a history or that there is a nature. He doesn't understand how it can be that every necessity turns into contingency and every contingency ends up in necessity. He says this and we, reading him, are dragged into this whirligig, from which we shall never extract ourselves. Yet it is not us he is questioning: he is too afraid we shall hit up against reassuring dogmatisms. This questioning will be something between himself and himself, because 'the writer has chosen insecurity'. Insecurity: our basic situation and, at one and the same time, the difficult attitude that reveals this situation to us. It is not appropriate for us to ask for answers from him; what he teaches us is how to deepen an initial enquiry; he reminds us, as Plato did, that the philosopher is the person who experiences wonderment, but, more rigorous in this than his Greek master, he adds that the philosophical attitude disappears the minute that wonderment ceases. Conversely, to those who predict that philosophy will one day take over the world, he replies that if man were one day happy, free and transparent to other men, we ought to be as amazed by that suspect happiness as we are at our present misfortunes. I would happily say, if the word did not seem suspect to him through overuse, that he had managed to rediscover the internal dialectic of questioner and questioned, and that he had pushed it as far as the fundamental question we avoid with all our alleged responses. To follow him, we have to give up two contradictory securities between which we constantly waver, for we reassure ourselves ordinarily by the use of two concepts that are opposite in nature but equally universal. Both of these take us as objects, the first telling each of us that he is a man among men and the second that he is an Other among others. But the former is worthless because man is constantly making himself and can never think of himself in his entirety. And the latter deceives us, because we are in fact similar, insofar as each of us differs from all. Jumping from the one idea to the other, the way monkeys jump from one branch to another, we avoid singularity, which is not so much a fact as a perpetual postulation. Severing our links with our contemporaries, the bourgeoisie confines us within the cocoon of private life and cuts us up with its scissors into *individuals*—that is to say, molecules without history that drag themselves from one moment to the next. Through Merleau we find ourselves singular again, through the contingency of our anchorage in nature and in history or, in other words, through the temporal adventure that we represent within the human adventure. Thus history makes *us* universal to precisely the same degree that we make *it* particular. This is the considerable gift Merleau bestows on us by his relentless determination to keep on digging in the same spot: starting out from the well-known universality of the singular, he arrives at the singularity of the universal. He it was who exposed the crucial contradiction:

every history is the whole of history; when the light-ning flash that is man blazes out, all is said: all lives, all moments, all ages—contingent miracles or misfires—are *incarnations*: the Word becomes flesh, the universal establishes itself only by way of the living singularity that distorts it as it singularizes it. We should not see here a rehashing of the 'unhappy consciousness': it is precisely the opposite. Hegel is describing the tragic opposition between two abstract notions, the very ones that are, as I said, the two poles of our security. But, for Merleau, universality is never universal, ex-cept for 'soaring' thought: its birth is dependent on the flesh and, as flesh of our flesh, it retains, in its most subtle degree, our singularity. This is the admo-nition anthropology—be it analysis or Marxism—should not forget. Nor, should it forget, as Freudians do too often, that every man is the whole of man and that we must have regard in all human beings for the *lightning-flash*, that singular universalization of univer-sality. Nor, as novice dialecticians do, should it be for-gotten that the USSR is not the mere beginning of the universal revolution but also its incarnation, and that 1917 will bestow ineradicable features on future social-

ism. This is a difficult problem: neither banal anthropology nor historical materialism will free themselves
from it. Merleau didn't think he was providing solutions. On the contrary, had he lived, he would have dug
down even further into the problem, spiralling as ever,
until he had radicalized the elements of the question, as
we can see in 'Eye and Mind' from what he says of primordial historicity.[122] He did not reach the end of his
thinking or, at least, he did not have time to express it
in its entirety. Is this a failure? No, it is something like
a taking-up of the initial contingency by the final contingency: singularized by this twofold absurdity and
meditating upon singularity from the beginning to his
death, Merleau's life takes on an inimitable 'style' and
justifies by itself the warnings contained in the work. As
for that work, which is inseparable from the life, a lightning flash between two chance events, lighting up our
darkest night, we could apply to it, word for word, what
he wrote at the beginning of this year:

> [I]f we cannot establish a hierarchy of civi-
> lizations or speak of progress—neither in
> painting nor in anything else that matters—it
> is not because some fate holds us back; it is,

rather, because the very first painting in some sense went to the farthest reach of the future. If no painting comes to be *the* painting, if no work is ever absolutely completed and done with, still each creation changes, alters, enlightens, deepens, confirms, exalts, re-creates or creates in advance all the others. If creations are not established advances, this is not only because, like all things, they pass away; it is also that they have almost all their lives still before them.[123]

As a question without an answer, a *virtú* without illusion, Merleau entered universal culture as something singular; he took his place as something universal in the singularity of history. Changing, as Hegel said, the contingent into the necessary and the necessary into the contingent, it was his mission to embody the problem of embodiment. On this question, we can all find a meeting place in his work.

I, who had other meetings with him, do not want to lie about our relations nor end on such fine optimism. I can still see his face that last night I saw him—we parted in the rue Claude-Bernard—a face disappointed, suddenly impenetrable. It remains with me, a painful wound, infected by regret, remorse and a little rancour. Transformed into what it will now be, our friendship is summed up in it for ever. Not that I accord the slightest privilege to the last moment, nor allot it the task of telling the final truth about a life. But everything was, in fact, gathered in that face: frozen in that silent expression are all the silences he met me with after 1950, and at times, I, for my part, still feel the eternity of his absence as a deliberate mutism. I can clearly see that our final misunderstanding—which would have amounted to nothing if I could have seen him alive again—is cut from the same cloth as the others: it jeopardized nothing, and in it you can just see our mutual affection, our shared desire not to spoil anything between us. But you can see also the way our lives were out of phase, so that the initiatives we took were always out of kilter; and then, adversity intervening, it suspended our dealings, without violence, *sine die*. Like birth, death is an embodiment: his death, a nonsense full of obscure meaning, brought into being, where we were concerned, the contingency and necessity of an ill-starred friendship. Yet there was something there worth striving for:

with our qualities and our shortcomings, the published violence of the one, the secret excesses of the other, we were not so badly suited. And what did we make of all that? Nothing, except that we avoided falling out. Everyone may apportion blame as they see fit: at any rate, we were not very guilty, so that sometimes I see in our adventure nothing but its necessity: this is how men live in our times; this is how they love each other: badly. That is true; but it is true also that it was we, we two, who loved each other badly. There are no conclusions to draw from this except that this long friendship—neither established nor undone, but simply wiped out at the point when it was either about to be reborn or break up—remains in me like an ever-open wound.

Les Temps modernes, special issue (October 1961).

Notes

1   André Gide, *Corydon* (Paris: Gallimard, 1925); *Cory-don* (Richard Howard trans.) (New York: Farrar, Straus & Giroux, 1950). *Voyage au Congo* (Paris: Gallimard, 1927); *Travels in the Congo* (Dorothy Bussy trans.) (New York: Alfred A. Knopf, 1929). [Trans.]

2   This was written in response to Albert Camus, 'Lettre au directeur des *Temps Modernes*', *Les Temps modernes*, 82 (August 1952). [Trans.]

3   Characters from Molière's play *Les femmes savantes* [The Learned Ladies, 1672]. Trissotin is described as a wit, Vadius as a classical scholar; they quarrel over the quality of Trissotin's poetry. Sartre's 'Who would have said, who would have believed' here is also a clear reference to the well-known exchange between Rodrigue and Chimène in Act III, Scene 4 of Cornielle's *Le Cid*. [Trans.]

4   Literally, 'passage of evil'. The great Catholic writer's third play—published by La Table ronde, Paris, 1948, and staged the same year—was a resounding critical failure. [Trans.]

5   You must have formed the habit of projecting the failings of your thought on to others to believe that Jeanson claimed to speak in the name of the proletariat.

6 Albert Camus, *L'Homme révolté* (Paris: Gallimard, 1951); *The Rebel*: *An Essay on Man in Revolt* (Anthony Bower trans.) (London: Hamish Hamilton, 1953). [Trans.]

7 *Accusateur public*: the Prosecutor of the French Revolutionary Tribunal. [Trans.]

8 Henry de Montherlant (1896–1972): novelist, playwright and essayist. [Trans.]

9 For you are bourgeois, Camus, like me; what else could you be?

10 David Rousset, a survivor of Buchenwald, was the first person to bring the Gulag system to light within the French Left. He was denounced by *Les Lettres Françaises* in 1949 as a 'falsifying Trotskyite', but went on to fight a successful libel action against this charge.

11 Sartre is referring to Senator Joseph McCarthy's anti-Communist campaign of the 1950s. [Trans.]

12 It isn't my place to defend those of Marx, but allow me to tell you that the dilemma into which you have boxed those ideas (either Marx's 'prophecies' are true or Marxism is merely a method) misses the whole of Marxist philosophy and everything in it that constitutes for me (who am not a Marxist) its profound truth.

13 This is a reference to Roger Troisfontaines, *Le Choix*

de Jean-Paul Sartre. Exposé et critique de 'L'Etre et le Néant' (Paris: Montaigne, 1945). [Trans.]

14 Jean-Paul Sartre, *Being and Nothingness: An Essay on Phenomenological Ontology* (Hazel E. Barnes trans.) (New York: Methuen and Co., 1957) [*L'Être et le néant: Essai d'ontologie phénoménologique* (Paris: Gallimard, 1943)—Trans.]

15 Albert Camus, *L'Étranger* (Paris: Gallimard, 1942); *The Outsider* (Stuart Gilbert trans.) (London: Hamish Hamilton, 1946). [Trans.]

16 Georges Bataille, 'Le Supplice', in *L'Expérience Intérieure* (Paris: Gallimard, 1943). [Trans.]

17 My translation of part of an enigmatic fragment from Stéphane Mallarmé, 'Igitur', in *Œuvres complètes* (Henri Mondor and G. Jean-Aubry eds) (Paris: Gallimard, 1945), p. 428. [Trans.]

18 Ménalque, like the Nathanael mentioned below, is a character in André Gide's *Les Nourritures terrestres* [1897; *The Fruits of the Earth* (Dorothy Bussy trans.) (New York: Alfred A. Knopf, 1949)], who reappears in *L'Immoraliste* [1902; *The Immoralist* (Dorothy Bussy trans.) (New York: Alfred A. Knopf, 1930)]. It has sometimes been suggested that Ménalque was based on Oscar Wilde, but André Maurois says Gide personally rejected this suggestion. [Trans.]

19 Albert Camus, 'Nuptials at Tipasa', in *Selected Essays and Notebooks* (Philip Thody ed. and trans.) (Harmondsworth: Penguin, 1967), pp. 71–2 (translation modified). [Trans.]

20 See note 3. [Trans.]

21 The epistolary novel *Obermann* was written by Étienne Pivet de Sénancour in 1804. [Trans.]

22 *Lettres à un ami allemand*, my emphasis, J-P. S. [1945; published for the first time in English as 'Letters to a German Friend', in *Resistance, Rebellion, and Death* (Justin O'Brien trans.) (New York: Random House, 1961—Trans.]

23 Ibid. [Trans.]

24 Albert Camus, *La Peste* (Paris: Gallimard, 1947); *The Plague* (Stuart Gilbert trans.) (London: Hamish Hamilton, 1948). [Trans.]

25 Passy is a leafy suburb in the fashionable 16th arrondissement of Paris. Boulogne-Billancourt is a working-class area in that city's Western suburbs. [Trans.]

26 This is not entirely exact. Some are doomed come what may.

27 These three quotations are from Camus, 'Nuptials', in *Selected Essays and Notebooks*, pp. 90, 97, 98 (the

translation of the passage cited on p. 97 has been modified). [Trans.]

28 Albert Camus, *La Chute* (Paris: Gallimard, 1956); *The Fall* (Justin O'Brien trans.) (London: Hamish Hamilton, 1956). [Trans.]

29 This is, presumably, a reference to the tuberculosis that he contracted in his youth. [Trans.]

30 Paul Nizan, *Aden, Arabie* (Paris: Francois Maspero, 1960 [1931]; *Aden, Arabie* (Joan Pinkham trans.) (New York: Monthly Review Press, 1960). Paul Nizan, *Antoine Bloyé* (Paris: Grasset: 1933); *Antoine Bloyé* (Edmund Stevens trans.) (Moscow: Co-operative Publishing Society of Foreign Workers in the USSR, 1935). [Trans.]

31 'Tu causes, tu causes, c'est tout ce que tu sais faire!' This is the refrain of the parrot in Raymond Queneau's *Zazie dans le métro* (Paris: Gallimard, 1959). [Trans.]

32 'Le lac', a poem by Alphonse de Lamartine (1790–1869), is one of the classics of French poetry routinely learned by French schoolchildren in this period. Similarly, the sermons of Jaques-Bénigne Bossuet (1627–1704) were taught as models of French prose style. [Trans.]

33 Antoine Pinay (1891–1994): a French conservative politician. He served as Prime Minister of France in 1952. [Trans.]

34 SFIO: Section Française de l'Internationale Ouvrière—the French Section of the Workers' International—was founded in 1905. A French socialist political party, it was designed as the local section of the Second International. After the 1917 October Revolution, it split (during the 1920 Tours Congress) into two groups, the majority creating the Section française de l'Internationale communiste (SFIC), which became the French Communist Party (PCF). [Trans.]

35 Georges-Augustin Bidault (1899–1983): a Christian-Democratic French politician, active in the French Resistance during World War II. After the war, he served as foreign minister and prime minister on several occasions between 1945 and 1953. [Trans.]

36 Jean-Paul Sartre, *La Nausée* (Paris: Gallimard, 1938); *Nausea* (Lloyd Alexander trans.) (New York: New Directions, 1959). [Trans.]

37 26th September 1958 saw a 79.2 per cent referendum vote in favour of the Constitution of the new Fifth Republic with de Gaulle as president. [Trans.]

38 Léon Brunschvicg (1869–1944): a French idealist

philosopher who taught at the Sorbonne. Sartre and Nizan were both students of his and he supervised Simone de Beauvoir's thesis on Leibniz. [Trans.]

39 Paul Nizan, *Les Chiens de garde* (Rieder, Paris, 1932); *Watchdogs: Philosophers and the Established Order* (Paul Fittingoff trans.) (New York: Monthly Review Press, 1972). [Trans.]

40 Paul Nizan, *La Conspiration* (Paris: Gallimard, 1973); *The Conspiracy* (Quintin Hoare trans.) (London: Verso, 1989). [Trans.]

41 Paul Nizan, *Antoine Bloyé* (Paris: Grasset, 1933), p. 299. All translations from this work are by me [Trans.].

42 The first-year class of the two-year preparatory course for the arts section of the École normale supérieure. [Trans.]

43 Georges Valois (1878–1945): a once prominent member of the monarchist Action française; the leader of France's first substantial fascist movement, Le Faisceau. [Trans.]

44 Paul Nizan, *Aden, Arabie* (Joan Pinkham trans.) (New York: Columbia University Press, 1987), p. 61 (translation modified). [Trans.]

45 See Paul Valéry, *Monsieur Teste* (Jackson Matthews trans.) (New York: Alfred A. Knopf, 1947); also

available in Jackson Matthews (ed.), *Collected Works of Paul Valery, Volume 6: Monsieur Teste* (Princeton, NJ: Princeton University Press, 1989). [Trans.]

46 Nizan, *Antoine Bloyé*, p. 310. It would seem that Sartre misquotes Nizan here, who does not write, as Sartre suggests, of the 'visage uniforme de sa vie', but of the 'visage informe de toute sa vie'—the *formless* countenance of his whole life. [Trans.]

47 Nizan, *Aden, Arabie*, p. 65. [Trans.]

48 Nizan, *Antoine Bloyé*, pp. 260–1. [Trans.]

49 Nizan, *Aden, Arabie*, p. 65. [Trans.]

50 Nizan, *Antoine Bloyé*, p. 273. [Trans.]

51 Nizan, *Aden, Arabie*, pp. 102–03. [Trans.]

52 Nizan, *Antoine Bloyé*, pp. 140–1. [Trans.]

53 Ibid., pp. 281–4. [Trans.]

54 The French expression here is *hurlait à la mort*, which reflects a folk belief that dogs have an intuitive sense of death. A particularly lugubrious style of barking is thought to derive from the dogs' perception that someone in the surrounding area is dead or dying. [Trans.]

55 Nizan, *Antoine Bloyé*, p. 271. [Trans.]

56 Ibid., p. 276. [Trans.]

57 Nizan, *Aden, Arabie*, p. 83. [Trans.]

58 Ibid. [Trans.]

59 Nizan, *Antoine Bloyé*, p. 137. [Trans.]

60 See Paul Nizan, *Les matérialistes de l'antiquité. Démocrite, Épicure, Lucrèce* (Paris: Maspero, 1965 [1938]). [Trans.]

61 Nizan, *Aden, Arabie*, p. 85 (translation modified). [Trans.]

62 Ibid., p. 159 (translation modified). [Trans.]

63 The quotation is from Mallarmé, 'Plusieurs sonnets, IV', *Œuvres complètes*, p. 68. [Trans.]

64 Nizan, *Antoine Bloyé*, pp. 135–6. [Trans.]

65 Ibid., p. 207. [Trans.]

66 Ibid., p. 285. [Trans.]

67 Sartre was at Brumath, Alsace, in November 1939 when he began writing the second of his surviving wartime notebooks, which were published as *Les carnets de la drôle de guerre* (Paris: Gallimard, 1995, second edition); *War Diaries: Notebooks from a Phoney War 1939–40* (Quintin Hoare trans.) (London: Verso, 1984). [Trans.]

68 Nizan, *Antoine Bloyé*, pp. 307–08. [Trans.]

69 Ibid., p. 310. [Trans.]

70 I do not know whether, in 1939, on contact with those whom their leaders refer to curiously as 'men', he regretted leaving the condition of simple soldier.

But when I saw my officers, those incompetents, I regretted my pre-war anarchism: since we had to fight, we had been wrong to leave command in the hands of those vain imbeciles. We know that, after the brief interim Resistance period, it remained in their hands; this in some measure explains our misfortunes.

71 Joseph Rouletabille was a fictional detective created by Gaston Leroux, now perhaps better known as the author of *The Phantom of the Opera*. [Trans.]

72 See Maurice Merleau-Ponty, *Signs* (Richard McCleary trans.) (Evanston: Northwestern University Press, 1964), p. 39 [Maurice Merleau-Ponty, *Signes* (Paris: Gallimard, 1960)]. Sartre is paraphrasing slightly. [Trans.]

73 Maurice Merleau-Ponty, *Phénoménologie de la Perception* (Paris: Gallimard, 1945); *Phenomenology of Perception* (Colin Smith trans.) (London: Routledge and Kegan Paul Ltd, 1962). [Trans.]

74 Maurice Merleau-Ponty, *Humanisme et terreur, essai sur le problème communiste* (Paris: Gallimard, 1947); *Humanism and Terror: An Essay on the Communist Problem* (John O'Neill trans.) (Boston: Beacon Press, 1969). [Trans.]

75 Not, as I did in 1942, by an eidetics of bad faith, but

by the empirical study of our historical allegiances and the inhuman forces perverting them.

76 Maurice Merleau-Ponty, 'La guerre a eu lieu,' *Les Temps modernes*, 1 (October 1945).

77 Ibid.

78 Ibid.

79 Pierre Courtade (1915–63), Pierre Hervé (1913–93) and Jean-Toussaint Desanti (1914–2002). [Trans.]

80 Sartre provides no references for these quotations, but this passage can be found in Merleau-Ponty, *Sens et non-sens* (Paris: Gallimard, 1996), pp. 201–02. [Trans.]

81 Merleau-Ponty, *Sens et non-sens*, p. 205. [Trans.]

82 He had not pronounced on this question in 1945: he thought the word too ambitious to apply it to the modest activity of *Les Temps modernes*.

83 Sartre writes '*nous-même*' here, singular, not '*nous-mêmes*', which suggests an authorial 'we' that refers to himself alone: the context seems to suggest, however, that he is thinking of those who remained at *Les Temps modernes* beyond its first beginnings, i.e. chiefly Merleau and himself. [Trans.]

84 Literally, 'cellar rats'—those who frequented the jazz-saturated cellar nightclubs of the immediate post-war years. [Trans.]

85 Sartre is referring to the article 'The USSR and the Camps', reprinted in *Signs*, pp. 263–73. It was published originally in January 1950. [Trans.]

86 Père Joseph—Father Joseph—was the *éminence grise* of the Cardinal de Richelieu. [Trans.]

87 Maurice Merleau-Ponty, *La guerre a eu lieu* (Paris: Éditions Champ social, 2007), p. 55. This work, originally published in *Les Temps modernes*, 1 (October 1945): 48–66, is also reprinted in *Sens et non-sens*. [Trans.]

88 RDR: Le Rassemblement Démocratique Révolutionnaire. [Trans.]

89 PCF: Parti communiste français—the French Communist Party. [Trans.]

90 Yves Farge (1899–1953): one of the founders in February 1948 of 'Les Combattants de la Liberté', the forerunner of the French Mouvement de la Paix, of which he was President until his death in a car accident near Tbilisi (Georgia, USSR). [Trans.]

91 Merleau-Ponty, *Signs*, p. 265.

92 Ibid., p. 266.

93 Ibid., pp. 267–8.

94 Ibid., p. 268.

95 Ibid., pp. 268–9 (translation modified).

96 Ibid., p. 268.

97 Ibid., p. 265.

98 Ibid.

99 Ibid., p. 269 (translation modified).

100 Ibid., pp. 32–3.

101 Paul Rivet (1876-1958): one of the founders of the pre-war Comité de Vigilance des Intellectuels Antifascistes, which was one of the organizations that contributed to the emergence of the French Popular Front. [Trans.]

102 Henri Martin: a French sailor who was arrested for sabotage in March 1950 in French Indochina. Though cleared of that charge, he was sentenced to five years' imprisonment for distributing anti-war propaganda. He was freed in August 1953 after a national campaign to liberate him, in which Sartre played a prominent role. The book to which Sartre refers here, and which contained contributions from Michel Leiris, Vercors, Francis Jeanson, Jacques Prévert and Hervé Bazin among others, is *L'Affaire Henri Martin* (Paris: Gallimard, 1953). [Trans.]

103 The Communist leader Jacques Duclos had been arrested after a demonstration. Two dead pigeons in his car were alleged to have been 'carrier pigeons' for communicating with Moscow. [Trans.]

104 Jean-Paul Sartre, 'Les Communistes et la paix', Part 1, *Les Temps modernes*, 81 (July 1952); Part 2, *Les Temps modernes*, 84–85 (October–November 1952); Part 3, *Les Temps modernes* (April 1954). Reproduced in Jean-Paul Sartre, *Situations VI* (Paris: Gallimard, 1964), pp. 80–384; *The Communists and Peace*, with *A Reply to Claude Lefort* (Martha H. Fletcher and Philip R. Berk trans.) (New York: Braziller, 1968). [Trans.]

105 In the other fields I would say not that the situation was reversed but that we worked together.

106 Lucien Rebatet (1903–72): a fascist, anti-semitic writer who had been a prominent journalist on the magazine *Je suis partout* before and during the Nazi Occupation. [Trans.]

107 Jean-Bertrand Pontalis, better known today as a Lacanian psychoanalyst and man of letters. [Trans.]

108 The pseudonym of François Emmanuel (1914–99), the Romanian-born journalist, critic and publisher. [Trans.]

109 The prolific writer Jean Cau (1925–93) was Sartre's secretary at this time. He was to win the Prix Goncourt in 1961 for his novel *La pitié de Dieu*. In later years, he switched political camps dramatically and became involved with GRECE and the so-called New Right. [Trans.]

110 Clearly, we could all be defined in this same way, except that the degrees of drift are variable and sometimes run in the opposite direction.

111 Merleau-Ponty, 'From Mauss to Claude Lévi-Strauss', in *Signs*, p. 123.

112 Merleau-Ponty, 'Man and Adversity', in *Signs*, p. 229.

113 Merleau-Ponty, *Signs*, p. 156. It was a question at that point of characterizing the present moment of philosophical research. Merleau lent it these two features: 'existence and dialectics'. However, a few months before, he had given a lecture at the Rencontres Internationales de Genève on the thought of our time. Remarkably, he did not say one word about Dialectics: rather, in referring to our problems, he avoided the word contradiction and wrote: 'Embodiment and the question of the other are the labyrinth of thinking and sensibility among our contemporaries.'

114 Maurice Merleau-Ponty, 'Eye and Mind', in James Edie (ed.), *The Primacy of Perception* (Carleton Dallery trans.) (Evanston: Northwestern University Press, 1964) [Maurice Merleau-Ponty, *L'Œil et l'esprit* (Paris: Gallimard, 1961)—Trans.]

115 Merleau-Ponty speaks of the eyes as *computeurs du monde*, 'computers of the world'. See 'Eye and Mind', *The Primacy of Perception*, p. 165. [Trans.]

427

116 *La Vie de Marianne*, begun in 1727, is an unfinished novel by Pierre de Marivaux. The novel was written in sections, eleven of which appeared between 1731 and 1745. [Trans.]

117 'Being' or 'the Being'. [Trans.]

118 Merleau-Ponty, 'Man and Adversity', in *Signs*, p. 240.

119 Merleau-Ponty, 'Reading Montaigne', in *Signs*, p. 202.

120 Maurice Merleau-Ponty, *Les aventures de la dialectique* (Paris: Gallimard, 1955); *Adventures of the Dialectic* (Joseph Bien trans.) (Evanston: Northwestern University Press, 1973). [Trans.]

121 This is presumably a reference to *Le visible et l'invisible, suivi de notes de travail*, published posthumously, together with Merleau's notes for its continuation, by his friend Claude Lefort (Paris: Gallimard, 1964). See Maurice Merleau-Ponty, *The Visible and the Invisible, Followed by Working Notes* (Alphonso Lingis trans.) (Evanston: Northwestern University Press, 1968). [Trans.]

122 See Merleau-Ponty, 'Eye and Mind', *The Primacy of Perception*, p. 161. [Trans.]

123 Ibid., p. 190 (translation modified).

PART THREE

the captive of venice

THE WILES OF JACOPO

Nothing. The life has sunk without trace. A few dates, a few facts and then the prattling of old authors. But we should not be discouraged: *Venice speaks to us*; this false witness' voice, shrill at times, whispering at others, broken by silences, is its voice. In the story of Tintoretto, a portrait of the artist painted in his lifetime by his native city, an unrelenting animosity shows through. The City of the Doges tells us she has taken a serious dislike to the most famous of her sons. Nothing is said openly: there are hints and suggestions and then it is on to other matters. Yet this unyielding hatred is as insubstantial as sand; it is not so much an open aversion as a coldness, a sullenness, the insidious dispersal of a rejection. And we ask no more: Jacopo fought a dubious fight against his countless enemies, was wearied by it and died defeated. That, in broad outline, was his life. We shall see the whole of it, in its sombre nakedness, if we sweep aside for a moment the undergrowth of tittle-tattle that blocks our access.

Jacopo was born in 1518. His father was a dyer. Venice immediately whispers in our ear that this was a very bad beginning: 'Around 1530, the boy entered Titian's studio as an apprentice, but, a few days later, the famous quinquagenarian saw genius in him and showed him the door.' Short and snappy, as accounts go. This anecdote recurs repeatedly, with an insistence that eventually seems conclusive. Titian doesn't come out of it well, you may say. And he doesn't, at least not *today*, not as *we* see things. But when Vasari narrated this anecdote in 1567, Titian had reigned for half a century: nothing is more respectable than a long period of impunity. And then, by the rules of the day, he was second in authority only to God in his own studio: no one would deny him the right to throw out a hireling. On the contrary, it is the victims who are presumed guilty: branded by misfortune, they have the evil eye—perhaps infectiously. In short, this is the first time an unhappy childhood figures in the *légende dorée* of Italian painting. I feel sure there is something to be made of this, but we shall come back to it later. The Voice of Venice never lies, provided one knows how to hear it; we shall listen to it when we have learnt better how to do so. For the time being, whatever may be the deeper truth, we must stress the implausibility of the facts.

Titian wasn't an easy man to get on with. That much is known. But Jacopo was twelve years old. At twelve, a 'gift' is nothing; the slightest thing can destroy it. Patience and time are needed to consolidate a fragile facility and turn it into talent. And even the touchiest of artists is not, at the height of his fame, going to take offence at a mere boy. But let us suppose the Master did jealously dismiss his apprentice. This is tantamount to killing him: to be cursed by a 'national treasure' is a very serious matter. All the more so as Titian did not have the frankness to make his true motives known: he was king, he frowned and all doors were closed to the black sheep thereafter; the very profession of painter was denied him.

It is not every day you see a child on a blacklist. Our interest is aroused and we'd like to know how he overcame such a dreadful eventuality. But all in vain: in every one of the books, the thread of the narrative breaks off at this point; we run up against a wall of silence—no one will tell us what became of him between the ages of twelve and twenty. Some have tried to fill the gap by imagining he taught himself to paint. But this at least we know to have been impossible, and past writers knew it better than we do: in the early sixteenth century, the art of painting was still a complex craft, hedged about by ceremony, beset by a welter of recipes and rituals: it was more a skill than a branch of knowledge, a set of procedures rather than a method, while everything—professional rules, traditions and trade secrets—combined to make apprenticeship a social obligation and a necessity. The biographers' silence betrays their embarrassment; incapable of reconciling the precocious fame of young Robusti[1] with his excommunication, they cast a veil over the eight years that separate the two. We may take this as an admission: no one threw Jacopo out. Since he did not die of boredom and pique in his father's dye-shop, he must have worked properly, normally, in the studio of a painter of whom we know nothing, except that that painter *was not* Titian. In distrustful, tight-knit societies, hatred is retroactive; if the mysterious beginnings of this life seem a premonition of its mysterious end, if the curtain that went up on a miraculously interrupted disaster comes down on an unmiraculous one, this is because Venice has arranged everything retrospectively to mark out the child for the old age that was to be his. Nothing happens and nothing lasts; birth is the mirror of death; between the two lies scorched earth; everything is eaten away by bad luck.

Let us move beyond these mirages; on the farther side, the view is clear and reaches to the horizon: what emerges is an adolescent who starts off in top gear and races towards glory. As early as 1539, Jacopo has left his master and set up on his own: he has *his own studio*. The young employer has gained his independence, fame and clients; he is taking on workers and apprentices in his turn. Make no mistake: in a city teeming with painters, where an economic crisis is threatening to stifle the market, to become a master at twenty is the exception. Merit alone cannot bring this, nor hard work and worldly wisdom; it takes a degree of good fortune. And everything is running in Robusti's favour: Paolo Caliari is ten years old, Titian is sixty-two.[2] Between the unknown child and an old man who will surely not be around for much longer, a lot of good painters are to be found, but only Tintoretto seems bound for excellence: in his own generation, at least, he has no equal, so the road ahead is clear. And, indeed, for a few years he makes untroubled headway: commissions flow in, he is popular with public, patricians and connoisseurs; Aretino deigns to compliment him personally; the young man has the preternatural gifts that Providence reserves for those adolescents who will die young.

But he does not die and his troubles begin. Titian turns out to be appallingly long-lived and displays elaborate malicious intent towards his young challenger. The old monarch is so spiteful as to designate his successor officially and, as one might have expected, that successor was Veronese. Aretino's condescension turns to bitterness; the critics nip, bite, scratch and howl; in a word, they become modernized. This would not matter at all if Jacopo still had the public's esteem. But suddenly the wheel turns. At thirty years of age, confident in his own powers, he comes into his own: he paints *St Mark Saving the Slave*, putting the whole of himself into the work. To astonish, to hit hard and take the world by storm—this was very much his style. For once, however, he will be the one to be disconcerted: the work stuns his contemporaries, but it scandalizes them. He finds he has zealous detractors, but not zealous defenders; one senses the presence of a cabal in the background: he is halted in his tracks.[3] As they square up to each other, both united and separated by a single malaise, Venice and its painter look each other in the eye and the understanding between them is gone. 'Jacopo,' says the city, 'has not fulfilled the promise of his adolescence.' And the artist says, 'The moment I revealed myself, they were disappointed. It wasn't *me* that they loved!' This misunderstanding degenerates into rancour on both sides: something is torn in the fabric of Venice.

1548 is the hinge year. *Before that date*, the gods were with him; *after it*, they were against him. No great misfortunes, just bad luck: you need to have a bellyful of it; the gods had smiled on the child the better to destroy the man. As a result, Jacopo changes into himself, becomes that frenzied, hunted outlaw, Tintoretto. Before this, we know nothing about him, except that he worked at breakneck speed: you cannot make a name for yourself at twenty without application. Afterwards, the application turns to rage; he wants to produce, to produce endlessly, to sell, to crush his rivals by the number and size of his paintings. There is something frantic in this upping of the pace: right up to his death, Robusti seems to be racing against the clock and it is impossible to say whether he is trying to find himself through work or flee himself in overwork. 'Greased-Lightning Tintoretto' sails under a pirate flag; for this speedy freebooter, all means are fair—with a marked preference for foul ones. Disinterested whenever disinterest pays, he lowers his eyes and refuses to quote a price, repeating like a lackey: 'You may pay whatever you like.' But lackeys are better placed than anyone to know that there's a tariff for carrying bags: they count on the client to fleece himself, out of generosity.

On other occasions, to secure a deal, he offers the merchandise at cost price: this bargain-basement contract will bring him other, more profitable ones. He learns that the Order of the *Crociferi* are to commission work from Paolo Caliari and, feigning ignorance of the fact, goes and offers them his services. They try to show him the door politely: 'We would be only too happy, but we want a Veronese.' 'A Veronese's an excellent idea,' he says, 'And who's going to paint you one?' 'But,' they reply with some surprise, 'We thought Paolo Caliari was just the man for the job . . .' To which Tintoretto, in turn astonished, replies: 'Caliari? What a strange idea. I'll do you a better Veronese than him. And cheaper.' The deal is struck and he is as good as his word. Twenty times he repeats the trick: twenty times he 'does' *Pordenones* and *Titians*—and always at a knock-down price.

The question that tormented him was how he could lower the costs. One day he found the answer— a mean-minded solution of genius—and it was to overturn a whole tradition. It was customary for the masters to have their paintings copied; the studio executed replicas and sold them at highly competitive prices, which meant there was also a secondary market for painting. To capture this clientele, Jacopo proposed to offer it something both *better* and *cheaper*. He did so by eliminating the originals. His painters would take their inspiration from his canvases, but would not *imitate* them. By simple, unvarying methods, his co-workers would produce something new without invention. To do this, they had merely to reverse the composition, to put the left on the right and the right on the left, to replace a female figure with an old man taken from another picture, leaving the woman to be re-used elsewhere. These operations required some training, but they took no more time than mere copying. And Tintoretto was able guilelessly to proclaim: 'You can acquire an original from me for the price of a copy.'

When they didn't want his paintings, he made a present of them. On 31 May 1564, at the Scuola San Rocco, the Brotherhood's ruling body decided to brighten up its meeting hall: the central oval of the ceiling was to be decorated with a painting on canvas.

Paolo Caliari, Jacopo Robusti, Schiavone, Salviati and Zuccaro were invited to submit sketches. Tintoretto bribed some servants and obtained the exact dimensions. He had already worked for the Brotherhood and I do not rule out the possibility that he even had accomplices within its governing *Banca e Zonta*. On the appointed day, each artist showed his drawing. When Robusti's turn came, the assembled company were thunderstruck: he climbed a ladder, removed a board and above their heads unveiled a stunning picture already finished and in place. Amid the rumblings of discontent, he explained: 'A sketch can be misleading. While I was at it, I preferred to complete the job. But if you don't like my work, Gentlemen, I shall make a present of it to you. Not to you, but to Saint Roch, your patron, who has shown me such kindness.' He had forced their hands and the old rogue knew it: the statutes of the Brotherhood forbade them to refuse any pious donation. All that remained was to register the event in the annals of the Scuola: 'On this day, the undersigned Jacopo Tintoretto, painter, has presented us with a picture: he asks no remuneration, undertakes to complete the work if required and declares himself satisfied.' And the 'undersigned', in his turn, writes: '*Io Jachomo Tentoretto pitor contento et prometo ut supra.*'

Contento? I'm sure he was! The donation spread panic among his competitors. It opened all the doors of the Scuola to him, delivering its immense, desert-like walls over to the furies of his brushwork and eventually bringing him an annual pension of a hundred ducats. So content was he, indeed, that he repeated the trick in 1571. At the Doges' Palace this time. The Signoria was looking to commemorate the Battle of Lepanto and had artists submit their competing sketches. Tintoretto brought a canvas and donated it. It was accepted with gratitude. Shortly afterwards, he sent them his bill.

The inclination will perhaps be to regard his shameful, though charming, craftiness as a feature of the age rather than of his character: Tintoretto wasn't personally a shark, but his century was one of sharp practice. In a way, this would not be wrong. If someone wished to condemn him on the strength of these anecdotes, I can see the defence that could be mounted. Beginning with the most serious argument:

namely, that no one could at the time *work on his own account*. Today, painting is a picture sale; in those days, it was a painter market. They stood in the public square, like the *braccianti*[4] in the little towns of southern Italy; the buyers arrived, examined them all, choosing just one to take off to their church, *scuola* or *palazzo*. You had to offer yourself, put yourself about, the way our theatre directors do; you had to accept any old work, the way they accept any old script in the wild hope of using it to show off what they can do. Everything was fixed by contract: the subject, the number, status and sometimes even poses of the figures depicted, the dimensions of the canvas; religious traditions and traditions of taste added their constraints. The clients had the moods and whims of our theatre producers; they also, sadly, had their sudden moments of inspiration: at a sign from them, the whole painting had to be redone. In the Medici palaces, Benozzo Gozzoli underwent long, exquisite torture at the hands of idiotic patrons;[5] where Tintoretto is concerned, one need only compare the *Paradise* in the Louvre with that in the Doges' Palace to see the degree of pressure he was under. Intransigence, a refusal to compromise and a proud self-imposed poverty didn't exist as possible solutions: the family had to be fed and the studio had to be kept running, the way machines have to be kept running today. In a word, you either had to paint to order or give up painting.

No one can blame Tintoretto for wanting to make money; certainly, in the middle years of his life he was rarely without work and there was no shortage of cash. This utilitarian's principle was that you don't do anything for nothing: painting would merely be a pastime if it didn't bring a monetary return. We shall see that, in later life, he bought himself a comfortable, plebeian residence in an unfashionable part of town. With this he had security; it was the crowning glory of his career. But it took all his savings and the Robusti children were forced to share a paltry inheritance: the studio equipment, a waning clientele and the house itself, which went to the eldest son and then to the son-in-law. Twelve years after her husband's death, Faustina bitterly recalled that he had left his family in dire straits. She was right to complain: Tintoretto had always been a law unto himself about such things.

There can be no doubt that he liked money, but he did so in the American way: he saw it merely as the outward mark of his success. Ultimately, this contract-chaser wanted just one thing: the means to carry on his profession. And then there was some justification for his dishonesties: they wouldn't even have been conceivable had he not at least had the upper hand in terms of professional skill, capacity for work, and speed. His 'sprinting' gave him his advantage: it took him as long to paint a good picture as others took to make bad sketches.

And if he plagiarized Veronese, Veronese did the same to him. We have to view their mutual borrow-ings as their contemporaries would have. For many of them, the great painters were mere trade names or corporate, legal persons. *We* want *this particular painting* first and foremost. And, through it, we get the whole man: we hang Matisse on our walls. But consider the *Crociferi*: they didn't care one whit for Caliari; they were after a certain style that suited their taste: a blissful stupidity, a pleasing splendour, and all trouble-free. They knew a trademark and a slogan: a picture signed by Veronese is a picture to set your mind at rest. That was what they wanted, nothing more. For his part, Caliari could do better and proved that he could: he painted an awe-inspiring Crucifixion.[6] But he was too good a businessman to overtax his genius. Given this state of affairs, it would be petty of us to blame Tintoretto for at times appropriating a style that belonged rightfully to no one. After all, he made an honest offer: 'You want mindless vivacity? I'll give it to you.'

I will happily concede all this. The point is not to judge him, but to establish whether his age felt itself unreservedly reflected in him. Now, the evidence on this score is quite plain: his methods shocked his contemporaries and they held them against him. They may perhaps have put up with a degree of unfair competition, but Tintoretto went too far. All over Venice, the same cry could be heard: 'That's too much!' Even in this merchant city, this excessively shrewd merchant was regarded as eccentric. At the Scuola San Rocco, when he had blustered his way to the commission, his fellow painters cried 'foul' so loudly that he felt the need to pacify them. The building, he pointed out, had other ceilings and walls; the work was only just beginning; once his donation was accepted he would slip away and leave the field to worthier men. Those unfortunate fellows didn't take long to discover he had been lying in his teeth: the Scuola was to become his fiefdom and no other painter set foot in it in his lifetime.

And yet this surely wasn't the beginning of their hatred of him. We may note, however, that the scandal occurred in 1561 and the first *Life* of Tintoretto appeared in 1567: the proximity of the dates adds the final touch of explanation to the origins and meaning of the spiteful gossip collected by Vasari. Were these the slanders of jealous rivals? But all the painters were frantically jealous of each other; why would these slanders all be against Robusti if he were not the 'black sheep' of the artists, if he did not represent in everyone's eyes the faults of their neighbours all gathered together in one single person and carried to extremes? The clients themselves seemed shocked by his methods. Not all of them, admittedly. But he had made a great many firm enemies. Master Zammaria de Zignioni, a member of the Brotherhood of San Rocco, promised fifteen ducats towards the decoration costs on the express condition that Jacopo did not undertake the work. And the annals of the Brotherhood indicate that after Tintoretto's *coup*, the *Banca e Zonta* held some sensitive and rather stormy sessions in the Scuola itself, with the embarrassing donation gleaming above their heads. Agreement was reached, but Master de Zignioni kept his ducats. Nor did the public authorities always seem well-disposed towards him. Tintoretto donated his *Battle of Lepanto* in 1571; in 1577, the painting was destroyed by fire. When it came to replacing it, it seemed reasonable for its painter to assume the Signoria would call on him to do the job. But, not at all: he was deliberately passed over in favour of the second-rate Vicentino. It may perhaps have been argued that the picture had not been greatly liked. But this is barely plausible: Jacopo kept his nose clean when he worked for the authorities; he 'did a Titian' and kept himself out of it. Moreover, since 1571, the government had commissioned several works from him. No, it wasn't that the Venetian administration intended to forego his services altogether, but it wanted to punish him for his sharp practice. In short, all were in agreement: he was an unfair competitor, a rogue painter; there must have been something rotten about him to have no friends at all.

You troubled fine souls who make the dead serve the edification of the living—and your own edification in particular—may treat his excess, if you will, as striking proof of his passion. But the fact remains that passions are as varied as the people who have them: there are the consuming and the reflective, the dreamy and the concerned, the practical, the abstract, the idling, the precipitate and a hundred others. I would term Tintoretto's passion practical, concerned/recriminatory and consuming/precipitate. The more I think about his lamentable tricks, the more convinced I am that they originated in a sickened heart. What a nest of vipers! There is everything in that heart: the delirium of pride and the madness of humility, thwarted ambitions and limitless confusion, dynamism and bad luck, the will to 'make it' and the dizzying sense of failure. His life is the story of a social climber gnawed at by fear; it begins merrily, briskly, with a solidly mounted offensive and then, after the grave reverse of 1548, the pace speeds up to an insane, infernal degree; Jacopo will fight on until his death, but he knows he will not win. Social climbing and anxiety—these are the two biggest vipers in the nest. If we really want to know him, we must draw closer and take a look at them.

No one is cynical. To heap reproaches on oneself without becoming wholly downcast is the pastime of saints. But only up to a certain point: these chaste individuals condemn their lewdness, these generous people denounce their avarice, but if they discover what is really blighting them—namely, saintliness—then, like all guilty men, they run for justifications. Tintoretto is not a saint; he knows the whole city frowns on his methods; if he stubbornly persists in them, this is because he feels *he* is in the right. But do not tell me he is conscious of his genius: genius, that foolish wager, knows what it dares but doesn't know its own worth. Nothing could be more wretched than that fretful temerity that longs for the moon and dies without ever having reached it: pride comes first, un-proven, unauthorized; when it becomes frenzied, you may call it genius if you will, but I don't really see what is to be gained by that. No: Tintoretto doesn't justify his roguishness either by the limited fullness of his skill or by the infinite void of his aspirations: he is de-fending his rights. Each time a commission goes to one of his colleagues, he feels a wrong is being done to him. He must be given his head: he will cover all the city's walls with his paintings. No *campo* will be too vast, no *sotto portico* too obscure for him not to wish to adorn them; he will plaster the ceilings with his pic-tures, passers-by will walk upon his finest images, his brush will spare neither the facades of the palazzi on the Grand Canal nor the gondolas, nor perhaps even the gondoliers. He is a man who feels he has received, as a birthright, the privilege of transforming his city into himself and we may argue, in a sense, that he is right.

When he begins his apprenticeship, painting is in a bad way. Florence is in open crisis. Venice, as is its wont, is saying nothing or lying. But we have clear proof that the sources of properly Rialtine inspiration have dried up. In the late fifteenth century, the city was deeply affected by Antonello da Messina's stays there: this is the decisive turning-point; from that point on, it imports its painters. I don't say it goes very far to look for them: but the most renowned of them come, nonetheless, from *terra firma*: Giorgione from Castelfranco, Titian from Pieve di Cadore, Paolo Caliari and Bonifazio dei Pitati from Verona, Palma Vecchio from Bergamo, Girolamo the Elder and Paris Bordone from Treviso, and Andrea Schiavone from Zara. And there are others I could mention. In actual fact, this aristocratic republic is, first and foremost, a technocracy; it always had the audacity to recruit its specialists from anywhere and the shrewdness to treat them as its own children. Moreover, this is the period when *la Serenissima*, thwarted on the seas and threatened by coalitions on the mainland, turns its attention to its hinterland and attempts to shore up its power by conquest: the new immigrants are, for the most part, natives of the annexed territories. All the same, with this massive importation of talent, Venice was betraying its unease. When you remember that most of the artists of the Quattrocento were born within its walls or at Murano, you cannot help thinking that the line could not have been carried on, after the Vivarini and Bellini families died out and after the death of Carpaccio, without an infusion of new blood.

Painting is like other trades: it was the patricians who made it easy for good craftsmen to come in; it was the patricians, demonstrating what we might call a cosmopolitan chauvinism, who saw the Republic of the Doges as a kind of melting pot. In the view of that jealous, distrustful aristocracy, foreigners made the best Venetians: if they adopted Venice, they did so because they had fallen in love with it; if they wanted to be adopted by it, they would tend to be compliant. But the local craftsmen certainly didn't see the newcomers the same way. And why should they? It was foreign competition. They were not so unwise as to protest and were outwardly welcoming, but there were still conflicts and, indeed, perpetual tensions and a resentful pride. Forced to bow to the foreigners' technical superiority, the native disguised his humiliation by insisting the more strongly on his prerogatives;

he agreed to give way to the more expert, more skilful craftsman, but he did so as a sacrifice for the
homeland: his rights remained intact. A Rialtan was
on home ground in Venice; German workers were better
at glassblowing, but they would never have the Venetian's birthright. Before they passed on, the great
painters of the Quattrocento had the bitter experience of seeing public taste desert them in favour of
young incomers who held them in contempt. That
foreigner Titian, for example, when he left one of the
Bellini brothers for the other (Gentile for Giovanni),
did so because he was in pursuit of another foreigner,
Antonello, that meteor who had rent the sky of
Venice and parted the waters of its lagoon twenty
years before. In Giovanni himself Tiziano Vecelli was
not interested at all: what he sought in him was a reflection. We have proof of this in the fact that he very
quickly left the master for his disciple and studied at
the feet of Giorgione: in the eyes of the second 'alien',
this third one seemed to be the true heir to the first.
Now, Tiziano and Giorgione belong to the same generation; it may even be that the student was older than
the teacher. Did the two Bellinis not realize at that

point that they had had their day? And what of Giovanni's true disciples? What did they say? And what did the others think, the true representatives of the school of Murano? Many of them were youths or men still young; they had all felt the influence of Antonello, but through 'Bellinismo'; the colours and light came from Messina, but Giovanni had acclimatized them; it was through him that they had become Venetian. It was a matter of honour to these young men to remain faithful, but fidelity was stifling them; they did their best to adapt to the new demands without abandoning the rather crude techniques they had been taught; but this was to condemn themselves to mediocrity. What bitterness they must have felt seeing two young interlopers joining forces to break with local traditions, to rediscover a Sicilian's secrets and carry painting effortlessly to the peak of perfection? Yet Giovanni still ruled the roost; that admirable artist's name was known throughout northern Italy. The barbarian invasion began only in his last years; after his death in 1516, the floodgates opened.

Now, it so happened that at the height of the invasion, the greatest painter of the century came into the world in the heart of this occupied city, in an alleyway on the Rialto. Dark plebeian pride, always humiliated and repressed yet ever watchful, jumped at the occasion and slipped into the heart of the only Rialtan who still had talent and lifted and inflamed it. Let us remember that he wasn't directly a child of the people, nor entirely a scion of the bourgeoisie. His father belonged to the comfortable artisan class. It was a point of honour for these petty-bourgeois not to work for others: had he been a worker's son, Jacopo would perhaps have remained the obscure collaborator of an artist; as the son of a master craftsman, he had to become one himself or fall in status. He would come up through the ranks, but the honour of his family and his class forbade him to remain in them. One can see why he wouldn't leave a good impression in the studio where he served his apprenticeship: he entered it with the intention of leaving as soon as possible, to attain the place preordained for him in the social order. And then, what? Schiavone (or Bordone or Bonifazio dei Pitati—it matters little which) no doubt regarded him as an interloper: but Jacopo in turn regarded his master as a foreigner—in other words, as a thief. He was a *native*, this Little Dyer; Venice was his by blood. Had he been mediocre, he would have remained modest, though resentful. But he was brilliant and knew it, so he wanted to outdo everyone. In the eyes of a Rialtan, the foreigners had only their professional worth to protect them: if Jacopo did better work than them, they would have to disappear, even if it meant murdering them. No one paints or writes without a mandate to do so: would we dare to if 'I' were not 'Another?'[7] Jacopo was mandated by an entire working population to recover, by his art, the privileges of the pure-blood Venetian. This explains his clear conscience: in his heart, popular recrimination becomes an austere, assertive passion; he has been entrusted with the mission of gaining recognition for his rights; for one with such a just cause, any means of achieving it are acceptable: no quarter is given or asked. The unfortunate thing is that his struggle against the undesirables leads him to fight the patricians themselves and their assimilation policy, on behalf of the indigenous artisans. When he goes down the street shouting 'Veronese to Verona!', it is the government he is challenging. As soon as he realizes this, he takes a step back and then, just as quickly, resumes his previous course. Hence this curious mixture of rigidity and flexibility: as the cautious subject of a police state, he always yields or pretends to; as the *native-born* citizen of the most beautiful of cities, his arrogance gets the better of him; he can yield to the point of servility without losing his stiff-necked pride. It is of no use: the plots he hatches against the aristocracy's protégés are either spoiled by his impatience and his irreparable acts of clumsiness or they rebound on him of their own accord. This sheds a new light on the grudge *la Serenissima* bore against him. Ultimately, he is only demanding what they would perhaps have conceded, but his quarrelsome submissiveness irritates the authorities: they see him as a rebel. Or they regard him at the very least as suspect and, in the end, they are not wrong. One has only to see what his first transport of emotion led him to.

First to that conscientious, almost sadistic violence I shall call the full employment of oneself. Having been born among the common people, who bear the weight of a heavily hierarchical society, he shares their tastes and fears: we can see their prudence even in his presumptuousness. His nearest and dearest, shrewd, spirited and a little cautious, taught him the price of things, instructed him in life's dangers, showed him which hopes are permitted and which forbidden. Precise and limited opportunities, a destiny marked out in advance, already legible, a future only half-open, imprisoned by transparency, a little posy of flowers too distinctly visible in the crystal of a paperweight—all these things kill dreams: you come to want only what you can have. Moderation of this kind produces madmen and gives rise to the fiercest ambitions, though short-term ones. Jacopo's ambition sprang into being all of a sudden, already booted and helmeted, with its particular virulence and forms; it is identical with that slim shaft of light, the possible. Or, rather, nothing is *possible*: there is the end and the means, the prescribed task. One will raise oneself above the heaviest, lowest clouds, one will touch a taut, luminous skin with one hand—this is the ceiling. There are other ceilings, clearer and clearer membranes, thinner and thinner ones. And perhaps, way up at the top, there's the blue of the sky. But Tintoretto couldn't give a damn about that; everyone has his own upward force and his natural resting place. He knows he is gifted; he has been told it is a form of capital. If he proves his ability, he will have a profitable enterprise to his name and will find the funds to equip it. He is set on his way with a long lifetime ahead; his time is already spoken for: there is this seam to be mined and he will do so until both seam and miner are exhausted. Around the same time, that other glutton for work, Michelangelo, turns his nose up at the opportunity; he begins the work and runs off without finishing it. Tintoretto *always* finishes his work, with the fearsome application of a man who always finishes his sentences, come what may. Death itself waited for him at San Giorgio, it let him apply the last brushstroke to the last painting or, at least, give the last instructions to his collaborators. He never in the whole of his life permitted himself a whim, a moment's distaste or a preference; not even the luxury of a dream. He must have repeated this watchword to himself on his tired days: to turn down a commission is to make a present to the competition.

One has to produce at all costs. On this point, the will of one man and that of a city are in agreement. A hundred years earlier, Donatello criticized Uccello for sacrificing creation to research and carrying the love of painting to the point of no longer producing pictures. But that was in Florence: Florentine artists had just launched themselves into the hazardous adventure of *perspective*; they were trying to construct a new plastic space by applying the laws of geometric optics to painted objects. *Autres temps, autres moeurs.* At Venice, with Titian reigning supreme, everyone was of the view that painting had just achieved the height of perfection, that there was simply no further to go: art is dead, long live life. The great barbarism begins with Aretino's foolish remarks 'How lifelike it is! How true it is! *You'd never think it was painted*!' In short, it was time for painting to take a back seat to *positive creations*: the inspired merchants wanted useful beauty. The art work must give pleasure to the *amateur*, bear witness before Europe to Venice's most serene splendour and strike awe into the populace. The awe has lasted to this day: when faced with Venetian cinemascope, we humble tourists mutter: 'It's directed by Titian, it's a Veronese production, it's a performance by Pordenone, a staging by Vicentino.'

Jacopo Robusti shares the prejudices of his age and our smart observers hold that against him. How many times have I heard it said, 'Tintoretto—mere theatrics!' And yet no one in the world, either before or after, has taken the passion for experimentation further. With Titian, painting flowers to the point of suffocation; it negates itself by its own perfection. Jacopo sees this death as the necessary precondition for a resurrection: everything is beginning, everything remains to be done; we shall come back to this. But—and here is his major contradiction—he will never tolerate his experiments restricting his productivity. Were there only a single wall left in Venice unpainted, the artist's duty is to paint it: morality forbids one to turn a studio into a laboratory. Art is both a serious profession and a bitter struggle against the invaders. Like Titian, like Veronese, Jacopo will serve up exquisite corpses. With one difference: these dead bodies have a feverishness about them that might be a revival of life or the beginnings of decay. And if he absolutely has to be compared to our film directors, it is *in this respect* that he is like them: he takes on mindless scenarios and then subtly loads his own obsessions on to them.

One must fool the buyer, give him more than his money's worth: he will have his Catherine, Teresa or Sebastian; and for the same price he can be in the picture, and with his wife or brothers if he insists. But underneath, behind the sumptuous, banal facade of this *creation*, Tintoretto carries on with his experimentation. All his major works have a double meaning: his narrow utilitarianism masks an endless questioning. In setting his research within the framework of the paid commission, he is forced to revolutionize painting while at the same time respecting the client's stipulations. This is the deep-seated reason for his overwork; it will later be the reason for his downfall.

And yet he still had to corner the market. We have seen that he worked at this. But if we go back, now, over his methods, they will show up in a fresh light. Tintoretto's rebellion becomes more radical: in revolt against the 'melting-pot' policy, he is forced to infringe guild rules or customs. Unable to eliminate competition, the advantages of which they do in fact acknowledge, the government strive to channel it through formal contests. If it is their taste that decides in the last instance, the rich and powerful will preserve public order and establish that flexible form of protectionism that is 'managed competition'. Are they sincere? Without a doubt, and everything would be perfect if we had proof of their capacities. But we have to take their word on that score. It does happen that they make the right choice, but at other times, they opt for Vicentino. For his part, Tintoretto always manages to escape the test. Is it because he denies them any competence? Absolutely not: he simply feels they have no right to treat a native-born Venetian on the same footing as interlopers.

The fact remains that these contests exist: by avoiding them, our rebel is deliberately seeking to destroy protectionism. He is in a corner: since the authorities claim to judge on the basis of value, and since he rejects their judgement, he has either to give up painting or to make his reputation by the quality of his painting. That is no problem; he finds other ways, pips his competitors to the post and presents the judges with a *fait accompli*; he deploys his skill, his speed and his collaborators' diligence to achieve a level of mass production that puts a bomb under all the price scales, allowing him to sell his canvases for

paltry sums—or even give them away. There is an avenue in Rome with two cheap clothes shops on opposite sides of the street; the shopkeepers have, I
imagine, come to some agreement to simulate a fight
to the death—unless the two establishments are
owned by the same person, a tragic actor, who enjoys
eternally pitting the two aspects of his nature against
each other. On the one side, there is a window criss-
crossed with funereal notices: *Prezzi disastrosi*! On the
other, little multi-coloured posters announce: *Prezzi
da ridere*! *da ridere*! *da ridere*! This has been going on for
years and I can never pass these shops without being
reminded of Tintoretto. Did he choose to laugh or
cry? Both, in my view, depending on the client. We
may even suppose that he sniggered a little in solitude,
and that he lamented when he was among his family,
complaining that he was being bled dry. All the same,
it was 'sale time' all year round in his studio, and his
clients felt the lure of these clearance prices. Having
started out to commission a tiny inset portrait, they
ended up giving him every wall in the house to paint.
He was the first to break the already crumbling bonds
of guild brotherhood: for this pre-Darwinian

Darwinist, fellow guild members became his closest enemies. He beat Hobbes to the slogan of absolute competition: *Homo homini lupus*. Venice was roused to indignation. If a vaccine couldn't be found against the Tintoretto virus, he would dissolve corporate good order and leave only a cloud of antagonisms and molecular solitudes. The Republic condemned these new methods, called them felonies, spoke of botched work, undercutting, monopoly practices. Later—much later—other cities, in another language, would honour these methods as 'the struggle for life' or as 'mass production', would speak of 'dumping' or 'monopoly practices', etc. For the moment, this notorious character lost on the swings everything he had gained on the roundabouts. He won commissions at bayonet point, but socially he was shunned. In a strange turnabout, he, the *native*, the hundred per cent Rialtan, was the one who seemed an interloper—and almost an undesirable—in his own city.

The inevitable consequence is that he will perish if he doesn't start a family. First, to stifle competition from within his studio: this champion of free markets reverses the biblical precept; he makes sure others can never do unto him as has done unto them. And then, he needs total approval; outsiders working with him might be frightened off or discouraged by the vague sense of scandal around him; how much time he might waste stiffening their resolve. From now on, this thunder will release only damp squibs of lightning. What need has he of disciples? He wants other hands, other pairs of arms and that is all. Through absolute competition to family-based enterprise: this is the path. In 1550, he marries Faustina dei Vescovi and, there and then, begins producing children. Doing so the way he produces pictures—with indefatigable bolts of thunder. And this excellent child-bearer has only one failing: she overdoes the daughters somewhat. Never mind, he will put them all in a convent, except for two: Marietta, whom he keeps by him, and Ottavia, whom he marries off to a painter. The thunder will fecundate Faustina as many times as necessary to get two sons from her, Domenico and Marco. But he didn't wait for them to come along before he taught the trade to his eldest daughter, Marietta. A woman painter in Venice is no everyday affair: what a hurry he must have been in! Finally, around 1575, it was mission accomplished: the new personnel consisted of his son-in-law Sebastian Casser, Marietta, Domenico and Marco. The symbol of a domestic association is the *domus* that shelters and imprisons it. At around this same date, Jacopo bought a house. He would spend the rest of his days there. In this little *lazaretto*, the leper would live in semi-quarantine amid his family, loving them all the more, the more *others* there were to detest him. Seen *in the home*, in his work, in his relations with his wife and children, we find quite a different side to him: what a stern moralist! And a little Calvinistic round the edges perhaps? He had all the attributes: pessimism and work, the spirit of lucre and devotion to his family. Human nature is marred by original sin; men are divided by their interests. The Christian will be saved by works: let him battle against all; let him labour unremittingly, being hard on himself and on others, to embellish the Earth God has entrusted to him; he will find the mark of divine favour in the material success of his enterprise. As for the stirrings of his heart, let him keep them for the flesh of his flesh: his sons. Did Venice feel the influence of the reformed religion? It certainly did. In the

second half of the century we find there a curious individual, Fra Paolo Sarpi. He has the ear of the patricians, is a friend of Galileo's, is hostile to Rome and
openly maintains close ties with foreign Protestant circles. But if, in some intellectual circles, we can detect
tendencies vaguely sympathetic to the Reformation,
it is more than probable that the petty-bourgeoisie
knew nothing of them. It would be more accurate to
say that *la Serenissima* reformed itself. And this reformation had been going on a long time: Venice's merchants lived from credit; they could not accept the
Church's condemnation of those it insisted on calling
usurers; they encouraged science when it brought
practical benefits and scorned Roman obscurantism.
The Venetian state had always affirmed the precedence of the civil authorities; that was its doctrine; it
would not change it. In practical terms, it was the state
that had control of its clergy, and, when Pius V took
it into his head to remove ecclesiastics from lay juris-
diction, the Senate rejected the move outright. And
for many reasons the government regarded the Holy
See more as a temporal, military power than a spiritual
one. Though this did not prevent it, when the interests

of the Republic were at stake, from cosying up to the Pope, hunting out heretics or, to please the Very Christian Monarch, organizing a sumptuous celebration in honour of Saint-Bartholomew. Tintoretto took his pseudo-Calvinism from his city itself: unwittingly, the painter tapped into the latent Protestantism one finds at the time in all the great capitalist cities.[8] The status of artists was particularly ambivalent in this period, especially in Venice. But let us try our luck; perhaps this very ambiguity will enable us to understand Jacopo's dark puritanical passion.

Vuillemin has argued that 'the Renaissance [had] lent artists the features that Antiquity reserved for men of action and with which the Middle Ages adorned its saints.'[9] This is not wrong. But the opposite seems to me at least as true: '[In the sixteenth century] painting and sculpture were still regarded as manual arts; all honour was reserved for poetry. Hence the efforts made by the figurative arts to compete with literature.'[10] There can be no doubt, in fact, that Aretino, that poor man's Petronius, that rich man's Malaparte, was the arbiter of taste and elegance for the bright young things of the Venetian patriciate, nor that Titian prided himself on being one of his circle: all Titian's fame was barely enough to make him the equal of Aretino. And Michelangelo? His weakness was the belief that he was a naturally patrician soul and this illusion ruined his life. As a very young man, he would have liked to have studied the classics and written: a man of the lesser nobility may take up the pen without losing status. He took up the chisel out of necessity and never got over it. Michelangelo looked down on sculpture and painting from the pinnacle of his shame; he had the awkward, empty joy of feeling superior to his occupation. Forced into silence, he attempted to give a language to the dumb arts, to create a profusion of allegories and symbols; he wrote a book on the ceiling of the Sistine chapel and he tortured marble to compel it to speak.

What conclusions are we to draw? Were the painters of the Renaissance demigods or manual labourers? Well, it just depends: it depends on the clients and the method of remuneration. Or, rather, they were manual workers *first*. After that, they became employees of the court or remained local masters. It was up to them to choose—or be chosen.

Raphael and Michelangelo were agents of the state; they lived haughtily but in a condition of dependence. Even a temporary fall from grace could put them on the street; on the other hand, the sovereign took care of their publicity. That sacred personage yielded a portion of his supernatural powers to his chosen ones: the glory of the throne fell on them like a ray of sunlight and they reflected it on to the people; the divine right of kings produced divine-right painters. With it, mere daubers were changed into supermen. And what were they, in fact, these petty-bourgeois whom a giant hand had plucked from the crowd and suspended between heaven and earth—these satellites who dazzled with a borrowed brilliance—but human beings raised above humanity? Heroes they were indeed: that is to say, they were intercessors, intermediaries. Even today, when they employ the word 'genius', nostalgic republicans still worship, through them, the light of that dead star, monarchy.

Tintoretto was a member of the other species: he worked for merchants, civil servants and parish churches. I am not saying he was uneducated: he was sent to school at seven and must have left it at twelve knowing how to read and count. And, most importantly, how could one not term 'education' that patient training of senses, hand and mind, that traditionalist practice of trial and error, which studio painting still represented in the years around 1530. But he would never have the cultural baggage of the court painters. Michelangelo wrote sonnets; it is said today that Raphael knew Latin; and the frequenting of intellectuals eventually gave Titian himself a veneer of refinement. Compared with these fashionable men, Tintoretto seems unlettered: he would never have the taste and leisure to engage in the life of ideas or the world of letters. He didn't give a fig for the humanism of the literate classes. Venice had few poets and even fewer philosophers: in his view, that was already too many and he didn't mix with any. Not that he avoided them: he simply knew nothing of them. He accepted their social superiority. Aretino had the right to congratulate him with protective benevolence: that lofty personage was *admitted to society*; he was part of fashionable Venice; he was invited to dinner by patricians who would not even greet a painter in the street. But did he have to envy him into the bargain? Did he have

to envy him *because he was a writer*? Jacopo felt that the
works of the mind had a highly immoral air of gratu-
itousness about them: God put us on the Earth to
gain our daily bread by the sweat of our brow, but
writers do not sweat. Do they even work? Jacopo
never opened a book, with the exception of his
missal; the bizarre idea of stretching his talent to compete with literature was not one that would have occurred to him: there is everything in his pictures, but
they have *no message to deliver*; they are silent as the
world itself. Ultimately, this craftsman's son respected
only physical effort and manual creation. What enchanted him in the painting profession was the fact
that occupational skill was taken to the point of prestidigitation, and the refinement of the product to the
point of quintessence. The artist was, for him, the
supreme worker: he tired himself out and exhausted
matter in order to produce and sell visions. This
would not prevent him working for princes if he liked
them. But when all was said and done, he didn't like
them: they frightened him without inspiring him. He
never tried to approach them or to make himself
known: one might say he made every effort to restrict

his fame to within the walls of Venice. It is not perhaps well-known that he never left the city, except once, in his sixties, to travel to nearby Mantua. Even then, he had to be begged to do so: they wanted him to hang his paintings himself and he was adamant he would not go unless he could take his wife with him. The demand attests, in part, to his strong conjugal feelings, but it says much, too, about his dread of travel. And we should not be deceived into thinking his Venetian colleagues shared the same aversion; they went gallivanting off in all directions. And a hundred years earlier Gentile Bellini did so by sea. What adventurers they were! He, by contrast, was a mole: he was at ease only in the narrow tunnels of his molehill. If he imagined the world, agoraphobia laid him low; yet, if he had to choose, he would still rather endanger himself than his paintings. He accepted commissions from abroad—and 'abroad' for him began at Padua—but he didn't go looking for them. What a contrast between this indifference and his passionate pursuit of work at the Doges' Palace, at the Scuola San Rocco and from the *Crociferi*! He entrusted the execution of these other works to his collaborators, overseeing these mass productions from a distance, refraining from putting his own hand to them, as though he feared for the tiniest scintilla of his talent to go outside his homeland: Europe would get only his 'B Pictures'. You can find Raphael, Titian and a hundred others at the Uffizi, the Prado, the National Gallery, the Louvre and in Munich or Vienna. All of them, or almost all, but not Tintoretto. He kept himself fiercely for his fellow-citizens and you will know nothing of him unless you go and look for him in his native city, for the very good reason that he didn't *wish* to leave it.

But we must clarify this point, for in Venice itself he had two very different clienteles. He laid siege to the public officials and, naturally, if the Senate gave him work, the whole of the studio got involved, including the head of the household. At the Doges' Palace, in lighting that shows them to advantage, you can still see the works of a strong collective personality bearing the name of Tintoretto. But if it's Jacopo Robusti who interests you, then leave the Piazzetta behind, walk across the Piazza San Marco, take the humpbacked bridges over the canals and wander around in a labyrinth of dark alleyways where there are still darker churches for you to enter. And there he is. In the Scuola San Rocco you have him—in person, without Marietta, Domenico or Sebastiano Casser. He worked there alone. These canvases are shrouded in a dirty mist, or reflections make it difficult to see them properly. Wait patiently till your eyes get used to the light: you will in the end see a rose in the shadows, a guardian spirit in the semi-darkness. And who paid for these paintings? Sometimes it was the church's congregation, sometimes the members of the Brotherhood: big and petty bourgeois. They were his real audience, the only one he loved.

There was nothing of the demigod about this commercial painter. With a little luck, he would be notorious, famous, but he would never gain genuine glory: his clientele of outsiders did not have the power to hallow him in that way. Of course, the renown of his august colleagues reflected on the whole of the profession and he shone a little too. Did he envy them their glory? Perhaps. But he did nothing of what would have been needed to acquire it. The favour of princes could go hang: it was something that enslaved you. Jacopo Robusti took pride in remaining a small master, a small trader in the Fine Arts, paid by the job, but in command of his own establishment. He made no distinction between the economic independence of the producer and the freedom of the artist. His scheming proves that he hoped somehow to revolutionize market conditions, to promote demand through supply: among the members of the Brotherhood of San Rocco did he not slowly and patiently create a need for art—for a certain art—that only he could satisfy? His autonomy was all the better preserved by the fact of working for collective bodies— such as consorteries or parishes—and by their taking their decisions by majority vote.

That false aristocrat Michelangelo and that son of the soil Titian felt the attraction of monarchy directly. Tintoretto was born in a milieu of self-employed workers. The craftsman is an amphibian: as a manual worker, he is proud of his hands; as a petty-bourgeois, the upper bourgeoisie exerts an attraction: it was that class which, by the mere play of competition, enabled some air to penetrate into a stifling protectionist system. There was in those days *hope for the bourgeoisie* in

Venice. It was a slim hope; the aristocracy had long since taken its precautions: in that stratified universe, you could *become* rich but you had to *be born* a patrician. But even wealth was limited: not only did the trader or industrialist remain confined to their class, but the most lucrative occupations had long been closed to them; the State granted the *appalto*—the hiring of galleys—to aristocrats alone. Sombre and dreamy bourgeoisie![11] Everywhere else, in Europe, the middle classes were turning against their own past—buying up titles and castles as quickly as they could. In Venice, they were denied everything, even the lowly pleasure of betrayal. They would, then, betray in imagination. Arriving from Piacenza, Giovita Fontana launched herself into business, earned a fortune and spent it on a *palazza* on the Canale Grande. There is an entire existence in these few words: a fierce desire, once satisfied, turns in latter years into snobbish reverie; a merchantess dies and is reborn as an imaginary patrician. The rich commoners thrashed around, hiding away their nocturnal fantasies. Grouped into confraternities, they consumed their energies in charitable works, their melancholy austerity contrasting with the melancholy orgies of a disenchanted patriciate.

For the Republic no longer ruled the seas. The aristocracy gradually began to decline, the bankruptcy rate increased, the ranks of the impoverished nobility swelled, while the other nobles lost the spirit of enterprise: these sons of ship-owners bought up land, became *rentiers*. Mere 'citizens' were already replacing them in certain functions: the galleys fell under the command of the bourgeois. The bourgeoisie was still far from regarding itself as a rising class; it didn't even dare to believe it could one day take over from the fallen nobility: let us say, rather, that it was seized by an obscure agitation that rendered its condition less bearable and made a resigned attitude more difficult.

Tintoretto didn't dream. Never. If people's ambitions are geared to the openness of their social horizons, then the most ambitious commoners in Venice were the petty-bourgeois, since they still had a chance of rising out of their class. But the painter felt deep affinities with his customers; he appreciated their commitment to hard work, their moralism, their practicality. He liked their nostalgia and, above all, he shared their deepest aspiration: they all, if only to produce, to buy and to sell, had need of freedom. These are the clues to his *arrivisme*: he was drawn on by an up-draught from the heights. Disturbances in the heavens, a distant, invisible ascent opened up a vertical future; he climbed, this Cartesian diver; with the new spirit in him, a draught of fresh air drew him upwards: since childhood he had thought like a bourgeois. But the contradictions of his class of origin were to limit his ambitions: as a small trader, he hoped to cross the line; as a 'worker', he sought to work with his hands. That was enough to mark out his place. There were—approximately—7,600 patricians in Venice, 13,600 citizens, 127,000 artisans, workers and small traders, 1,500 Israelites, 12,900 servants and 550 beggars. Leaving aside Jews, nobles, beggars and servants, Tintoretto focussed exclusively on the ideal demarcation line that divided the commoners into two groups: 13,600 on one side, 127,000 on the other. He wanted to be the first among the latter and the last among the former: in a word, the humblest of the rich and the most distinguished among the purveyors to the rich. In the heart of troubled Venice, that made this artisan a false bourgeois who was more genuine than the genuine article. What the Brotherhood of

San Rocco would love in him and his paintings would be the beautified image of a bourgeoisie that was not disloyal.

Even when working for the Supreme Pontiff, Michelangelo would think he was demeaning himself. That contempt sometimes afforded him a critical distance: this nobleman had some cavalier ideas on art. Tintoretto was entirely the opposite; he operated at a level beyond that of his birth. Without art, what would he be? A dyer. It was his own strength that had lifted him out of his native condition and what kept him at that level was his dignity. He had to work or fall back to the bottom of the pile. Objectivity? Critical distance? Where would he acquire such things? He hadn't the time to examine his thoughts about painting? Who knows if he even *saw* it? Michelangelo thought too much: he was a Marquis de Carabas, an intellectual. Tintoretto didn't know what he was doing: he painted.

So much for his *arrivisme*: the destiny of this artist was to embody bourgeois Puritanism in a declining aristocratic Republic. In other places, this sombre humanism was the order of the day; at Venice, it would disappear without even having become conscious of itself, though not without arousing the distrust of an ever watchful aristocracy. The surliness that official, bureaucratic Venice society displayed towards Tintoretto was the same surliness the patriciate showed towards the Venetian bourgeoisie. These quarrelsome merchants and their painter represented a danger to the order of *La Serenissima*: an eye had to be kept on them.

One may find a degree of disdainful pride in the stubborn refusal to compete: 'I know of no one to rival
me and I accept no judge.' Michelangelo would perhaps have said that. The unfortunate thing is that Tintoretto did not. On the contrary, if he were invited to
submit a sketch, he would rush to comply. After that,
we know he flung his thunderbolts. More or less in the
way a squid squirts out its ink. Lighting bolts have a
blinding effect and the spectators weren't able to make
out his painting. And, indeed, everything was arranged
so that they never needed to view it, nor, particularly,
evaluate it. When the dazzle had dissipated, the canvas

was hung and the gift recorded. They had been completely hoodwinked. Either I am very much mistaken or this is an evasion on his part; it seems as though he was afraid to confront his adversaries. Would he go to such ingenious lengths if he were confident that his talent would win out? Would he deign to astonish his contemporaries with the quantity of his output if they unreservedly admired its quality?

And then this passion for asserting himself through suppressing his own personality was even more striking in competitions. But it was his style, his trademark: the slightest comparison offended his sensibilities; being set alongside others troubled him. In 1559, the Church of San Rocco commissioned from him *The Impotent Man at the Pool of Bethesda* to go alongside a Pordenone. No one asked him to imitate the style of his predecessor and there could be no competition between the two painters.[12] Antonio de' Sacchis[13] had been dead for twenty years. If he could in the past have influenced the younger man, the time for influences was over: Jacopo was now the master of his art. Yet, the urge was too strong to resist: he had to 'do' a Pordenone. A very good account has been given of how he 'exaggerated the baroque violence of gestures . . . by the clash between the monumental figures and the architecture into which they were intimately inserted' and how he 'achieved this effect by lowering the ceiling of the hall . . . by [using] the columns themselves . . . [to] arrest the gestures and freeze their violence'.[14]

In short, he trembled at the idea of being eternally imprisoned in an inert face-off: 'Compare, if you will, the Pordenone with the Pordenone; I, Jacopo Robusti, am not here.' He contrived, of course, that the false de Sacchis would crush the genuine one. His withdrawal was no rout: he departed with a defiant shout on his lips: 'I take them all on, ancients and moderns, and defeat them on their own home ground.' But here precisely lies the element that will seem suspect: why does he need to play their game, to submit to their rules, when he would only have to be himself to crush them? What resentment there is in his insolence: he is a Cain murdering all the Abels who are preferred to him: 'You like Veronese? Well, when I deign to imitate him, I can do better; you see him as a man, but he is merely a method.' What humility too: from time to time, this outcast slips into the skin of another to experience, in his turn, the sweetness of being loved. And then sometimes you'd think the courage to display his scandalous genius had deserted him; weary of the struggle, he leaves it in the semi-darkness and attempts to prove it by *reductio ad absurdum*: 'Since I paint the best Veroneses and the best Pordenones, just imagine *what I can do* when I consent to be myself.' In fact, he very rarely gave himself such consent, unless he was shown total trust from the start and left quite alone in an empty room. The origin of this lay, of course, in the hostility displayed towards him. But the painter's timidity and the bias of his fellow-citizens both originated in the same disturbing moment: in 1584, at Venice, at the hand of Tintoretto and before the patricians, art-lovers and aesthetes, *painting gave itself a fright*.

A long process of development began here and it was everywhere to substitute the profane for the sacred: cold, sparkling and frosty, the various branches of human activity will emerge one after the other from their sweet intermingling in the divine. Art was affected: out of a bank of mist emerged the sumptuous disenchantment that was painting. It still remembered the time when Duccio or Giotto showed God the Creation exactly as it had left His hands: as soon as He had recognized His works, the affair was in the bag and the world was, for all eternity, in a frame. Between the picture—the realm of the Sun—and the supreme Eye, monks and prelates would sometimes interpose their transparent forms; they would come on tiptoe to see what God Himself saw, and then they would excuse themselves and leave. It was over: the Eye was closed, the Heavens blind. So what happened? First, there was a change of clientele: so long as one was working for clerics, all was well; the day the biggest of the Florentine bankers formed the curious notion of decking out his house with frescoes, the Almighty retreated, sickened, into his role as Lover of Souls. And then there was the great Florentine adventure: the conquest of perspective. Perspective is a profane thing—sometimes, even, a profanation. Take Mantegna's Christ, painted lengthways, his feet in the foreground and his head at the back of beyond. Do you think the Father could be happy with a foreshortened Son? God is absolute proximity, the universal embrace of Love: can one take the universe that

He made—and that He constantly preserves from annihilation—and show it to Him *from a distance*? Is it
for Beings to conceive and produce Non-Being? Is it
for the Absolute to engender the Relative? Is it right
that Light should contemplate Shade? That Reality
should take itself for Appearance? No, this is the eternal story beginning again: Innocence, the Tree of
Knowledge, Original Sin and the Casting-out from the
Garden. Only, this time, the apple is called 'perspective'. But the Adamites of Florence merely nibble at
it rather than eating, which prevents them from learning immediately of their Fall: in mid-Quattrocento,
Uccello still believes himself to be in Paradise, and
poor old Alberti, the theorist of the 'perspectivists', is
still presenting Geometric Optics as an Ontology of
Visibility. When all is said and done, he remains so
guileless as to demand of the divine Gaze that it approve perspective's 'lines of flight'. To this absurd re-
quest Heaven remained silent: the creature was
smartly consigned to that nothingness which is properly his own and which he had just rediscovered. Distance, banishment, separation—these negations mark
our limits; only man has a horizon. Alberti's window

opens on to a measurable universe, but that rigorous miniature depends entirely on the point that defines our anchorage and dispersal: namely, on our eyes. In his Annunciation, between the Angel and the Virgin, Piero della Francesca shows us an unfathomable arrangement of columns: this is an appearance; in themselves and for their Creator, these inert masses of white, each the same and each incomparable, continue their slumber: perspective is a violence human weakness inflicts on God's little world. A hundred years later in the Netherlands, they will rediscover the Being in the depths of Appearing and appearance will recover its dignity as emergence: painting will have new aims; it will find a new meaning. But, before Vermeer can give us the sky, the stars, day and night, the moon and the earth in the form of a little wall of bricks, the burghers of the North will have to win their greatest victories and forge their humanism.

In Italy in the sixteenth century, artists' hearts are still aglow with faith; that faith combats the atheism of the eye and the hand. Through wishing to cleave ever more keenly to the Absolute, they have developed techniques that throw them into a relativism they detest. Mystified dogmatists that they are, they can neither press forward nor go back. If God no longer looks at the pictures they paint, who will bear witness for them? They reflect man's powerlessness back to him: where will he find the strength to stand surety for them? And then, if painting's only purpose is to gauge the extent of our short-sightedness, it isn't worth an hour's trouble. Showing man to the Almighty, who deigned to raise him from the mire, was an act of thanksgiving, a sacrifice. But why would you show him to Man? Why show him *as he is not*? The artists of the end of the century—those born around 1480: Titian, Raphael and Giorgione— reached an accommodation with Heaven. We shall come back to this. And then the wealth and effectiveness of means still concealed the baleful indeterminacy of ends. We may presume Raphael had some premonition of this: he didn't give a damn for anything; chased after loose women, sold cheap prints, and, out of *Schadenfreude*, encouraged his collaborators to make obscene etchings: his was a suicide by facility. In any event, the joy of painting disappears with these legendary figures. In the second quarter of the

century, painting runs wild, led astray by its own perfection. In the barbarous taste contemporaries affected for great *realizzazioni*, we can discern an unease:
the public calls for all the splendours of realism to be
used to conceal one's subjectivity; for the author of
the work to efface himself before life itself, to let himself be forgotten. The desirable thing would be to
come across paintings unawares, on the edge of a
wood, and for the characters in them to tear themselves from the canvas and, in a shower of broken
fragments of picture frame, to jump at the throats of
passers-by. The object should reabsorb its visibility,
should contain it within itself, should deflect attention from it by a continuous appeal to all the senses
and, in particular, to touch. Everything should be
done to replace *representation* by an implicit participation of the spectator in the spectacle; horror and tenderness should throw men up against their simulacra
and, if possible, in the midst of these, desire, cutting
through all restrictions of perspective, should discover
that *ersatz* of divine ubiquity: the immediate presence
of the flesh. The Reason of the eye should be respected, and yet it should be combated by the reasons

of the heart. What was wanted was *the thing itself*, and that it should be a crushing presence; that it should be bigger than nature, more present and more beautiful. Such a desire is a desire for Terror. But Terror is a sickness of Rhetoric. Art, ashamed, will seek to hide itself once it has lost its letters of credit. Tied down now under the surveillance and restrictions of State, Church and taste, the artist, though beset perhaps with more attention and honour than ever before, for the first time in history becomes aware of his solitude. Who gave him his mandate? Whence does this entitlement he claims for himself derive? It is Night, and God has expired: how is one to paint in the darkness? And for *whom*? And *what*? And *why*? Art's object remains *the world*, that absolute: but reality is giving way, and the relation of the finite to the infinite has been overturned. The wretchedness of bodies and their fragility had been sustained by an immense plenitude. Now, fragility is becoming the only plenitude, the only security: the Infinite is the void, the blackness both within creatures and outside them. The Absolute is absence, it is God having taken refuge in souls: it is the desert. It is too late to *show*, too late to *create*; the painter is in hell; something is being born, a new damnation: genius—that uncertainty, that insane desire to pass beyond the Night of the world and contemplate it from the outside and crush it on to the walls, on to the canvases, bathing it in a previously unknown light. Genius, a new word in Europe, a conflict between the relative and the absolute, between a limited presence and an infinite absence. For the painter well knows he will never leave the world behind. And then, even if he were to, he would take with him everywhere this nothingness that runs through him: one cannot transcend perspective until one has granted oneself the right to create other plastic spaces.

Michelangelo dies a haunted man, summing up his despair and contempt in two words: original sin. Tintoretto says nothing; he cheats: were he to admit his loneliness to himself, he would not be able to bear it. But, for this very reason, we can understand that he suffers from it more than anyone: this false bourgeois working for the bourgeois does not even have the excuse of fame. This is the nest of vipers: a little dyer quivers, afflicted with that character neurosis Henri Jeanson so aptly terms 'the terrifying moral health of the ambitious'; he sets himself modest goals: to raise himself above his father by the judicious exploitation of his gifts, to dominate the market by flattering public taste. Cheerful *arrivisme*, ability, speed and talent—he lacks nothing, yet all is gnawed at by a dizzying absence, by Art without God. That Art is ugly, wicked, nocturnal; it is the mindless passion of the part for the whole, a wind of ice and darkness howling through pierced hearts. Sucked towards the Void, Jacopo is swallowed up by a journey that goes nowhere, and from which he will never return.

Genius doesn't exist: it is the shameful audacity of the nothingness. The little dyer does exist and he knows his limitations: this sensible boy wants to repair the tear in the fabric. All he asks is a modest fullness: what does he care for the infinite? And how would he admit to himself that the tiniest brushstroke is enough to challenge the competence of his judges. His stubborn, petty ambition would unravel in the Night of Unknowing. It isn't his fault, after all, if painting is a stray dog with no collar:[15] later, there will be madmen who will rejoice in their abandonment; in the middle of the sixteenth century, the first victim of monocular perspective was concerned, first of all, to conceal his own. Working alone and to no end was a terrifying thing. He needed judges. At any price. A panel of judges. God was silent; that left Venice: Venice which stopped up the gaps, filled in the holes, blocked up the outlets, stopped the haemorrhaging and the leaks. In the Republic of the Doges, good subjects were answerable to the state for all their activities; if it happened that they painted, they did so for the adornment of the city. Jacopo put himself into the hands of his fellow citizens; they had a certain, highly academic conception of Art, which he rapidly adopted. All the more rapidly for the fact that it had always been his own. Since his earliest childhood, he had been told—and had believed—that a craftsman's worth is measured by the number and size of the commissions he receives and the honours paid to him. He would hide his genius behind his *arrivisme* and take social success as the only clear sign of mystical victory. His bad faith was patent to the blindest; on earth, he played his hand of cards and cheated; and then there was the dice-throw against heaven, in which he didn't cheat. Now if he wins in this world, with all the

aces he pulls from his sleeve, he dares to claim he will
have won in heaven; if he sells his canvases, it is because he will have caught the world in his trap. But
who could hold this great mischief against him? It was
the nineteenth century that declared the divorce between the artist and the public. In the sixteenth, it is
true that painting was going mad: it had ceased to be
a religious sacrifice. But it is *no less true,* that it was becoming more rational: it remained a service performed for society. Who in Venice would dare, then,
to say. 'I paint for myself, I am my own witness?' And
are we sure that those who say this today are not lying?
Everyone is a judge and no one is: make of that what
you can. Tintoretto seems more unfortunate than
guilty: his art rends the age with a fiery dart, but he can
see it only with the eyes of his times. The fact remains
that he has chosen his own hell: at a single stroke the
finite closes on the infinite, ambition upon genius and
Venice on its painter, who will never again leave it. But
the captive infinite gnaws away at everything: Jacopo's
reasonable *arrivisme* becomes a frenzy; it had merely
been a matter of rising in society; now he must *prove*
something. Having voluntarily placed himself in the

position of defendant, the unfortunate man has become embroiled in an endless trial. He will mount his own defence, making each picture a witness in his own cause and never ceasing to plead his case: there is the city of Venice to convince, with its magistrates and burghers who, alone and with no possibility of appeal, will decide on his mortal future and his immortality. Now, he and he alone brought about this strange conflation. He had to choose: he could either rely on himself alone and legislate without appeal to anyone else or transform the Most Serene Republic into an absolute tribunal. Having said this, he took the only option he could—to his great misfortune. But how well I understand the indifference he felt towards the rest of the universe! What need did he have of German or even Florentine support? Venice is the finest, richest city; it has the best painters and critics, the most enlightened art lovers: it is *here* the game has to be played, with every move an irrevocable one; *here* in a brick corridor between a thin strip of sky and the stagnant waters, beneath the blazing absence of the sun, Eternity will be won or lost in a single life, forever.

All well and good, you may say, but why cheat? Why put on Veronese's fine plumage? If he wants to dazzle them with his genius, why snuff it out so often? And why apportion judges for himself if it is only to corrupt and deceive them?

Why? Because the tribunal is biased, the cause lost, the sentence passed and because he knows it. In 1548, he asks Venice to sanction the infinite; it takes fright and refuses. What a destiny! Abandoned by God, he has to cheat to find himself judges; having found them, it takes further skulduggery to get the trial adjourned. He will spend his life keeping them in suspense, at times running away, at others turning round to blind them. It is all here: the pain and the anger, the arrogance, the pliability, the furious effort, the rancour, the unbending pride and the humble desire to be loved. Tintoretto's painting is, above all else, the love affair between a man and a city.

In this tale of madness, the city seems even madder than the man. Since she managed to honour all her painters, why display such sourness, such sullen distrust towards the greatest of them all? Well, quite simply because she loves another. *La Serenissima* is hungry for prestige: her fame was for many years assured by her ships. Weary now and having gone down in the world a little, she vested her pride in an artist. Titian was worth a whole fleet by himself: stealing brilliance from the gleaming crowns and tiaras, he had wreathed himself in it. His adopted country admired him *more than anything* for the respect shown him by

501

the Emperor: it felt it saw its own glory in the sacred light—still awesome, but perfectly inoffensive—that shimmered around his brow. The painter of kings could not but be the king of painters: the Queen of the Seas regarded him as her son and, thanks to him, recovered a little majesty. She had, in the past, given him a profession and a reputation, but, when he worked, the radiance of his divine right streamed through the walls and reached as far as the San Marco district. She knew then that he gave back a hundred-fold what she had given him: he was a National Treasure.

Furthermore, the man was as long-lived as the trees; he went on for a century and gradually transformed into an institution. The presence of this one-member Academy, born before their time and determined to outlive them, demoralized the young; it exasperated and discouraged their ambitions. They felt their city could confer immortality on the living, but that it had reserved that favour for Titian alone. As a victim of this misunderstanding, Tintoretto demanded the city regard him as the equal of his renowned predecessor, on the fallacious pretext that he was every bit as worthy. But worthiness was not at issue: it is, by right, a question for hereditary monarchies, but not a matter for republics. Jacopo was mistaken when he criticized the City of the Doges for shining all its lights on the baobab of the Rialto. The opposite was the case: that old trunk was illuminated by a beam that had its source in Rome, Madrid or, at any rate, somewhere outside the city's walls; only then did it spill over on to Venice, dragging it from its shadows. It was indirect lighting, so to speak.

I was going to call this chapter 'In the Shadow of Titian', but that was mistaken too, *for Titian cast no shadow.* Just reflect on this: when Jacopo was born, the old man was forty-one years old; when the younger man first attempted to make a name for himself, he was seventy-two. This might be the moment to yield to youth; he could bow out gracefully at that point. But he was having none of it! The indestructible monarch reigned for another twenty-seven years. When he died, aged a hundred, he had the supreme good fortune to leave behind him an unfinished *Pietà*, the way young hopefuls do who are cut down in their prime. For more than half a century, Tintoretto-the-Mole

scuttled around in a maze whose walls were bespat-
tered with glory; up to the age of fifty-eight, this creature of the night was hounded by the sunlight radiated
by Another, blinded by His implacable celebrity.
When that brilliance was finally extinguished, Jacopo
Robusti was himself of an age to die. He stubbornly
outlived the tyrant, but he was to gain nothing by it:
Titian's trick was to combine two contradictory functions and make himself a court painter while retaining
the independence of a small master: such a happy
conjuncture would not be found often in history. At
any rate, we are a long way from it with Tintoretto
who put all his eggs in the same basket.

Take a look at the two tombs and you will see
what putting his country before all else still costs him,
even today. The radioactive corpse of the Old Man
was buried under a mountain of lard at Santa Maria
dei Frari, effectively the cemetery of the Doges; Tintoretto's body lies beneath a slab in the obscure shade
of a local parish church. Personally, I find this entirely
appropriate: the lard, sugar and nougat go to Titian:
this is poetic justice and I would have been even happier if he had been buried in Rome beneath the mon-

ument to Victor Emmanuel, which, with the exception of Milan Central Station, is the most hideous building in the whole of Italy. To Jacopo, the honours of bare stone: his name suffices. But, since this is a strictly personal opinion, I would understand if an indignant traveller were to call on Venice to justify itself: 'Ungrateful city, is this all you could do for the best of your sons?' Why so petty-mindedly surround that Titianesque opera, *The Assumption*, with a bank of lights and yet so meanly begrudge Robusti's canvases electricity? I know what Venice's answer will be: we find it as early as 1549 in Aretino's correspondence: 'If Robusti wishes to be honoured, why does he not paint like Tiziano Vecellio?' Jacopo would hear that refrain every day of his life; it would be repeated before every one of his canvases, before and after his death, and it is still repeated today:

Where has he gone wrong? Why does he stray from the royal road when he has had the good fortune to find it opened up for him? Our great Vecellio raised painting to such a high degree of perfection that it should never again be changed: either the newcomers will

505

follow in the footsteps of the Master or Art
will fall back into barbarism.

Capricious Venetians, illogical bourgeois! Tintoretto
is *their* painter; he shows them what they see and feel
and they cannot abide him; Titian doesn't give two
hoots for them and they adore him. Titian spends the
better part of his time reassuring princes, attesting by
his paintings that all is for the best in the best of all
possible worlds. Discord is merely an illusion; the
worst of enemies are secretly reconciled by the colour
of their coats. Violence? A ballet danced without
much conviction by pseudo-toughs with gentle woolly
beards: thus are wars justified. The painter's art verges
on apologetics and becomes theodicy: suffering, injustice and evil don't exist. Nor does mortal sin: Adam
and Eve transgressed only to gain the opportunity to
know—and show us—that they were naked. In a
great, four-pronged gesture, at once noble and languid, God leaning down from on high and Man
sprawling backwards reach out to one another. Order
reigns; perspective, tamed and enslaved, respects the
hierarchies: with some discreet adjustments, the best
places are reserved for kings and saints. If someone is
lost in the distance, in the foggy reaches of a waste-

land or the smoky lamplight of some dubious quarter, it is never by chance: the darkness corresponds to the obscurity of his condition and it is, moreover, needed to set off the bright lights of the foreground. The paintbrush pretends to be relating an event, but in fact what it depicts is a ceremony. Sacrificing movement to order and relief to unity, it doesn't so much shape bodies as caress them. Of all the bearded men applauding the Assumption, none has an individual existence. The group appeared first, with its raised arms, its legs—a burning bush; after which this single substance was given a measure of diversity by the production of these transient figures that just stand out from the collective background, but which can, at any moment, be absorbed back into it: this is the condition of the ordinary folk; Titian reserves individuality for the Grandees. Even then he takes care to smooth their corners: relief isolates and distances; it is a form of pessimism. The courtier, a professional optimist, indicates that relief, then mists it over and sets all his colours to sing the glory of God in unison. After which, he sets about polishing his painting: scratching out and buffing up, lacquering and varnishing. He will spare no effort to conceal his labour. In the end he vanishes altogether: you walk into a deserted picture, stroll amid flowers beneath a righteous sun, but the owner is dead; the walker is so alone that he disappears, oblivious. All that remains is that greatest of treacheries: Beauty.

For once the traitor has the excuse that he believes in what he is doing: he isn't a man of the city, but a peasant who has 'made it'; when he came to Venice it was from the countryside and his childhood, from the depths of the Middle Ages. This yokel had for many years felt the people's reverential love of the nobility; he passed through the bourgeoisie without noticing them, joining his true masters in the upper social reaches, all the more certain of pleasing them for the sincerity of his respect. It is often said he regarded himself secretly as their equal: I do not believe this at all. Where would such a conception have come from? He is a vassal: ennobled by the glory only kings can dispense; he owes everything to them, even his pride. Why would he turn this round against them? His impudent happiness, the hierarchy of powers and the beauty of the world are, in his eyes, merely reciprocal reflections; as sincerely as one might ever imagine, he takes the bourgeois techniques of the Renaissance and places them in the service of feudalism: he has stolen the toolkit.

Yet bourgeois and patricians both admire him: he provides Venice's technocrats with an alibi; he speaks of happiness, glory, pre-existent harmony at the very moment when they are making the most praiseworthy efforts to conceal from themselves their decline. All the merchants, whether of lowly or noble birth, are enchanted by these beatific canvases that reflect to them the calm repose of kings. If all is for the best, if evil is merely a fine illusion, if everyone retains forever their hereditary place in the divine and social hierarchy, then none of the events of the last hundred years has happened: the Turks haven't taken Constantinople; Columbus hasn't discovered America; the Portuguese haven't even dreamed of dumping their spices on the world market and the continental powers haven't allied themselves against *la Serenissima*. People had thought that the Barbary pirates were rife on the high seas, that the African source of precious metals had dried up, that the scarcity of money during the first half of the century had put a brake on trade and then, suddenly, that Peruvian gold flowing down in torrents from the great Spanish tank had driven prices up again and swamped the market. But it was merely a dream: Venice still rules over the Mediterranean; it is at the height of its power, wealth and greatness. In other words, these troubled people want Beauty because it is reassuring.

In this, I can understand them. I have flown more than two hundred times now, though I never get used to it. I am too used to crawling about the earth to find flying normal and, from time to time, the fear resurfaces—most particularly when my flying companions are as ugly as I am. But it only takes a beautiful young woman to be on the flight, or a handsome young man, or a charming, loving couple and my fear vanishes. Ugliness is a prophecy: there is in it some unidentifiable extremism that wants to raise negation to the point of horror. The Beautiful seems indestructible; its sacred image protects us: so long as It will remain among us, the catastrophe will not happen. So it was with Venice: the city was beginning to fear it would collapse into the slime of the lagoons; it took the notion of rescuing itself through Beauty, that supreme frivolity; it looked to its palaces and paintings to serve it as life-rafts and rescuing floats. Those who ensured Titian's success were the same people who deserted the sea, who fled disenchantment in orgies, who preferred the security of ground-rents to the profits of commerce.

Tintoretto was born in a distressed city; he breathed the air of Venetian disquiet and it ate away at him; it was all that he knew how to paint. In his place, his severest critics would have acted no differently. But they were not in his place: they could not help but feel this disquiet, but they didn't want to have it shown to them; they condemned the pictures that *represented* it. Jacopo was doomed by ill fate to be the unwitting witness to an age that refused to know itself. This time we discover the meaning of that destiny and the secret of Venetian ill-feeling at a single stroke. Tintoretto displeased everyone: the patricians because he revealed to them the Puritanism and dreamy agitation of the bourgeois; the artisans because he destroyed the corporate order and revealed the seething of hatreds and rivalries beneath the veneer of occupational solidarity; the patriots because, by his hand, the frenzied distraction of painting and the absence of God disclosed an absurd, chance-governed world to them, where anything could happen—*even* the death of Venice. But surely this newly bourgeois painter was at least palatable to his adoptive class. Unfortunately not: the bourgeoisie didn't accept him unreservedly: he constantly fascinated them, but often he scared them. This was because they were a class that was not yet self-aware. Master Zignioni doubtless dreamed of betrayal; he was obscurely seeking the means of joining the patricians, in short, of leaving behind that bourgeois reality which he contributed, despite himself, to producing: what he loathed most in Robusti's paintings was their radicalism and their demystifying power. In short, Tintoretto's testimony had at all costs to be rejected, his efforts presented as a failure and the originality of his experimentation denied: *he had to be got rid of.*

When we look at what he was criticized for, it was *first and foremost*, for working too quickly and leaving the mark of his hand everywhere; it was polished, finished work that was wanted—above all something *impersonal.* If the painter revealed himself in the work, he put himself at issue; and if he put himself at issue, he posed a challenge to the public. Venice imposed the

Puritans' maxim on its painters—'no personal remarks': it would make every effort to confound Jacopo's lyricism with the haste of an overworked
supplier who performs slapdash work. Then there is
the following piece of tittle-tattle reported by Ridolfi:
Tintoretto is said to have written up on the walls of
his studio: 'Titian's colour and Michelangelo's representation of relief.' This is stupid: that formula is
found only at a very late date, being coined by a Venetian art critic with no reference whatever to Robusti. In
fact, Tintoretto could have known Michelangelo's
works only through Daniele de Volterra's reproduc-
tions—hence in 1557 *at the earliest*. And who do they
take him for? Do they think he would *seriously* devote
himself to concocting such an absurd potion? It is, in
fact, a fantasy of the period: in the face of the Spanish threat, the cities of northern and middle Italy
sought to unite, but did so too late. Yet the awakening
of a national consciousness—rapidly put to sleep
again—was not without its transient influence on the
Fine Arts. 'Michelangelo and Titian' means Florence
and Venice. How fine that would be: painting unified!

There is nothing serious in this, as we can see: the dream is a harmless one so long as it remains everybody's. But those who claim to see it as the obsession of Robusti *alone* must have wanted to tear that artist in two by lodging an explosive nightmare in his breast. Colour is *Jean-qui-rit*, the representation of relief is *Jean-qui-pleure*. On the one hand, unity; on the other, a permanent risk of disorder. On the one side, the harmony of the spheres; on the other, abandonment. The century's two Titans hurl themselves at each other, grab each other by the throat and attempt strangulation: Jacopo is the theatre of operations. At times Titian wins a round, but only just; at others Michelangelo is the victor, but with difficulty. In any event, the loser has enough strength left to spoil the victor's triumph: the result of the Pyrrhic victory is a failed painting. Failed from excess: Tintoretto seems to contemporaries like a Titian gone mad, devoured by the dark passion of Buonarroti, shaking with Saint Vitus' Dance—a case of possession, a curious dual personality. In a sense, Jacopo does not exist, except as a battlefield; in another sense, he is a monster, a misbegotten creature. Vasari's story now has a strange light cast upon it:

Adam Robusti wanted to taste the fruit of the tree of knowledge and the Archangel Tiziano, with outstretched finger and beating wings, drove him out of Paradise.

Even today, to be the victim or the bringer of bad luck is one and the same thing in Italy. If you have recently had financial difficulties, a car accident or a broken leg, or if your wife has just left you, don't expect to be invited to dinner: a hostess will not lightly expose her other guests to premature baldness, a head cold or, in extreme cases, to the risk of breaking their necks on her stairs. I know a Milanese who has the evil eye; it was discovered last year: he no longer has any friends and dines at home alone. Jacopo is like this: a caster of fate, because his fate has been cast— or his mother's, perhaps, when she was carrying him. In fact, the *jettatura* comes from Venice: the city, accursed and worried, produced a worried man; it curses its own worrying nature in him. The unfortunate man is desperately in love with a city that is in despair but will not admit it: the love-object is horrified by such love. When Tintoretto passes, people draw aside: he reeks of death. This is perfectly true. But what do the

patrician festivals, the bourgeois charity and the docility of the people smell of, if not the very same thing?
Or the redbrick houses with their flooded cellars and
their walls striped with horizontal rat-runs? What do
these stagnant canals smell of, with their urinal-style
watercress and these grey mussels locked in their foul,
gooey coating beneath the quays? At the bottom of a
rio, there is a bubble stuck to the clay; it is shaken clear
by the backwash from the gondolas and rises through
the muddy water, emerges on the surface, revolves,
glistens, bursts with a silent fart and everything dies
with it: bourgeois nostalgias, the grandeur of the Republic, God and Italian painting.

Tintoretto led the mourning for Venice and for a
world. But when he died, no one lamented his passing
and then silence descended. Hypocritically pious
hands covered his canvases in veils of mourning. If
we tear down this black veil, we shall find a portrait
started over again a hundred times. The portrait of
Jacopo? Of the Queen of the Seas? As you like: the
city and its painter have but a single face.

Les Temps Modernes, 141 (November 1957).

giacometti's paintings[16]

'Several naked women, seen at the Sphinx, as I am sitting at the back of the room. The distance separating us (the shiny floor that seemed impassable despite my desire to cross it) impressed me as much as did the women.'[17] The result: four inaccessible figurines, balanced on a massive wave that is, in fact, a vertical floor. He made them as he saw them—*distant*. But here are four tall girls with a substantial *presence*, surging up from the ground and about to crash down on him, all together, like the lid of a box: 'I saw them often, particularly one evening, in a little room on the rue de l'Échaudé, very close and threatening.' In his eyes, distance, far from being an accident, is part of the intimate nature of the object. These whores twenty—impassable—yards away are forever fixed in the glare of his hopeless desire. His studio is an archipelago, a disorder of diverse distancings. Against the wall, the Mother-Goddess retains the nearness of an obsession; if I retreat, she advances; she is closest when I am most distant. This statuette at my feet is a passer-by glimpsed in the rear-view mirror of a car, disappearing from sight. It's no use my approaching; he keeps his distance.

These solitudes push the visitor back the whole insuperable length of a room, a lawn or a glade that one has not dared to cross; they attest to the strange paralysis that grips Giacometti at the sight of his fellow creatures. Not that he is misanthropic: the torpor is the effect of a surprise mixed with fear, often with admiration and sometimes with respect. He is, admittedly, distant. But, after all, it was man who created distance and it has meaning only within a human space; it separates Hero from Leander and Marathon from Athens, but not one pebble from another pebble. I understood what it was one April evening in 1941: I had spent the previous ten months in a POW camp or, in other words, in a sardine tin, and had experienced absolute proximity there. The boundary of my living space was my skin; day and night I had felt the warmth of someone's side or shoulder against me. This was no great annoyance: the others were still me. On this first evening of freedom, as a stranger in my native town and not yet having met up with my old friends, I pushed open the door of a cafe. Suddenly, I was afraid—or almost. I couldn't understand how these squat, bulbous buildings could conceal such deserts within them. I was lost: the few drinkers seemed more distant than the stars; each of them had a great area of seat to himself, a whole marble table, and to touch them, I would have had to have crossed the 'shiny floor' that separated me from them. If they seemed inaccessible to me, these men shimmering comfortably in their tubes of rarefied gas, it was because I no longer had the right to put my hand on their shoulders or their thighs and call them 'kiddo'. I was back in bourgeois society; I had to re-learn life 'at a respectable distance' and my sudden agoraphobia betrayed my vague sense of regret for the 'unanimous' life from which I had just been definitively separated.[18]

So it is with Giacometti: in his work distance isn't a voluntary isolation, nor even a stepping back: it is a demand, a ceremony, a sense of difficulties. It is the product—he has said so himself[19]—of the forces of attraction and repulsion. If he cannot cross these few metres of shiny floor separating him from the naked women, that is because shyness or poverty keep him rooted to his chair; but if he feels so much that those few metres are uncrossable, this is because he wants to touch the sumptuous flesh. He refuses to mingle and rejects relations of good neighbourliness, because he wants friendship and love. He does not dare to take, because he is afraid of being taken.

His figurines are solitary, but if you put them together in any way at all, their solitude unites them; they suddenly form a little magical group: 'Looking at the figures, which, to clear the table, had been placed randomly on the ground, I noticed that they formed two groups which seemed to match what I was looking for. I mounted the two groups on bases without the slightest change . . .' A Giacometti exhibition is a populace. He has sculpted people crossing a public square but not seeing one another; they pass each other by, irremediably alone, and yet *they are together*: they are going to be lost forever, but they would not be lost if they had not sought each other. He defined his universe better than I could when he wrote of one of his groups that it reminded him of, 'a corner of a forest seen over many years, whose trees, with their slender, bare trunks . . . always seemed to be like people halted in their tracks and talking to each other.' And what is this circular distance—which speech alone can cross—but the negative notion, *the void* ? Ironic, wary, ceremonious and affectionate, Giacometti sees emptiness everywhere. Not everywhere, you will say. There are objects that touch. But this is the point: Giacometti is sure of nothing; not even of that. He was fascinated for weeks by the feet of a chair: they did not *touch* the ground. Between things, between people, the bridges are broken; emptiness slips in everywhere, each creature secretes its own void.

Giacometti became a sculptor because he is obsessed with emptiness. One statuette he called 'Me rushing along a street in the rain'.[20] Sculptors seldom make busts of themselves; if they attempt a 'portrait of the artist', they look at themselves from the outside, in a mirror: they are prophets of objectivity. But imagine a lyrical sculptor: what he wants to convey is his inner feeling, that boundless void that grips him and separates him from shelter, his abandonment to the storm. Giacometti is a sculptor because he carries his void the way snails carry their shells, because he wants to convey this in all its facets and in all dimensions. And sometimes he gets on well with the tiny state of exile he carries with him everywhere, and sometimes he is horrified by it.

A friend moves in with him: Giacometti, happy at first, quickly begins to worry: 'In the morning, I open my eyes: he had his trousers and his jacket *on my empty space.*' At other times, however, he keeps tight to the walls, clings to them: the void around him portends fall, landslip or avalanche. In any event, he must bear witness to it.

Will sculpture alone be able to do this? As the figure leaves his fingers, it is 'ten paces away', 'twenty paces away' and, whatever you do, it stays there. It is the statue itself that determines the distance from which you must see it, just as court etiquette determines the distance from which you must address the

king. The *real* engenders the no-man's-land that surrounds it. A Giacometti figure is Giacometti himself
producing his little local nothingness. But all these tiny
absences, which belong to us the way our names or
our shadows do, are not enough to make a world.
There is also the Void, that universal distance of
everything from everything else. The street is empty,
in the sun: and *in this void* a person appears suddenly.
Sculpture *sets out from fullness* to create emptiness: can
it show fullness emerging in the midst of a former
emptiness? Giacometti has tried to answer this question a hundred times. His composition *The Cage* represents 'his desire to abolish the base and to have a
limited space for creating a head and a figure.' This is
the whole problem: the—immemorial—void will always predate the beings that populate it if it is first
enclosed between walls. This 'Cage' is 'a room I saw,
I even saw curtains behind the woman . . .' Another
time, he makes 'a figurine in a box between two boxes
that are houses'. In short, he frames his figures: with
regard to us, they retain an imaginary distance, but
they live in a closed space that imposes its own distances on them, in a prefabricated void which they do

not manage to fill and do not create, but submit to. And what is this framed, populated void if not a picture? Lyrical when he is sculpting, Giacometti becomes objective when he paints: he attempts to pin down the features of Annette or Diego as they appear in an empty room, in his deserted studio.

I have tried to show elsewhere that he came to sculpture like a painter, since he handled a plaster figurine as though it were a figure in a painting: he confers a fixed, imaginary distance on his statuettes. Conversely, I can say that he approaches painting as a sculptor, for he would like us to see the imaginary space delimited by the frame as a *genuine* void. He would like us to see the seated woman he has just painted through several layers of emptiness; he would like the canvas to be like still water and us to see his figures *in* the picture the way Rimbaud saw a drawing-room in a lake—showing through it.[21] Sculpting the way others paint and painting the way others sculpt, is he a painter? Is he a sculptor? He is neither. And both. He is a painter and a sculptor because the age will not allow him to be a sculptor and an architect. As a sculptor in order to restore everyone's circular solitude and a painter in order to put men and things back into the world—that is to say into the great universal Void—it so happens that he sometimes models what he initially wanted to paint.[22] But on other occasions he knows that sculpture (or, alternatively, painting) alone enables him to 'realize his impressions'. At any rate, the two activities are inseparable and complementary: they enable him to treat the problem of his relations with other people in all its aspects, according to whether the distance comes from them, from him or from the universe.

How can you paint emptiness? Before Giacometti no one seems to have tried. For five hundred years, paintings have been packed to the gunwales; the whole world has been crammed into them. Giacometti begins by expelling people from his canvases: his brother Diego, all alone, lost inside a great shed, is sufficient. And this character still has to be distinguished from the things around him. Normally, this is done by emphasizing his outline. But a line is produced by the intersection of two surfaces, and emptiness cannot count as a surface. Even less can it count as a volume. You separate the container from the content by means of a line: but emptiness isn't a container. Can we say that Diego 'stands out against' this dividing wall behind him? We cannot: the 'figure/ ground' relation exists only for relatively flat surfaces; unless he leans against it, this distant wall cannot 'serve as a background' to Diego; when all is said and done, he has no connection with it whatever. Or rather, he has: since man and object are in the same picture, there have to be some appropriate relationships (colours, values, proportions) that confer unity on the painting. But these correspondences are simultaneously erased by the nothingness that interposes itself between them. No, Diego does not stand out against the grey background of a wall; he is there and the wall is there— and that is all there is to it. He is not enclosed or supported or contained by anything: he *appears* all alone in the immense frame of emptiness. With each of his pictures, Giacometti takes us back to the moment of creation *ex nihilo*. Each of them raises again the old metaphysical question, 'Why is there something rather than nothing?' And yet there is something: there is this stubborn, unjustifiable, supererogatory apparition. This painted figure is mind-boggling because he is presented in the form of an *interrogative apparition*.

But how is he to be pinned down on the canvas without putting some sort of line around him? Is he not going to burst in the void like a fish from the abyssal depth brought up to the surface of the water? Indeed he is not: the line represents an arrested flight; it marks a balance between outside and inside; it forms around the shape the object adopts under pressure from outside forces; it is a symbol of inertia, of passivity. But Giacometti doesn't regard finitude as a limitation imposed upon him: the coherence of the real, its plenitude and its determination are one single effect of its inner affirmative power. 'Apparitions' both affirm and limit themselves as they take on definition. Like those strange curves studied by mathematicians that are both encompassing and encompassed, the object is its own envelope.

One day, when he had set out to draw me, Giacometti exclaimed in astonishment: 'What density, what lines of force!' And I was even more astonished than he was, since I believe I have, like everyone, a rather flabby face. But he saw every feature as a centripetal force. The face coils back on itself, it is a loop closing. Move round it and you will never find an outline: only fullness. Lines are the beginnings of negation, the transition from being to non-being. But Giacometti sees the real as pure positivity: *there is* being, and then, suddenly, there no longer is: but from being to nothingness no transition is conceivable. Observe how the many lines he traces are *internal* to the form he is describing; see how they represent the intimate relations of being with itself: folds in a jacket, wrinkles in a face, the protrusion of a muscle, the direction of a movement. All these lines are centripetal: their aim is to pull things tighter, they force the eye to follow them and bring it back always to the centre of the figure; you would think the face were retracting under the influence of some astringent substance: in a few minutes it will be the size of a fist or a shrunken head. And yet the limit of the body is nowhere marked: sometimes the heavy mass of flesh ends obscurely, stealthily, in a vague brown nimbus, somewhere beneath the tangle of lines of force—and sometimes it literally has no end: the outline of the arm or hip is lost in a shimmering of light that conjures it away. Without warning, we are made to watch a sudden dematerialization: here is a man crossing his legs; so long as I focussed only on his head and shoul-

ders, I was convinced he had feet; I even thought I
could see them. But if I look at them, they unravel;
they fade into luminous mist and I no longer know
where body ends and void begins. And don't go thinking this is one of those disintegrations that Masson
attempted, so as to give objects a kind of ubiquity by
spreading them all over the canvas. If Giacometti did-
n't delimit the shoe, that wasn't because he believed it
to be limitless but because he's counting on us to supply a limit. And in fact the shoes are there, heavy and
dense. To see them you simply have not quite to look
at them.

To understand this technique, let us examine the
sketches he sometimes makes of his sculptures. Four
women on a base: well and good. Now let's look at
the drawing. Here is a head and a neck, drawn with
full strokes, then nothing, then nothing, then an open
curve revolving around a point: the belly and the navel.
Here again is the stump of a thigh, then nothing, then
two vertical lines and, lower down, two others. This is
all. The whole of a woman. What have we done here?
We have used our knowledge to re-establish continuity and our eyes to stick these *disjecta membra* together:

we *saw* shoulders and arms on the blank paper; we saw them because we had *recognized* the head and the belly. And these limbs were there in fact, even though no lines supplied them. In the same way we sometimes conceive lucid, fully-formed ideas though no words supply them to us. Between the two extremities, the body is a shooting current. We are confronted with the pure real, the invisible tension of the blank paper. But isn't the void also represented by the whiteness of the paper? Precisely: Gicaometti rejects both the inertia of matter and the inertia of pure nothingness. Emptiness is fullness relaxed and spread-out; fullness is oriented emptiness. The real flashes like lightning.

Have you noticed the profusion of white lines scoring the torsos and faces? This Diego isn't solidly stitched: he's simply basted together as the dressmakers say. Or might it be that Giacometti wants to 'write luminously on a dark background'? Almost. It's no longer a matter of separating fullness from the void but of painting plenitude itself. Now, plenitude is both singular and diverse: how can it be differentiated without being divided? Black strokes are dangerous: there's a danger they will efface being or fissure it. If we use them to outline an eye or encircle a mouth, we shall be exposed to the belief that there are little pockets of emptiness within reality. These white striations are there as inconspicuous indications: they guide the eye, force it to move in a particular way, then melt beneath our gaze. But the real danger lies elsewhere. We know how successful Arcimboldo was, with his heaps of vegetables and piles of fish. What is it that appeals to us in these trick images? Might it be the fact that this is a technique we have long been familiar with? What if our painters were all, in their way, Arcimboldos? They would not, admittedly, stoop to making a human head out of a pumpkin and some tomatoes and radishes. But do they not each day make faces with a pair of eyes, a nose, two ears and thirty-two teeth? What is the difference? To take a sphere of pink flesh, make two holes in it and ram an enamelled marble into each hole; to shape a nasal appendage and plant it, like a false nose, beneath the eye sockets; to pierce a third hole and fill it with white pebbles—isn't this precisely to replace the indissoluble unity of a face with a jumble of heteroclite objects? Emptiness seeps in everywhere; between the eyes and the eyelids, between the lips, into the nostrils. A head becomes an archipelago in its turn. You may say that this strange assemblage corresponds to reality, that the oculist can remove eyes and the dentist can extract teeth? Perhaps. But what should painters paint? That which is? That which we see? And what do we see? Some painters have depicted this chestnut tree beneath my window as a great, self-contained, quivering ball; others have painted its leaves one by one, with the veins showing. Do I see a leafy mass or a multitude of leaves? Individual leaves or foliage? Heaven knows, I see both; it's neither entirely the one nor the other; and I am tossed endlessly from the one to the other. As regards the leaves, I do *not* see them right to the end; I think I am going to apprehend them all, but then I lose them. And when I can hold the foliage in view, it breaks up into leaves. In short, I see a teeming coherence, a dispersion folded back on itself. Try painting that!

And yet Giacometti wants to paint what he sees, just as he sees it. He wants his figures, each set in their original voids on his static canvas, perpetually to move from the continuous to the discontinuous. He wants the head to be isolated, since it rules the body, but he wants the body to reclaim it, so that it is merely a periscope of the belly, in the same way as Europe is described as being a peninsula of Asia. He wants the eyes, the nose and the mouth to be leaves in a leafy mass, at once separate and merged together. And he manages to do it: this is his great achievement. How? By refusing to be more precise than perception. It isn't a question of painting *vaguely*; on the contrary, he will suggest a perfect precision of being beneath the imprecision of knowing. In themselves, or for others with better eyesight—for angels—these faces conform rigorously to the principle of individuation; they are determined down to the tiniest detail. We know this at first glance: moreover, we immediately recognize Diego and Annette. This alone, if such a thing were needed, would absolve Giacometti of the charge of subjectivism. But at the same time we cannot view the canvas without unease: despite ourselves, we want to ask for a torch or, quite simply, a candle. Is there a mist, or is evening falling, or are our eyes getting tired? Is Diego lowering or raising his eyelids? Is he dozing? Is he dreaming? Is he peeping?

Of course we ask these same questions at an exhibition of bad paintings, when faced with some poor portrait done so hazily that all answers are possible without any particular one requiring our assent. But that clumsy indeterminacy bears no relation to Giacometti's calculated indeterminacy: and indeed, should we not better term the latter over-determinacy? I turn to Diego and, from one moment to the next, he is sleeping, awake, looking at the sky and then staring at me. All these things are true and all are clear: but, if I bend my head a little and change the angle of my gaze, the obvious truth vanishes and is replaced by another. If, wearying, I want to settle on one single opinion, I have no recourse but to leave as quickly as I can. Even then, it will still be only fragile and probable: for example, when I find a face in the fire, an inkblot or a swirl of drapery, that shape, emerging suddenly, tautens and forces itself upon me. Yet, though *I* cannot see it differently, I know others will. But the face in the flames has no truth to it: what irritates and at the same time enchants us in Giacometti's pictures is *that there is* a truth and we are sure of it. It is there, within my grasp, if only I search it out. But my vision blurs, my eyes tire and I give up. Particularly as I am beginning to understand: Giacometti has us in his grasp because he has stood the problem on its head.

Take a painting by Ingres. If I look at the tip of the Odalisque's nose, the rest of the face becomes blurred, a pink butter, flecked with a delicate red by the lips. Now, if I turn my gaze on the lips, they will come out of the shadow, moist and parted, and the nose will disappear, consumed by the lack of differentiation of the background. But no matter: reassuringly, I know I can conjure it up again at will. With Giacometti, the opposite is the case: for a detail to seem clear and reassuring, I have—I have only—not to make it the explicit object of my attention; what inspires confidence is what I glimpse out of the corner of my eye. The more I observe Diego's eyes, the less able I am to decipher them; but I can sense slightly sunken cheeks and a strange smile playing about the corners of his mouth. If my unhappy taste for certainty leads my eyes down to that mouth, everything immediately eludes me. What is it like? Hard? Bitter? Ironic? Open? Pursed? His eyes, on the other hand, have almost passed out of my visual field and I now *know* they are half-closed. And there is nothing to stop me from moving on further, obsessed by this phantom face that is perpetually forming, unforming and re-forming behind me. The remarkable part is that you believe in it. As in hallucinations: in the beginning you glimpse them from one side and, when you turn around, they are gone. Ah, but on the other side . . .

Are these extraordinary figures—so perfectly immaterial that they often become transparent, and so totally, fully real that they hit you unforgettably like a physical blow—in the process of appearing or disappearing? They are doing both at the same time. They seem so diaphanous at times that we no longer even dream of enquiring about their faces: we pinch ourselves to find out if they really exist. If we persist in staring at them, the entire picture comes to life: a dark sea surges over and submerges them; nothing remains but a surface smeared with soot; and then the wave rolls back and we see them again, white and naked, shining beneath the waters. But when they reappear, it is with a violent affirmation, like muffled cries that reach the top of a mountain and which we know, when we hear them, have somewhere been shouts for help or cries of pain. This play of appearance and disappearance, of flight and provocation lends them a certain coquettish air. They remind me of Galatea, who fled from her lover beneath the willow trees and, at the same time, wanted him to see her. Coquettish, yes, and graceful, since they are all action, and sinister because of the void that surrounds them, these creatures of nothingness attain to the fullness of existence by escaping our clutches and mystifying us. Every evening an illusionist has three hundred accomplices: the spectators themselves and their second natures. He attaches a wooden arm to his shoulder in a fine red sleeve. The audience asks of him two arms in sleeves of identical material. It sees two arms and two sleeves and is contented. Meanwhile, an unseen real arm, wrapped in black material, will pull out a rabbit, a playing card or an exploding cigarette. Giacometti's art is akin to the prestidigitator's: we are his dupes and his accomplices. Without our eagerness, our thoughtless haste, the traditional unreliability of our senses and the contradictions of our perception, he would not succeed in bringing his portraits to life. He works 'by eye', from what he sees, but especially from what he believes we will see. It is not his aim to present us with an image, but to produce simulacra which, while presenting themselves as what they are, arouse feelings and attitudes in us that are normally produced by encounters with real human beings.

At the Musée Grévin, you may either be irritated or frightened when you mistake a waxwork figure for the museum attendant. Nothing could be easier than to weave elaborate practical jokes on this theme. But Giacometti doesn't particularly like jokes. Except for one. One single practical joke to which he has dedicated his life. He understood many years ago that artists work in the imaginary realm and we create only illusions; he knows that the 'monsters imitated by art' will never produce anything but factitious fears among spectators. Yet he has not lost hope: one day he will show us a portrait of Diego that is in appearance just like the others. We shall be forewarned; we shall know it is merely a fantasy, a vain illusion, captive within its frame. And yet on that day, as we stand before the mute canvas, we shall feel a shock—a tiny shock. The same shock we feel when we are coming home late and a stranger comes towards us in the dark; then Giacometti will know that he has, by his paintings, given rise to a real emotion, and that his simulacra, while remaining illusory, will, for a few moments, have had *genuine* powers. I wish him success in pulling off this memorable practical joke soon. If he doesn't manage it, that will be because no one can. In any event, no one can go further.

Les Temps modernes, 103 (June 1954).

the unprivileged painter

Since Goya's time, killers have gone on with their slaughter and right-thinking souls with their protests. Every five or ten years, a painter comes along and updates *Disasters of War* by modernizing the uniforms and the weaponry. Without success: there can be no doubting the indignation in the painter's heart, but it doesn't transmit itself to the brush.

Lapoujade's undertaking is of a quite different order.[23] His aim is not to fix art in some set form by subordinating it to the needs of Good Intentions, but to interrogate painting *from the inside* about its movement and its scope. Since the point almost a century ago when creation became a critical endeavour, it has been audacious, and has examined its own audacity and judged it. Lapoujade, drawn along by the developments in Painting that he himself has effected, has been led to bestow presences on us that are both at the heart of each composition and beyond them all. Figurative art wasn't appropriate for manifesting these presences: the human figure, in particular, concealed men's suffering. It has disappeared now and, in the very fabric of art, something has been born from its death: tortured victims, flattened cities, massacred crowds; the torturers, too, are present everywhere. Victims and persecutors—the painter has painted our portrait. The portrait of the century. At the same time, the object of his art is no longer the individual. Nor the typical. It is the singularity of an age and its reality. How has Lapoujade, obeying the very demands of 'abstraction', achieved what the figurative has never managed to pull off?

Since pictures won the freedom to subject themselves to the laws of Painting alone, the artist has been able to reassert the fundamental, inviolable bond between his work and Beauty. Whatever its origin, a picture will either be beautiful or will not exist at all;

when a canvas has simply been daubed with paint, painting has not taken place, and that is all there is to it. In that case, the eye sees only a daub. The Beautiful is not even the goal of art: it is its flesh and blood, its being. Everyone has always said this and everyone claims to know it. All well and good. But it is true, nonetheless, that this pure fundamental concern, concealed at the beginning of the century by an alchemist's dream—the desire to produce a real absolute—is rediscovering its primal purity in abstract art. As a result, the old 'Art for Art's sake' chestnut has returned with vigour: yet how silly it is! For no one 'makes art' merely for the sake of doing so, or in order that Art should exist. People simply make art and that is all there is to it. Lapoujade doesn't paint his canvases in the hope of adding a few square inches to the surface area of Beauty. But he will derive his motifs, themes, obsessions and purposes from the very movement of his art: when the world of the plastic arts has dissolved its figurative constraint, what exigencies will sustain its continued existence? It must be said that all the works we see here have no other source: Lapoujade's *Hiroshima* was called forth *by Art*.

Some will find this shocking. It is a long time since politicians first got into the habit of asking little favours from artists. Beribboned renegades long ago proved that painting dies the moment it is made to serve alien purposes. Up until now, in fact, if painters wanted to depict man's inhumanity to man, they were suddenly faced with this unfortunate alternative: they could either betray painting without any great gain for Morality or if, despite everything, their work seemed beautiful, they could betray men's suffering and anger to Beauty. There was betrayal at every turn.

Fine sentiments incline a painter towards academicism. If you wish to communicate a legitimate indignation to the public, that public has above all to be able to decipher the message; the disquieting aspects of art will, in that case, be subordinated to its false securities. Living Beauty is always a work in progress: so as not to perplex the public with experimentation, the artist will choose a dead form; the most readable style will be adopted, which is necessarily an old one that has become conventional. As for showing torture, bodies with torn flesh, living bodies racked, tormented and burned, some have tried it but they have not, I think, repeated the experiment. In fact, reawakening our visual habits, they have presented us with the disturbing imitation of reality and inclined us, as a result, to react as we would in reality—with horror, anger and, above all, with that silent sympathy that causes every human being to feel the wounds of others as so many gaping holes in his own body. An unbearable spectacle and one that drives the spectator away. After that, the painting may be an ingenious composition, with carefully judged proportions and harmony, but that is of little consequence since we have already fled and shall not return. And if we were to return, the punctured eyes and scabby wounds—everything—would break apart, disintegrate; beauty would never be restored. The attempt would have failed.

Such painters will surely be criticized for their lack of tact: if they revisit these scabrous subjects, they should do so with both delicacy and caution. Tact was the outstanding feature of Titian's work, if I may be permitted to mention that great figure. Princes could commission a painting of a massacre committed to their orders and sleep soundly in their beds: he would turn it into a procession or a ballet. And it was beautiful, of course! If one paints tortures following his methods, they become tortures absent from the canvas, just as Mallarmé's poetic rose was the 'rose absent from all bouquets'. The torturers will be shown in the richest fabrics, fine strapping *Reiter* overseeing the operation, with perhaps, at a pinch, the entrancingly beautiful, unharmed bare foot of a victim whose legs, trunk and head are hidden. On these grounds, I regard Tiziano Vecellio as a betrayer: he forced his brush to render tranquil horrors, painless pain and deathless dead: it is his fault that Beauty is a traitor to humanity and that it sides with kings. If a pig-headed painter with a room overlooking a triage camp paints fruit bowls, then that is not so serious: he sins by omission. The real crime is to paint the triage camp as though it were a fruit bowl.

I concede that there have been two exceptions. But the first is merely apparent: racked by remorse and revolt, the uncertain Goya, that tormented visionary, painted not war but his visions. He had no desire to enlighten the masses, being a man himself so unenlightened that the horrors of battles and executions gradually became, in the depths of his heart, the unvarnished horror of being Goya.

Guernica is different: here the artist most reliant upon chance took advantage of the most unprecedented good fortune. In fact, the painting combines some incompatible features. Effortlessly. The picture, an instance of unforgettable revolt, the commemoration of a massacre, seems, at the same time, to have striven only after Beauty; and indeed achieved it. The bitter accusation contained in the painting will remain, but that will not disturb its calm formal beauty. Conversely, the beauty does not betray the accusation, but *helps to make it*. This is because the Spanish Civil War, a crucial moment in the pre-war years, broke out at a point when *this* painter's life and *this* style of painting were reaching their decisive moment. The negative force of Picasso's brush was exhausting the 'figurative' and clearing the way for its systematic destruction. In this period, figures were still intact, for the goal of experimentation was precisely to render the movement that brought about their disintegration. This violence did not need to hide or transform itself;

it became merged, as violence, with the disintegration of human beings by their own bombs: thus an experimental method became the singular meaning of a revolt and the denunciation of a massacre. The same social forces had made a painter the negation of *their* order and had distantly prepared the ground for the fascist acts of destruction and *Guernica*. This stroke of fortune allowed the artist not to cajole the Beautiful. And if the crime, in entering the 'plastic arts', still remains an odious one, this is because it explodes, and because, to use a term coined by André Breton, Picasso's beauty is 'fixed-explosive' in nature. The miraculous throw of the dice couldn't occur again: when, after the 1939 war, the painter wanted to start over, his art had changed and the world had too; there was no meeting of the two. All in all, we are still in the same bind: when it is a matter of human beings and their suffering, we can neither accept the figurative representation of horror nor its disappearance beneath magnificent display.

For Lapoujade, the alternative no longer even exists; there no longer are any problems. I borrowed the foregoing examples from the figurative dimension.

Paradoxically, if the human figure is imitated, the demand for justice comes from outside; if imitation no longer takes place, this demand comes from Art itself.

This is the most recent stage in a long journey. For years we have been discovering the nudes, couples and crowds that force themselves on his brush. Look at his adolescent girls: they lack nothing. Yet the flesh has now lost its surround: the imitated outlines of a body. Even so, it has not scattered to the four corners of the canvas. Outlines, volumes, masses, perspectival effects—there was actually no need for all this, then, to *put us in the presence* of a naked body? Obviously not. Or, rather, the opposite is the case: the picture requires *on its own account* that we sense the delicacy of a flesh tint at the very moment that it has been rid of alien forms.

The starting point is the restlessness of Art; the painter is freeing himself from an academic tradition: he wants to be able to cultivate his garden to the fullest extent, that plane surface that has come down to him. He wants to be able to transform the old routine farming of that surface into intensive cultivation. And then he will suppress the customs barriers and tolls, the roadblocks and detours imposed by imitation: this means both increasing the number of ways in which the work is determined and, at the same time, tightening its unity. The deep motive for the experimentation lies in this: giving Beauty a tighter grain, a firmer, richer consistency. The artist's only concern should be art. And when we see Lapoujade's work, he doesn't seem to be looking for another way to paint but to be giving painting a new nature. The rest follows, of course. But the serious changes in all the arts are material first and the form comes last: it is the quintessence of matter. Lapoujade belongs to a generation of builders. After what he himself calls the 'disintegration of the figurative' by Picasso, Braque and a whole generation of analysts, all that was left for the newcomers was a teeming of colours and rhythms—shattered wreckage. They had no choice: these thinned-down, ductile materials permitted of, and were crying out for, integration into new wholes. Up to this point, these young people were a group and the same task awaited them all. Afterwards, each was alone: it was for each to question the new art as to its ends and resources. Lapoujade chose to restore the world to us. In my opinion, this was a decision of the first importance. But let us be assured that the world had asked nothing of art: if it made its return, bloody and new, that was because Painting demanded it.

Beauty is not a single-layered entity. It requires two unities, the one visible and the other secret. If a moment were to come, albeit at the end of a very long quest, when we summed up a work in a single view of it, the object would be reduced to its inert visibility, Beauty would vanish and ornament alone would remain. To put it more precisely, the unification the brush constantly strives after, and our eye in its wake, must itself take as its goal the permanent reconstitution of a certain presence. And that presence, in turn, can yield its indecomposable unity to us only in the medium of Art, through the painter's effort—or our own—to construct or reconstruct the beauty of a whole. The act is purely aesthetic, but, to the very extent that no one concerns himself with it, the Whole insinuates itself into the visual syntheses, ordering and confirming them. In fact, the paths traced out by the painter for our eyes are paths that *we* must find and undertake to travel along: it is up to *us* to embrace these sudden expansions of colour, these condensings of matter; *we* must stir up echoes and rhythms. It is at this moment that Presence, that rejected intuition, comes to our aid: it does not itself determine the itinerary but overdetermines it. To *construct*, it will be enough to establish visible relationships. To safeguard that construction, to protect it from total absurdity, a transcendent unity is necessary. This unity ensures that the movement of the gaze will never stop: it is this constant roving of the eyes that produces the permanence of invisible unity. We shall, then, keep on moving around; if we were to stop, everything would break to pieces.

If you ask what this Presence is, I can reassure you right away: Lapoujade is no Platonist and neither am I. I don't think he is pursuing an Idea through his compositions. No, the regulative principle makes its appearance in each canvas and remains inseparable from that canvas: neither can be said to exist elsewhere. This abstract painter wants a concrete presence in every picture. And if the same name has to be given to all these presences, let us say that each of his works has sought a meaning for itself and has, in each case, found one. But, above all, let us avoid confusion here: a meaning is not a sign or a symbol or even an image. When Canaletto paints Venice, the likeness is perfect: as half-sign and half-image, the Queen of the Seas has taken care to avoid any confusion: you can't mistake it. Hence the painting has no meaning. No more than does an identity card. When Guardi paints rags and the weathering of bricks by the most corrosive of lights, the chosen alleyways or canals are not, as they say, very meaningful. It's a stretch of wharf of a kind you find everywhere or a studied deformation of light. Canaletto uses his brush in the service of his native city; Guardi is concerned only with plastic problems, with light and matter, with colours and light, with achieving the unity of the multiple by means of a rigorous imprecision. As a result, Venice is present in each of his paintings; present as it was for him and as it is for us; and also as everyone *feels* it but as no one has seen it. One day, I visited a writer in the fine garret of a brick *palazzio* beside a *rio*. None of the forms that Guardi loves to paint was to be seen. Yet as soon as I saw the place, as soon as I glimpsed the condition of my host, I thought of the painter: I rediscovered Venice, my Venice, all of our Venices, and I have experienced the same feeling about other people, other objects and other places. The same? Well, not quite: meaning depends on the matter in which it surfaces; Guardi will always say more than we feel, and say it differently. The fact remains that 'figurative' painting was the first to submit itself to the double unity rule. But, paradoxically, the incarnation of the invisible presence is more or less concealed in that form of painting by a brutal, mechanical bond which subordinates the portrait to its model in a manner external to the work of art. When an artist paints grapes, the belief is that the bunch of grapes is *incarnated* in his work. As though, ever since Apelles, the artist's only ambition were to deceive birds. Yet when Van Gogh painted a field, he didn't claim to transfer it to his canvas: he was attempting, by way of a deceptive figuration and with no other concern than for art, to embody in the application of paint to a vertical surface an immense, full world in which there were fields and people, Van Gogh among them. Our world.

Let us note that Van Gogh never tried to make us see a field with crows nor, even less, fruit trees, for the simple reason that these objects are not even representable. They provide an aesthetic material for the incarnation of that presence that defies the brush: the world covering itself with fields, the world spurting forth, all sap and flowers, from a magic wand. And the image still has to be very far removed from the model or else the world will not be 'captured' in it. It was essential that Van Gogh should begin by distorting everything, if he wanted to show us through art that the most tender, most innocent of natural gracilities is inseparable from horror. There are, then, three elements in 'the figurative': a guide-reality, which the canvas claims to confront; the representation made of this by the painter; and the presence that eventually descends into the composition. One can understand that this trinity might have seemed awkward. It is. The guide-reality, ambiguous in its essence, guides nothing at all: it floats, belly up, and nothing will be done for it, nothing can be made of it unless it is rendered entirely real or, in other words, made into an imaginary object. No field will impart the charm or horror of the world unless it is seriously reconstructed; or, rather, it will impart both: together and separately. It will reflect everything, but incoherently: there will be no sureness of touch, but merely approximations, a hotchpotch, confusion. This dreary disorder will not, without some forcing, render the complex structures of the *felt* universe: what the painter will add to the canvas will be the days of his life, passing time and the time that does not pass. These powerful reagents will transform the represented object: it will not be the inert particularity of the model that passes into the picture but nor will the form traced take on the generality of the type or sign. The world's action on a human being and the human being's long passion for the world, both summed up in the mendacious flash of a snapshot, will endow these few acres of clay with a biographical singularity. It will fall to them to evoke the adventure of living, of contemplating the very outbreak of madness, of hurtling towards death. At the same time, this chance form, integrated, for want of anything better, into a composition, will undergo art's planings and filings, its removal of rough edges. Vincent says he 'is doing' a field, but isn't under any illusions: he creates order on a canvas without ever entirely wishing to restore to it the gentle yielding of the corn to the wind, nor entirely to call on to his canvas that enormous, intimate presence that is man, heart of the world, embraced by the world, heart of man. When at last he puts down his palette, when the presence is embodied in the composition, what has become of the representation of the object? It is a transparency, a memory, barely more than a magnificent allusion to the object represented. And the field, finally, the simple field the artist was trying to represent, would be eliminated from the canvas if the world did not come to its aid and incarnate itself, as unfigured swaying corn and harvests, in this thick paste of a rimless sun or in this wheel of suns at ground level that are the picture's only real inhabitants and the only true vestiges of the creative act.

In figurative painting, conventions have scarcely any importance: it is enough simply to convince us that the figure proposed is, within *this* reference system, the best representation of the object. The best: that is to say, the strongest, densest, most meaningful. It is a matter of skill or good fortune. However, since the last century, with every new option, the gap has widened between figure and represented object. The greater the distance separating the two, the stronger the internal tension of the work. At the point when resemblance is thrown overboard entirely, when notice is given that all similarity between image and object is purely fortuitous, then meaning, liberated by the collapse of *representation*, manifests itself in its negative aspect. Meaning is the mark of this failure of representation and shines out through the dissemblances, lacunae, approximations and intentional indeterminacies. Though itself invisible, it has a blinding effect because it dissolves figures into its non-figurable presence. Such are the meanings that haunt our world too: they both obliterate detail and feed on it. Every brick wall, if it stands alone, hides Venice from me; I shall sense the city through the necessary disappearance of its palaces, the gathering of its plumage into a single feather that I do not see. On the canvas, the artist still offers us the figurative elements of an intuition but he strikes them out immediately: roused to life by this rejection, the Presence—which is the thing itself without details in a space without parts[24]—will take on body. But this is a trap set by the artist: he introduces other figures, whose nature is alien to that of the object designated, other material—paper, sand, pebbles—and other allusions; he wishes to produce a new entity: a presence all the more austere for still being fuelled by an absence, but an absence already secretly falsified by substitutions. How many painters between the wars dreamed—as simultaneous chemists and alchemists—both of forcing gold into being and of imparting to it the character of base metal? One of them wished for a double transmutation; he wanted to paint a wardrobe that would be a frog without ceasing to be a wardrobe: a chosen signal would have made it possible—this was his hope—to take each of these objects as, in turn, plastic substance or incarnation. The aim was a suspect one: the intention was not to flush out the scattered meanings of the world and have us experience them, but to create others that had never existed. These were insignificant tricks, uninspired sleights of hand. At the end of this long crisis, in which artistic creation sank into illusionism because it had failed to understand that the imaginary is the only absolute, figuration had the good sense to explode. And meaning?

Did that also disappear at the same time? Quite the reverse: as we have seen, there was no true connection between the two. Once released, the incarnate presence revealed itself as the most rigorous exigency of abstract art.

Images that break and fall to pieces are not a studied option on the part of the new painters but an event in progress, the consequences of which are not all known. This permanent deflagration is a chain reaction from one canvas to another: painters see it as both their problem and their material. Art gives them an explosion to govern. They will do so by an explosive order. Their elders sowed the wind; those who wish today to master the whirlwind will have to become cyclones within the cyclone and organize the tiniest straw in that wind with implacable rigour. This pulverulence has to be preserved and reduced by invented laws and by a visual logic. They have to seek out the manifold unity of multiplicity and acquire a new sense of the canvas. They have to know how to give full value there to these dilations and thickenings, these revolving fields of flame, these black flecks, these spots, pools and smears of blood in the sun—and also how to contain them. They have to know how to employ these fluidities and densities as part of the overall ceremony of the artwork, using the most rigorous process of selection and pruning. There is no more hiding, no more fakery and no details are negligible any longer; there is simply a superabundance in which everything is of equal value. But, though he confines himself to experimenting with colours, to strengthening lines, to discovering opportunities and exploiting them, to structuring the whirlwind and, lastly, to counterbalancing local turbulences by pursuing a rigorous equilibrium, the painter will give definitive form to a tremendous event: at worst, we shall see a rose-window, at best a graceful merry-go-round.

To maintain the rhythm of the explosive space, to prolong the vibration of colours, to exploit to the full the strange and terrifying disintegration of being and its whirlwind movement, it is essential that the brush impose a meaning on it and impose that meaning on us. No mobility without a path and no path without a direction—who will decide these vectoral determinations if the artist does not de-condition sight? But a very powerful motive has to be found for the eye to

undertake the unification of this sumptuous dispersion, without seeking a figure or a likeness in it. Only
one such motive exists: the secret unity of the work.

This is, so to speak, in the picture itself. There is,
said Éluard, another world and it is in this one. But
we shall not find this unity if we do not ourselves proceed to unify the canvas. Each time we effect new syntheses or the eye establishes local unities, the presence
is revealed a little more. We shall never have the whole
of it, for it consists only in the work itself, regarded as
an organism. Lapoujade was invited by Art to reject
the false unity of the figurative. Barely had he done so
when he understood what was being asked of him:
chance must be driven out and this indefinitely divis-
ible surface must be endowed with the indivisible
unity of a Whole.

Some have felt as he did on this. They have chosen lyrical unity. The painter hurls himself into his
canvas with all his *élan*, only then to resurface from it
and hurl himself at us. He has painted the way one
strikes a blow: the presence embodied in the work is
his own. He gives his work the lithe unity of an as-
sault. Lapoujade doesn't think lyrical painting wholly

561

impossible. It is feasible; it has been done. Done already. For his part, he would be afraid that this self-projection into the pure medium of art may not be readable. And, of course, despite what is too often said of it, Art is not a language. But it isn't true either that we communicate only by signs. We *experience* through others what others *experience* as we do; we are, for our fellow creatures, a shared source of experience. And these painters aspire precisely to impart the unity of their emotions—an impulse or a release—to the canvas; in short, they choose the exhibition-going public as the people to whom to impart the experience of their own particular adventure. Is this possible without some prior unanimity? Singularity can be discovered only as a differentiation from what is common to all. If it were just a matter of painting, everyone could take their chance: art would remain intact, even if it locked itself up in hermeticism. But lyrical painting presents itself also as an act that sets its indispensable seal on multiplicity. Art demands that I repeat that act; Beauty doesn't occur unless I have repeated it.

Since the eye's immediate motive is communication and since communication represents both the completion, endlessly recommenced, and the perpetual animation of the abstract work, the painter must have a direct, constant concern for it. Since meaning is revealed through unification, and since it becomes unified in revelation, it must by nature be communicable. To set conditions without giving oneself the means to fulfil them is to run the risk of ultimate failure, of the work sinking into indeterminacy.

This, I believe, is Lapoujade's deepest conviction: painting is a great avenue of communication; at every crossroads it finds the presences it embodies. And yet it doesn't have to go looking for them. If the artist wishes to gather meanings, they are to be had by the dozen; the eye will perhaps read them, but languidly, without becoming spellbound by their obviousness or their necessity. If they are not both necessitated by the tremors of a material in process of organization and by urgent imperatives shared by painter and viewers, how could they be imposed upon us? These obvious facts meet; the artist is there and we all come together. If he hears the confused murmurings of the highways and byways, without even straining his ear to catch them, this is because he is himself a crossroads, as we all are. Yet there are still some deserted or disused avenues here and there. Lapoujade, that infinitely diverse crossroads of man and world, is a traffic jam, a marking-of-time suddenly interrupted by shouts or silence, who stubbornly restarts after mysterious asphalt-hued moments of suspense. He believes solitude doesn't suit painting and his canvases have convinced me of it.

One day, said Marx, there will not be any painters: just human beings who paint. We are a long way from that. But Lapoujade is this strange contradiction: with a number of other artists of the same age, he is the man who has reduced painting to the sumptuous austerity of its essence. Yet, amidst the human presences embodied in his canvases, he is the first not to claim any privilege. As a painter, through his painting, he tears off the artist's mask; there remain only human beings and this one, with no special prerogatives, a man among other men, the painter abnegating himself by the splendour of his work. Look: he has painted crowds. He is not the first to do so: with people on canvases it was always 'the more the merrier'. But the old masters kept themselves safely tucked away: they worked at the prince's right hand and on a dais. Or, at a pinch, facing the populace and on a level with it, but protected by soldiers. There was no mistaking what the work was meant to say: 'I'm a painter, I belong to you, the rich and powerful; I'm showing you—from the outside—the rabble you govern, from which your favour has removed me for all time.' The age was responsible, but 'figurative painting' was too. How was one to paint the crowd as seen by itself, as it experienced and made itself, here and everywhere; what curve could one impart to space to inscribe in it that infinite circle whose centre is everywhere, merging everywhere with its circumference? How could each individual be depicted as both driver and driven? And what shapes, what colours would show that each of these human molecules is incomparable to the others and that all are interchangeable? What system of reference could one choose to make art-lovers understand that a crowd receives a painter into itself only by undoing him; that he finds he is not allowed the minuscule distance, the tiny independence of eye that makes for reliable testimony; that the alerted masses refuse to open themselves up to witnesses and that you have to go in there entirely naked, without any special badges of honour, simply as a man. You have to take part in everything, to flee or to charge, to become a driven driver, to be both active and passive. You have to bear the weight of twenty or a hundred thousand other 'selves' to be able to come back to one's painting with, in the best of cases, a memory that is violent but formless. The internal reactions of a mass gathering are not visible to the eye: they invade you, you experience them and, in the end, you notice you are having those reactions. Just try and depict that figuratively!

Here, then, is the new painter of crowds: he can embody their presence only by refusing to represent them. Of course, when he drives the Figure from his studio, he, like all artists, pronounces that vow of poverty that Beauty has always demanded and always will. But he does much more: he spurns the dais; as a man, he refuses to be excluded by the privileges of his mission and to contemplate his species from outside. The figurative is a double exile, the rejection of

the painter by the model and vice versa. By deforming the figure, anarchistic bourgeois artists spoke to
us with gentle irony of their solitude: you see, there is
no communication!

On the other hand, if one is Lapoujade, communicating is what one does first. One is a real, stormy,
troubled crowd; one *exposes oneself to it* and, after the
progressive elimination of the detail, there remains
the *meaning* of the demonstrations at the Place de la
République, of the police charging on 27 October.[25]
The meaning: an experience had by thousands of
strangers, certain that it was the same for each of
them. To embody that experience, a material is required: language is not enough; it breaks down a multiplicity of facts, each of which derived its meaning
from the others. Provided that he, as a painter, attempts
to set down only his diverse, multifarious adventure as
an interchangeable human being, Lapoujade will lend
his crowds a material form that is shifting but rigorously unified within dispersion. The unification of the
atomized particles brings something beyond them
into being: the explosive unity of the masses. On the
basis of which, the crowd is, in each individual, called

upon to recover the detailed totality of a life. The painter guides us: there are, he says, immediate data of expression:[26] the sombre, dense heaping-up of colours in the lower part of the canvas, a raising of matter, the joyful upward spurting of light, a hundred others, a thousand others: they are the key elements of the *dispositif*. But their appeal is solely to the heart. The singularity of the paths traced by the brush is what is essential. Compact in places, rarefied in others, laid on thick at times and liquid at others, the matter of the painting doesn't claim to make the invisible visible, to achieve that metamorphosis around us, and through us, of a clearing in the scrubland, the steppes or the virgin forest. By its texture and its itineraries, it merely *suggests*. The contrast between the rigorous determination of the artwork and the relative indeterminacy of the experience or ordeal, serves the painter; the tight patches of paint seem to move apart from each other; a new path, suddenly uncovered, forces the colours to pale by establishing new relations between them: we shall, in the end, through these metamorphoses, grasp the presence 'without parts' of the demonstration as it is embodied with all its densities at once. And then, suddenly, there is a streak of asphalt: the void. This overflows and runs off to the bottom of the canvas. But is there a top or a bottom? The space is itself *a meaning*; it is composed by the crowd and is determined as a function of the crowd's acts. This streak is, simultaneously, a thick downward plunge and a flight to the horizon; it matters little which. It is the sudden opening-up of the void: the police are charging. Are we going to run or resist? Whatever we do, the space exists with all its dimensions in one: it is distance—which shrinks on one side and, on the other, seems interminable. But what good are words, the patch of paint is enough: the meaning is resuscitated. Not, as in the age of the conjurors, a faked-up presence, such as a fish/wardrobe or a wolf/table: the real presence, but indecomposable—that is to say, both general and particular, enriched for everyone by everything he has succeeded in putting into it, by everything the man who paints has put into it.

Man amid men, men amid the world, the world amid men: this is the unique presence claimed by this unmastered explosion; this is the single—particular and general—test that Lapoujade undergoes with us, by us and for us; the single communication that we are a part of from the outset and that illuminates the canvas even before being illuminated by it. But this rejection of privilege, identical to the rejection of figuration, is a commitment by the painter and the man: it leads Lapoujade, as he passes from one painting to another, towards the most radical consequences of the undertaking. And, first, if the painter is no longer a contemplative being, if he is thrown out into the midst of all his peers—other human beings—the constant bond that unites him with, or sets him against, each and every one is *practice*. He acts, suffers, frees himself and dominates or is dominated; contemplation was merely passive; the brush must render action: not from the outside but as the ordeal of the Other suffered by the man who paints him: the Meaning will be the incarnation of the Other, as known from the change he is made to undergo, and of the painter himself discovering himself through that change which *he* undergoes or inflicts. However it is painted, the inertia of a Nude is generally distressing: the woman is alone, with the painter at the other end of the room. No one in real life—and particularly not the painter—has contemplated such a docile Nudity from such a distance. Lapoujade paints couples. He has, at times, evoked the tenderness of adolescent flesh. But in the erotic series he entitled *le Vif du Sujet,* he has tried to suggest woman as men approach her, as she appears in the act of love. A Nude, when all is said and done, is something in which two people are involved. Even if the only presence is female, the male is suggested in the very movement of the colours; that is what gives *this particular* presence to the female in-habitant of the paintings. By becoming the totalizing unity of the bursts of colour and matter, action, the many-sided relation between human beings, brings an ultimate precision to the painter's project: the non-figurative offers its visible splendours to the incarnation of the non-figurable. The abstract order initially seemed limiting; in fact, it reveals a new field and novel functions for painting.

The other consequence of this option is clearly the decision the unprivileged painter makes to mark his solidarity with other human beings. This solidarity is something self-evident: he has only what they have; wants nothing more than they do; is nothing more than they are. And then, this is a kind of permanent act: woman appears on his canvases through love, men through the common struggle. The most surprising but simplest truth is that the choice of abstraction should, in the very name of art, reinstall man on Lapoujade's canvases. Not, as he was for centuries, in the guise of prince or prelate, but modestly, anonymously, in his patient, stubborn struggle to escape hunger, to free himself from oppression. Man is everywhere in Lapoujade's paintings: he has, in fact, never stopped painting human beings or deepening his depiction of them. At the present moment, he understands that Man, seen by an unprivileged eye, is primarily neither great nor small today, neither beautiful nor ugly: art commands him to set the human realm on his canvases in all its truth. And the truth of that realm today is that the human race comprises torturers and their accomplices, and martyrs. The torturers are few in number, the accomplices far more numerous; the majority is made up of torture victims or candidates for torture. Lapoujade has understood this: no one can speak of men in 1961 without dealing first with persecutors; no one can speak to the French of the French unless he first speaks of tortured Algerians: this is the face we show to the world today; let us contemplate it as it is; afterwards we shall decide whether to retain it or operate on it.

Lapoujade chooses to show torture because it is our deeply ingrained truth—alas, our ignoble truth. At the point when he attempts to paint it, he notices that his art, which called forth the unity of this 'meaning', was the only art that permitted such a depiction. The triptych is beautiful without reserve; it may be so without remorse. This is because, in non-figurative painting, Beauty does not conceal, but *shows*. The picture will not present anything to be *seen*. It will allow the horror to descend into it, but *only if it is beautiful.* By this I mean, if it is organized in the richest, most complex way. The precision of the scenes evoked depends on the precision of the brushwork; in the tight drawing and grouping of this concert of striations, of these beautiful but sinister colours, lies the only way of making us feel the meaning of their agony for Alleg and Djamila.[27] But, though it enhances the plastic vision, meaning does not, as I have said, bring in new elements that are foreign to the ensemble as seen.

Meaning will embody itself: in this frenzy of colours, we shall apprehend bruised flesh and unbearable suffering. But that suffering is the suffering of the victims. Let us not claim it is—in this discrete, imperious form—unbearable to look at. Nothing appears other than (behind a radiant Beauty, and thanks to it) a pitiless Destiny, which human beings—which *we*—have made for humanity. The success is total; this is because it originates in painting and its new laws: it conforms to the logic of the abstract. It is, I believe, quite a noteworthy event that a painter has been able to give such visual pleasure by showing us, unvarnished, the shattering bereavement of our consciences.

Méditations, 2 (second quarter 1961). On an exhibition by Lapoujade entitled *Foules* (Crowds).[28]

masson[29]

The artist is a suspect; anyone can question him, arrest him and drag him before the judges; all his words and works can be used against him. He has some major advantages, but, in exchange, every citizen has the right to call him to account. If Masson painted his children, he would be asked whether he loved them. And why paint his children rather than a potter, a fuller or a Gaulish warrior wounded at Vercingetorix's side? He prefers to draw Titans and hence he will be asked the preliminary question: do you believe in your mythology? If he were not sincere, he would lose any chance of making an emotional impact. Of course, we don't require a contemporary French painter to have the faith of Hector Hippolyte, the Vodou priest who painted Goddess Erzulie and Baron Samedi as he saw them every day. But there are many different ways of believing. If these monsters had come from his pen of their own accord and his own will had played no part in them, if he had remained the mere witness of this automatic drawing and seen it as expressing his hidden desires and unconscious terrors, I would say he believes in them. But this is not the case: if he acknowledges that 'some subjects appeared unexpectedly', he adds afterwards that they 'came in by accident, swelling the initial river'. What is more, he is not the witness to his work: he has no need to learn its meaning, since he knows the meaning as he makes the work: 'There isn't one of these drawings in which I can't explain the symbolism. It would even be easy, with most of them, to make out an origin . . . [they are], in short, the products of my culture and my dealings with the world . . . Moreover, reminiscences of things seen.' There is nothing here that presses itself upon him in the manner of an obsession: Nature and other people have supplied him with pretexts. But perhaps what is at issue here is a conventional language he has deliberately adopted, which he regards as alone capable of symbolizing the world of eros: wouldn't that be another way of believing? No; what do they symbolize, these bleeding eagles wresting themselves from the earth? The difficult break with the past and with custom, with instincts and our animal natures, with traditions and conformism? The painful, abstract solitude of pride? Transcendence? The trauma of birth? 'The horror of the earth in which its plumage is caught' (Mallarmé)?[30] Everything and nothing, anything you like. On the contrary, these giants came to him from a friendly conversation on Bachofen. Since Masson knows this, he is no longer an adherent of symbolism; he is clothing a body of knowledge. He is doing what he likes doing: the pencil launches out, sketches the curves that come easiest; the form emerges, unfinished and ambiguous. In a single movement, Masson deciphers that form and traces it out; he invents the interpretation from the figure and subjects the figure to the interpretation. In a sense, he believes so little in what he is doing that this little piece of pyrotechnics is a farewell. Masson has made these drawings in order to take his leave of all mythology.

Should we condemn him for this? Should we see this imagery merely as a literary conceit? Far from it. It is by taking his images seriously that he can be said to be making literature. Since reality can be approached without the aid of metaphors, why, then, disguise it in a tawdry get-up? It isn't a painter's business to invent symbols for the libido or the Oedipus complex: mental patients take care of this and will do a much better job of it. Masson's bestiary is born of a more profound, more technical concern. It is a provisional response to the question his painting raises for the painter. Are we saying, then, that a mythology can resolve a problem of technique? Yes, if the technique and its problems are themselves born of a myth. Masson is mythological in his essence—every bit as much as Bosch or Hippolyte. But his myths lie well this side of sexuality, at the level where, to speak like sociologists, 'nature' and 'culture' are indistinguishable, where one cannot separate the project of painting from the project of being a man.

Depending on their temperaments, poets and artists employ two main types of inspiration, the one expansive, the other retractile. There is avarice and fear in this latter: one gathers together, delimits, stifles, confines and corsets within outlines; one does what one can to persuade oneself and others that things are absolutes, that space is a shadow, a conceptual order and that plurality is merely an appearance donned by unity. One autumn day, Coppée accompanied Mallarmé on his daily walk. The following year, Mallarmé wrote to him: 'My walk reminds me by its autumn . . .' There is a large degree of avarice in this: all walks heaped into a single one. I see Mallarmé's walk—he had his wife, his daughter, his cane and his walk—as a re-volving ball: the seasons, days and hours are lights that tint it delicately. This Platonism is a myth. And the outline is an analogous myth in painting: you won't find 'in Nature' those window-leadings that frame Rouault's faces; they express nothing visible but, rather, a holy terror, the hatred of change and plural-ity, a deep love of order, which aims, beyond the lac-erations of time and space, to restore their calm everlastingness to objects. Rouault paints the world as God made it, not as we see it, while Cézanne paints Nature 'as God lays it out before our eyes' and Gris paints 'that initial idea, that notion of the object which is equal for all and which, in our example of the table, is shared by the housewife, the carpenter and the poet.' If the notion is shared by all, it belongs to no one as his own: Gris' table is the table seen by an abstract, universal subject.

We may contrast Rimbaud: 'Dawn, like a flight of doves' or 'its scarlet and black wounds shine forth from glorious flesh. The true colours of life deepen, dance and detach themselves around the Vision in the making.'[31] This is what I shall term the unity of fragmentation. Far from the plurality of substances being concealed, it is emphasized; even where it is not visible, there is an assumption of diversity, but that diversity is then made to represent the unity of an explosive power. The poet who sees the dawn as a flock of doves explodes the morning like a powder keg and says: this deflagration is the morning. For thinkers of this particular bent, beauty becomes 'fixed-explosive'.[32] The impenetrability and corpse-like rigidity of space will, by the poet's artifices, become a conquering force, its divisibility to infinity a glorious efflorescence. Every object extends everywhere, through everything. To be is to quiver in an infinite agonizing struggle and to be a part, while clinging on to oneself, of the furious terrestrial tide which at every moment claims new regions of being from the nothingness. This dionysian myth causes us to swell pleasantly and fills us with a sense of our power; in the poet it draws its source from an infernal pride that agrees to die in order to be everything, from a self-assured generosity both giving and losing itself. A creator's myth: one thinks of the Jesus Patibilis of the Manichees, crucified on matter and making the entire world 'the Cross of Light'. But for those who want to change the world and reinvent love, Jesus simply gets in the way. Or, rather, the Saviour who, in all things, shows his 'pathos-laden face' is man himself; their aim is to pin the exteriority of Nature down to reflecting human transcendence back to man.

These are myths, then, and myths, also, the fragmentation wrought by Impressionism, its exploding of forms and negation of outlines. And the dynamism of Masson is a myth too. The painting of Cézanne, Rouault and Gris reveals their belief, admitted or otherwise, in a divine almighty power; Masson's is characterized by what Kahnweiler terms 'the intrusion of the existential element'.

But do not look for anguish in it—at least not first and foremost. No; but while the painters of forms seek to paint Nature without human beings and still believe the experimenter can withdraw from the experiment to contemplate it from without, Masson knows the experimenter is an integral part of the experimental system, that he is a real factor in the physical event and that he modifies what he sees—not in his mind, as idealists contend, but out there in the world—by the mere fact of seeing. This artist wants to put the painter in the painting and show us the world with man in it. The temptation will be to call him a painter of movement, but that isn't quite exact. He is trying not so much to represent a real movement on a still canvas as to reveal the potential motion of stillness. He has not, for many a long year, thought of eliminating outlines, so powerful is the influence of Cézanne and Cubism on the painters of his generation; but he struggles immediately to transform their meaning. At the same time as he is attempting to pin down this perpetual upheaval, these serial protoplasmic explosions that seem to him to form the innermost contexture of things—their substance—he is trying to metamorphose the line that surrounds them into an itinerary, trying to make it the arrow which, on a map, indicates the movement of an army, a mission or the winds. But whose itinerary? The movement of whom or of what? This is where Masson's original myth is to be discovered, his myth of the human being and of the painter.

Imagine a line drawn on a blackboard: all its points exist simultaneously; this means, among other things, that I am free to travel along the series in any direction. And no doubt I have to 'pull' this line and my eyes have to 'follow' it from one end of the blackboard to the other. But, as they move from right to left or from bottom to top, I still have in my mind—and even in my eye muscles—the felt possibility of moving them from top to bottom or from left to right, so that the movement they carry out seems to me to be the pure effect of my whim and has nothing to do with the figure under consideration: the line is inert. However, in certain cases and for certain reasons, it may be that my eyes are compelled to obey a definite itinerary in following this line: it then becomes a vector. In that case, my gaze slides from one point to another like a glass alley on an inclined plane and its motion is accompanied by a sense that no other motion is possible. But since I can no more travel backwards along this line than one can travel backwards in time, this impossibility confers on space, in one specific region, the irreversibility that properly belongs only to time: I project the movement of my eyes into the line at the same time as I carry it out. It seems to me that the movement comes from the line, and I make this slipstream of light one of its properties. The line both exists already and forces me to trace it out. Succession is, in this way, embodied in juxtaposition; space absorbs time, becomes imbued with it and reflects it to me. And since causality is merely the unity of the moments of an irreversible series, the line ceases to be inert and manifests a kind of inner causality. Each point on the line seems to me the effect of the points I have passed through to arrive at it and the cause of the points I shall pass through thereafter. Being pushed out from the preceding segment, it seems to project the following segment out in front of itself, when in reality it merely projects my gaze forward. The mind strings the points together into a synthetic unity of apperception, at the same time as, in each of them, causality plays the role of a disintegrative power; in this way, the vector appears both as substance and event; it seems to be its own cause since it both *is* already and creates itself through our vision.

But let us come back to painting: if the outline of painted objects is merely a line, everything sinks into the eternity that is a timeless inertia; but if the painter can turn the outlines into vectors, then the viewers' eyes could be said to confer on them the living unity of a chain of melody. This is Masson's dream: that his painting should be more urgent, more insistent than that of the Cubists or the Fauves, that it should contain an additional exigency. This is his ideal: that everything should organize and create itself before your eyes if you read it the right way round; that everything should scatter into chaos if you read it against the grain. And this is his problem: how to compel us to grasp the lines in his pictures, and particularly the outlines of objects, as vectors. In other words, what are the psychological factors that can prevail on us to see a mountain or a road going in one particular direction?

The answer is clear: a line becomes vectorial only when it reflects back to me my own power to move my eyes along it. It seems at each point both to retain its past and to outrun itself towards its future but in fact it is *I* who outrun myself; the orientation of the vector is merely the provisional definition of my immediate future. But as the line is, in itself, a mere juxtaposition of points, the demand it exerts is not the product of its physical structure but of its human signification. I can see the road that runs beneath my window as a strip or as a flow. In the former case, I view it in its material aspect; in the latter I consider it in the totality of its meaning, like the wake left behind by marching crowds, or a static vehicle that will shortly carry me to my place of work; I incorporate into this whitish strip the oriented labour of the road-builders who made it or the road-menders who maintain it, the quickening force of the lorries that run along it, the call of the great factories of eastern France that it 'serves'. Its vectorial nature is, if you will, 'frozen human labour'. But, you may say, a mountain is not something made by man and yet I can choose to see it as something rising up or as a mass of fallen earth. Yes, but that depends on whether some precise motive compels me to 'read' it from base to summit and find in it the movement of an arrogant ascent, or from summit to base, when it reflects the image of the social forces crushing me and my secret prostration. In a word, the line or surface will force themselves upon me as vectors only if they manage, by some particular means, to reflect human transcendence. Every vector is already a myth because it secretly appeals to anthropomorphism: it is a sacred space.

If the painter wants to breathe life into his picture, let him project human transcendence on to things, let him unify them—even more than by colour harmonies or formal relations—by sweeping them all up together in a single human movement; let them form the act of taking, rejecting, fleeing—in a word, let man, visible or hidden, be the magnetic pole that draws the whole canvas towards himself. This is Masson's intention; but in him, ends and means are mingled: if the human dimension haunts his paintings and engravings, that is because he sees Nature through man; the thunderbolts that streak across his paintings express the initial choice this Dionysian artist made of himself, his refusal to wrest himself from the world to see it from some Olympian height, his desire to plunge into the heart of being and to paint the tracks left by his descent into the world. Man is the refractive medium through which Masson sees things and wants to make us see them, the deforming mirror that reflects faces back to him. For in Masson's work, man himself is seen through man. If a painter of the last century wanted to represent some horrible character, he would give him the forms and colours he thought likely to inspire horror in us: Masson wants to imbue his monsters with the horror they inspire, not offer them with all the deformations our horrified gaze produces in them. Where Titian or Rubens painted a woman as desirable, he wants to paint her as desired. Man's desire slips into this female flesh, acts as a leaven on it, makes it 'rise', stretches it, shapes it; the outlines of a breast are traced by a caressing hand; the entire body becomes a thunderbolt, the lightning flash of a ravishment, it bears the marks of the havoc wrought upon it. There are no circles any longer, but whirlings. No vertical lines, but ascents or falls or downpours. No light any more, but simply grains of energy. 'Cosmogonies, germinations, insect dances in the grassy jungle, eggs hatching, eyes bursting within the mother-earth, in the recesses of the female earth.'[33] The outlines must dance; there is only one goal to this immense witches' sabbath: to decompress the tightly knit grain of being and free its internal energies, to introduce succession into bodies. Masson wants to paint time.

How will he paint it? How, in fixing on the canvas these neutral, inert surfaces, which we can choose to regard as still or mobile, will he compel us never again to see them at rest? How will he force us to see them, once and for all—and even against our will—as these turgescences, these erections, these screes, these flows, these funnel-shaped whirls, moulding the substance of being? I saw this mountain as a great dormant heap. How will he transform it for me into this sharp ascending mass that suddenly breaks off, slants away and runs off towards the east? He is constantly searching for ways and means, for solutions. What if he abandoned the line? No, he won't give it up until he has worn it threadbare. Though a prisoner of the outline, which is a halting, a finitude, he wants his canvas to be one whole outburst, one whole blossoming; this fertile contradiction is at the origin of all his advances.

From this point of view, his mythologies are ultimately just one of the solutions he has tried, and perhaps the most naïve. One day he trapped the sun.[34] The mousetrap that captures the sun in its steel jaws has no other goal than to manifest that heavenly body's 'intensibility' and its 'coefficient of adversity': once caught, the planet turns into a mouse and this gentle round mass rolls in a rumpled ball along an iron bar. It has become prey; the giant instrument bears witness to the human presence even in intersidereal space; a proof of the existence of man, just as the ordered movements of the heavens were for so long a proof of the existence of God. A rather literary proof. Masson soon abandons this approach and moves on to riddle-drawings: since Man alone infuses Nature with spirit, it is the human form he is going to inscribe everywhere, the human form he will have shine out for a moment atop everything and break down into vegetal sprays and mineral splashes. The tree here is a hand:[35] don't try to work out what Masson means. That would be to descend into literature. Masson doesn't engage in literature; he means nothing but what he says: the branches are fingers because only fingers spread apart, open up or clench, so as to take and grip; he asks of fingers only that they transform foliage into a gesture. If the shales here[36] evoke the image of a skeleton, this is because only man—and a few apes—stands upright: they represent a standing mountain. Look at this *Paysage de la Martinique* [Martinique landscape]:[37] the hills are thighs, calves, sexual organs; the roots are hands, without ceasing to be roots; you can see this as a tangle of limbs or a panorama, as you please. But it would be futile—and dangerous—to see this as the indication of some pansexualism: we would be falling back into metaphor. Legs and calves here assume the function of those arrows that are drawn on battle-plans, on the plans of strategic operations: they transform the lines of the mountain tops, the outlines of the hillocks into vectors. The best thing would be for us to sense these half-hidden muscles that silently drive the whole painting forward without our eyes actually noticing them. As for the female sex organ, which we find in so many pictures, it evokes neither fecundity nor rutting for Masson—or, at least, not initially. It represents discord, the gaping void, the explosive dislocation of a body. As early as 1922, in his *Croquis de femme* [Sketch of a Woman], he gave the parted legs of his models the role of suggesting the action of two forces applied at the same point, pulling in opposite directions. The sex was the bursting-out of the rent flesh as an effect of that tension; this is why Masson's pencil will so often transform it into a wound. We shall, at any rate, meet it again in most of his landscapes. Merely hinted at or highlighted, this tortured sex between parted legs is neither sign nor symbol but, rather, a motive schema. For, as Limbour has rightly underscored, it is discord that characterizes Masson's pictures. Not that Masson is particularly aggressive: but this balanced unbalancing will alone express that human transcendence he wishes to paint on to things, which is always both ahead of and behind itself, both particle and wave at the same time, still caught in the toils of being and yet already far off in the future, already laying siege to the places the bulk of the herd will come to occupy later. This discord blossoms into a mythology, for it imposes on Masson his forms and his subjects. Since we retain outlines and want to make the line signify the opposite of what it manifests ordinarily—not finitude but explosion, not the slumped inertia of being, which is what it is and nothing else, but a certain way of being all that one is not and never being quite what one is—we are led to make the line itself an ambiguous reality, like those double lines which, at places where a circle meets another, belong to the circumference of both and are, at one and the same time, themselves and other than themselves, themselves and their own wresting from themselves. Limbour has already pointed out how 'the main actor in the picture is a movement, clean lines which, with a lively—even a rash—*élan,* catch in their loops and at their extremities on to a number of individual attributes in which we recognize animals: heads and mouths, crests, feathers, tufts of fur, claws, etc.'[38] But this cannot be enough for Masson: it is by no means sufficient that the line is an arrow flying from one point to another; it has also, at each of its points, to be a becoming, an intermediary between one state and another: if all its inertia is to be expelled, the outline must enwrap a metamorphosis that is occurring, and we must never know whether it ends as a man or a stone because, within its confines, the stone becomes a man. In Masson's works, things are thus doubly human: they change into human beings so that the brushstrokes portraying them may suggest both movements and qualitative alterations. Masson comes, in this way, to retrace a whole mythology of metamorphoses: he brings the mineral, plant and animal kingdoms into the human realm. And, still in the same spirit, to unite these ambivalent forms by intimate relationships that are, at the same time, repulsions and dissonances, he devises a way of counterpoising them in the indissoluble unity of hatred, eroticism and conflict. When he draws *Two Trees* in 1943, it is not enough for these trees to be half man and woman: they have to make love into the bargain. And in *The Rape* in 1939, the two characters fuse to each other in the gaping, pained unity of a single wound, a single sex. This is how his subjects—rapes, murders, single combats, disembowellings and manhunts—are born.

But this monstrous universe is simply the complete representation of *our* universe. All this violence is there not to symbolize the savagery of our appetites and instincts: it is needed to fix our gentlest, most human acts on the canvas. It takes every bit of this frenzied eroticism to depict the most innocent of our desires. Sadism, masochism—all is in the service of movement. We have to see this fantastical, tortured fauna as the most ordinary of animals, plants and human beings. Masson believes in these nightmares, but they are the effects of his atheistic realism. Such are rocks, plants and man himself for man if God does not exist.

The drawings he offers us today make up his ultimate mythology. In them, a self-conscious art aims to express all the phases of movement. One should look to them for the graphic representation of movement and becoming. Not for anything else: that is certainly enough. Look at drawing no. 15, *Winged men caught in blocks of ice, breaking free from this Himalaya of polyhedrons only at the price of their skins.* First, what is it? A spurting forth: a sheaf of arrows, a divergent, ascending movement.

Why do these men have wings? Why are these winged creatures men? Because, without wings, the men would appear to be standing, not rising: the earth would be their support; they would, in the end, be obeying gravity and one might, with a certain malice, still see them hunkering down, bearing weight on their own feet. But the wing crowns the movement and completes it: it is not dynamic in itself and acts only through its signification. Look closer at these wings: they are an encumbrance; they fall down and turn inside out like umbrellas in the wind; only the human body will be able to represent effort and breaking free. And why are these men headless? Because the head arrests movement or channels it, diverts it to its advantage; even when only roughed out, it assumes too much importance: the force will be the greater for being blind. These creatures are made to be seen, not to see; a single gaze and everything would congeal. And why the blood, why the polyhedral crystals? Blood, pain and clenching of the muscles represent resistance; they communicate a grasping power to the pure matter: even the inert is a clutch, a claw. But, on the other hand, these claws have to be inert; the contrast between mineral and muscle has to be pushed to extremes; and what better symbol of the unalloyed, sombre obstinacy of the mineral than these polyhedra of ice? Wings, blood, crystals—here we have imagery in the service of movement: the human body, by contrast, provides the direct representation of soaring flight.

The eye is everywhere tugged apart by contradictions to the point where it explodes: the adolescent here is bowed down, like Atlas, beneath the weight of the world; he is leaning over to pick a flower. Is he leaning over, is he bowed down? You can see either as you please, and the contesting of the one by the other: this is already a metamorphosis. And here is a tiny little man in the hands of a giantess. Look at him: he is leaning up against a rock, the whole of the Titaness becomes a rock; her back, her powerful shoulder-blades are petrified. Now raise your eyes and look at the giantess herself. The semblance of petrification disappears; all is movement and there is no Titaness any more: a woman is soaring skywards. Similarly, these enormous hands holding tiny women represent the ambiguity of the human condition rather well;

look at them: the woman becomes a statuette, an amulet, an inert plaything. Look at the woman: her hands stiffen, they are marble hands, mere material supports. And it is our eye that operates the transubstantiation, our eye that leaves the flesh haunted by the memory of marble and the marble by a ghost of animal warmth. Everywhere we find thwarted, disappointed expectations, a deliberate transmutation of sensations: this sexual organ explodes, this head bursts into bloom, this female body trails off into a fog and the fog bleeds. Nowhere has Masson handled lines better, nowhere has he better lightened his outlines, made them mobile; nowhere are the slidings and swirlings of his surfaces more palpable. He is the perfect master of his mythological technique.

It is for this reason that he will abandon it. He doesn't know clearly, when he makes them, that his drawings are farewells and yet he isn't entirely unaware of it. He feels he has perfected his craft: it was a solution to his problem; he has to find others, he cannot content himself with a happy find which, once perfected, runs the danger of degenerating into a mere procedure. As a painter of movement, his art must itself be movement. He has a clear insight into what he is doing, now that he is no longer diverted by the difficulties of execution from seeing himself, and he discovers that his mythology is 'rigged': there is more here besides the drawing; it combines with significations that reach beyond graphic art; to animate his engravings or canvases Masson notices that he has resorted to symbols. To communicate a troubling softness to his female figures, to make us feel one sinks into them, he has used mist. That is to say, he has used all the associations of ideas and feelings that fog evokes in the viewer. He has only partly traced the outline of this misty woman: she is an open figure. But if he has given up the line, if he has cast off the brushstroke, this is because the misty substance he chose to paint gave him permission to abandon them. What if he gave up the guard-rails and safety-nets— all these protections by which his art is still hemmed in? What if, by simple decree, he rejected outlines?

He had, in fact, been patiently trying to wear them down for a long time. Between 1940 and 1947 he tried to eliminate their value and their function while persisting in drawing them: let them remain on the canvas or the paper if they like, but they are to stop signifying finitude. 'All determination,' said Spinoza, 'is negation.' It is this negation Masson is attempting to deny. Sometimes he scores the interiors of the bodies with thick lines, at the same time as he thins to the ultimate degree the external trace that delineates their shape: the accent is then put on substance and the furrows, striations and dividing lines look like internal movements of the flesh while the outer line that delimits that flesh—thin, dead, inert—seems an entirely temporary halt to its expansion.[39] At other times, the creature will spurt up from the earth in a kind of spiralling and the outline, knotted back on itself, caught in this live coiling, sticks to it, spirals with it and, far from looking like a barrier raised against the internal forces, seems drawn towards the 'inner space'.[40] At yet, at other times, he will cover his drawing with tangled curves, hatchings, fleckings: and the outline properly so-called, lost in the middle of this forest, devoured by the greenery, will lose both its autonomy and its discriminative function. Is it one of the countless crossed lines that depict the 'inside' of the face or one of those making up the background? Without abandoning it, he eliminates the graphic form by excess. During this time, by an osmosis occurring through this flimsy, impotent membrane, the background will penetrate into the form and the form will seep into the background. Even more boldly, he will double the outline and paint a face as though projected out in front of itself. It is the form this time that begins to break up and wrest itself from itself. One further step remained: it has now been taken. From 1948 onwards, the outline gives way; living substance breaks out of its shells and spreads across the picture. There is nothing left to stop Masson revealing his myth in all its Dionysian purity. 'If a leg falls into the sea,' the Stoics said strangely, 'the whole sea becomes leg.' In his latest canvases, legs, thighs and breasts fall into the sky, into the water: all the water, all the sky, the walls and the ceiling become breasts or thighs. The mythology is now redundant: there is no need to draw a mountain as a twisted, muscular leg any longer, since everything is in everything, the leg in the mountain and the mountain in the leg. 'Imagine a head of hair compared with a waterfall . . .' he wrote in 1947. But if he wanted to transform the waterfall into a head of hair, it was so as to make it more of a waterfall, so that the sensual impact of disarranged hair would make us feel the gentle, restless voluptuousness of the falling water. These comparisons are no longer necessary now. We do, admittedly, still see metamorphoses. But no longer the successive phases of a bird changing into a man: the metamorphosis is now that of something changing into a bird. 'I heard,' wrote Conrad one day, 'a rattling . . . muffled sounds . . . it was the rain.' This is what Masson wants to paint now: neither the taking-flight nor the pheasant, nor the pheasant taking off, but a taking-flight that becomes a pheasant. He goes into the field and a flare explodes in the bushes: this pheasant-explosion is his picture. He has retained everything of his earlier experimentation, but arranged everything in a new synthesis. Only now is it the time for us to look back at his 1947 drawings; only now can we understand them.

In 1947, they were simply a perfect accomplishment that seemed complete in itself: this was Masson's very own style, which had its limits and its outlines. Today, the engravings explode and they move us because we can see heralded in them, uncertainly as yet, a new and different approach.

Introduction to André Masson, *Vingt deux Dessins sur le thème du Désir* (Paris: F. Mourlot, 1961).

fingers and non-fingers

I got to know Wols in 1945.[41] He was bald and had a bottle and a knapsack. In the knapsack there was the world, his concern; in the bottle, his death. He had been handsome but he wasn't any longer: at thirty-three you would have taken him for fifty, were it not for the youthful sadness of his eyes. No one, himself included, thought he would live to a ripe old age. He made this clear himself on several occasions, taking no satisfaction from it, to point out his limitations. He had few plans: he was a man who was always beginning again, eternal in every moment. He always told you everything right off, and then he told you it again differently. Like 'the little waves of the port/that repeat without repeating'.[42]

His life was a rosary of battered beads, each of which embodied the world; the string could be cut at any point without doing any harm—that was how he put it. I now believe he had thrown himself into a short-term project, a single one, which was to kill himself, being convinced you can express nothing without destroying yourself. The bottle makes its appearance very early on in his drawings. He wasn't proud of this. Though sick and poor, stoicism and voluntarism were totally alien to him; he wasn't even contemptuous of his miseries: he spoke about them, rarely, but unrestrainedly—with a great deal of distance and a degree of collusion. To put it more accurately, he found them normal and, when all is said and done, insignificant. His real torments lay elsewhere, in the depths of him.

He couldn't get over the fact of belonging to our species: 'I am the son of man and woman, or so I've been told; that surprises me . . .'[43] He treated his fellow humans with a suspicious courtesy, preferring his dog to them. In the beginning, we hadn't perhaps been without interest, but something had got lost along the way. We had forgotten our *raison d'être* and launched ourselves into a frenzied activism which he, with his usual politeness, called 'scheming'. His nearest and dearest themselves remained so alien to him that he could work right there among them, despite their shouting and yelling. A coral among corals, he lay down on his bed, closed his eyes and the image 'gathered in his right eye'. He sketched crowds that are animal colonies: the people touch each other and perhaps smell one another; they certainly do not see or speak to each other, absorbed as each of them is in a solitary gymnastics of elongation. He had every reason to bear a grudge against us: the Nazis had driven him out, the Falangists had put him in prison, then expelled him, the French Republic had interned him.[44] But he never said a word about this and never, I believe, gave it a thought: these were our 'schemings' and they didn't concern him. Generous without warmth and attentive out of indifference, this princely tramp pressed on with his fruitful suicide night and day. At the end, his friends had to carry him, each day, to the Rhumerie martiniquaise and bring him back in the middle of the night, a little more dead each day, and each day a little more visionary. And why not? That is living.

When he opened up his bag, he pulled out words, some found in his head, most copied from books. He made no distinction between the two, though he scrupulously insisted on putting the author's name at the foot of every quotation: there had, after all, been an encounter and a choice. A choice of thought by man? No, in his view, it was the other way about. Ponge once said to me at about this time, 'One doesn't think, one is thought.' Wols would have agreed with him: the ideas of Poe or Lao-Tzu belonged to *him*, insofar as they had never belonged to *them*, and insofar as *his* ideas didn't belong to *him*. What were they about, these twenty-four maxims he carried around with him? Like his gouaches, about absolutely everything. Torn out of a book or from an individual's speech, cut adrift from all the surrounding circumstances, they seemed infinite or, rather, indefinite, unless one took the view that Wols was to be found in them *in person*. He was very attached to them. Though less than to the products of his paintbrush: for one thing, he was distrustful of words, those 'chameleons'. And rightly so. And yet we have to trust them or write nothing. His poems are not especially inspired. Above all, I sense that he used language to *reassure* himself: hardly any of the chosen phrases is without a little flash of mystery; the gilded verses of a white pantheism serve as commentaries to the blackest of works. He escaped horror by speaking. He knew this, I think. He left more than a hundred and fifty pictures, thousands of gouaches and two dozen maxims—never changed—which he had taken for his own in what were perhaps happier times, if he ever had any happier times. Before his de-tox, which came eight months before his death, he was starting to become muddled in his speech. He would sit down beside me in the morning, talk confusedly, become irritated, groan and suddenly pull out his little black book, place between us the wisdom of Lao-Tzu or the Bhagavadgita and calm down immediately. The sentences floated before my eyes, dead and inert; they were the lifebelts of this slumberous, tragic genius. Though truer to himself than anyone I have known, no one more roundly made me feel that 'I is another'. He was suffering; his thoughts and images were being stolen from him; atrocious ones were being put in their place and they filled his head or gathered in his eyes. Where did this come from? From what childhood? I do not know. The only thing that is sure is that he felt he was being manipulated. I have never been able to look at *La Pagode* [The Pagoda], his gouache of 1939, a self-portrait of the painter, without thinking of Sherrington's experiment: that dog's head, cut from its body, but artificially perfused, just about surviving on a tray. Though not severed from his body, Wols' head was just as pained: the eye is closed; and there can be no doubt he is being used in an experiment: wires, membranes and clusters of pipes driven into his skin plug the sleeper into an entire little world—a butterfly, a horse, cockroaches, a violin, etc.—which he suffers, unseen, *from the inside* and which inflicts his sleepwalking on him. *Le Pantin* [The Jumping Jack]—another self-portrait—one-armed and open-eyed this time, seems to be activated by a strange, complicated, antiquated apparatus that regulates his movements and his vision *from behind*: from the top of a post, a circus strongman oversees operations. Tormented, hounded, haunted by woodlice and cockroaches, he could do nothing but give himself up unreservedly to these simple hallucinations and transcribe them there and then. He hesitated over the results. He was in no doubt that he had to give them all he had. But would they be beautiful? Recopied in his own hand, these words of Maeterlinck show that he was still trying to hope:

> If the matter on hand is the making of a pipe, the shoring of a tunnel, the construction of cells or boxes, the building of royal apartments . . . the plugging of a chink through which a thin current of air might penetrate or a ray of light filter—these being calamities to be dreaded above all—it is again to the residue of their digestion that they have recourse. One might say that they are first and foremost transcendental chemists whose learning has triumphed over every prejudice, every aversion; who have attained the serene conviction that nothing in nature is repugnant, that all can be reduced to a few simple bodies, chemically indifferent, clean and pure.[45]

Did he really share this serene conviction? On some days, yes, he wanted to share it. Pantheism, whatever form it takes, is the permanent temptation of the possessed: they are inhabited, the cockroaches run around at night from kitchen to attic; the enemy is in solid occupation of the cellars: they will escape that enemy if they blow up the building or if they plunge themselves into the Great All. Being different anyway—it is their lot to be so—they will substitute the being-other of substance for that of the finite mode. Wols, that proud termite, built palaces from his droppings, by order. The beast dreamt of his own decomposition, along with the decomposition of his products, dreamt that nothing would remain of either but the original purity of their elements. His gouaches bear witness to this: they are frightening and they are beautiful. But one cannot decide whether the beauty is a promise or the ghastliest dream of the termite's nest.

Klee is an angel and Wols a poor devil. The one creates or recreates the marvels of this world, the other experiences its marvellous horror. All Klee's good fortune conspired to create his one misfortune: happiness remains his limitation. All Wols' misfortunes gave him his single piece of good fortune: his misery is boundless. Yet it was in Klee that Wols recognized his own self, when he was about nineteen years old. Let us say, rather, that he found lights in Klee's work and projected them on to his own darkness: those lights illuminated a swarming and wriggling that already troubled him and, phantasmagorically, covered over with human significations the spontaneously inhuman meaning of his original intentions. If we want to retrace the path he followed, we must start out from Klee.

'The artist,' said Klee,

is better and more subtle than a camera, he . . . is a creature on earth and a creature in the Universal: a creature on a star among the stars. These facts progressively manifest themselves in a new conception of the natural object . . . that tends to become totalized . . . By our knowledge of its inner reality, the object becomes much more than its mere appearance . . . Beyond these ways of considering the object in its depth, other paths lead to its humanization, by establishing between the 'Thou' and the 'I' a relation of resonance that transcends any optical relation: first, by way of a common rooting in the earth which, from below, conquers the eye; second, through a common participation in the cosmos which comes from above. Paths that are metaphysical in their conjunction.[46]

The artist refuses to *anatomize:* however rigorous the analysis, it merely expresses the inevitable 'natural' illusion of a subject that regards itself as absolute, with no ties or limitations. Klee is too much the realist to accept that the pure void becomes a gaze and that objects parade, like fashion-models, before an invisible lorgnette. Whatever the objects of his attention, the painter will not make them say what *they* are without thereby learning what *he* is. The sea which, from twenty thousand feet and at six hundred miles per hour is hardened, frozen and shrivelled, damns with the denunciation of its secret solidity the aircraft whose speed leaves it behind. The whole of the sea is aircraft, the whole aircraft is sea. This reciprocity of reflections will be crushed on a canvas; the sky and the earth will plunge into its abyss, dragging human beings down with them—those solitary voyagers revolving around a spinning planet. This is the place:

this is where an organic—or, as Klee puts it, 'physiological'—painting is born. The painter and his model belong equally to the totality that both governs their true relations and is, on the other hand, entirely embodied in each of them. The object reveals itself in its functional relation to the world and, at the same time, reveals the artist in his physiological relation to the indivisible whole. The Seer is something seen; his Seeing is rooted in visibility. By contrast, the artist gives that which he does not have—his being. No sooner does he project it outward than this lacework of shadows is reflected back by the ribs and veins of the object. And this plastic object, by its ambiguity, achieves a shared rootedness in the earth, a shared participation in the cosmos; it unites the 'Thou to the I', revealing, by way of the other, the presence within each of that notable intruder, the Whole.

Wols' gouaches of 1932 can be cited as sufficient proof that he came to a discovery of himself through ideas of such purity: in them he is a creature on a star, reproducing other equally astral creatures; he has understood that the experimenter is necessarily part of the experiment and the painter necessarily part of the picture. A little later, he gives *The Circus* a significant subtitle: 'Simultaneous Filming and Projection'; these lines by Klee could serve as a commentary to it:

> All paths meet in the eye, at a point of convergence from which they are converted into Form, to end in the synthesis of outer gaze and inner vision. At this meeting point are rooted forms shaped by the hand that are entirely distinct from the physical aspect of the object and yet which, from the standpoint of the Totality, do not contradict it.

This is a text which Wols seems to be trying to illustrate in 1940 with his *Janus Bifrons Carrying the Aquarium*. Here, the circus tumbler has two faces, two pairs of eyes, simultaneously seeing the world in front and a world behind; the union of these two views is effected somewhere outside by the hand of the monster that is busy choosing a head from inside its portable fish tank. Yet this gossamer universe, studded with its suspect, transparent areas, is not Klee's world: it is frightening. And then, can the artist *see*? Janus' eyes are blank. He seems to be being led: a cockroach is tugging at his sleeve. The foul beast is doubtless going to force him to choose a cockroach.

The affinities will seem clearer and the disparity the more marked in those gouaches of his youth that claim to show our 'shared participation in the cosmos'.[47] There can be no doubt that Wols was attempting here—as in each of his works—to present both the world and himself in the form of other creatures. But he turns his attention, this time, to heavenly paths. His angelic master often took this route: 'The higher path involves the dynamic order . . . It is the aspiration to free oneself from earthly bonds that leads on high: one is striving to attain an unfettered mobility beyond that of swimming or flight.' Wols takes his inspiration from this, but, if we look at them closely, his bottle imps are very far from moving freely. Klee's little figures enjoy a spontaneous weightlessness; at other times, 'a little genie holds out his hand' to draw the artist into a celestial region where 'objects fall upwards'. There is nothing of that kind here: neither outstretched hand, nor reversal of gravity. For this 'Sylph of the Cold Ceilings', one may rise up but one cannot escape the earth's attraction. His little figures rise and fall as the current takes them, light but inert, some way short of the liberty afforded by swimming or flight. Around 1939, they will disappear. By contrast, the 'shared rootedness' will increasingly assert itself. It is that rootedness that will integrate the upward aspiration into itself; that aspiration will become the upward thrust of his tied-down crowds, solitary marshmallows, stretching out in vain towards the zenith. Above their heads, as a last incarnation of 'unfettered mobility', is a teeming of flies, fleas and flying bugs, of floating pustules, jumping beans and spider's threads. This horrible swarm mocks the efforts of the human plants to shake off their roots. Rootedness, impotence, horror and vain desire—these shadows, slowly accumulated in a crystal paradise that they are going to explode, are Wols discovering himself 'in person' through the work of Klee.

We can see at a glance what the two artists have in common. Both are totalitarian and cosmic. For each of them, the plastic arts perform a function of ontological revelation: their works aim without exception to pin down the being of their author and the being of the world in a single movement. And there is no doubt, with each of them, that there is an underlying religious experience to this. But this very experience separates them: they didn't undergo it in the same way nor do they share a common conception of the 'pre-history of the visible'.

Klee justifies his totalitarian realism by an explicit recourse to Creation: 'The being [of the fundamental things of life] . . . lies in the precise function they perform in what we might still call "God".' Moreover, of the artist he says:

> His progress in the observation and viewing of nature leads him gradually to a philosophical vision of the universe that enables him freely to create abstract forms . . . In this way the artist creates—or takes part in the creation of—work that is in the image of the works of God . . . Art [is], as a projection of the original supra-dimensional ground, a symbol of Creation. Clairvoyance. Mystery.

The painter and his object communicate at the deepest level; they are produced, sustained and integrated into the totality of being by the synthetic unity of an act which they both *are* and perform, at the same time as *it* makes *them*: the All is the manifold sign of a single *fiat* which the artist encounters in himself as the source of his existence and which he continues through his work. The fundamental thing remains *praxis*, and being is defined as the functional relation of the parts to the continuing Creation by which they are totalized. In this sense, Klee's mysticism is the very opposite of quietism and Jean-Louis Ferrier is right to call it an 'operative realism'. If everything is actual, active and perpetually reactivated,

> the door is open to exact research . . . Mathematics and physics provide the key in the form of rules to be observed or avoided . . . these disciplines impose the salutary obligation to concern oneself first of all with the function and not to begin with the finished form . . . one learns to recognize the underlying forms; one learns the prehistory of the visible.[48]

It might be thought that Wols was responding to the words I quoted above—'what we might still call "God"'—when, in *Reflets*, he writes: 'It is superfluous to name God or to learn something by heart.' The whole difference between the two men can be seen here. Though free of all catechisms, Klee nonetheless retains a Christian, Faustian view of the universe: *Im*

Anfang war der Tat.[49] This is not the case with Wols. This sorcerer of being begins by rejecting the Act: 'At every moment, in every thing, Eternity is present.' Then he rejects the *Logos*: 'The Tao that can be named is not the real Tao.' Art crumbles to dust at the same time as its guarantee, divine Creation. Wols' realism will not be 'operative', because any kind of operation is repugnant to him: after his first attempts, he will give up painting on canvas for many years (twelve in all). 'It's ambition and gymnastics, I don't want it.' What he condemns in any undertaking is not simply the plan and the execution, but also—and above all—the construction, the style and all the forms of inter-pretation and transposition: 'When you see, you mustn't focus eagerly on what you could do with what you see, but see what *is*.' The plastic object is increate, insofar as the eternal is manifested in it. So, there will be no composition: vision will of itself make itself visible, since seeing and showing are one and the same thing. This fierce invalid begins by amputating his practical reason: 'Not to do, but to be and to believe.' There is only one choice to be made: to squander one's energies in 'scheming' or to gather oneself into a still waiting. By denying Being that virulence which, in Klee's hand, brings it close to a pure act, is Wols opting for a contemplative quietism? In fact he is not, but rather for that introverted *praxis* I term passive activity. His infinitives are disguised imperatives: we are, and yet we *must* be. He liked to cite the following maxim from the Bhagavadgita: 'All existences obey their [own] nature.' Here 'ought' merges with 'is' and nature with norm. Klee's 'philosophical vision' gives way to *the metaphysical attitude*. One *assumes* an attitude and one *retains* it. Through this tension, Wols will generate the inflexible law that both governs and remains alien to him. It is a contradictory striving: he both raises himself up—hence the endless teeming of phalluses in his gouaches—and overdoes obedience, so as to efface himself, and so that the heteronomy of his will disappears with him. This is a recipe for dissension: the eternal rends immanence asunder, explodes our categories, 'Thou' and 'I', subject and object. To be is to 'see what is', to discover one's nature in the being of the Other. And to see is to be: the being of the Other appears only to the Being-Other of one's own inwardness.

It is also to *dream*: 'the experience that nothing is explicable leads to dreaming.' Not the experience, but the lofty refusal to explain, to break down being into causal series that reach back *ad infinitum*. Entire and gathered together, Wols welcomes the inexplicable, which is whatever comes; on each occasion, the world is embodied in it. Fully. So, to dream is to see. 'They who dream by day are cognizant of many things which escape those who dream only at night.'[50] They see being, that ambiguity of things, and it matters little to them whether it appears from the outside— root, potsherd, pebble or paving stone—or wells up from their innermost depths to 'accumulate in their right eyes'. What counts is opening oneself up, waiting, grasping the ungraspable or, rather, being seized by it. And then, if need be, fixing it, without moving—or almost: 'You have to squeeze the space up more tightly.' The inner vision will externalize itself on to 'a tiny little sheet' by an imperceptible agitation of the fingers. An imaginary thing shows on the surface of the paper: the *manner of being* of a cryptogam, a passion, a woodlouse, Wols or the world—all indistinguishable from each other.

The being of the part resides in its relation to the whole. Klee says the same thing, but, colluding in Creation, he argues that this relation is a practical one: the part 'works' in an ongoing totalization and the philosopher-artist lucidly plays a part in the permanent unification of reality. Wols knows nothing of unification: he 'has in his sights a path towards unity'. That *unity* is *already* there and always has been. But totalization is there none: the Whole hangs in the air, alone, finished, never begun. He refuses to see the synthetic relating of the detail to the totality as an active, dynamic participation in the universal project. It is a stable structure of reciprocity: the part cancels itself out in favour of the whole; in each part the whole is embodied and imprisoned. Being yields itself up through this dual relation: neither shifting nor stable, eternity is erected in advance; it is a force that is suppressed as it produces and maintains inertia, an inertia shot through with the horrible dream of acting.

For Klee the world is, inexhaustibly, to be made; for Wols, it is made—and with Wols in it. Klee, active and a 'computer of being', comes to himself from afar; he is himself even in the Other. Wols suffers his own being: that being, which is other than himself even in the very depth of himself, is his being-other; external things reflect this back to him to precisely the degree that his—unnameable—inside has projected it on to them. He quoted me once: 'Objects . . . touch me; it is unbearable. I am afraid of coming into contact with them.'[51] It matters little here what these words mean for me: what *he* means is that objects touch him because he is afraid of touching himself in touching them. They are himself outside of himself: to see them is to dream himself; they hypnotize him. Kelp and hart's tongue reflect his nature back to him; he deciphers his own being from the knots in a piece of bark, from the fissures in a wall; roots, rootlets, the teeming of viruses under a microscope, the hairy furrows of women and the turgescent flaccidity of male fungi compromise him; he finds, in them, that he is fissure, root, hart's tongue and kelp. By contrast, when his eyes are closed and he withdraws into his own darkness, he experiences the universal horror of being-in-the-world; the vile hatching of a wart in stone, the crabbedness of a larval flora and fauna, accentuated by the impossibility of rejecting existence—

everything accumulates in that retina of his which is steeped in darkness. These are two paths that are but one: fascination and automatism. He is spellbound by external objects when they seem to him like products of his *écriture automatique*; his automatism is merely the spellbound attention he devotes to his own products when they present themselves to him as external objects.

For the 'horrible workers' whose 'I' is an other, being is defined by otherness: it is in the nature of things not to be what they are.[52] Up to 1940 or thereabouts, Wols took familiar figures from the tangible world—men and women, plants, animals, doors, houses and towns—and applied the principle of nonidentity to them. His aim was not to breathe life into this imagery but to unsettle it. A single subject treated a thousand times: the fixed shimmering of the elusive, both manifested and hidden in the uncertain relation of part to whole and of whole to part, in the double incompleteness of the One and multiplicity. In these rigorous, complicated little systems throng forms whose careful individuation merely underlines their radical indistinctness: they offer themselves to the gaze, the better to elude it; each is in contact with all, directly or through one of the countless transmission belts striating the gouache. As for localizing the point of contact, that is impossible: one can barely determine more or less extended zones where the contact probably takes place. Taken in isolation, each thing changes, immutably, into its opposite; each one affirms and denies itself simultaneously; the composition runs out of steam and falters: it is decomposition interrupted. A particular densely painted patch imposes itself, then straggles off in a spidery rumpling of threads; it 'takes light' the way a leaky boat 'takes water' and then tightens again, dark and impenetrable. Yet nothing has moved, except our eyes. On this stake, at its upper edge, an athletic figure is impaled; this is the pointed crown of a pillar that sits heavily on the earth; from the eye's lower edge, we see it come apart halfway down: farewell to weight and gravity; it ends in bamboo tubes bound together with string. In *The General and His Family*, the three figures are floating, falling and walking all at the same time in a suddenly emergent space that has both a continuity which unites them and inner divisions that separate them forever. The son has a bloated, full face: a head-of-hair-that-becomes-a-nose, a buccal proboscis; importance puffs up his cheeks, dulls his little elephant eye and then, suddenly, there is nothing—a wreath is wound around the empty space and, inside, the eye vanishes, unfinished perhaps, or swallowed by that omnipresent gap, the sky.

Despite the beauty of his gouaches, Wols is still simply a virtuoso of prestidigitation. So long as he uses those most magical of objects, the human face and the human body, then he will be able, in whatever way he distorts them, to trick us at will. If he relies on our habits, summons up our commonest expectations, our nocturnal fears, our desires, if he evades or deflects our attention with sham and pretence, then these deceitful analogies will bring us up against impossible syntheses, which we shall continue to assent to, despite having recognized their impossibility. This is the three-card trick, the prestidigitator's force of suggestion. There is no deliberate intention to deceive; no one has less of a method, as I have said, than the author of these *trompe-l'oeil* works: he simply shows what he sees. Nonetheless, around 1940, he developed a distaste for his way of seeing: to reveal the 'supra-dimensional, trans-optical foundation' of things and depict it in images, the visionary has to apply himself to seeing—and, hence, to being—more profoundly. Wols' *attitude* became radicalized. Yet he would never entirely give up drawing towns, people, animals and plants: what changed was the function he assigned to them. Earlier, he used everyday objects to construct traps, to suggest the 'ungraspable' as something that lay beyond their contradictions. After 1940, with different means employed to call it up, *being* appears first and those objects are suggested allusively. Everything turns around: being was something one divined; it was the flip-side of man; now, it is man that is the flip-side of being. Let us re-open Wols' bag and filch this further quotation from it:

> Taking fingers to illustrate the fact that fingers are not fingers is less effective than taking non-fingers to illustrate the fact that fingers are not fingers. Taking a white horse to illustrate the fact that horses are not horses is less effective than taking non-horses to illustrate the fact that horses are not horses.

The universe is a finger. Everything is a horse.

For anyone attempting to understand them through their author, Chuang-Tzu, these remarks remain fairly obscure; they do, however, become clear when related to Wols' work, and cast a new light on it.

There are two ways of illustrating the otherness of being. The first of these is to reveal, in a finger, the cancerous presence of Everything. Dubuffet excels at this: he paints women as pink purulences, as glandular, visceral blossomings, as honest, hard-working beasts with a meatus, two breasts and the fine stripe of the sex. They are non-women, a purely organic entity, its swathing of myth stripped away, a naked palpitation on the surface of inorganic matter. Wols set off down this track at first, but he did not have Dubuffet's powerful, harsh materialism to sustain him: the microscopic structures of matter fascinate him, as we know, but they do so because of the being they attest to. As a result, he will have little difficulty changing tack in 1941 or thereabouts, and moving on to his second style—revealing the being-other of the finger by deliberately painting non-fingers.

Non-fingers whose being-other will indeed be the finger—a finger never seen and never named, but always present. Is he going to go back to Klee again? To attain: 'the philosophical vision of the universe that . . . enables one freely to create abstract forms'? Yes and no. The universe is certainly in question; and experience, revealing the nature of things to Wols, enables him to embody the world in objects that are not met in the world. But, more faithful than ever to automatism, both before and after 1941 he rejects the name of creator or artist. An exhibitor of shadows or of being—those are his titles. These new figures are, no doubt, imaginary. But the imagination is not creative: in the metaphysical attitude, Being becomes its law, it is the mere plastic objectivization of that Being. Moreover, its products *are*: they manifest the strict equivalence of Martian fauna as it might appear to the members of our species, and of the human race as it might appear to Martians. As both man and Martian together, Wols strives to see the earth with inhuman eyes: it is, he thinks, the only way to universalize our experience. He would not, admittedly, call the unknown—or too well-known—objects that now figure in his gouaches 'abstract forms', since they are as concrete for him as those of his first period. This comes as no surprise: they are the same in reverse. He has, for example, retained the stretched-out character of his forsaken crowds; only it is no longer human beings that are stretched out, but unnameable, rigorously individuated substances that symbolize nothing or no one and seem to belong simultaneously to the three kingdoms of Nature—or perhaps to an as yet unknown fourth one. Yet they do concern us all the same: being radically *other,* it is not our lives they manifest to us, nor even our materiality, but our raw being, perceived from the outside—though from where?—without complicity, alien, repellent, but *ours.* It is impossible to view this being that we are without a sense of dizziness, this being that is captive in these substances like the being that they are.

If being-other is the law of being, it will not be so hard to show that a finger is not really a finger, that it betrays its essence in every way: we know that essence, but how is it with the non-fingers, those unknown objects of which we know nothing? How can we perceive that *they* are other than themselves? How does Wols go about making us feel this? This question is directed at writing itself and it is writing that will supply the answer. We come now to a gouache, *The Great Burning Barrier*[53] that I cannot view without a sense of anxiety. Let us examine it.

Space has become more sober here: this continuous, three-dimensional, very respectably Euclidian milieu has rid itself of the cleavages, the dark dungeons, the cavings-in, the multifarious curves that cross-hatched it in the earlier period. And necessarily so: as long as the people had human faces, the onus was on the space to unsettle them. Now the container must seem all the more familiar for the fact that the content is so much less ordinary: the Thing comes to us, unnameable, through the realist space in which we believe we live; it asserts thereby that it belongs to our world: when the trap has closed again, we shall notice, too late, that the being's virulence gnaws at the frame that was lent to it: so long as it is *nothing*, the void is itself for as far as the eye can see; it alters as soon as you fill it.

Here, the Thing is red. At first glance, you would think it was painted wood. Red oxide. Pastilles of blood. An open-work fence. Or a fence blown to pieces—by a bomb or by time. Planks nailed to posts, rough-hewn tree trunks. Beneath this makeshift barrier, other trunks lie unused. This initial sense breaks down almost at once: the shadows, a gradual alteration of the colours and the movements forced upon our eyes effect a transformation and turn the dead wood into stone. This horizontal creature, half-way up the gouache is, without a doubt, ligneous in nature. But now it breaks off at ninety degrees and forms a right angle: a wooden leg looms out at us. But it is not wooden. Grey and grey-green flecks betray the mineral essence of the enormous foot on the end of it, which twists round towards the right. Where did the transformation occur? Everywhere and nowhere. The lower part is a wooden beam, the higher part granite, but the undeniable unity of form compels us to *see* the unity of substance, cleverly denied by the internal evidence: a single entity forms and unforms simultaneously before our eyes. it is both rocky and ligneous, but there is no conflict: just a still wavering of matter, suspect at every point. All the more so as a sinuous creature, on the other side of the central axis (powerfully marked by a red, phallic upward thrust), smoothly takes over and extends the stiff, constrained movement of the stone ankle-boot and darts out towards the far right, with its pink belly and grey or grey-green back, a climbing plant or a crawling beast . . . No, that is going too far: it would be more accurate to assign it some pre-biological status. This time the forms are distinct, but the unity of values, colours and orientation drags the stony wood towards life, transforms its inert density into tension, revealing— with two white cavities and hairs that are suddenly clearly visible—that the stone ends in the rudimentary outline of a muzzle. The opposite is also true: the minerality on the left of the axis turns into dead weight; its passivity binds the creature on the right— conger-eel or snake—in the chains of the inorganic. Every dead tree is a cliff, every cliff a leg; every leg is a reptile and all life, instantly paralysed, is merely an instantaneous process of petrification: being-other strikes immediately, crumbling otherness to dust. But let us be careful not to mistake for a method what has to be termed permanent transubstantiation: that is the law of this improvisation.

And here is the second law: everything is fixed, outlined, its contours are set; nothing either is or can be located in space. Substance has undergone some inward accident: in the places where the hue darkens, marking the increased density and thickening of being, the opaque matter resolves into translucency; through it we can make out the contours of the bodies it should hide, *does hide*. It is not the only effect of this artful play of transparencies to bestow a porous impenetrability on the visible; it also ends up jumbling the picture planes. A single object seems simultaneously *in front of* and *behind* the others, like this hooded monk—or unhooded male member—apparently walking slowly, to the right of centre, in the lower half of the gouache: how is he/it to be situated in relation to the recumbent figures? Is he/it in the foreground, the background or the middle distance? There is no answer to this question: by its emergence, the Thing produces a radical indeterminacy of location; it creates distant objects only to hurl them to the very forefront of the picture. And the identity of these entities is something merely approximate: are there two fallen trunks at the bottom of the picture or three? Is the rearing snake, which hisses and sticks out its bent tongue on the far right of the gouache in front of the upright post, part of that post or separate from it? Everything is subtly constructed to render these questions futile. By imperceptible transformations of being, nearness takes a backward jump and becomes distance: the last fallen tree trunk seems right up against us over two-thirds of its length; on the other side of the post, on the right, the line becomes stronger and is braided with a chalky white; the object terminates abruptly; it is a cliff twenty leagues distant. In the dazzling centre of the gouache, the otherness intensifies; it is the crossroads of uncertainties: straddling forms, inert spurtings, transparent opacities, metamorphoses, dead wood, tumescent organs, knots of vipers—everything is hissing, everything is wresting itself from a rootedness that exists only as a result of the multiple effort expended on   escaping it. In this monument of uncertainties, heaviness flies and inertia strains and tautens; nothing is certain, except that perfect precision leads to the most rigorous imprecision.

Right now, what do I see? First, allusions that make me think the universe is the right way up: these slashes in the stone are eyes, a wooden mouth opens, a one-legged man soars upward. But no, it is a cruci-

fixion with two or three crosses, the recumbent figures are fresh corpses, I am witness to a slaughter, I
catch three specks of blood on the rigid transparency
of what is indubitably a male member—or, there
again, it is perhaps a fire. But, to retain their consistency, these hints have to remain marginal or one's
eyes have to slide rapidly over the picture. Under examination, they contradict these impressions or are
contradicted: the one-legged man was a mirage, I mistook this fire-coloured strip of unknown substance
for the stump of a leg, the eyes are holes, mere gaps,
exposed as such by other holes, which are almost like
them but empty. Hardly have they substituted themselves for the crucified figures when a horrible bunch
of rods, mushrooms and sea-serpents crumbles in its
turn. These things never quite *are*. Summoned up and
rejected by *contamination*, the allusion never raises itself to the status of signification; rather, it sinks in
swells, beneath the skin, like a multiple meaning I cannot pin down. But, for the mere relation of meaningless proximity everywhere to produce false signs that
devour each other in a permanent reciprocity of con-
testation, the apparent contiguity of forms has, in reality, to manifest the plastic unity of a whole. If I seek

it out, this unity eludes me, but the details send me back to it constantly: by its incessant, congealed metamorphosis, it reveals itself as *integral to* a totality that is omnipresent in its absence, which is the Thing itself. There is the Thing, a materialization in *this* world, which comes to me, implicating me, in *my* space; and simultaneously there is that very world in which it unfurls itself, our world, which has now become an object for some unknown gaze, for *my* gaze. What *I,* the world's prisoner, see is, from the outside, the very world in which I have remained; it is I. I am the burning, bleeding other side of this thing that glows red. The 'vibratory disappearance' of allusions leaves me alone before this packet of ectoplasm, while at the same time conditioning my gaze: no, this sickening structure isn't a massacre or a martyrdom or a cauldron of hatred, but, since it is nothing else, hatred, misfortune, blood and anguish seem to me, through the fleetingness of these false signs, to be *its other meaning.* As though our human and cosmic condition—the condition through which we ordinarily sleep-walk— disclosed its unbearable horror only to eyes that have no connivance about them—naïve, alien eyes—or as though the truth of that horror were *my* being-other, raised within myself and ascending into my vision to alter it. I feel myself to be *over there*, a captive of the gouache and seen, with my comrades in hell, by a clear, demystified gaze; and at the same time I feel that I am *here*, in my own gaze, alienated from that of Wols, fascinated by his own fascination, as though his 'automatic writing' prompted an automatic reading within me. Inside and outside, angel and madman, other object and different subject: this ambiguity relates to me and, for that reason, is a persistent worry. All the more so as we are not speaking of an inert ambivalence that I could just register serenely. The two terms of the contradiction doubtless interpenetrate more than they are opposed, but since they cannot, in spite of everything, remain together, the Thing discloses to me—beyond action and passivity—its instantaneous imminence: *in a moment*, one of these two aspects of being will be absorbed into the other; this will mean *mental* alienation unless a frosty, angelic gaze declares my alienation from the object; *in a moment*, either I shall be entirely alone and 'other' in this world or the world will confess its deep alterity: the asylum or hell on earth. *In a moment*: but in the moment—an over-ripe fruit that is always on the point of bursting—Eternity is embodied as the being-other of temporal succession; this suspended urgency is time caught in flight; it is time halted and it is the formless sketching-out of a before and an after. For this reason, the Thing in the gouache eludes contemplation: to see it is to produce it and await it, to be torn between prior rejection and fascinated acceptance. In it Destiny becomes the being-other of Eternity.

That the finger is not a finger was what had to be demonstrated. Wols proved this brilliantly: by the non-finger. In so doing, he showed how he differed from the Surrealists, who had influenced him greatly. For the latter, painting and poetry are one and the same; to paint 'melting watches' or to write 'soluble fish' or 'butter horse' amount to the same thing. We know the importance they attach to titles; in their best works, words roll between canvas and paint like those puns that govern the phantasmagoria of our dreams: the Word is king. The superiority of Wols lies in the fact that the Things in his gouaches are unnameable: this means they do not fall within the ambit of language and that the art of painting has freed itself entirely from literature. Wols' titles do not designate the object: they accompany it. To cite just one, what does *Pyrate Roots* mean? There is a play on words here, of course, but it happens after the gouache has been produced, and to one side of it: the work has produced its title, a vague reflection of a mood, of an inexpressible, forever obscure meaning. In short, the painter, with nothing in his hands or his pockets, allows himself to be frisked and relieved of all his words. To convince and to horrify, he has only the resources of the plastic arts: 'the five living pigments: point, line, surface, chiaroscuro and colour.' With these elements of form, in 'this little grey place where the jump from chaos to order can be successfully made,' he allows his forever-alienated thought to organize itself into the plastic thought of alienation. This vigilant, dumb automatism doesn't unleash itself in bolts of lightning; it is a directed ripening. And at last the object appears: it is being and it is the world, it is anxiety and the Idea, but it is, first and foremost, a self-improvised gouache whose only reference is to itself. It is all very well for Wols to mock Art and artists: by driving out literature, he condemns himself simply to draw more than ever on that sign-less writing commonly known as Beauty. Beauty, silent proof, cosmic unity of parts and whole: it is always the world—or at least a possible world—that is realized by beauty's particular density and by its rigour. So long as he is narrating, Wols relies on the familiar appearance of objects to persuade us. Afterwards, he employs one single, but constant argument: the Beautiful. Not one of his gouaches is not beautiful. But this absolute end serves him as a means. Or, rather, if in secret he admits it is an end, this is because he has first belittled it and is using it; it is because he has made it the likeness of horror. Werner Haftmann is right to compare his gouaches to 'those creatures of an abominable beauty (one sees) in the aquariums of Naples or Monte-Carlo'. Though it is abomination, Beauty in Wols' work—that flower of evil—is never betrayal: it does not save; it attenuates nothing. Indeed, it reinforces the sense of anxiety since it is the very substance of the Thing, its texture, the coherence of being. The strict integration of forms and their marvellous, delicate hues are there to make manifest our damnation.

Preface to *En Personne: Aquarelles et Dessins de Wols* (Paris: Delpire, 1963).

a fine display of capuchins[54]

Three o'clock: the storm catches me on the Nomen-
tana in the north-west of the city. It is a raging of
birds: a whirl of plumage, a screeching, black feathers
flying up to the sky. When calm has returned, I feel my
jacket. It is dry. A straw sun is already breaking
through the grey-blue cotton wool of the clouds. To
the west, broad and empty, a street climbs between
the houses and ends in the sky. I can never resist the
temptation to ascend these little hills to see what's on
the other side. The finest in Europe is rue Roche-
chouart, when viewed from Boulevard Barbès. Once
you've crested the pass, you almost expect to glimpse
the sea. The rain is coming down again and bouts of

spray hit me as I climb. A smear of bitumen sprawls down from the top of the hill and settles against the sickly pallor of a wall. That wall puts an end to Rome's imposture: beyond it, there is a cabbage patch, an expanse of acid light, the last vestige of humanity; and then wilderness. A wilderness in the rain. Far away, the blue-black ink of the Alban Hills fades into the sky. This land-locked city is more alone in the environing lands than a boat on the sea.

Taxi to the Via Vittorio Veneto, autumnal and bourgeois. The street of the rich foreigners. But the rich foreigners are hiding in their hotels. On the pavements and on the steps of Santa Maria della Concezione, the plane trees, shaken by the storm, have shed their leaves, which are the colour of Roman walls. You might think the *palazzi* were moulting. Ochre, bright red, chrome yellow in the puddles: a marinade of dead skins. Santa Maria della Concezione is the Capuchin church. I go in. The nave is deserted. Silence, nothing. St Michael is noiselessly crushing the Devil's head; gilded chandeliers ring the altar. At the far end, on the right, near the sacristy, forestalling my questions, a sullen friar puts his left index finger to his

lips and points me to a stairway plunging underground. His left hand, suspended for a moment in the
air, is rounded, cupped and pressed against my stomach. I give him twenty lire and pass along. I go down
some stairs and find myself in a gallery of catacombs:
the crypt. But no: the left-hand wall has some barred
windows in it; stretching up, I can see a little garden
through the bars: I am in a hospital corridor. There is
a thoroughly Italian ambiguity in this: I am on the
ground floor in the cold, clear light of autumn and in
the basement in the yellow glow of electric light bulbs.
On the right, the corridor runs past four small rooms
of unequal size: mortuary chapels, little cells protected
by low balustrades that remind me both of communion rails and of the ropes that cordon off the drawing-rooms in stately homes. For that reason, as I come
closer, the chapels become drawing-rooms. Four little
rococo boudoirs, whose walls, white beneath the
grime, are flanked by dark niches, alcoves or divan-
beds in their lower part and, in the upper section, decorated with pleasing, artless arabesques, with rosettes,
ellipses and stars, all quite crudely executed. The only
odd thing about the decoration and the furnishings is

the material they are made of: it is bone. What inge-
nuity! To make a cherub takes just a skull and two
shoulder-blades; the   shoulder-blades will be the
wings. By tastefully piling up skulls and femurs, you
get rock-work niches. The old chandeliers themselves,
providing an illumination that pales in the daylight,
are bundles of tibias hanging from the ceiling by
chains. Each *salotto* has its own inhabitants: standing
by its bed, a skeleton in a homespun robe salutes me;
a mummy sits up on its couch. You might think these
corpses were for sale: there are tickets on their robes,
but no prices marked, just their names and social rank.
Here is the Grim Reaper above my head, floating,
with his hourglass and scythe: I'm not sure whether
he's swimming or flying, but the air around him co-
agulates into a troubling gelatinous mass. Between the
three walls of each *salotto*, beneath a blackish compost,
its grains shining and tightly packed—anthracite dust
or caviar?—a number of more privileged monks are
taking their rest. This humus is the soil known as
consecrated ground: an inscription on a cross planted
bang in the middle of the sacred plot tells us as much,
like the tags indicating plant names in a botanical

garden. *Terra Sancta*: a species of tufa not native to these parts: it is found principally in Palestine, with other varieties in Lhasa, Mecca and elsewhere. I gaze at the baroque incrustations on the walls and wonder why the Capuchins have broken the nitrogen cycle and preserved these organic products from dissolution. Did they wish to show that everything sings the glory of God, even those peculiar pipes we are made of? I should like to think so. But why these exceptions? Why perch that skeleton on this pile of sticks that once were men? Why provide this carefully reconstructed prior with such a bed of bones? The living have used other dead bodies to serve those that are themselves mere dust and grimaces. It reminds me of a postcard I used to look at in the window of a newsagent's on the Boulevard Saint-Michel when I was a child: from a distance you could see the head of the Little Corporal, Napoleon Bonaparte. Closer up, the head began to swarm; it became a tangle of maggots. Nearer still, and the maggots were nudes. The delight in humiliating great men—the eye of the victor of Austerlitz was nothing but a buttock—combined with the delights of humiliating women: the most beautiful woman in the world, pressed up against a great many others, is worthy only to serve as conjunctive tissue for the male. It is not God we find in these chapels, but the image of a circle of hell: the exploitation of one dead man by another. Bones circle around other bones, all alike, making up that other rose-like figure: a skeleton. I am startled by someone speaking next to me. 'Good heavens! To think you can make human beings out of thigh bones, shins and skulls.' A fat Italian with fierce eyes falls to one knee, crosses himself, springs nimbly to his feet and scurries away. Two French women are torn between admiration and terror.

'My sister-in-law found it upsetting, but I don't. Does it upset you?'

'No, it doesn't.'

'No, me neither. It's so . . .'

'So well-ordered. So well-presented.'

Well-presented is right. And above all, it's made from nothing. I imagine Picasso would be delighted. 'A box of matches!' he said once. 'A box of matches that would be a box of matches and, *at the same time,* a frog!' He would like these elbow-bones that are both elbow-bones and the spokes of a wheel. In fact, the material counts more in this masterpiece than the form. It is a sorry material, but sufficient to horrify. It is not really brittle or friable; and yet how fragile it is: it has that dull life you find in hair that keeps on growing after death. If I tried to break it, it would crack lengthways against my palm, a bundle of splinters that would bend without breaking. Faced with this dubious joinery, dead and alive, rough and smooth, I draw back and slip my hands into my pockets: touch nothing, brush against nothing. I have sealed up my mouth hermetically, but there are always the damned nostrils: in all such dubious places, they dilate and the surroundings come streaming in in the form of a smell. There's a hint of a smell of bones. It's a mixture: one quarter old plaster, three quarters bug infestation. And for all that I tell myself I am imagining it, there's nothing to be done: I have four thousand Capuchins up my nose. Because there were four thousand of them that had to be dug up one by one. I would locate somewhere around 1810 the germinal frenzy that triggered this sadistic lyricism among honest monks and drove them to dash around on all fours sniffing the ground to unearth these sizeable truffles. It seems other examples are to be found. There is one at Palermo, I'm told. Towards the end of the French occupation, the order of Capuchins must have caught a heavy dose of pre-Romanticism.

'They've no right to do this!'

Upset and angry, a very beautiful woman stops on the bottom step and turns towards her ageing husband coming down behind her.

'They've no right!'

She has spoken too loudly: the Frenchwomen are staring at her. Embarrassed, her husband smiles apologetically.

'Well, they were monks . . .'

She raises here lovely, rancorous eyes to the cherubs:

'It's not permissible,' she says emphatically.

I smile at her; she is right: it is not permissible. But who or what is to forbid it? Christianity, perhaps, but not the Church, which makes a profit from this *capucinade*.[55] Yet surely it isn't Christian to play jigsaws with an ossuary. Desecration of graves, sadism, necrophilia—this is all blatant sacrilege. My compatriots cross themselves: these ladies are under a misapprehension: they have come to pay their respects to death in a place where death is scoffed at. I forgive them: beneath their dresses, they may perhaps have stockings worn threadbare at the knees on the steps of the Scala Santa; perhaps, this very morning, they saw the telegrams piling up at Santa Maria di Aracoeli around a doll swaddled in gold cloth; you need to be hard-headed in Rome to distinguish religion from witchcraft. If these good mothers had not, without realizing it, been changed into witches, they would not confuse the thrill they feel with the pious disgust preachers inspire when they describe the decay of the flesh. The lofty condemnation of the body we find in some Spanish paintings—that is good Catholicism. Shall we show kings eaten by worms? Well and good! The maggots make a shimmering silky surplice for their torn purple robes; clumps of macaroni are coming out of their eye sockets and despite that—because of that—these bodies remain ghastly images of ourselves: they are men decomposing; death is a human adventure. In short, it is permissible to mock a corpse, but only down to the bones. The flesh flows aside and frees the threepenny-bits that were concealed in the pudding; after that, with your soul in heaven and your mineral remains on earth, you have earned your rest. Look, rather, at the calm face of death, the tidy decease to which the feminine bones of the Protestant cemetery attest: those old maids are pure mineral. But here, the Capuchin canker attacks the bones. What heresy! To show such zeal over these rotten scraps, you would have to believe they still have a soul in them. And what hatred! These Capuchins are the ancestors of the Milanese crowd that slapped the face of Mussolini when he was dead and hanging by his feet. For hatred, death is a scandal: deprived of its prey, it is left dumbfounded before the detested corpse, like a man who has just been cured of his hiccups. These monks preserve human remains in order to extend the pleasure, they refuse to let human beings become nondescript, in order to be able to treat them like things; they wrest bones from their mineral fate so as to enslave them to the caricature of a human order;

they exhume them with great pomp to turn them into building materials. Monks used to consider beauty diabolical when it was merely worldly, but when it is a question of preferring everything, even beauty, to their neighbour, they turn into aesthetes. They deck their chapels out with human relics the way the guards at Buchenwald made lampshades from human skin. Approaching a notice, I find the words: 'No writing on the skulls.' Really? Why not? Armchairs, couches, rock-work, chandeliers, altars . . . why shouldn't these bones also be used as paper, paperweights or blotting paper? It would complete the degradation if one of these bald heads bore the inscription: 'Pierre and Maryse made love here.' But no: the Capuchins' best trick is to have forced the living to adore their victims. The two ladies have left, the beautiful Italian woman is going off down the corridor with a handkerchief pressed to her nose; and I am going too, leaving behind this debris of bones bewitched by a hatred stronger than death. The Capuchin friar is still there, sullen and bearded, by the sacristy. I pass by without glancing in his direction, a little embarrassed, like a client passing the brothel-keeper's assistant: he knows what I have just been seeing; my skeleton walks past his. I go outside. It's raining. All cities are the same in the rain. Paris is no longer in Paris, or London in London; but Rome remains in Rome. A black sky has settled over the houses, the air has changed to water and it is difficult now to make out shapes. But thirty centuries have impregnated the walls with a sort of phosphorus: I walk along in the rain between soft shafts of solar light. The Romans are running among these drowned suns, laughing and waving some ancient implements they don't quite seem to know how to use: umbrellas. I emerge into an underwater square amid drowned carcases. The rain stops, the earth emerges: the carcases are ruins: a temple, an obelisk—in a word, skeletons. I walk round the pillaged Pantheon; the metal-tipped obelisk is supported by an elephant that doesn't look at all happy. This whole African ensemble is there to the glory of Christianity. And here is Rome, emerging from the water, already dry: the whole thing an accursed ossuary. The Church rounded on the monuments of Antiquity the way the Capuchin friars rounded on their colleagues; when the Popes stole the bronze of the Pantheon to ensure

Christ's triumph over the pagans, it was the same desecration of graves. Antiquity *is alive* in Rome, with a hate-filled, magical life, because it has been prevented from dying entirely so that it can be kept in bondage. From this it has gained this insidious eternity and has been able to enslave us in its turn: if we are tempted to sacrifice ourselves to these stones, it is because they are bewitched; the order of the ruins fascinates us because it is both human and inhuman: human because it was established by men, inhuman because it stands alone, pickled in the alcohol of Christian hatred, and because it is self-contained, sinister, gratuitous, like the display of Capuchins I have just left.

France-Observateur, 115 (24 July 1952).

venice from my window

The water is too well-behaved: you don't hear it. Growing suspicious, I lean out: the sky has fallen in there. The water hardly dares move and its millions of creases confusedly rock the sullen Relic, which blazes up intermittently. Over towards the East, the canal comes to a stop and the vast milky pool begins that reaches as far as Chioggia. But on that side, it is the water that has taken the day off: my gaze skids over a glazed surface, slides over it and peters out towards the Lido, in a dismal incandescence. It is cold; a nondescript day is ushered in in chalky tones; Venice thinks it is Amsterdam once again; those grey pallors in the distance are palaces.

That's how it is here: the air, water, fire and stone are continually mingling or changing places, exchanging their natures or their natural locations, playing 'puss in the corner' or 'off-ground tag': old-fashioned games, with nothing innocent about them; we are seeing the training of an illusionist. To inexpert tourists, this unstable compound holds many surprises: while you are putting your nose in the air to see what the weather will be like, the whole of the heavens with its clouds and atmospheric phenomena may well be lying at your feet distilled into a silvery ribbon. For example, it may very well be that an early morning Assumption has spirited the lagoon away today and placed it where the sky ought to be. I look up: no, there is nothing there but a vertiginous hole, with neither light nor shade, rent solely by the colourless beams of cosmic rays. On the surface of this upturned abyss, a pointlessly frothing foam conceals the undoubted absence of the Sun. As soon as it can, that celestial body slips away; it is fully aware that it is undesirable and that Venice persists in regarding it as the hated image of personal rule. In fact, the city consumes more light than Palermo or Tunis, especially if you count the amount absorbed by the high-walled, dark alleyways; but Venice will not have it said that she owes her illumination to the liberality of a single source.

We must here consult the legend: in the beginning, the lagoon was plunged into perpetual radiant night; the patricians liked to view the constellations, whose equilibrium, based on mutual mistrust, reminded them of the benefits of aristocratic rule. All was for the best: the Doges, kept under close surveillance, were resigned to being no more than the straw men of commercial capitalism. One of them, Faliero, cuckolded and publicly mocked, did rebel against this briefly, but he was immediately thrown into jail. His judges had no difficulty in persuading him of his guilt: he had incurred the death penalty by attempting to impede the forward march of the historical Process, but, if he acknowledged his guilt, posterity would honour his misplaced courage. So he did, indeed, die craving the people's forgiveness and praising the justice that was to be done to him. Since then, no one had disturbed public order; Venice was peaceful beneath her seven stars.

The Grand Council decided to decorate its Council Chamber by having the high frieze painted with the portraits of past Doges, and, when they came to Faliero, these vindictive merchants ordered that his picture be covered with a veil bearing the insulting words: *Hic est locus Marini Falieri decapitati pro criminibus.* Now the poor lamb really lost his temper: was this what he had been promised? Not only was posterity not rehabilitating him but his memory was forever to be execrated. Suddenly, his severed head rose on the horizon and began to revolve above the city; the sky and the lagoon became tinged with purple and the proud patricians on the Piazza San Marco hid their eyes behind horrified fingers and cried out: '*Ecco Marino*'. Since then, he has returned every twelve hours, the city has been haunted and, as ancient custom demands that the Doge-elect appear on his balcony to throw jewels and florins to the crowd, the murdered Potentate ironically casts waves of gold sullied with his blood across the squares.

This myth has today been shown to be without foundation; beneath the vestibule of the chapel of the Madonna della Pace, in SS Giovanni e Paulo, a sarcophagus was discovered containing a human skeleton with its head on its knees. So, everything returned to normal, except that the Venetians, unyielding in their resentment, immediately converted the sarcophagus into a water-trough. No matter; we can judge the people's state of mind and their animosity against the day star by this story, which the gondoliers willingly relate. The city certainly likes to see the treasure it has won on the seas reflected in the golden sky, but only provided that it remains skewered up above it like the straggling mark of its greatness, or summer embroiders it in emblematic flashes across the heavy green draperies that stretch, by its good offices, down into the Canal. In Rome, that great inland village, I am, in fact, always happy to be present at the birth of an earthbound king. But when I have spent some time drifting around the canals of Venice, and seen copper-coloured fumes rising above the Rio or ephemeral glimmering lights take flight above my head, I can only admire this system of indirect lighting and it is not without a sense of unease that I step out again on to the Riva degli Schiavoni and see the great, worn face of Marino Faliero floating above the subtle shimmerings of the town.

No sun today, then. It is playing at being Louis XVI in Paris or Charles I in London. By disappearing, the great golden orb has disturbed the equilibrium; what remains are shafts of light, with no top or bottom to them; the landscape revolves, and I revolve with it, now hanging by my feet above an absence, beneath the frescoes of the Canal, now standing on a promontory above a shipwrecked sky. We revolve, the ceiling, the floor and I, who am the Ixion on this wheel, in the most absolute immobility. I end up feeling seasick: the emptiness is unbearable. But there you are: in Venice, nothing is simple. Because it is not a city, but an archipelago. How could you forget that? From your little island you look enviously across at the one opposite. What is there over there? A solitude, a purity and a silence which, you could swear, are not to be found over here. Wherever you are, you always find the real Venice is elsewhere. At least, it's like that for me. Normally, I'm reasonably happy with my lot, but, in Venice, I fall prey to a sort of jealous madness. If I didn't restrain myself, I'd be constantly on the bridges or in gondolas, madly seeking out the secret Venice on the other bank. Needless to say, as soon as I reach that bank, everything withers. I turn around and the mysterious peace has now descended on the other side. I have long been resigned to this: Venice is wherever I am not.

Those princely houses opposite are *rising out of* the water, are they not? It's impossible for them to be floating—houses don't float—or for them to be resting on the lagoon: it would sink under their weight. Or for them to be weightless: you can see they are built of brick, stone and wood. What, then? You cannot but *feel* them emerging. To look the palaces on the Grand Canal up and down is to discover that they are caught in a sort of frozen upthrust, which is, if you like, the reversal of their density, the inversion of their mass. A surge of petrified water: you would think they had just appeared and nothing had been there before these stubborn little erections. In short, they always have something of the *apparition* about them. With an apparition, you guess what it might be. It might be said to come into being instantaneously, the better to hammer home the paradox: pure nothingness still persists, but this entity is already there too. When I look at the Palazzo Dario, leaning to one side, seeming to leap out aslant, I always feel that it is—

very much—there, but, at the same time, nothing is. All the more so as it sometimes happens that the whole city vanishes. One evening, when I was coming back from Murano, my boat was alone for as far as the eye could see. There was no Venice any longer. Where the disaster had occurred, the water was covered in dust beneath the gold of the sky. For the moment, everything was clear and precise. All those fine plumes of silence were present and correct, but they don't *satisfy you* the way a great rugged mountain landscape does, tumbling down beneath your windows, in utter abandon. Are they waiting or defiant? These pretty things have a provocative reserve about them. And then, what is there facing me here? The *Other* pavement of a 'residential' avenue or the *Other* bank of a river? In any event, *it is the Other.* If truth be told, the left and right of the Canal are not so dissimilar. The Fondaco dei Turchi is, of course, on one side and the Ca' d'Oro on the other. But, broadly speaking, you have the same little boxes, the same marquetry work, interrupted here and there by the roar of those great white marble city halls, eaten away by tears of dirt. At times, as my gondola slid down between these two funfairs, I wondered which was the reflection of the other. In short, it isn't their differences that separate them: quite the opposite. Imagine you were to go up to a mirror; an image forms in it: your nose, your eyes, your mouth, your suit. It is you, it *should* be you. And yet there's something in the reflection—something that is neither the green of your eyes, nor the shape of your lips, nor the cut of your suit—that makes you suddenly say they have put *someone else* in the mirror, in place of my reflection. This is roughly the impression the 'Venices opposite' make at any time of day. Nothing would stop me believing today that *our* funfair is the real one and the other merely its image, blown off slightly to the East by the Adriatic wind. Just now, as I opened my window, I made a similar window open on the third floor of the Palazzo Loredan, which is this building's double. Logically, I should even have appeared in it, but it was, instead, a woman who poked her head out, leaned over towards the water, unfurled a carpet like a roll of parchment and began to beat it abstractedly. And this matutinal beating, the only movement to be seen, soon abated; it was swallowed up by the darkness of the room and the window closed upon it. Forsaken, the miniatures are carried off in a motionless glide. But this isn't what troubles me: together, we are drifting. There is something else, a very slight, systematic strangeness, which vanishes whenever I attempt to pin it down, but returns as soon as I start to think of something else. When I look out of my window in Paris, I often find it impossible to understand the merry-go-round of sparkling little people gesticulating on the terrace of the *Deux Magots* and I never knew why, one Sunday, they leapt out of their seats and ran over to a Cadillac parked by the pavement and jostled it, laughing. No matter: what they do, I do with them; from my lookout post, I too shook the Cadillac, because they are my natural crowd. I need only a minute, at the very most, to be down there with them; and when I lean out to look at them, I am already among them, looking up at my window, with their crazy ideas running through my head. I can't even say precisely that I *look* at them, since, when it comes down to it, I have never seen them. I *touch* them. Why? Because there is a terrestrial path between us, the Earth's reassuring crust. The *Others* are beyond the seas.

The *other* Venice is beyond the sea. Two women in black come down the steps of Santa Maria della Salute. They scuttle across the square, accompanied by their pale shadows, and on to the bridge that leads to San Gregorio. They are suspect and marvellous. They are women, but women as distant as those Arabs I saw from Spain, bowing down upon the soil of Africa. *Weird and wonderful*: they are the inhabitants of these untouchable houses, the Holy Women from Beyond the Seas. And here is another untouchable, the man who has planted himself in front of the church they have just left and who is looking at it, as is no doubt their wont on this unknown island. He is, horror of horrors, *mon semblable, mon frère*; he has a *Blue Guide* in his left hand and a Rolleiflex slung over his shoulder. Who could be more bereft of mystery than a tourist? Well, this one, frozen in his dubious stillness, is as troubling as the savages in horror films who part the rushes, watch the heroine go by with a glint in their eye and then disappear. He is a tourist from the Other Venice and I shall never see what he sees. Opposite me, these brick and marble walls have the fleeting strangeness of those solitary hillside villages you see from a train window.

All this is on account of the Canal. Were it just an honest stretch of sea, candidly admitting that its function was to keep human beings apart, or a raging river that had been tamed, carrying its little craft along reluctantly, there would be nothing to make a fuss about: we would just say there's a certain city over there, different from our own and, by that very token, entirely like it. A city like any other. But this Canal claims to *bring people together*; it presents itself as a watery path, deliberately made for walking on. The stone steps that run down to the roadway, like the white front steps of the pink villas in Baltimore, the carriage entrances that should open to let out a pony and trap, the little brick walls protecting the garden from the curiosity of passers-by and the long tresses of honeysuckle running along the walls and trailing down to the ground— all this is prompting me to run across the carriageway and establish that the tourist on the far side really is one of my own kind and that he isn't seeing anything I can't. But the temptation vanishes before it has altogether taken shape; it has no effect other than to heighten my imagination: I can already feel the ground opening up; the Canal is just an old branch, rotting away beneath its moss, beneath the dry black hulls covering it, which crack if you set foot on them. I am going under, I am sinking, with my arms upraised, and the last thing I see will be the indecipherable face of the Unknown Man on the Far Bank, who has now turned round to look at me, anxiously gauging his impotence in the situation or enjoying the sight of me falling into the trap. In short, this false connection only pretends to bring things together, the better to keep them apart; it thwarts my plans with ease and gives me to believe that communication with my fellow men is impossible; even the tourist's proximity is an optical illusion, like the striped creatures that the 'Newly-Weds of the Eiffel Tower' mistook for bees when they were actually desert tigers.[56] Venice's water lends the whole city a mildly nightmarish coloration: it is in nightmares that tools let us down, that the revolver levelled at the mad killer doesn't go off; it is in nightmares that we are running with a deadly enemy at our heels when suddenly the road starts to melt as we try to cross it.

The tourist, still shrouded in mystery, leaves the scene. He goes on to the little bridge and disappears. I am alone above the motionless Canal. The far bank seems even more inaccessible today. The sky has rent the water, which is in tatters; who would believe the Canal had a bottom to it? Through the great grey lagoons with which it is studded, I see the sky shining beneath the water. Between the two quays there is *nothing*: a transparent sash hastily thrown across a void. Those cottages are separated from ours by a crevice running across the whole of the earth. Two halves of Europe are separating. They move apart gently at first, then faster and faster; as in *Hector Servadac*,[57] now is the time to wave handkerchiefs. But the far quay is deserted, all the windows are closed. Already there are *two* human races, their destinies already dividing for all time, but no one knows it yet. In an hour's time, a maid will step out on to some balcony to beat the carpets and will be aghast to see the void beneath her and a great yellow and grey mass revolving ten thousand leagues away. Venice is constantly breaking up; whether I'm on the Riva degli Schiavoni, looking towards San Giorgio, or on the Nuova Fondamenta looking towards Burano, I always have a Land's End opposite me, emerging from a chaotic sterility, from some vain interstellar agitation.

This morning, the precious architecture opposite, which I never took entirely seriously before, seems fearfully austere: these are the smooth walls of a human world moving away; a little world, so limited, so enclosed, rising up definitively like a thought in the middle of a desert. *I am not in it.* The floating island is the whole earth, round and overloaded with human beings; it is moving away and I am left on the quay-side. In Venice and a few other places, you have the time to view the destiny of man from outside, with the eyes of an angel or an ape. Sadly, we weren't there for Noah's Ark. Of course, last summer, off the North Cape, we had this impression even more strongly: it seemed a fact or almost. We were bouncing around; to the south the last claws of Europe scratched at the sea, to our north were millions of grey waves, the solitude of a dead star. I ended up thinking I was in interstellar space, a satellite revolving around an inaccessible Earth. You don't feel the same anxiety in Venice and yet Humanity moves away from you, sliding off over a calm lake. The human race—or, who knows, the historical Process—retracts, to become a little seething ferment, limited in space and time. I see it whole, from some point out-side time and space, and very gently, very treacher-ously, sense my abandonment.

The present is what I touch; it is the tool I can handle; it is what is acting on me or what I can change. These pretty chimeras are not my present. Be-tween them and me there is no simultaneity. All it takes is a little sun to turn them into promises; per-haps they are coming to me from the depths of the future. On some spring mornings, I have seen them advancing towards me, a floating garden, still *other*, but like a portent, a presage of what I shall be to-morrow. But the sullen brightness of this morning has killed their colours and walled them up in their finitude. They are flat and inert; the general drift of things carries them away from me. They are definitely not part of my experience; they well up from the dis-tant depths of a memory that is in the process of for-getting them—a strange, anonymous memory, the memory of sky and water. In Venice, the tiniest thing is enough to turn light into a gaze. A certain light has only to envelop this imperceptible insular distance, this constant gap between things, for that light to

seem like a thought; it kindles or erases the meanings
scattered about the floating clusters of houses. This
morning I read Venice in the eyes of another; a glassy
stare has settled on the false grove, wilting the sugar
candy roses and the lilies made of bread dipped in
milk; everything is in a glass case; I am present at the
awakening of a gloomy memory. From the depths of
an ancient gaze my eyes try to dredge up sunken
palaces, but retrieve only generalities. Am I perceiving
or remembering? I see what I know. Or, rather, what
another already knows. *Another* memory is haunting
mine, Another's recollections well up before me, a
frozen flight of dead parakeets; everything has a
weary air of the past, of having been seen before. The
San Gregorio Abbey garden is just greenery, the sim-
plified rose windows mere working drawings; the facades, those sad, severe colourwashes beyond a glacial
lake, offer themselves with perfect clarity—almost
too perfect, crystalline—but I cannot pin down any
detail. Little houses, little palaces, fine follies, bankers'
and ship-owners' whims, the Capriccio Loredano, the
Barbaro folly—you are all virtually digested, almost
half-way dissolved into generalities. The Gothic Idea

is applied to the Moorish Idea; the Idea of marble joins with the Idea of pink; the garnet-coloured blinds and the rotting wood shutters are merely now a water-colourist's brushstrokes: a little green, a patch of burnt topaz. What will remain in this memory, as little by little it forgets? A long red and white wall, then nothing. The palaces, even now being forgotten, are beyond waiting for: they are no longer on the far side of the water, but in a very recent past, yesterday perhaps, or a moment ago; without moving they grow distant, they have lost the naïve brutality of presence, that silly, peremptory smugness of a thing that is there *and cannot be denied.* All that it is possible to love when we love something: chance features, scars, gashes, the poisonous softness of moss, water and old age—is condensed, nay erased, by this urgent, superficial light; there is no space in these things now, but a kind of extension without parts: they are things known, their matter is worn to the point of transparency, and the joyous coarseness of being attenuates to the point of absence. They are not there. Not entirely there. I see their architects' plans and drawings. The dull, false gaze of death has frozen these winsome sirens, fixing them in a supreme contortion. Wherever I go today, I am sure to arrive five minutes too late and to meet only with the impersonal memory of the disaster, sky and water merging again, recalling for a moment a drowned city, before breaking up and scattering into a pure spray of space. How superfluous I am going to feel, as the only presence amidst universal obsolescence, and at great risk of exploding, like one of those deep-sea fish when they are brought to the surface, because we are used to living under infinite pressure and such rarefactions are no good to us. There are days like this here: Venice is content merely to remember itself and the tourist wanders in bewilderment through this *cabinet fantastique* in which water is the central illusion.

A hope: a false ray of sunshine, born of an absence somewhere, a mere refraction of the void, lights up the copper figure of *Fortuna* on the Customs House globe, lathers up the soapy whitenesses of Santa Maria, repaints naïve and minutely tufted foliage through the abbey's iron railings, changes the idea of green into wooden shutters and the idea of topaz into old blinds eaten into by salt and sky. It passes a languid finger over the dried-out facades and brings the entire clump of roses into bloom. This whole suspended little world awakens. At the same time, a heavy black hull appears in the west: a barge. In its excitement, the water comes alive beneath its burden of sky, shakes its white plumage and turns over; the sky, disturbed, cracks and, pulverized, studs the waves with gleaming maggots. The barge turns and disappears into the shadow of a rio; it was a false alarm; the water reluctantly calms itself and gathers its disorder into heavy, trembling masses; already large patches of azure are re-emerging . . . A sudden re-lease of pigeons: the sky, crazed with fear, is taking flight, the landing-stage beneath my window creaks and attempts to mount the wall: the *vaporetto* goes by, its passage announced by the lowing of a conch. This long, beige cigar is a throwback to Jules Verne and the Exhibition of 1875. There is no one on deck, but its wide wooden benches are still haunted by the bearded gentlemen of the *Cronstadt* who opened the Exhibition. On a little beige-coloured zinc roof over the rear deck, wreaths are lying in piles of three: per-haps they are thrown into the water as floating monuments to commemorate drownings. On the bow, a winged victory in a fur coat abandons herself to the winds. Around her blonde hair, she has knotted a muslin shawl which flaps against her neck: a dreamy passenger from 1900. There is no one to be seen, except this dead woman who knew Wagner and Verdi. A miniature ghost ship is carrying an Italian countess, who died in the wreck of the Titanic, between two ancient celebrations. This is not surprising: each morning the Grand Canal is covered with anachronisms. It is a floating museum: the managements parade collectors' items in front of the loggias of the great hotels—the Gritti, the Luna, the Bauer-Grunewald. The water laughs gleefully, it plays: beneath the boat's stem, there's a general stampede; moorhens jostle, flap away clucking, their panic coming to rest at my feet. Gondolas and other boats caper around the great, barbarous gilded posts, their stripes like those of American barbers' poles. The *vaporetto* is far in the distance by now, but I am witness to a whole nautical cavalcade—spume, water nymphs, sea horses. On the quay, the ray of sunshine has vanished, plunging the buildings back into generality. The silence

proudly rises in red bricks above this impotent chatter. A distant trumpet sounds and falls silent. This is
a picture for the tourists: eternity ringed by becoming
or the intelligible World floating above matter. There
is still some squawking beneath my windows, but
never mind: silence has cut down the noises with its
icy scythe. In Venice, silence is visible; it is the taciturn
defiance of the Other Bank. Suddenly, the entire sea-
borne parade sinks; the water is like a dream, with no
continuity to its ideas: it is suddenly smooth again and
I am leaning out over a great clump of torpor; it is as
though it envied the corpse-like rigidity of the palaces
on its banks. The defiant sky has not re-descended
from the celestial vault; the fake corpse is turning
green between the quays and I can already see the pale
reflection of the Palazzo Dario emerging on the right.
I look up: everything is as it was. I need massive,
weighty presences; I feel empty when faced with these
fine feathers painted on glass. I'm going out.

Verve, 27–28 (February 1953).

Notes

1   Until quite recently, it was thought that Tintoretto's real name was Jacopo Robusti and this assumption informs the whole of Sartre's text. It is now believed that Robusti was a nickname and that the family name was actually Comin. [Trans.]

2   Paolo Caliari is better known as Veronese. [Trans.]

3   Ridolfi even claims that the Scuola San Marco rejected the canvas and Tintoretto had to take it back home.

4   Day-labourers.

5   Benozzo Gozzoli (1421–97): a Florentine painter. In his early years, he was an assistant to Fra Angelico. [Trans.]

6   It hangs in the Louvre. The funniest part is that it was inspired by the real Robusti.

7   A reference to Arthur Rimbaud's famous dictum, ' "Je" est un autre' ('I' is another). [Trans.]

8   That latent Protestantism that inoculates Italian cities against the Lutheran disease and leads Italy to carry out its own religious revolution under the name of the Counter-Reformation.

9   Jules Vuillemin, 'La personnalité esthétique du Tintoret', *Les Temps modernes*, 102 (1954).

10 These are the words of Eugenio Battista in an excellent article on Michaelangelo—'Michelangelo: credeva nell'arte ma disperava della sorte dell'uomo' —published by *Epoca* 8(360) (25 August 1957): 35–50.

11 There is an allusion here to Pierre Drieu la Rochelle's novel of 1937, *Rêveuse bourgeoisie* (Paris: Gallimard, 1937). [Trans.]

12 Ridolfi, deceived by the stylistic resemblance, said the picture was painted 'in concorrenza con il Pordenone' [in competition with Pordenone—Trans.].

13 Giovanni Antionio de' Sacchis was the actual name of the painter known as Pordenone. [Trans.]

14 Vuillemin, op cit., p. 1974. See also Tietze, p. 372, Newton, p. 72. [These are probably references to the following editions: H. Tietze, *Tintoretto: The Paintings and Drawings* (London: Phaidon Press, 1948); Eric Newton, *Tintoretto* (London: Longmans, Green and Co., 1952)—Trans.]

15 This phrase clearly echoes the title of Gilbert Cesbron's *Chiens perdus sans collier*, a bestseller on the theme of juvenile delinquency in which the central character is an orphan. Cesbron's novel appeared in 1954, three years before this essay. [Trans.]

16 On an exhibition of Giacometti's paintings at the Galérie Maeght. [Ed.]

17 Letter to Matisse (November 1950).

18 This would seem to be a reference to the 'unanimism' of Jules Romains, a doctrine initially presented as an antidote to modern individualism, though later refined somewhat. [Trans.]

19 Letter to Matisse (November 1950).

20 The New York Museum of Modern Art lists this work, rather strangely, as 'Walking Quickly Under [*sic*] the Rain' (1949). [Trans.]

21 In Arthur Rimbaud, 'Délires II', *Une saison en enfer* (1873); 'A Season in Hell' (Louise Varèse trans.), in *A Season in Hell and The Drunken Boat* (New York: New Directions, 1952). [Trans.]

22 For example, *Nine Figures* (1950).

23 Robert Lapoujade (1921–1993): one of the foremost French painters of his generation. After the exhibition *Choses vues* (1969), which largely contained canvases inspired by the events of May 1968, he devoted his time to writing and cinema, becoming an experimental filmmaker of considerable note and notoriety. He returned to painting in the 1980s and, in his latter years, taught at the École supérieure des arts décoratifs. [Trans.]

24 This would seem to be a (contradicting) echo of Locke's observation that '. . . the mind is not able to frame the idea of any space without parts.' See John Locke, *An Essay Concerning Human Understanding* (Roger Woolhouse ed., introd. and annot.) (London: Penguin, 1997 [1689]). [Trans.]

25 Presumably a reference to the demonstrations of 27 October 1960, which was a national day of action for Algeria called by the major trade unions. [Trans.]

26 *Les données immédiates de l'expression*: the phrase echoes Bergson's 'Les données immédiates de la conscience' (The Immediate Data of Consciousness). See Henri Bergson, *Essai sur les données immédiates de la conscience* (Paris: F. Alcan, 1889); reprinted in Henri Bergson, *Œuvres complètes,* VOL. 1 (Geneva, Skira, 1945–46); *Time and Free Will: An Essay on the Immediate Data of Consciousness* (F. L. Pogson trans.) (London: George Allen and Unwin, 1910). [Trans.]

27 Henri Alleg and Djamila Bouhired, two of the most prominent victims of torture in the Algerian national liberation struggle. Alleg published the memoir, *La Question* [Paris: Editions de Minuit; *The Question* (John Calder trans.), London; John Calder Publishers Ltd, 1958] in 1958. Both the book and an article which Sartre wrote about it in *L'Express* (March 1958) were

subjected to various forms of censorship by the French government, including an official banning order which appears to have been relatively ineffective. [Trans.]

28 The exhibition in question at the Galérie Pierre Domec, 10 March–15 April 1961, seems in fact to have been entitled *Peintures sur le thème des Emeutes, Tryptique sur 1a torture, Hiroshima* (Paintings on the Theme of the Riots, Tryptich on Torture, Hiroshima). [Trans.]

29 André Masson (1896–1987): one of France's leading Surrealist painters before breaking with André Breton in 1929 and pursuing a more structured style. During the war years, he escaped to the USA where he developed a strong interest in African-American and Native American mythological themes. He was close to many writers, collaborating on the review Acéphale with Georges Bataille (his brother-in-law), Roger Caillois and Pierre Klossowski. In 1946, he designed the sets for the first production at the Théâtre Antoine of Sartre's play *La Putain respectueuse* [The Respectful Prostitute] (Paris: Nagel, 1946). [Trans.]

30 From Stéphane Mallarmé, 'Le vierge, le vivace et le bel aujourd'hui', in *Œuvres Complètes I*. [Trans.]

31 From Arthur Rimbaud, 'Being Beauteous', in *Illuminations* (Louis Varèse trans.) (New York: New Directions, 1957).

32 French: 'explosante-fixe'. André Breton, *L'Amour fou* (Paris: Gallimard, 1937) [*Mad Love* (Mary Ann Caws trans.) (Nebraska: University of Nebraska Press, 1937)]. Breton contrasts this type of beauty with two others: the 'veiled-erotic' and the 'circumstantial-magical'.

33 Georges Limbour, *André Masson et son univers* (Geneva: Editions des Trois Collines, 1937), p. 103.

34 *Piège à soleil* [Sun Trap] (1938).

35 Limbour, *André Masson et son univers*, p. 38. See also *Deux Arbres* [Two Trees] (1943). [Trans.]

36 André Masson, 'A la cime de l'Être', in *Mythologies, Volume 3: Mythologie de l'Être* (1939) (Paris: Éditions de la revue Fontaine, 1946).

37 1941.

38 Georges Limbour, 'Georges Braque à Varengeville', in *Dans le secret des ateliers* (Paris: L'élocoquent, 1986). [Trans.]

39 *Portrait de Georges Limbour*, 1946; *Sur le point de parler*, 1946.

40 *Au travail*, 1946.

41 The pseudonym of Alfred Otto Wolfgang Schulze (1913–1951). [Trans.]

42 From a poem by Wols.

43 This is a line from Comte de Lautréamont which he made his own.

44 From September 1939 to October 1940, Wols was incarcerated as an 'enemy alien'. [Trans.]

45 Maurice Maeterlinck, *The Life of the White Ant* (Alfred Sutro trans.) (London: George Allen & Unwin, 1927), p. 71.

46 Paul Klee, *The Thinking Eye. The Notebooks of Paul Klee,* VOL. 1 (Jurg Spiller ed., Ralph Manheim trans.) (New York: G. Wittenborn, 1961), pp. 63–7. [Trans.]

47 Cf. *Les ludions* [The Bottle Imps], 1932; *Tous volent* [All Fly], 1937.

48 Paul Klee, 'Exacte Versuche im Bereich der Kunst', *Bauhaus. Zeitschrift für Bau und Gestaltung,* 2(2/3) (1928). [Trans.]

49 'In the beginning was the deed', one of the most widely quoted lines from Goethe's *Faust.* [Trans.]

50 Wols quoting Edgar Allan Poe from the short story, 'Eleonora' [first published in the 1842 edition of *The Gift: A Christmas and New Year's Present*, an annual publication; reproduced in G. E. Woodberry and

E. C. Stedman (eds), *The Works of Edgar Allan Poe, Volume 1: Tales* (Chicago: Stone and Kimball, 1894–95), pp. 203–11—Trans.]

51 Sarte, *Nausea*, p. 10. [Trans.]

52 The phrases 'horribles travailleurs' and 'Je est un autre' are taken from Rimbaud's letter to Paul Demeny of 15 May 1871, first published in *Nouvelle Revue Française* (October 1912). [Trans.]

53 The title of this gouache from 1943–44 was not chosen by Wols.

54 The French title of this piece, 'Un parterre de Capucines', plays on the word *capucine*, which means both a Capuchin nun and a nasturtium. [Trans.]

55 Though the term is used more freely here, it generally means a dull sermon or address. [Trans.]

56 *Les Mariés de la Tour Eiffel* (1921) is a one-act ballet written to a scenario by Jean Cocteau. [Trans.]

57 Jules Verne, *Hector Servadac, voyages et aventures à travers le monde solaire* (Paris: Pierre-Jules Hetzel, 1877); *Hector Servadac; Or the Career of a Comet* (Ellen Frewer trans.) (New York: Scribner Armstrong, 1878). [Trans.]